D1600460

STUDIES IN THE HISTORICAL BOOKS OF THE OLD TESTAMENT

SUPPLEMENTS

TO

VETUS TESTAMENTUM

EDITED BY

THE BOARD OF THE QUARTERLY

J. A. EMERTON - W. L. HOLLADAY - A. LEMAIRE

R. E. MURPHY - E. NIELSEN - R. SMEND - J. A. SOGGIN

VOLUME XXX

LEIDEN

E. J. BRILL

1979

STUDIES
IN THE HISTORICAL BOOKS
OF THE OLD TESTAMENT

EDITED BY

J. A. EMERTON

LEIDEN
E. J. BRILL
1979

BS
1205.2
.S78
1979

80033153

ISBN 90 04 06017 0

Copyright 1979 by E. J. Brill, Leiden, The Netherlands

All rights reserved. No part of this book may be reproduced or translated in any form, by print, photoprint, microfilm, microfiche or any other means without written permission from the publisher

PRINTED IN THE NETHERLANDS

CONTENTS

PREFACE

Most of the articles in this volume were submitted for publication in *Vetus Testamentum*. Since, however, they are all concerned with the historical books of the Old Testament, and since there would have been a long wait before they could all appear in ordinary issues of the journal, it was thought that it would be helpful to collect them together and publish them as a *Supplement to Vetus Testamentum*. Dr H. G. M. Williamson has kindly prepared the indexes.

J. A. Emerton

JOSHUA: THE HEBREW AND GREEK TEXTS [1]

by

A. G. AULD

Edinburgh

In the book of 1914 whose title this article has borrowed, the Oxford scholar S. Holmes and the Press of Cambridge University were responsible for a study that was modest yet of far-reaching implications [2]. It was a response to a German debate begun by J. Hollenberg's 1876 study of the character of the Alexandrian translation of the book of Joshua [3] which "was in many passages favourable to the LXX" while on the whole upholding "the general superiority of the MT". With the exception of C. Steuernagel [4] subsequent scholars, signally A. Dillmann [5], had adopted a much less favourable attitude to the Greek. Apart from his rebuttal of specific arguments of Dillmann and others, Holmes claimed to advance "distinctly fresh reasons . . . in favour of the superiority of the LXX" (pp. 1-2): (1) It can hardly be accidental that the LXX often lacks two or more instances of a given word or expression in the MT. (2) The circumstance that in several cases where the two texts vary from one another each text is consistent with itself suggests the hypothesis of a deliberate and systematic revision. Then (3) even some confused passages in the LXX, when turned back into Hebrew, give an intelligible text manifestly earlier than the MT.

He did have some immediate following. G. A. Cooke, in his revised edition of the Cambridge Bible volume on Joshua [6], paid tribute to Holmes and adopted many of his conclusions. Then many of his results were endorsed by C. D. Benjamin in a thesis published in 1921 [7]. But there has followed a long period of neglect.

---

[1]) This is a version of a paper read to the Summer Meeting of the SOTS in Cambridge, 1977.

[2]) *Joshua, the Hebrew and Greek Texts* (Cambridge, 1914).

[3]) *Der Charakter der alexandrinischen Übersetzung des Buches Josua und ihr textkritischer Werth* (Moers, 1876).

[4]) *Das Buch Josua* (Göttingen, 1899).

[5]) *Die Bücher Numeri, Deuteronomium und Josua* (Leipzig, 1886).

[6]) *The Book of Joshua* (Cambridge, 1917).

[7]) *The Variations between the Hebrew and Greek Texts of Joshua: Chapters 1-12* (Philadelphia, 1921).

The first edition of Martin Noth's commentary on Joshua was published in 1938 [8]). The freshness of its attack might have weakened even more dangerously the malevolent grip of Hexateuchal criticism on that book had that not received a new lease of life in the same year from G. von Rad's essay on "The Form-critical Problem of the Hexateuch" [9]). An important year for modern study of the book of Joshua, 1938 saw too the publication of the last part of M. A. Margolis's uncompleted *Book of Joshua in Greek* (Paris, 1931-8). This has been well described as the outstanding example of an attempt to recover the proto-LXX version of the text of an Old Testament book [10]). Its handling of the Greek and other versions is superb. But it is much less clear that Margolis's all-too-brief comments are sound on the relationship between his reconstructed first Greek version and the Hebrew tradition. In almost every case of divergence he opts for the priority of the Hebrew. Noth had been responsible for the text of Joshua in the 3rd edition of Kittel's *Biblia Hebraica*, and in the commentary (p. 7), while he mentions Holmes, his statement that the Greek has shortened and simplified its original at several points is an endorsement of Margolis's view. Margolis apparently never cited Holmes; and this—given the brilliance of the main part of his study—may have contributed to that neglect of Holmes which it also shares.

Despite H. M. Orlinsky's paper at the Rome Congress on "The Hebrew *Vorlage* of the Septuagint of the Book of Joshua" *Supp. to VT* 17 (1969), pp. 187-95, and its plea for a return to Holmes's starting-point, all recent studies have continued to take the *Hebraica veritas* as their point of departure. E. Otto's work on the festival of unleavened bread at Gilgal [11]) and M. Wüst's on the geographical texts relating to the settlement of the Transjordanian tribes [12]) are both eclectic in their use of the LXX. J. A. Soggin's commentary [13]) is fairly scrupulous about noting variants, but seldom discusses their significance. F. Langlamet's *Gilgal* shows careful attention to detail, devoting a dozen pages to variants within Jos. iii-iv. Yet these, with

---

8) *Das Buch Josua* (Tübingen, 1038).

9) *Das formkritische Problem des Hexateuchs* (Stuttgart, 1938).

10) F. M. Cross, *The Ancient Library of Qumran and Modern Biblical Studies* (New York, 1958), p. 130.

11) *Das Mazzotfest in Gilgal* (Stuttgart, 1975).

12) *Untersuchungen zu den siedlungsgeographischen Texten des Alten Testaments: I. Ostjordanland* (Wiesbaden, 1975).

13) *Joshua* (London, 1972) = *Le Livre de Josué* (Neuchâtel, 1970).

Margolis and Noth, are mostly found to be simplifications, harmonisations, or arrangements of a *texte de base* of whose complexity the translator was only too conscious[14]). Holmes's name is beginning to reappear in the bibliographies of studies on Joshua. Yet that normally tells us more about the completeness of the bibliography than about the attention paid to Holmes's work.

Holmes occasionally noted the relevance of his observations to the literary analysis of Joshua (pp. 15-16, 37-8, 49); and it was concern with this problem that led me to a scrutiny of the LXX in Joshua before I knew of Holmes's work. There is no room in one article to discuss his detailed conclusions, although most of them appear to be accurate or at least responsibly argued. Some of the arguments presented here will corrobate his case. Yet it will be with regard mainly to outstanding problems of literary analysis that this paper will offer some characterization of the shorter Greek and fuller Hebrew of Joshua.

These vary from the very beginning. In the following translation from the first chapter those elements in the MT not reflected in the LXX are italicized:

> 1 After the death of Moses *the servant of Yahweh*, Yahweh said to Joshua the son of Nun, Moses' minister, 2 "Moses my servant is dead; now therefore rise, go over *this* (LXX: the) Jordan, you and all this people, into the land which I am giving to them, *to the people of Israel*. 3 Every place that the sole of your foot will tread upon I have given to you, as I proclaimed to Moses: 4 the desert and *this* Lebanon as far as the great river, the river Euphrates, *all the land of the Hittites*, and as far as the great sea towards the setting sun; it will be your territory."

In this opening of the book there is no "plus" in the LXX reflecting a longer text than the corresponding phrase in the MT. (It offers *Anti*lebanon in *v.* 4; but that will be an interpretation of the same text.)

Of such brief pluses, there are about twice as many in the MT as in the LXX in Jos. i-iv, vi, viii-ix, xiii-xvi, xviii, xx-xxi, and xxiv; while in chapters v, vi, x-xii, xvii, xix, and xxii-xxiii they are four or five times as numerous. But are we dealing with additions in one tradition or omissions in the other or a mixture of both? It is fair to observe throughout the book, as in the verses rendered above,

14) Langlamet, *Gilgal et les Récits de la Traversée du Jourdain* (Paris, 1969).

that the shorter Septuagint is seldom an intrinsically unsatisfactory text; while the fuller Hebrew appears to possess an accumulation of detail and pedantry. Small *is* beautiful—but is shorter also earlier?

The LXX's accounts of the capture of Jericho in Jos. vi and of Ai in Jos. vii-viii are considerably shorter than those in the MT. There are several divergences in the material common to them; but the most noticeable difference is that of length. A useful sample is viii 9-17 which takes up the story after the instructions given by Joshua for an ambush of Ai by "thirty thousand mighty men of valour". In the following translation the common tradition (which is also the shorter LXX) is given in the left-hand column, while the MT's pluses are to be found on the right.

9 So Joshua sent them forth; and they went to the place of ambush, and lay between Bethel and Ai, to the west of Ai	but Joshua spent that night among the people.
10 And Joshua rose early in the morning and mustered the people, and went up, with the elders	of Israel
before the people to Ai	
11 And all the fighting men who were with him went up, and drew near before the city,	and encamped
on the east side (MT: north side)	of Ai, with a ravine between them and Ai.
12	And he took about five thousand men, and set them in ambush between Bethel and Ai, to the west of the city.
13	So they stationed the forces, the main encampment north of the city
with the ambush (MT: rear guard) west of the city.	But Joshua spent that night in the valley.
14 And when the king of Ai saw this, he and all his people	the men of the city,
made haste and went out early	to the descent toward the Arabah
to meet Israel in battle; but he did not know that there was an ambush against him behind the city.	
15 And Joshua and all Israel saw this and fled before him	in the direction of the desert.
16	So all the people who were in the city were called together to pursue them;

and they pursued Joshua, and were themselves drawn away from the city.	
17 There was not a man left in Ai who did not go out after Israel; they left the city open, and pursued Israel	or Bethel

Small may be beautiful. But is the shorter Greek here a better (i.e. earlier) text or an improved (i.e. later) text? One of the all too few and all too brief fragments of Joshua from Qumran (cave 4) is of viii 3-18 [15]). This Hebrew text is much shorter than the MT and shares a number of minuses with the familiar LXX. Now if the Hebrew tradition which our Greek has rendered *did* omit from the story of Ai the material in our right-hand column it would cast suspicion on some at any rate of the other passages where the Greek differs from the Hebrew (MT) text. The LXX is free from the discrepancy of the numbers of the men in ambush; and one cannot help thinking that this has been the main reason why scholars have assented to the alleged inferiority of the Greek text. Yet if such difficulty had been felt, the simple expedient was open of making the numbers correspond. An editor or translator prepared to omit several words to avoid a difficulty was equally capable of altering a single number for the same end [16]). It is certain that at some stage in the growth of our familiar Hebrew tradition a complicated account of the capture of Ai was produced, perhaps in an attempt to do justice to conflicting information. Why not at a late stage in the MT tradition, rather than assume that a complicated account was first produced and then simplified in the LXX tradition? At this stage in the discussion only one further point will be noted: that viii 9, 13 share characteristics with MT pluses elsewhere. They attest the same pedantic concern for the location of the camp and the precise whereabouts of Joshua himself at any given moment as we find in x 15, 43 (both absent from the LXX): "Then Joshua returned, and all Israel with him, to the camp at Gilgal." A further example of such specification in the MT will be mentioned below in connection with v 10.

The LXX's pluses with respect to the common tradition are by no means homogeneous, but as a group they are of a different order

[15]) J. A. Callaway, "New Evidence on the Conquest of Ai", *JBL* 87 (1968), p. 319, n. 35.

[16]) Compare Holmes's discussion, p. 13.

from those of the MT. Three of them are clearly MT omissions: After xv 59 the Greek preserves the list of towns in Judah around Bethlehem; and after xxi 35 the list of Levitical towns from the tribe of Reuben. The topographical gap in the MT's chapter xv and the numerical asymmetry in ch. xxi leave no other option. Thirdly it may be argued that the longer conclusion of the LXX to the Danite town list xix (47-48) is not only prior to the shorter MT but also the source of the information in Jud. i 34-35 (Holmes, pp. 15-16). At no point within the LXX tradition of Joshua has there occured an obvious substantial omission like these from the Hebrew. It is attractive to view this as a token of the greater reliability of this shorter tradition in its witness to a mostly shorter "original". If the text common to both Hebrew and Greek is also largely the original from which both have diverged, then the Greek is a version of a Hebrew tradition which has occasionally "extended" this text, mostly with additional historical detail; while the MT represents a Hebrew tradition that has thoroughly "expanded" it.

Commentators have often observed that the familiar Hebrew text of Joshua contains unnecessary detail. Noth for example describes many words and phrases as "literary" or "secondary additions". Yet there is little recognition in his textual notes that many of these are MT pluses. A similar observation can be made about Langlamet's *Gilgal*, where he detects nine layers in Jos. iii-iv. In none of the cases where he prefers the longer text of the MT and Holmes the shorter LXX does Langlamet ascribe the MT plus to any of his six narrative or catechetical sources. All are deemed to belong to one or other of the three redactional phases. Now, even if Holmes is correct, Langlamet is still close to the truth; for where a plus in the MT is also an *addition* to the *common* tradition, it does represent a redactional phase. The choice then is between asserting that the LXX reflects an improved edition in which unnecessary verbiage of earlier editors has been pruned, and asserting that the verbiage now in the MT accumulated at a stage after the separation of the *Vorlage* of the LXX. Of course, if Otto's subsequent *Mazzotfest in Gilgal* is to be believed, Jos. iii-iv should be divided almost without remainder into two parallel sources. And yet his account of Jos. viii 1-29 is a further illustration of our case (pp. 26-50, 89). Within the story of the capture of Ai he assigns *vv.* 3a, 12, 13, 20b to his later source B and the remainder to A. All these are absent from the Greek apart from *v.* 3a, and that part-verse only disturbs the reader whose suspicions have been triggered by the Hebrew's *vv.* 12,13.

In short, it appears we should disqualify our familiar Hebrew text from serving as a sure base for a close examination of the literary structure and relationships of the book of Joshua. It is from the more-or-less "original" common text that better answers may come to our literary questions about the completed book of Joshua. This finds particularly clear confirmation in Jos. v with its discussion of the circumcision and first passover in Canaan.

The divergence over passover in *vv.* 10-12 is more straightforward and may be studied first. The central column below offers a retroversion of the LXX into a Hebrew as close to the MT as appears compatible with the Greek rendering:

10	10	10 ויחנו בני־ישראל
Καὶ ἐποίησαν οἱ υἱοὶ Ισραηλ	ויעשו בני־ישראל	בגלגל ויעשו
τὸ πασχα τῇ τεσσαρεσκαι-	את־הפסח בארבעה	את־הפסח בארבעה
δεκάτῃ ἡμέρᾳ τοῦ μηνὸς	עשר יום לחדש	עשר יום לחדש
ἀπὸ ἑσπέρας	בערב	בערב
ἐπὶ δυσμῶν Ιεριχω	בערבות יריחו	בערבות יריחו
ἐν τῷ πέραν τοῦ Ἰορδάνου	בעבר הירדן [17]	
ἐν τῷ πεδίῳ		
11 καὶ ἐφάγοσαν ἀπὸ τοῦ	11 ויאכלו מעבור	11 ויאכלו מעבור
σίτου τῆς γῆς	הארץ	הארץ ממחרת הפסח
ἄζυμα καὶ νέα	מצות וקלוי	מצות וקלוי
ἐν ταύτῃ τῇ ἡμέρᾳ	בעצם היום הזה	בעצם היום הזה
12 ἐξέλιπεν τὸ μαννα	12 (וי)שבת המן	12 וישבת המן ממחרת
μετὰ τὸ βεβρωκέναι αὐτοὺς	באכלם	באכלם
ἐκ τοῦ σίτου τῆς γῆς	מעבור הארץ	מעבור הארץ
καὶ οὐκέτι ὑπῆρχεν	ולא היה עוד	ולא היה עוד
τοῖς υἱοῖς Ισραηλ μαννα	לבני ישראל מן	לבני ישראל מן
ἐκαρπίσαντο δὲ	ויאכלו מתבואת	ויאכלו מתבואת
τὴν χώραν τῶν Φοινίκων	ארץ כנען	ארץ כנען
ἐν τῷ ἐνιαυτῷ ἐκείνῳ	בשנה ההיא	בשנה ההיא

The LXX plus in *v.* 10 offers a commonplace specification of the location of Jericho. As for the MT's plus in that verse, its concern to specify the location of the camp at any given time has already been discussed in connection with its pluses in viii 9, 13 and x 15, 43.

---

[17]) Haplography in MT?

However quite the most significant difference is over chronology, and concerns the similar MT pluses in *vv*. 11, 12—"from the morrow (after the passover)". For the tradition behind the LXX the eating of unleavened bread from Canaanite grain was part of keeping the passover on the fourteenth day of the month. Hardly surprising that a book with so many Deuteronomic features should describe the first passover in Canaan according to the calendar in Deut. xvi 1-8. This text was economically altered through two neat additions to correspond to the "Priestly" calendar of passover in Lev. xxiii 5-6, where passover belongs to the fourteenth and the beginning of the feast of unleavened bread to the fifteenth day of the month. In both versions, *bʿṣm hywm hzh* has a strengthening function: in the Hebrew, to underline that it was on the *following* day that unleavened bread was eaten; in the Greek, where the sentence division is earlier, to anticipate *bʾklm* . .—to highlight the coincidence of the feast and the end of manna (on the fourteenth). The deliberate nature of these "corrections" to the tradition, and the consistency of the MT's interest in Joshua and the camp, put us on the ready to detect further examples of corrective reformulation of the text.

As for *vv*. 2-9, the most important difference between our versions is over the candidates for Joshua's circumcision as described in *vv*. 4-6a:

4 ὃν δὲ τρόπον περιεκάθαρεν	4 וזה הדבר אשר מל	4 וזה הדבר אשר מל
Ἰησοῦς τοὺς υἱοὺς Ισραηλ	יהושע את־בני־ישראל	יהושע
		כל־העם היצא ממצרים
		הזכרים
		כל אנשי המלחמה
		מתו במדבר בדרך
		בצאתם ממצרים
	5	5 כי מלים היו
		כל־העם היצאים
ὅσοι ποτὲ ἐγένοντο	כל הילודים	וכל־העם הילודים
ἐν τῇ ὁδῷ	בדרך	במדבר בדרך
καὶ ὅσοι ποτὲ ἀπερίτμητοι	וכל הערלים	
ἦσαν τῶν ἐξεληλυθότων	בצאתם	בצאתם
ἐξ Αἰγύπτου πάντας	ממצרים	ממצרים
τούτους περιέτεμεν Ἰησοῦς	אלה מל יהושע [18]	לא מלו

[18]) The underlining points to similarities in consonantal texts with quite contradictory meanings.

6 τεσσεράκοντα γὰρ καὶ δύο	6 כי ארבעים ושנים	6 כי ארבעים
ἔτη ἀνέστραπται Ισραηλ	שנה הלך ישראל	שנה הלכו בני־ישראל
ἐν τῇ ἐρήμῳ τῇ Μαδβαριτιδι	במדבר	במדבר
διὸ οἱ ἀπερίτμητοι ἦσαν	לכן ערלים היו	עד תם
οἱ πλεῖστοι αὐτῶν	רבים מהם	כל־הגוי
τῶν μαχίμων τῶν ἐξεληλυ-	אנשי המלחמה	אנשי המלחמה
θότων ἐκ γῆς Αἰγύπτου	היצאים מארץ	היצאים
	מצרים	ממצרים
οἱ ἀπειθήσαντες	אשר לא שמעו	אשר לא שמעו
τῶν ἐντολῶν τοῦ θεοῦ	בקול האלהים [19]	בקול יהוה
...	...	...

The MT and LXX agree that circumcision had not been practised while the people wandered in the desert. But while the Greek is quite matter-of-fact in talking of others than the children of the desert requiring circumcision, the Hebrew is at pains to deny that any at the time of the exodus had not been circumcised: did it hold that the rite was not universally practised among the Israelites in Egypt? or did it hold that circumcision was practised later in life, perhaps at puberty, so that its second category of candidates were still children at the exodus? In any case, there is no motive for Greek translators or prior Hebrew editors to have gone out of their way to alter a text to imply that the Israelites did not universally practise circumcision while in Egypt. The MT is not only longer, but more strident and more orthodox; and it is fair to assume that this text has been reformulated for dogmatic reasons, and probably in the light of God's command to Abraham (Gen. xvii) that the rite should be carried out universally and after but one week of life. This helps us to understand the alteration to *v.* 2:

2 . . .	2 ...	2 ...
Ποίησον σεαυτῷ μαχαίρας	עשה לך חרבות	עשה לך חרבות
πετρίνας ἐκ πέτρας ἀκρο-	צרים	צרים
τόμου καὶ καθίσας περίτεμε	ושב ומל	ושוב מל
τοὺς υἱοὺς Ισραηλ	את־בני־ישראל	את־בני־ישראל שנית

A combination of the Hebrew pluses in *vv.* 4, 5, that all were circumcised in Egypt and that (only) the adults of the exodus generation died in the desert, leads to the conclusion that those who left as

[19]) The underlining points to a type of variation to be discussed at the end of the article.

children were now being recircumcised. Hence the addition in *v.* 2 of *šnyt* to guarantee the now proper understanding of *wš(w)b*. Its original sense of sitting can be illustrated from ancient and recent Egyptian practice, and may be taken to imply circumcision of adolescents [20]).

Confirmation from this earlier part of the chapter that orthodoxy has been at work on the text of Jos. v at some stage after the completion of the common text of the book, and inspired by the "Priestly" Gen. xvii, invites a final comment on the MT's report of the passover. Amongst the older literary critics, and their followers today, it is precisely the phrase *mmḥrt hpsḥ* that leads to these verses being claimed for the "Hexateuchal" P-source. Our account of the textual history of the chapter has shown that this judgement is in a sense both right and wrong: right in that both chronology and phraseology have been drawn from "P" contexts in the Pentateuch; wrong in that the phrase was no part of the once complete original book—nor part of any P-document's Joshua-story.

The detailed examples so far used in this paper have been of individual passages in which it could be shown that the Greek tradition was shorter and/or preferable—in the sense of a better witness to the "original" book of Joshua. To conclude the discussion it may be useful to mention a number of recurrent variations. Some of these concern the designations of an individual tribe.

Tribes are called not only *šbṭ* and *mṭh*; they are referred to also by their proper name, or that name can have *bny* or *mṭh bny* prefixed. In Jos. xiii-xix there are 69 references to individual tribes in the tradition common to Hebrew and Greek, with 12 more peculiar to the MT. Of the 69 common instances, 52 appear in the same *form* in both traditions while there is divergence in the case of 17. When the evidence is tabulated, some conclusions become clear:

	Common (*52*)	*LXX* (*17*)	*MT* (*17*)	*MT+* (*12*)
"simple" name	*20*	*8* (3^{A}+ 5^{B})	2^{C}	*3*
bny	*25*	*3* (2^{C}+ 1^{D})	*7* (5^{B}+ 2^{E})	*6*
mṭh	*0*	3^{F}	1^{G}	*1*
mṭh bny	*7*	*3* (2^{E}+ 1^{G})	*7* (3^{A}+ 1^{D}+ 3^{F})	*2*

---

20) J. B. Pritchard (ed.), *The Ancient Near East in Pictures Relating to the Old Testament* (Princeton, 1954), no. 629; and L. Durrell, *Balthazar* (London, 1958), p. 157.

1) Tribal names alone or construed with *bny* are much more common than forms including *mṭh*.

2) The MT not only boasts 12 "additional" instances, but also uses a longer form in 12 of the common instances—the LXX has a longer form in only 5 [21]).

3) There is no instance in the common tradition of the tribal name construed with *mṭh* within the actual descriptions of allocations—only in the outer framework in xiv 1-5 and xix 51.

4) There is no case in which *bny* is used in one tradition and *mṭh* in the other.

5) Apart from the "framework" passages already noted under 3), *mṭh* and *mṭh bny* forms are used only in the opening and concluding formulae of individual allocations. It is to the same and similar contexts that all the Hebrew pluses and variants including *mṭh* belong. A decision on their reliability is indispensable before analyis can begin of the growth of this geographical material to its originally completed form, and before serviceable historical sources can be reconstructed. One likely conclusion of such analysis would be that *mṭh* is most securely embedded in the formula that concludes the regularly patterned reports in Jos. xix of the allocations to the last six tribes (cf. Holmes, p. 68); other reports will have been partially adjusted to this pattern.

Two recurring divergences can be detected in references to the deity. The first concerns the possessives construed with "God". The situation here too can be readily tabulated:

	Common	*MT variants*	*LXX variants*	*MT* + 's	*LXX* + 's
my	1	0	1	0	0
our	4	0	10	2	1
your(s)	3	1	0	0	0
your(pl)	15 [22])	10	0	5	0
their	1	0	0	0	0

[21]) The figures underlined in the above table are the totals within each tradition of each of the four forms of designation. The figures within brackets, with a letter from A to G attached, point to the specific types of divergence that have occurred. The key to the letters is as follows:

A	xviii 11, xix 24, 40	E	xix 9, 16
B	xiii 24, xviii 11, xix 9, 10, 32	F	xiii 15, xv 1, xvi 8
C	xvii 7, xix 1	G	xvii 1
D	xviii 21		

[22]) This total masks one verse (i 11) where the MT has "your God" and the LXX "God of your fathers".

The Hebrew tradition most often offers the second person plural suffix, both in its own pluses and where it differs from the Greek. In nine of the eleven cases of difference the Greek attests the *first* person plural. Of course inner-Greek corruption was a ready possibility as soon as the *īpsilon* of *īmōn* (your) became indistinguishable in pronunciation from the *īta* of *īmōn* (our). Yet if pronunciation affected the scribes one would expect more divergence within the Greek textual tradition which in this matter is remarkably unified (the text of LXX^B has been followed here and throughout this article). Then, whether the Greek or Hebrew tradition is in the end to be preferred, the variation has occurred in only one direction. Further, *hymōn* (your) overlaps perfectly with the Hebrew second plural suffix in all ninety or so instances throughout Joshua—and that is with all nouns. However, of the fifty-four instances of *hēmōn* (our), no less than thirteen are in passages where the Hebrew reads the second not first person suffix—in the nine cases already mentioned with "God" and four more. The reason can hardly be accident. The very regularity of the Hebrew second person usage with the deity, given its already noted propensity to systematise, is suspicious in face of the Greek testimony. And our final topic too shows the Hebrew tradition ready to alter terminology for the deity.

The use of the proper name *yhwh* for the deity is almost completely regular in the book of Joshua. In the MT, (*h*)*'lhym* refers independently to the God of Israel just three times. However ten further such instances are attested in the LXX. Seven of these are in chapters whose concentration of MT pluses and differences is much heavier than the norm for the book; while in the case of the other three the difference in divine name is not the only one in the verses in question. (One of the ten cases closes our earlier quotation from v 6a.) Happily in two passages there is more than just general indirect evidence for the priority of "God" over "Yahweh" (against Holmes, p. 50).

According to Jos. ix 27 (MT) Joshua concludes the affair of the Gibeonites by making them hewers of wood . . . "for the altar of Yahweh, to continue to this day, in the place which he should choose". The Greek differs in two respects: in reading "the altar of *God*", and in adding the subject "Yahweh" to the final clause—"for the altar of God, to continue to this day, in the place which Yahweh should choose". It is easy to understand the Hebrew's omission of the final Yahweh as unnecessary once "God" had been altered to read "Yahweh" earlier. The alternative assumption, that the verse first suffered "elohistic" corruption and then received a gratuitous "Yahweh", is much harder to entertain.

Then there are two instances in connection with the famous poetic fragment in Jos. x:

> 12 Then Joshua spoke to Yahweh in the day when *Yahweh* (LXX: God) gave the Amorites over to the men of Israel; and he said in the sight of Israel,
>
> "Sun, be still at Gibeon,
> and Moon, in the Valley of Ayalon."
>
> 13 And the sun was still, and the moon stopped, until *the nation* (LXX: God) took vengeance on its enemies. *Is this not written in the Book of Jashar*? (not in LXX) The sun stopped in the midst of heaven, and did not hasten to go down for about a whole day.
>
> 14 There has been no day like it before or since, when *Yahweh* (LXX: God) listened to the voice of a man; for Yahweh fought for Israel.

The tradition is united that Yahweh figures in the first and last comments. As for the LXX's three instances of "God", its witness is to be preferred in *v.* 12 and *v.* 14. However in *v.* 13 its *theos*/God is a simple inner-Greek corruption of *ethnos*/nation—but a corruption facilitated by the presence of *theos* in the text immediately before and after [23]).

Here is another textual conclusion with literary implications: it becomes likely that "God" belongs to the "source" of our poetic fragment—the "Yahweh" notes at beginning and end will be the contribution of the Joshua editor, and Massoretic tradition will have later removed the resulting inconsistency. The Hebrew tradition which twice altered the divine name, and which —as we saw earlier—added the following *v.* 15, also cited in *v.* 13 the name of our "source": but perhaps on no stronger authority than its editor's observation that David's elegy over Saul and Jonathan is similarly introduced in 2 Sam. i 18. Claims that we are dealing here in Jos. x with a fragment of an early *Yahweh*-epic and that we know that epic's name must be received with double caution [24]).

The evidence is far from exhausted [25]). Many more textual *cruces*

---

[23]) Holmes (p. 50) conjectures that the original *gwy* was corrupted into *yhwh*, which was rendered *theos*.

[24]) Cf. P. D. Miller, *The Divine Warrior in Early Israel* (Cambridge, Mass., 1973); and F. M. Cross, *Canaanite Myth and Hebrew Epic* (Cambridge, Mass., 1973), p. 70.

[25]) For discussion of other details, see my "Judges I and History: a Reconsideration", *VT* 25 (1975), pp. 261-85; "A Judaean Sanctuary of 'Anat (Josh.

could be studied, some of them with significance for the literary criticism of the book: normally only negative significance, in that they foreclose options.

Of course any shorter or variant text ought to be assessed on its merits. However criteria—or at least local criteria—are often lacking for a firm decision. Awareness of the whole context is vital. And in the case of the book of Joshua that means giving the Greek, not the Hebrew, the benefit of the doubt. . . . But not fanatically! I am not yet persuaded that its "Shiloh" should be preferred to Massoretic "Shechem" at the beginning of ch. xxiv—that would entail the re-writing of too many books.

15:59)?", *Tel Aviv* 4 (1977), pp. 85-6; "The 'Levitical Cities': Texts and History", *ZAW* 91 (1979), pp. 194-206; and "Textual and Literary Studies in the Book of Joshua", *ZAW* 90 (1978), pp. 412-17.

THE LEGAL BACKGROUND TO THE RESTORATION OF MICHAL TO DAVID

by

ZAFRIRA BEN-BARAK

Haifa

At the height of a long and bitter war between the House of Saul and the House of David (2 Sam. ii 12 — iii 1) a singular episode claims the attention of the biblical narrative:

> Then David sent messengers to Ish-bosheth Saul's son, saying, "Give me my wife Michal, whom I betrothed at the price of a hundred foreskins of the Philistines". And Ish-bosheth sent and took her from her husband Paltiel the son of Laish. But her husband went with her, weeping after her all the way to Bahurim. Then Abner said to him, "Go, return"; and he returned (2 Sam. iii 14-16).

By way of a royal command Eshbaal [1]) takes Michal, Saul's daughter, from her husband Paltiel the son of Laish and gives her to David, in accordance with the latter's demand.

This narrative passage gives rise to three fundamental questions:

A. *Why does Eshbaal agree to hand over Michal, who is under his authority, to his most dangerous adversary, David?*

The first question has a clearly political character. After the defeat at Gilboa, with the death of Saul and his sons, Israel was divided into two units. The first, "Israel", included most of the tribes of Israel and was under the rule of Eshbaal, the only remaining son of Saul (2 Sam. ii 8-10). The second unit, "Judah", consisting of the tribe of Judah and tribal elements in the South, was under the leadership of David, who was crowned at Hebron (2 Sam. ii 2-7, 11). This political rift between "Israel" and "Judah" was accompanied by a civil war, in which superiority lay with David's forces (2 Sam. iii 1) [2]).

---

[1]) Eshbaal, the correct form, is preserved only in 1 Chr. viii 33, ix 39. Ish-bosheth is a scribal alteration. See S. Loewenstamm, "Eshbaal", *Encyclopaedia Biblica* 1 (Jerusalem, 1955), pp. 749-50 (Hebrew); E. Lipiński, "*ʾšbʿl* and *ʾšyhw*, and parallel personal names", *OLP* 5 (1974), pp. 5-13.

[2]) On "Israel" and "Judah" under David see M. Noth, *Geschichte Israels* (2nd edn, Göttingen, 1954), pp. 167-72 = E. tr. *The History of Israel* (revised edn, London and New York, 1960), pp. 181-6; J. Bright, *A History of Israel*

David's motives for demanding the restoration of Michal are obvious, and fit in well with his aim of obtaining complete control over Israel. His marriage to a daughter of Saul king of Israel would bestow legitimacy upon his rule, and would act as a bridge between the two hostile factions.

There can be no doubt that all this was not lost on Eshbaal, who was well aware of the advantages to be gained from this marriage for an adversary who was going from strength to strength, and of the danger it heralded for his tottering rule. This was especially so since Eshbaal actually had no legal right to the throne, in view of the fact that in Israel the dynastic principle had not yet been established as a part of the institution of kingship [3]). Indeed, his ascent to the throne was unaccompanied by any act of sanctification (Noth, p. 169; E. tr., p. 183). One would therefore expect that he would strenuously resist any such union and spare no effort to frustrate the execution of an act so pregnant with danger not only for his kingdom but perhaps for his very life. It is thus all the more astonishing that he does not oppose the handing over of the king's daughter to David, and that he himself orders that David's request be complied with and sees to its execution [4]).

B. *How are Michal's marriage first to David and then to Paltiel and her remarriage to David to be explained?*

The second question is on the plane of social ethics. Twice Michal is given to a different man, in the lifetime of her husband, and on both occasions by the legal authority, the king. On the first occasion Michal, as David's wife, is given to Paltiel the son of Laish by King Saul (1 Sam. xxv 44). On the second occasion Michal, as the wife of Paltiel the son of Laish, is given in his lifetime to David, at the command of Eshbaal king of Israel. This repeated offence against one of the sacred principles of society is in need of explanation. A

(2nd edn, London, 1972), pp. 190-3; S. Herrmann, *Geschichte Israels in alttestamentlicher Zeit* (Munich, 1973), pp. 185-90 = E. tr. *A History of Israel in Old Testament Times* (London, 1975), pp. 145-9.

[3]) For the opinion that with Saul's reign the dynastic principle had not yet been established in Israel see J. Pedersen, *Israel, its Life and Culture III-IV* (London and Copenhagen, 1940), p. 58; R. de Vaux, *Les institutions de l'Ancien Testament* I (Paris, 1958), pp. 145-6 = E. tr. *Ancient Israel: Its Life and Institutions* (London, 1961), pp. 94f.; Bright, p. 191.

[4]) The response of Eshbaal to Abner in the matter of Saul's concubine (2 Sam. iii 6-8) demonstrates his great sensitivity to the stability of his kingdom and to anything that could endanger it.

basic social principle in Israel, as in every ancient Near Eastern society, was the prohibition of any sexual relations between a married woman and another man. Its breach was an offence punishable with death, for both the adulterer and the woman [5]). The prohibition is laid down in the severest manner in a legal context—in the Ten Commandments two are devoted to the subject: Exod. xx 14, 17; and Deut. v 17, 18 (cf. Lev. xx 10; Deut. xxii 22). The same state of affairs, with punishment of equal severity, prevails in the ancient Near Eastern Law codes, e.g. the Code of Ḫammurabi, §§ 129-132 [6]); the Middle Assyrian Laws A §§ 12-18, 22-24 [7]); the Hittite Laws B §§ 197, 198 [8]).

The biblical narratives provide us with detailed cases in which the offender incurred the most drastic penalty, no matter whether it was an ordinary citizen or the king himself. In the patriarchal narratives an adulterous relationship is seen as an offence also against God, which results in both individual and collective punishment, as in the traditions concerning Sarai and Pharaoh (Gen. xii 10-20), Sarah and Abimelech (Gen. xx), and Rebekah and Abimelech (Gen. xxvi 6-11; cf. Prov. ii 16-19, v 3-14, vi 24-35, vii 5-27). The story of the marriage of Samson and the woman of Timnah (Jud. xiv-xv), which contains remarkable parallels to the story of the marriage of Michal and David, describes the disaster which was caused as a result of the giving of a man's wife to another, albeit by her own father. To no avail were the father's attempts to minimize his deed, nor his willingness to give Samson his younger daughter. The consequences were terrible: the burning of the father and his daughter, the wife of Samson (Jud. xv 6). The episode of David and Bathsheba (2 Sam. xi-xii 25) is a classic example of the outrage that results from the abduction of another man's wife [9]). The importance of this

---

[5]) For the great severity of the prohibition against taking another wife see R. Patai, *Sex and Family in the Bible and the Middle East* (New York, 1959), pp. 80-91; de Vaux, pp. 62f. (E. tr., pp. 36f.); cf. S. Greengus, "A Textbook Case of Adultery in Ancient Mesopotamia", *HUCA* 40/41 (1969-70), pp. 33-44.

[6]) G. R. Driver and J. C. Miles, *The Babylonian Laws* I (Oxford, 1952), pp. 281-4; II (Oxford, 1955), pp. 50-3.

[7]) G. R. Driver and J. C. Miles, *The Assyrian Laws* (Oxford, 1935), pp. 36-55, 386-97.

[8]) A. Goetze, "The Hittite Laws", in J. B. Pritchard (ed.), *Ancient Near Eastern Texts Relating to the Old Testament* (2nd edn, Princeton, 1955), p. 196.

[9]) On the story of David and Bathsheba see H. W. Hertzberg, *Die Samuelbücher* (Göttingen, 1956), pp. 245-55 = E. tr. *I and II Samuel* (London, 1964), pp. 305-17; P. R. Ackroyd, *The Second Book of Samuel* (Cambridge, 1977), pp. 99-115.

example is manifold: it is based on historical reality, it is close in time to the events of the Michal and David episode, and the hero, David, is involved in both cases. From the outset it is emphasized that even the king did not dare openly to seduce the wife of Uriah the Hittite. He spares no effort to conceal what he is doing, and finally prefers murder of the husband to public exposure of his misdeed. The harsh reaction of the prophet Nathan and his condemnation of David shows that society would brook no compromise in matters of this nature (2 Sam. xii 7-12).

To return to the case of Michal, the reaction of her husband Paltiel the son of Laish is all the more astonishing by comparison. The story emphasizes the depth of his grief and his inability to take his leave of her, but at the same time his conduct shows that he accepts the decision. This is difficult to comprehend, for it is reasonable to suppose that he would appeal to the king or the leaders of the community, that he would put up a bitter and unyielding struggle, and that he would most certainly not accompany his wife on her way to another man. And no less incomprehensible is the absence of reaction of the community and its dignitaries, particularly in view of the fact that it took place within the sovereign territory of Israel and under the king of Israel.

C. *How can David's remarriage to his former wife Michal be reconciled with the law in Deut. xxix 1-4?*

The third question is of a legal nature. The law expressly forbids remarriage where the wife has been married to another man in the interim:

> ... Then her former husband, who sent her away, may not take her again to be his wife...[10])

The woman was thought to be impure to her husband and their conduct as a whole was considered an abomination before God and a defilement of the land verse (4b) [11]). Confirmation of this strict prohibition comes from Jer. iii 1:

> If a man divorces his wife and she goes from him and becomes another man's wife, will he return to her? Would not that land be greatly polluted?

[10]) See G. von Rad, *Das fünfte Buch Mose. Deuteronomium* (Göttingen, 1964), pp. 106-8 = E. tr. *Deuteronomy* (London, 1966), pp. 149f.; Z. W. Falk, *Hebrew Law in Biblical Times* (Jerusalem, 1964), pp. 154-7.

[11]) See M. Weinfeld, *Deuteronomy and the Deuteronomic School* (Oxford, 1972), pp. 269f.

The presentation of this instance as an outstanding example of sin in a society is evidence that such a prohibition was well known to the society and was one of the principles whose breach it would not tolerate.

All the three significant questions have to be answered. Failure to resolve them, or even any attempt to explain them away, will call into question several of the basic principles of Israelite society at the beginning of the monarchy.

I

The passage 2 Sam. iii 14-16 discussed above is part of a scattered biblical account which centres on one story: "the marriage of Michal daughter of Saul to David" (1 Sam. xvii 25, xviii 17-19, 20-29, xix 11-17, xxv 44; 2 Sam. iii 12-16, vi 16, 20-23, xxi 8-9) [12]). The outstanding features of this story are its various stages and the vitality and dynamism of the narrative. Nonetheless, as some scholars see in some of the texts parallel or late traditions, it must be asked to what degree they are authentic and inter-connected, and by the same token how relevant are the questions which were raised above, since those problems arise only if the story itself is authentic and complete. Within the story, it is possible to distinguish the following stages.

> Firstly, 1 Sam. xvii 25: "... And the man who kills him the king will enrich with great riches, and will give him his daughter".

King Saul's promise, then, signifies the start of the long chain of events.

The next stage is 1 Sam. xviii 17-19, the marriage of Merab the daughter of Saul to David. According to the Masoretic text, Saul offers his elder daughter Merab to David in marriage, on condition that David fight the wars of the Lord. At the end of this passage it is stated without any explanation that Merab is given as wife to another, to Adriel the Meholathite [13]).

The next stage, 1 Sam. xviii 20-29, is the account of Michal's marriage to David. The motive for this marriage is Michal's love for David. The condition which is demanded of him this time for his marriage with Michal is a marriage-gift (*mohar*) of a hundred

---

[12]) For these writings see M. H. Segal, *The Books of Samuel* (Jerusalem, 1956), pp. 134-58, 203, 248f. (Hebrew); Hertzberg, pp. 109-31, 162, 204-8 (E. tr., pp. 142-68, 205, 254-60); P. R. Ackroyd, *The First Book of Samuel* (Cambridge, 1971), pp. 136-58, 199f., and *The Second Book of Samuel*, pp. 39-44; H. J. Stoebe, *Das erste Buch Samuelis* (Gütersloh, 1973), pp. 312-65, 451, 460, and "David und Mikal. Überlegungen zur Jugendgeschichte Davids", *BZAW* 77 (Berlin, 1958), pp. 224-43.

[13]) Ackroyd, *The First Book of Samuel*, p. 153.

foreskins. David fulfils the condition twice over, bringing two hundred foreskins. As a result, "Saul gave him his daughter Michal for a wife" (verse 27).

The two stories of the marriages of David to Saul's daughters give rise to a number of reservations, the basic question being whether we have before us a reflection of historical reality, i.e. that David was offered first the hand of one of Saul's daughters and later of another, or whether they are two versions of David's marriage [14]). In the view of most scholars the Michal narrative is authentic and reflects historical reality, while the Merab narrative is dismissed as a colourless imitation [15]). Even among those scholars who uphold the trustworthiness of the Michal narrative, however, there are doubts as to the tradition which places Michal's marriage to David in the reign of Saul [16]). In our view, the account of Michal's marriage to David taking place in Saul's lifetime and at his initiative is rooted in historical reality. This story is linked in all its details to everything else that is written about the affair as a whole. It is not possible to understand any of the biblical passages on Michal's marriage to David, which are accepted as reliable by most biblical scholars, without the original passage in 1 Sam. xviii 20-29, which indicates that the marriage took place in Saul's lifetime and at his initiative. A further decisive fact is that throughout Michal is explicitly referred to as David's wife: 1 Sam. xix 11, xxv 44; 2 Sam. iii 14. Thus the words of Ahimelech clearly establish that the marriage took place in Saul's reign (1 Sam. xxii 14).

The following stage is 1 Sam. xix 11-17, where Michal saves David's life. This incident shows that Michal is living in David's house, and emphasizes her devotion to her husband—she is the one who presses him to flee, and hides his escape. When rebuked by Saul, she does not hesitate to give a deceitful answer [17]).

The next stage is 1 Sam. xxv 44, where Saul gives Michal the wife of David to Palti the son of Laish from Gallim. This piece of informa-

---

[14]) Hertzberg, p. 123, n. 4 (E. tr., p. 159, n. a.).

[15]) This view is in accord with Codex Vaticanus, which makes no mention of the Merab tradition (1 Sam. xviii 17-19). Cf. Stoebe, *Das erste Buch Samuelis*, pp. 550f., and "David und Mikal", pp. 224-43. In his view the whole question is one concerning the traditions about David's youth, in which are reflected the motifs of the patriarchal narratives, the marriage of Jacob to Leah and Rachel, the daughters of Laban.

[16]) Noth, p. 170, n. 1 (E. tr., p. 184, n. 1); Stoebe, *Das erste Buch Samuelis*, p. 352, and "David und Mikal", pp. 227f., 234f.

[17]) Hertzberg, p. 130 (E. tr., pp. 166f.).

tion was apparently inserted at this point in connection with the account of David's other wives, and because it is related to the difficult situation in which David finds himself [18]).

The final stage is 2 Sam. iii 12-16, the restoration of Michal to David. This passage has also given rise to misgivings—is this a single narrative or two versions? But even if there were two traditions concerning the manner in which Michal was returned to David, it does not affect the historical fact that Michal was formally restored to David. She could return to him only by order of Eshbaal, the king [19]).

The following three conclusions may be drawn from the discussion so far:

1. The narrative of Michal's marriage to David is reliable and is based on historical reality, and its stages are consistent with one another.
2. The fundamental questions which were posed at the beginning of this discussion are relevant, but remain unanswered. Proof of the authenticity of the narrative is what causes these questions to arise and serves to emphasize their difficulty.
3. At the same time it has become clear from the discussion that the biblical source alone cannot provide the answers to these questions.

II

Legal documentary material from Mesopotamia reveals a remarkable practice which has significant implications for the case of Michal and David.

In the Laws of Eshnunna, (paragraph 29, 19th century B.C.) we find the following law:

> If a man has been [*made prisoner*] during a raid/or an invasion, or has been carried off forcibly, (and) [*dwelt*] in another land for a l[ong] time, another indeed took his wife and/she bore a son—whenever he returns, he will [*take back*] his wife [20]).

The law [21]) deals with the case of a man who is forcibly displaced by an enemy force and against his will lives for a considerable time

[18]) Cf. J. Morgenstern, "Additional Notes on '*Beena* Marriage (Matriarchat) in Ancient Israel' ", *ZAW* 49 (1931), pp. 54f.

[19]) Two further passages may be seen as supplements to the story of the marriage of Michal and David. The first, in 2 Sam. vi 16-23, indicates the rift between Michal and David and the fact that she had no children. The second, 2 Sam. xxi 8-9, is the handing over of Saul's offspring to the Gibeonites. Here are mentioned the five sons of Michal whom she bore to Adriel the Meholathite. See pp. 26-7.

[20]) This translation follows R. Yaron, *The Laws of Eshnunna* (Jerusalem, 1969), pp. 34f.

[21]) Cf. Yaron, pp. 109f., 134f.

in a foreign country. His wife who is left on her own is allowed to remarry. A son is born of the second marriage. The first husband upon his return receives back his wife. The law is laconically phrased and important details are missing (cf. Yaron, p. 134).

Paragraph 135 of the Laws of Ḫammurabi (c. 18th century B.C.) informs us:

> If the man takes himself off and there is not the (necessary) maintenance in his house, (and) before his return his wife enters another man's house and then bears sons, (if) her husband afterwards returns and regains his city, that woman shall return to her first husband; the sons shall follow their (respective) fathers [22]).

This law, like that of Eshnunna, discusses the case of a woman whose husband is taken by force and lays down the same ruling. However, it adds two important details: first the reason for the wife's second marriage, second the rule for children born of the second marriage [23]).

Paragraph 45 of tablet A of the Middle Assyrian Laws [24]) deals with the same case. But while the earlier sources from Eshnunna and Babylon are brief and give only the main points of the case, the Middle Assyrian tablet discusses the subject at length, adds important details and presents different aspects of the law:

> If a woman has been given (in marriage), and her husband has been taken by an enemy, (and) she has no father-in-law or son, she shall belong to her husband for two years; during these two years, if there is not enough to eat, she shall come and declare it. If she is a villager of a palace, her [palace?] shall feed her, and she shall do its? work. If she is the [wife?] of a *ḫupšu*, [.....] shall feed her, [..........]; and, [if she is a free woman? and there is] a field and [a house at her disposal (?)], she shall come [and declare it] saying: "[I have nothing] to eat". (Then) the judges shall ask the mayor (and) elders of the village whether the field and house belong in that village, (and) they shall sell the field and house for her maintenance during the two years, on her behalf (-*še*). She is "in waiting" and they shall write a tablet for her (to that effect). She shall complete two years, (and) then she may be "in waiting" for the husband of her

22) This translation follows Driver and Miles, *The Babylonian Laws* II, pp. 52f.

23) For this law see Driver and Miles, *The Babylonian Laws* I, pp. 284-90; II, pp. 215-17; T. J. Meek, "The Code of Ḫammurabi", *ANET*, p. 171.

24) Cuneiform text in O. Schroeder, *Keilschrifttexte aus Assur verschiedenen Inhalts* (Leipzig, 1920), I, col. VI, 46-88 (p. 10); Driver and Miles, *The Assyrian Laws*, pp. 212-28, 256-66, 412-15; G. Cardascia, *Les lois assyriennes* (Paris, 1969), pp. 217-26; J. N. Postgate, "Land Tenure in the Middle Assyrian Period: A Reconstruction", *BSOAS* 34 (1971), pp. 496-520. For the date of the Laws see Driver and Miles, pp. 4-12.

choice, (and) they shall write a tablet for her as if she were an *almattu* ("widow").

If, after a time, her lost husband returns to the land, he shall take (back) his wife who was married outside (his household), (but) he shall have no claim on any sons she bore to her later husband—it is her later husband who takes (them). The field and house which she had sold outside (his household) for her maintenance, if it? has not entered the... of the king, he shall pay as (much as) was paid (for it before), and shall take (it back); and, if he has not returned, (but) died in another land, the king shall give (away) his field and his house wherever he wishes to give (it) [25].

From this document we are given to understand that the wife has no father-in-law or sons who will provide for her or look after her in her husband's absence. The tablet deals with three cases of women in this situation, over two of whom it pauses only briefly, these being women from the lower classes, the wife of a villager-dependant of the Palace, whom the Palace is obliged to support in return for her employment there, and the wife of a *ḫupšu*, who is also required to work in return for her maintenance. The third case, which is the central concern of the law, is that of a free woman whose husband possesses an estate and who belongs to a higher social class than the other two. This woman is not required to work for her living, and thus she finds herself in distress. The judges, the mayor and the elders of her village, sell her estate, and in return supply her needs (see Postgate, p. 506). She remains in this situation as a deserted wife for two years, and then she is allowed to remarry. Finally, upon the return of her first husband she goes back to him and her children remain with their natural father. The tablet concludes with the right of the first husband to redeem his estate.

The three sources discussed above, from Eshnunna, Babylon and Assyria, reveal the existence of a similar custom [26]. The fact that the sources are dispersed over a very long period of time and derive from different peoples may be evidence that this practice was widely accepted throughout Mesopotamia. Some development may be discernible in it: from the brief Eshnunna law through that of Babylon to the Assyrian law which drew upon the two earlier laws and enlarged upon them. It is possible from these sources to sketch a clear and comprehensive picture of the practice and to lay down the following principles:

[25]) This translation follows Postgate, pp. 502f.

[26]) Cf. E. Szlechter, "Effets de la Captivité en Droit Assyro-Babylonien", *RA* 57 (1963), pp. 181-92.

1. The basis of the law and its essential condition is that the husband has been forcibly taken by an enemy and now is absent from his home and his city against his will, by reason of *force majeure*. This basic element is found in all three sources and is what determines the law.
2. The wife is left without any means of sustenance and in need of assistance. This clause, which is lacking in Eshnunna, is expressly stated in the Babylonian and Assyrian laws. The Assyrian law brings to light the woman's situation and why she is left without means of maintenance even though she belongs to a high social class.
3. It is remarkable that in all the sources discussed there is no mention of the wife's father. It is reasonable to presume from this that after her marriage the wife belonged to her husband's household and her father was no longer obliged to look after her. The fact that the document does not mention the woman turning, in the hour of her need, to her father's house for help, but only, it would appear, to the local authority, shows that her father has ceased to be the source of her maintenance and protection. The matter is not made to depend on the social status of the father, nor on his economic situation [27]).
4. The wife was obliged to make a declaration of her condition and thus came under the protection of the local authorities. This clause is lacking at Eshnunna and Babylon. It reveals the responsibility of the authorities towards the deserted wives especially the free woman from the upper class.
5. At least two years were set as the period during which the woman had to remain as wife of her first husband. This is according to the Assyrian law; the law from Eshnunna remarks only that the husband may be absent for a long time, while the Babylonian law makes no mention of the time involved.
6. After two years the woman receives the status of an *almattu*, a "widow". The term refers to a woman who has not only lost her husband but also has no father-in-law or adult sons to maintain her, and thus is left without support from her husband's house. Only after receipt of a tablet confirming her as an *almattu* is she entitled to remarry. This clause is likewise only found in the Assyrian law [28]).

[27]) See Driver and Miles, *The Assyrian Laws*, p. 217, n. 1. From the Mesopotamian custom of bestowing a *šeriktum* upon a daughter of the family on the occasion of her marriage we may conclude that this was her share of the paternal estate, and that she had no right to additional claims thereafter.

[28]) See Postgate, p. 504. Cf. Driver and Miles, *The Babylonian Laws* I, p. 294, and *The Assyrian Laws*, pp. 212f.

7. The woman marries a second time. This basic element is found in all the sources (cf. Szlechter, pp. 186-91).
8. The woman has borne sons to her second husband. This clause appears in all the sources, and emphasizes that she was free to build a completely new life in the home of her second husband.
9. With the return of the first husband, the woman is obliged to come back to him.
10. The children that were born to the second husband remain with him. The law recognized that offspring belonged to the family of their natural father.

In summary, according to the sources from Eshnunna, Babylon and Assyria the law was in essence that a woman whose husband had been taken under constraint, i.e. by *force majeure*, and who was left without means of support was allowed to remarry. Nonetheless, from the legal point of view she belongs to her first husband and although her second marriage is lawful it is immediately and incontestably invalid upon the return of the first husband, and the woman returns to the latter.

III

The Mesopotamian practice discussed above is important for an understanding of Michal's marriage to David, for a closer examination will demonstrate the similarity of the Mesopotamian practice's principles, particularly the Assyrian law, to the biblical narrative.

David is forced against his will to abandon his home and flee for his life, to wander in the desert and go into exile in a foreign land. There appears *prima facie* a difficulty in comparing David's situation with the main principle of the law: while the Mesopotamian law is concerned with a man who has been taken by an enemy, David is said to have fled himself. We have already emphasized, however, that the law in question is based on a single criterion, namely whether the situation in which the man finds himself was imposed upon him against his will, by *force majeure*, or whether he created it of his own free will. In the case of David it is made abundantly clear that his departure was involuntary, by *force majeure* to no less an extent than that of a captive. The narrative lays stress on Michal's initiative in smuggling David out of the house (1 Sam. xix 11-12) and thus removes any similarity to paragraph 136 of the Laws of Ḫammurabi. Likewise it cannot be compared with paragraph 30 of the Laws of Eshnunna (cf. Yaron, p. 136, n. 105). On the contrary, this narrative is a link in the special complex of relations between Saul and David, wherein David continually shows feelings of loyalty, love and honour towards Saul (1 Sam. xxiv 6, 9-15, 22, xxvi 9-11, 17-20, 22-23), while Saul on the one hand shows his love for David, raises him above the people and makes him his son-in-law, and on the other seeks to kill him and pursues him (1 Sam. xvi 21-22, xviii 13, 17, 27, xix 11-15, xxii 1-8, xxiii 13-21, xxiv, xxvi) [29]). So far as this reflects a conflict, one reason may be David's elevated position (son-in-law of the king, hero of Israel and the person to whom the people give precedence—1 Sam. xviii 7), which defines it as a court conflict over the succession to the throne.

Michal is left alone in her husband's house; she has no sons, and her father-in-law, David's father, is forced to find refuge with the king of Moab (1 Sam. xxii 1-4). We might also suppose that David's household could not afford to support her in a fitting way, in view of David's sudden flight. Michal's status is similar to that of the free women of the upper class whose only protector is the formal authority. It should also be remembered that the woman no longer belongs to her father's household; it is not clear, moreover, what the relations between Saul and Michal were after she helped David to escape. At all events, Michal, without father-in-law, and sons, was in the eyes of the law without means of support and therefore entitled to marry another man. The accounts of David's wanderings point to his being away from home for years. According to the Assyrian law, which lays down a period of two years for the time that the wife still belongs to her first husband, Michal would be formally free to remarry. It is possible to understand Saul's action as that of a ruler who is responsible for her fate and assists her in remarrying, and not at all because he is her father. It would be proper in the matter of a woman of the status of a king's daughter that the palace should deal with it. His action must be recognized as a customary official act and not as the arbitrary act of Saul giving his daughter in marriage.

With the return of the missing first husband the wife was by law obliged to come back to him. In like manner David demands Michal.

One is not informed whether or not Michal had sons from her second marriage, except for the knowledge that she returned to David without sons (2 Sam. iii 16-17). It may be possible to conclude that she did from a piece of information that is the subject of dispute:

[29]) See Pedersen, *Israel* ... *III-IV*, pp. 50-7; and Bright, pp. 187-9.

> And the King took ... the five sons of Michal the daughter of Saul, whom she bore to Adriel the son of Barzillai the Meholathite (2 Sam. xxi 8).

It is usually thought that there is an error here, and that "Merab" should be read instead of "Michal", on account of the name of the husband, Adriel the Meholathite, who is referred to in 1 Sam. xviii 19. It is difficult to accept that there was a mistake in the name of Michal, however, and it is possible that the mistake is actually in the name of the second husband (who is of secondary importance in the narratives), which should be Paltiel the son of Laish. Stoebe suggests that "Adriel" and "Paltiel" are the same name. "Paltiel" is the Hebrew name, while "Adriel" is Aramaic and has the same meaning: "God is the saviour". It would appear that there are several different versions of the name of Michal's second husband: Palti (1 Sam. xxv 44), Paltiel (2 Sam. iii 15), Adriel (2 Sam. xxi 8) [30]. With the aid of the Mesopotamian custom one may explain the passage of events; Michal bore sons to her second husband and they remained with their natural father after the return of the first husband. It is for this reason that it is stated that Michal had no sons (2 Sam. vi 23).

The following is a chart comparing the principles of the Mesopotamian law to the Michal and David narrative.

Legal Principles	Eshnunna	Babylon	Assyria	The Marriage of Michal to David
1. Husband is absent from home and city by reason of *force majeure*	x	x	x	x
2. Wife is without means because she has no father-in-law or sons.	x	x	x	x
3. Two years (minimum) laid down as time she must wait for return of her husband.	x		x	x
4. Wife marries a second time.	x	x	x	x
5. Wife bears sons to second husband.	x	x	x	x
6. First husband returns and his wife goes back to him.	x	x	x	x
7. Children remain in house of second husband.		x	x	x

[30]) See Stoebe, *Das erste Buch Samuelis*, p. 451, and "David und Mikal", pp. 228-32.

Comparison of the Mesopotamian law and the biblical narrative thus shows that identical principles were involved. We may therefore conclude that the same practice that was widespread in Mesopotamia was known and followed in Israel, at least at the beginning of the monarchic period.

Conclusion

In the light of this conclusion let us now attempt to answer the fundamental questions which were raised from the biblical narrative.

A. The first question was: why does Eshbaal agree to hand over Saul's daughter Michal to David? David's demand for the return of his wife on the strength of his being her first husband rests on the basic law and custom of the society. Its breach was liable to tarnish the reputation of Eshbaal the king, marking him as a ruler who attacked the legal foundations of society, and in consequence as unconcerned for social order and lawfulness in his kingdom [31]). There can be no doubt that Eshbaal was especially sensitive to his name in this delicate period, when the very existence of his kingdom was in question. It is reasonable to suppose that he would try his utmost to prove to Israel that they were right in making him king. Thus his desire to create the image of a king who preserves law and order was balanced against his fear of the advantages that a daughter of Saul would give to his adversary David. And the former considerations proved decisive. Only thus can Eshbaal's action be understood.

B. The second question is: how can we explain Michal's repeated remarriage? Only in the light of the Mesopotamian law can we understand not only that was there not a crass breach of one of the sacred principles of society, the prohibition against taking another man's wife, but that all the parties in this case were acting in accordance with law and custom. After Michal has been living for years in the house of her husband David who is absent, and has been without husband, sons, or father-in-law, she is married to her second husband Paltiel the son of Laish. Her remarriage to David is to be understood in the same way. With his return to his country David, Michal's first husband, claims his wife and received her in accordance with the law. Again, only by reference to the Mesopotamian law can the

[31]) It was an official preoccupation of oriental monarchs that their names should be synonymous with order, justice and preservation of the law. See D. J. Wiseman, "Law and Order in Old Testament Times", *Vox Evangelica* 8 (1973), pp. 5-21.

conduct of her second husband be explained. From the beginning of their marriage Paltiel knows that, as long as there is no positive knowledge of her first husband's death, the latter retains a claim to his wife. When the time comes, he acts as a responsible citizen in accordance with custom, albeit openly showing his deep distress. This is the reason for the absence of any reaction from the leaders of Israel. Not only is it not to be expected that they will side with Paltiel the son of Laish, her husband, but as representatives of law and order in the society it is their duty to see that the transfer is carried out, even at the price of causing pain and suffering to a respected citizen. Their silence is to be taken as assent.

C. The third question was: how can David's remarriage to his former wife after her marriage to another be explained in the light of the express law in Deut. xxiv 1-4? In the Mesopotamian sources (Laws of Eshnunna paragraph 30; Laws of Ḫammurabi, paragraph 136) it is expressly stated that if a man leaves his wife and his city of his own free will and his wife marries another he has no further right to her and is not entitled to take her back. Thus in the biblical law (Deut. xxiv 1-4) it is expressly stated that the man sends away his wife of his own free will and at his own initiative and afterwards she marries another—contrary to David's case. The biblical law adds the fact that she married another man and is therefore forbidden to her husband, for whom it is a sin:

> ... after she has been defiled, for that is an abomination before the LORD, and you shall not bring guilt upon the land which the LORD your God gives you for an inheritance (Deut. xxiv 4b).

The language of this addition is clearly Deuteronomistic [32]), and evidently the law was not yet in force in David time. Likewise the reference to this law in Jer. iii 1 as one of the customary laws is evidence for the lateness of the law and its connection with the Deuteronomist (cf. Weinfeld, p. 359).

In sum: the Mesopotamian law mentioned above contributes to our understanding of Michal's marriage to David and places it in its proper social and legal contexts. The biblical story, as a result, is seen to be based on a custom known and accepted throughout Mesopotamia as well as in Israel. Only in the light of this Mesopotamian legal practice can one adequately answer the questions posed at the beginning of this study.

---

[32]) On Deuteronomic phraseology see Weinfeld, pp. 323, 340f., 359, 362.

DIE LIST JOABS UND DER SINNESWANDEL DAVIDS*

Eine dtr bearbeitete Einschaltung in die Thronfolgeerzählung: 2 Sam. xiv 2-22

von

R. BICKERT

Marburg

I. *Zur Einführung*

Unter dem beherrschenden Einfluß des Rost- von Radschen Verständnisses der Thronfolgeerzählung [1]) 2 Sam. ix-xx und 1 Reg. i-ii [2]) galten lange Zeit die aus diesem Werk erwachsenden exegetischen wie theologischen Fragen als im wesentlichen beantwortet. Seine literarische Einheitlichkeit wurde (abgesehen von 2 Sam. xi 27b-xii 15a) bis vor kurzem im allgemeinen nicht angezweifelt [3]), bis eine Monographie von E. Würthwein, die inzwischen weitgehende Zustimmung gefunden hat, nachwies: Ein gegebener (antidavidisch-antisalomonischer) Erzählungszusammenhang hat eine umfangreiche (prodavidisch-prosalomonische) Überarbeitung erfahren [4]). Ergänzt wurde dieser Nachweis durch Beobachtungen von T. Veijola, der eine Reihe kleinerer dtr Zusätze in der Thronfolgeerzählung feststellte [5]), und von F. Langlamet [6]). Der vorliegende Beitrag möchte in einem begrenzten Abschnitt der von Würthwein aufgezeigten Überarbeitung der Thronfolgeerzählung die kritische Analyse weiterführen.

---

* Für Anregungen und Förderung bei dieser Arbeit bin ich Herrn Prof. E. Würthwein zu Dank verpflichtet.

[1]) L. Rost, *Die Überlieferung von der Thronnachfolge Davids* (Stuttgart, 1926); G. von Rad, „Der Anfang der Geschichtsschreibung im alten Israel", *AkultG* 32 (1944), pp. 1-42 = *Ges. Studien* 1 (München, 1958), pp. 144-88.

[2]) So die gewöhnliche Abgrenzung in der neueren Literatur. Nach E. Würthwein, *Die Erzählung von der Thronfolge Davids — theologische oder politische Geschichtsschreibung*? (Zürich, 1974), p. 58, n. 97, beginnt die Thronfolgeerzählung jedoch mit 2 Sam. x.

[3]) Lediglich bei H. Schulte, *Die Entstehung der Geschichtsschreibung im alten Israel*, *BZAW* 128 (Berlin-New York, 1972), werden kleine Zusätze aus der restlichen Thronfolgeerzählung entfernt: 2 Sam. xvi 10, xix 22 f., „und vielleicht" xv 25 f. (p. 180).

[4]) Zu Würthwein vgl. oben die n. 2.

[5]) T. Veijola, *Die Ewige Dynastie. David und die Entstehung seiner Dynastie nach der deuteronomistischen Darstellung* (Helsinki, 1975).

[6]) F. Langlamet, „Pour ou contre Salomon? La rédaction prosalomonienne de I Rois, I-II", *RB* 83 (1976), pp. 321-79, bes. pp. 329-51.

Würthwein zählt zu jener Überarbeitung auch 2 Sam. xiv 2-22, Verse, die er einen „weisheitlichen Einschub" [7]) nennt. Er begründet diese Auffassung von 2 Sam. xiv 2-22 zwar nur knapp, aber überzeugend [8]).

Es ist nun, über Würthwein hinaus, möglich zu zeigen, daß der von ihm herausgelöste Text in sich selber nicht einheitlich ist [9]). Zuletzt hat J. Hoftijzer schon auf mancherlei Unstimmigkeiten und Ungereimtheiten sowie eine teilweise unangemessene Breite im Stil bei diesem Abschnitt hingewiesen, ohne allerdings daraus literarkritische Folgerungen zu ziehen [10]). Aber eine konsequent angewandte Literarkritik vermag m.E. die durch 2 Sam. xiv 2-22 aufgegebenen Probleme zu klären und damit das literarische Rätsel dieser Verse zu lösen [11]).

Mittels der folgenden literarkritischen Schritte soll dabei die

---

[7]) Würthwein, p. 46.

[8]) Vgl. ibid. pp. 46 f.: 1. ergibt sich schon aus 2 Sam. xiii 39 Davids Sinnesänderung, und da „dieser Sinneswandel schon vorliegt, ist es überflüssig, David durch eine vorgespielte Komödie zu etwas zu bewegen, was er sowieso will" (p. 46); 2. hat der Einschub 2 Sam. xiv 2-22 die Funktion zu „zeigen, wie sehr Joab aktiven Anteil an der Rückkunft Absaloms hatte" und soll „damit seine Verantwortung für die folgenden Verwicklungen hervorheben" (p. 47); 3. stellt der Einschub Joabs Antrieb zum Handeln genau umgekehrt dar wie die alte Erzählung: „Wenn Joab Absalom zurückholte, so nach der ursprünglichen ThFE nicht um des Sohnes, sondern um des Vaters willen. Die Anekdote von der weisen Frau aus Thekoa stellt die Sache umgekehrt dar, so als ob das Interesse Joabs primär dem Sohn gegolten habe" (p. 47).

[9]) Damit erweist sich an 2 Sam. xiv 2-22 beispielhaft die Berechtigung der Auffassung Langlamets vom „caractère encore incomplet de la critique littéraire entreprise" im Rahmen der Thronfolgeerzählung. Langlamet fordert darum zugleich dazu auf „à poursuivre le travail dans la direction indiquée par Wuerthwein", *RB* 83 (1976), p. 348. Vgl. auch *RB* 83 (1976), p. 117: „. . . le travail n'est pas achevé."

[10]) „David and the Tekoite Woman", *VT* 20 (1970), pp. 419-44. Die zentralen Schwierigkeiten des Textes sucht Hoftijzer, dem sie voll bewußt sind, mittels einer psychologisierenden und harmonisierenden Exegese zu entschärfen und so zu überspielen. Damit ist dem schwer zugänglichen literarischen Befund freilich nicht gerecht zu werden.

[11]) „Die Rede ist voll von Ungereimtheiten und gibt unlösbare Rätsel auf, solange man sie rein als Rede der Frau verstehen will". Dieser ganz richtige Satz Delekats (aus "Tendenz und Theologie der David-Salomo-Erzählung", *Fs L. Rost*, *BZAW* 105 [Berlin, 1966], p. 35) leidet nur darunter, daß er die "ungereimten" Partien der Rede auf Zusätze des Verfassers der Thronfolgeerzählung zurückführt und sie für eine "versteckte Äußerung des Erzählers" (ibid.) hält. Das ist ein Irrtum. Das Richtige ahnt dagegen Veijola, p. 47, n. 3, der sich „das langatmige Gespräch des klugen Weibes aus Thekoa mit David in 2 Sam. 14:4-20" so erklärt, daß „eine spätere Erweiterung . . . nicht von vornherein von der Hand zu weisen" ist.

Diskrepanz ihre Erklärung finden, die darin besteht, daß einerseits Joab sich der klugen Frau bedient, indem er sie zu seinem Sprachrohr macht, und daß andererseits diese Frau über weite Strecken ein selbständiges Gespräch mit dem König zu führen scheint — was dazu geführt hat, daß 2 Sam. xiv 2-22 stets unter die Überschrift „Die weise Frau und David" anstatt „Joab und David" gestellt worden ist [12]).

II. *Literarkritische Analyse von 2 Sam. xiv 2-22*

Im Gespräch zwischen König David und der klugen Frau aus Tekoa bereiten dem Verständnis besonders große Schwierigkeiten die bereits von Hoftijzer in den Mittelpunkt seiner Ausführungen gestellten V. 9 und V. 13-17. Neben diesen *offensichtlich* der Erklärung bedürftigen Stellen gibt es jedoch noch weitere, nicht sofort erkennbare und von Hoftijzer auch nicht erkannte Textteile, die ebenfalls einen literarkritischen Eingriff notwendig machen.

Ein Hinweis Veijolas gibt den Ansatz für die Erörterung des V. 9 [13]). Zwar hat sich auch Hoftijzer dem in seinem Kontext außerordentlich schwierigen Vers eingehend gewidmet [14]); doch trotz zahlreicher förderlicher Erkenntnisse gelingt Hoftijzer keine überzeugende Erklärung dieses Verses.

1. Welche Stellung nimmt V. 9 in seiner Umgebung V. 4-8, 10-11 ein? In V. 4 hat die Frau aus Tekoa das Zetergeschrei erhoben; damit hat sie einen Hilferuf ausgestoßen, der bekundet, daß sie sich in Not befindet und nach Rechtsbeistand verlangt [15]). Die verwandte Formulierung in 2 Reg. vi 26bβ zeigt, „daß das Zetergeschrei mit dem Hilferuf *hôšî'āh* eingeleitet wurde" [16]). Wie in 2 Reg. vi 28a,

---

[12]) So durchweg in der Literatur (einschließlich Würthwein). Einzelnes gelegentliches Schwanken, ob nicht doch Joab anstelle der Frau der wahre Partner Davids in diesem Text sei, wie es bei R. N. Whybray, *The Succession Narrative. A Study of II Sam. 9-20 and I Kings 1-2* (London, 1968), pp. 43, 59, 86, oder bei Veijola, p. 47, n. 3 („Es ist aber zweifelhaft, dass hier die weibliche Zungenfertigkeit dargestellt wird, weil ja nach V. 3 *Joab* die Worte dem Weibe in den Mund gelegt hatte") begegnet, hindert dennoch nicht, die Szene 2 Sam. xiv 2-22 am Ende stets mit "Die weise Frau und David" zu überschreiben.

[13]) Veijola, p. 75, n. 166, stellt ganz zu Recht fest: „2 Sam. 14:9 ist in seinem Kontext eine völlig widersinnige Aussage" und fährt fort: „. . . die Betonung der Unschuld Davids und seines Königtums erinnert stark an DtrG (vgl. 2 Sam. 3:28)."

[14]) Vgl. Hoftijzer, pp. 424-8.

[15]) Vgl. dazu und zum Folgenden bei H. J. Boecker, *Redeformen des Rechtslebens im Alten Testament* (Neukirchen, 1964), den Exkurs 3, pp. 61-6, bes. pp. 63 f.

[16]) ibid. pp. 63 f.

so folgt jetzt in V. 5a mit *măh-lāk* die direkte Reaktion des Königs, auf die hin, vergleichbar mit 2 Reg. vi 28b-29, in V. 5b-7 die Frau ihre Notlage schildert. Damit will sie erreichen, daß der König etwas unternimmt; er wird also um eine Rechtsentscheidung angegangen. Tatsächlich gibt der König in 2 Sam. xiv unmittelbar anschließend eine solche, nämlich in V. 8, 10, 11, wobei der verbindliche Rechtsspruch aber erst, wie Hoftijzer richtig gesehen hat [17]), in V. 11 ergeht. Den V. 8-11 zufolge muß die Frau, wie es scheint, dem König seine Entscheidung zu ihren Gunsten erst abringen: denn in V. 8 äußert er sich ganz unbestimmt; die Frau trägt darauf in V. 9 ein Bekenntnis der „Schuld" vor, das den König und seinen „Thron" von „Schuld" freispricht; danach drückt sich in V. 10 der König schon viel entschlossener in einem für die Frau positiven Sinne aus; aber immer noch, in V. 11a, läßt die Frau nicht vom König ab, und jetzt endlich, in V. 11b, fällt dann das eindeutige königliche Wort zu ihren Gunsten, durch einen Eid bekräftigt [18]). Der Gesprächsablauf in V. 8-11 wäre demzufolge einfach und klar und von einer Klimax bestimmt.

Aber — sind die V. 8-11 wirklich in dieser Weise zu deuten? Dagegen erheben sich starke Bedenken. Denn der König träfe ja dreimal, wenn auch mit unterschiedlich großem Nachdruck, seine Entscheidung, nachdem die Frau ihm ebenfalls dreimal ihr Anliegen, wenn auch jeweils in anderer Form, vorgetragen hätte, so daß also dieselbe Angelegenheit dreimal kurz hintereinander zur Sprache gebracht worden wäre. Überdies steht durchaus nicht fest, daß sich V. 9, in dem eine „Schuld" bekannt und gleichzeitig von „Schuld" freigesprochen wird, in den Rahmen der V. 8-11 fügt. Daß in V. 8-11 der König sachlich stets denselben positiven Entscheid auf das Rechtsbegehren der Frau von V. 5b-7 (, 9, 11a) ausspräche, ist

---

[17]) Vgl. Hoftijzer, p. 422: „The woman's intention in presenting her fictitious case . . . is, that the king may give the ruling that the culprit will neither be executed nor exiled, but may stay at home. This means that he will go unpunished. David actually gives this ruling . . . (v. 11), confirming this decision by an oath." So auch p. 424 und pp. 428 f.

[18]) Vgl. dazu Hoftijzer, p. 424: „First he gives a ruling of a vague character, the second ruling is more outspoken. The third time she induces him to confirm the last one on oath." Ebenso W. Schottroff, *‚Gedenken' im Alten Orient und im Alten Testament* (Neukirchen, 1964), pp. 168 f.: „Die erste Zusage Davids (V. 8) erfolgt . . . Aber die Frau ist mit ihrem Redeschwall noch gar nicht am Ende und fährt . . . im selben Atemzug fort V. 9) . . . Wieder überhört sie die Zusicherung des Königs, um endlich ihre Rede mit einer bittenden Anrede an den König abzuschließen (V. 11). Auf diese Bitte läuft ihr ganzer Redeschwall hinaus, nun erst kann sie innehalten, um den König zu Wort kommen zu lassen."

somit keine so überzeugende Erklärung für den dreifachen Redewechsel in diesen Versen, wie es auf den ersten Blick erscheint.

Diese Deutung geht im Gegenteil im Ansatz fehl. Denn sie übersieht, daß die Antworten in V. 8 und V. 10 miteinander konkurrieren. Nach V. 8 nämlich schickt der König die Frau nach Hause, während er selbst in ihrer Sache Befehl erteilen will; er behält sich mithin allein die Lösung des ihm vorgetragenen Falles vor. Er nimmt ihn der Frau aus der Hand und in die seine. Die Frau spielt dabei keine Rolle. Was der König zu tun gedenkt, bleibt ungesagt, d.h. er fällt keinen Rechtsentscheid, was die Frau doch begehrt. Anders in V. 10! Hier fordert der König die Frau auf, auch ihrerseits etwas in ihrer Sache zu unternehmen und so zu der von ihr vom König verlangten Hilfe mit beizutragen, indem sie ihren Widerpart vor ihn bringt. Dann sagt er ihr offen seinen Schutz zu (V. 10bβ). Damit erhält die Frau den gewünschten Rechtsbeistand des Königs! Jedoch nicht nur in V. 10; noch größeres Gewicht hat, daß gleich darauf (V. 11b) auch der Sohn unter königlichen Schutz gestellt wird. V. 10, 11b gehören also unbedingt zusammen: Zusammen sind sie das auf V. 5b-7 hin zu erwartende Urteil des Königs. — Daß V. 11a diesen Zusammenhang nachträglich unterbricht, wird sich unten erweisen. Und weiter: Hatte David sich in V. 8 entschlossen, persönlich einzugreifen, ohne die Frau dabei in Anspruch zu nehmen, dann war der Fall damit erledigt und es überflüssig, sie, wie in V. 10, doch noch an dem zu beteiligen, was zur Behebung ihrer Not zu geschehen hatte. Davids Worte in V. 10 kommen dann nach denen des V. 8 zu spät. So ist V. 8 ein Vorgriff, unvereinbar mit V. 10. — Damit ist V. 8 dem Grundbestand von 2 Sam. xiv 2-22 abzusprechen.

Demnach ergibt sich als unmittelbare Fortsetzung von V. 7 und Antwort auf V. 5b-7 *nur* V. 10, 11b. Was soll dann aber V. 8? Nun, offenbar steht er um des V. 9 willen da! Denn V. 9 ist für sich allein genommen ja in seiner Umgebung nicht verständlich [19]). V. 9 ist ein isolierter Satz; immerhin erhält er zu seiner Einführung in den Kontext mit V. 8 eine notdürftige Vorbereitung: Die V. 8f. lassen jetzt den Eindruck entstehen, als habe der König zunächst (V.8) eine ausweichende Antwort auf V. 5b-7 gegeben, um die Frau loszuwerden; diese habe sich dadurch aber nicht erschüttern lassen, sondern sich jetzt erst recht (V. 9) durch (scheinbare!) Übernahme jeder mit ihrem Fall zusammenhängenden „Schuld" und der Entlastung des

[19]) Vgl. dazu oben die n. 13.

Königs davon im vorhinein dessen Schutz anheimgegeben und so ihre Sache um so hartnäckiger verfochten [20]. Tatsächlich aber ist ganz unklar, welche auch nur scheinbare „Schuld" hier vorliegen soll! [21] V. 9 wird innerhalb seines Kontextes auch durch V. 8 nicht wirklich verständlicher. Er muß (wie nachher zu sehen ist) anders eingeordnet werden. — Daß V. 9 nicht durch V. 10 fortgeführt wird, geht daraus hervor, daß in V. 10 der König überhaupt nicht auf die starken Worte der Frau aus V. 9 eingeht. Während er in V. 10 das Verhältnis der Frau zu ihrem Widersacher aus V. 7 aufgreift, geht es in V. 9 bei der Selbstbeschuldigung der Frau und der Entlastung des Königs durch sie allein um die Stellung dieser beiden zueinander, so daß V. 10 keinerlei gedankliche Verbindung zu V. 9 hat. Es bleibt von V. 10 her also ebenfalls dunkel, warum die Frau in V. 9 unvermittelt die „Schuld" auf sich und ihre Familie nimmt und die „Unschuld" des Königs und seiner Dynastie beteuert. V. 9 ist und bleibt eine Digression; und wenn diese, wie gesehen, durch V. 8 vorbereitet wird, so sind die V. 8f. also gemeinsam ein Einsatz zwischen V. 7 und V. 10 und entfallen dann *beide* für den Grundbestand von 2 Sam. xiv, 2-22. Auf V. 7 folgt dort sofort V. 10! Damit erledigt sich auch der Vorschlag von Budde und Eissfeldt [22], zwischen V. 7 und V. 8 die V. 15-17 einzustellen. Die V. 15-17 sind an ihrem Ort zu lassen und da zu erklären (dazu gleich mehr). Das Bemerkenswerte an V. 8f. ist, daß diese Verse die Frau aus Tekoa und David vom Kontext abweichend auftreten lassen: David ist in seinen recht unverbindlich kurzen Worten ziemlich distanziert gegenüber der Frau; diese wiederum erweist sich gegen David höfisch-devot wie in so auffälliger Weise sonst nur noch in V. 4aβ (dazu s.u.).

---

[20] Gegen Hoftijzer, der das Schuldbekenntnis in V. 9 meint uneigentlich verstehen zu sollen, p. 427: „. . . one may say that often a confession of guilt is a part of a plea for forgiveness or for another favour, and is meant to further this plea . . . If this is so, the central point . . . is *not* who takes (or has to take) the responsibility in the case under consideration", sondern man hofft „by doing so to further the chance that the( ) request will be granted"; ähnlich p. 428. Aber diese Deutung ist zu künstlich, um zu überzeugen.

[21] Gegen Delekat, p. 35: „Die Frau hatte die eventuelle göttliche Strafe für die Amnestierung des Brudermörders auf sich genommen . . ." Ebenso gegen Schottroff, pp. 168 f.: „(V. 9): bei einer Entscheidung zu ihren Gunsten sei sie und die Sippe ihres Vaters bereit, die ungesühnte Blutschuld auf sich zu nehmen."

[22] K. Budde, *Die Bücher Samuel* (Tübingen und Leipzig, 1902), p. 267 (im Anschluß an S. A. Cook); O. Eißfeldt in *HSAT* I (Tübingen, 1922), p. 461, und n. e.

Der Gang der Wechselrede in V. 5b-7, 10 erscheint störungslos klar. Um so schwieriger ist der Anschluß des V. 11a an V. 10. Daß die Frau den König bei Jahwe beschwört, wirkt so, als ob sie sich Davids Geneigtheit für ihre Sache noch erkämpfen müsse, obwohl sie David doch, wie V. 10 beweist, bereits auf ihrer Seite hat. Auch ist das *hărbôt*[23]) auffallend, da ja doch gar keine weiteren Akte der Blutrache in Betracht kommen. Endlich ist der Bluträcher als *Individuum* nachträglich neu eingeführt, nachdem in V. 7 die Sippe als *Kollektiv* sich zur Blutrache anschickte. V. 11a verdoppelt allem nach V. 7 und muß (samt dem *wăjjo'mær* aus V. 11b) darum Zusatz sein. Seine Entfernung aus dem Grundtext von 2 Sam. xiv 2-22 hat wie die von V. 8f. noch einen weiteren günstigen Effekt: Die Weitschweifigkeit und Geschwätzigkeit im Redegang V. 8-11 verschwindet[24]). V. 11b schließt direkt an V. 10 an.

2. Die nun folgenden V. 13-17 leiden unter besonders großen rhetorischen Mängeln und z.T. geradezu unter Unverständlichkeit. Das hat auch Hoftijzer gesehen[25]) und sich daher mit V. 13-17 im zweiten Teil seiner Ausführungen intensiv befaßt[26]). Was in V. 13-17 gesagt wird, ist zu verworren, als daß es zu einer klugen Frau, die ja hier reden soll, paßte[27]).

Die Verse sind umständlich breit und schwerfällig: a) V. 13 enthält zwei Vorwürfe der Frau an den König, die beziehungslos nebeneinander stehen, denn V. 13a gilt einem Kollektiv, V. 13b dagegen einem Einzelnen; b) unvermittelt kommt V. 14a hinzu, bei dem es

---

[23]) Lies das Qere anstelle des Ketib *hărbăjt*; s. *BHS*.

[24]) Damit ist die in der älteren Literatur beliebte und beispielhaft bei Budde, p. 265 („9 ff. Die Verse bieten ein köstliches Bild weiblicher Geschwätzigkeit und Zudringlichkeit und königlicher Langmut") vertretene Auffassung zur Aufklärung der literarischen Schwierigkeiten in V. 9-11 zurückgewiesen. Vgl. auch Veijola, p. 47: Es „erscheint die Beweiskraft einer solchen Argumentation nicht zuletzt deswegen als fragwürdig, weil nicht sicher ist, ob die alttestamentlichen Erzähler dieselben Vorurteile über die weibliche Psyche hegten wie heutige Exegeten."

[25]) Auf viele Probleme in Einzelheiten, besonders bei den V. 13-17, macht Hoftijzer, p. 420, ausdrücklich aufmerksam.

[26]) Hoftijzer, pp. 429-42.

[27]) Auch für V. 13-17 ist Buddes Wort von „weiblicher Geschwätzigkeit und Zudringlichkeit und königlicher Langmut" (vgl. oben die n. 24) völlig unangebracht und kann allein schon mit dem Satz Veijolas (vgl. ebenfalls oben die n. 24) entkräftet werden. Vgl. aber außerdem auch Hoftijzer, p. 429: „The words the woman speaks here are very difficult, especially vv. 14-17. Some commentators describe her here as highly talkative and as a chatterbox ... In my opinion this interpretation is impossible and incompatible with the way in which the author introduces her."

sich um einen „fast fatalistischen Gemeinplatz" [28]) handelt; an ihn schließt sich antithetisch V. 14b an, der mit V. 13 locker verbunden ist durch die Aussage, Gott selber werde sich um das Geschick des Verbannten kümmern; c) die Rechtfertigung der Frau vor David V. 15-17, daß sie zum König vorgedrungen sei, ist überfüllt.

Zuerst zu c). In V. 15a begründet die Frau ihren Schritt mit ihrer Furcht vor dem *ʿămm*, in V. 16 aber mit der Sorge um ihre und ihres Sohnes Sicherheit vor dem (individuellen!) Bluträcher. V. 15a und V. 16 sind offenbar Doppelungen. Ebenso konkurrieren auch die durch die Begründungen jeweils vorbereiteten Fortsetzungen V. 15b und V. 17a miteinander. Da nun V. 16 den Zusatz V. 11a kennt, muß auch V. 16 sekundär sein. Es ergibt sich von hier aus eine Entwirrung der unübersichtlichen V. 15-17: V. 15a ist ursprünglich gegenüber V. 16; V. 15b ist ursprünglich gegenüber V. 17a. Die V. 16, 17a gehören also nicht zum Grundbestand von 2 Sam. xiv, 2-22! Da ferner der V. 17b den V. 17a voraussetzt, muß auch V. 17b für jenen Grundbestand entfallen. V. 17bα verdoppelt zugleich in störender Weise V. 20b; die Herausnahme des V. 17b beseitigt diese Doppelung. — So bleibt aus V. 15-17 allein V. 15 beim Grundtext von 2 Sam. xiv 2-22. Freilich können einem auch an dieser Zuweisung des V. 15 Zweifel kommen, wenn man nämlich den *ʿămm* mit Hoftijzer (pp. 438f.) mit der Verwandtschaft der Frau in V. 7 identifiziert. Dann griffe V. 15 wieder auf den von ihr vorgetragenen Rechtsfall zurück, der sich mit V. 13 bereits als fiktiv erwiesen hat, und dann gälte in der Tat: „. . . die Frau hat nun . . . die Maske einmal fallen lassen und sie kann sie jetzt nicht wieder anlegen" [29]). Aber hat der *ʿămm* in V. 15 wirklich etwas mit der Verwandtschaft in V. 7 zu tun? Nein! Das ist deshalb unwahrscheinlich, weil (mit Ehrlich) auch der *d^e^băr ʾ^a^mātô* in V. 15 „nicht ihre Bitte in Betreff ihres vorgeblichen Falles" (p. 308) meint, sondern die dem V. 15 unmittelbar vorangehenden Worte der Frau. V. 15 geht also nicht hinter V. 13 zurück! Man verfährt dann auch im Blick auf den *ʿămm* des V. 15 besser so, das, was *ʿămm* hier bedeutet, allein aus V. 15 selbst zu erheben. Bedenkt man, daß die Frau mit dem *König* redet, so liegt es nahe, unter dem *ʿămm* den für das Handeln des Königs aufgrund entscheidender Rechte und Pflichten mitverantwortlichen Teil der Bevölkerung, die Vollbürger, zu verstehen. Die Frau gibt nun in

---

[28]) So die Formulierung G. von Rads in *Weisheit in Israel* (Neukirchen, 1970), p. 252.

[29]) A. B. Ehrlich, *Randglossen zur hebräischen Bibel* 3 (Leipzig, 1910), p. 308.

V. 15 vor, diese (und nicht Joab!) hätten sie veranlaßt, den König aufzusuchen! Die Frau will also ihren wahren Auftraggeber verbergen. Offenbar gehört auch dies zu dem klugen Verhalten, das sie bis dahin schon gegenüber David gezeigt hatte. Freilich wird David (V. 18f.) den Ablenkungsversuch der Frau (V. 15) durchschauen; aber das gibt der vorgetragenen Deutung des V. 15 nur Recht. — V. 15 bleibt also beim Grundbestand von 2 Sam. xiv 2-22, während die V. 16f. als sekundär ausscheiden. Bei dieser Lösung ist auch eine Umstellung der sonst an ihrem jetzigen Ort problematischen V. 15-17 zwischen die V. 7 und 8, wie sie Budde und Eissfeldt angeregt haben [30]), unnötig. — Die V. 18-21 sind offensichtlich intakt. So umfaßt denn der unbearbeitete Text der V. 13-21 zunächst: V. 13-15. 18-21.

Wie aber ist nun die oben unter a) genannte Doppelung in V. 13 zu beurteilen? Hoftijzer erwägt, ob „the first sentence should, strictly speaking, refer to an other subject than the second one. This last one refers to the king being guilty insofar as he violates his own ruling on fratricide, and so clearly has a bearing on the basic facts of the case presented by the supposed widow." Hingegen würde „the first sentence . . . refer . . . neither to the basic facts nor to the ruling" (p. 431). Hoftijzer entscheidet sich dann aber doch gegen eine solche Auffassung der „first sentence" und meint, es sei „preferable to let both sentences refer to one subject and not to different ones" (p. 431). Damit weicht er jedoch einer kritischen Lösung des literarischen Problems aus! Die Spannung zwischen der „first sentence" (sc. V. 13a) und der „second sentence" (sc. V. 13b) ist ernst zu nehmen; es besteht nur die Möglichkeit alternativer Wahl zwischen ihnen. Hat V. 13b Bezug zu den „basic facts" des fiktiven Rechtsfalles, so gehört V. 13b zum Grundtext; V. 13a jedoch, dem es an einem solchen Bezug fehlt, muß dann Zusatz sein. — Wie steht es mit dem oben unter b) aufgeführten V. 14? Sein Sinn ist: Gott läßt den Verbannten nicht in der Verbannung sterben; das soll der König wissen. Die Berufung auf Gott soll die Entscheidung Davids zugunsten seines Sohnes erreichen. Damit widerspricht V. 14 aber V. 13b, der den König durch Behaftung bei seinem eignen Wort zur Rückholung seines Sohnes zwingen will. V. 14 kann also V. 13b nicht fortsetzen und muß wie V. 13a Zusatz sein. — Also umfaßt der Grundbestand der V. 13-21: V. 13b, 15, 18-21 — ein straffer Text, der der gern für

[30]) Vgl. oben p. 35 und die n. 22.

die V. 13-17 bemühten weiblichen Redseligkeit zur Erklärung entraten kann [31]).

3. Nunmehr sind noch die nicht sofort erkennbaren und bisher unerkannt gebliebenen Textteile zu behandeln, die einer literarkritischen Untersuchung bedürfen. Zunächst noch einmal zu V. 16! Dieser Vers kennt, wie gesehen, den V. 11a. Beiden Versen ist im besonderen gemeinsam der Gebrauch des Verbs *hišmîd*. Eben dieses Verb findet sich wieder in *V.7aβ*. Einmal auf diese Spur gebracht, kommt man alsbald auch darauf, daß V. 7aβ nicht recht als Fortsetzung zu V. 7aα paßt. Denn ging es der Sippe in V. 7aα um die Einhaltung der der Blutrache gemäßen Gerechtigkeit, so ist sie jetzt in V. 7aβ nur auf Erbschaft aus [32]). Es ist aber etwas sehr Verschiedenes, ob die Herausgabe des Mörders verlangt wird, weil der Mord gerächt werden, oder deshalb, weil ein Erbe ausgeschaltet werden soll. V. 7aβ bringt daher ein ganz neues Anliegen in die Klage der Frau V. 5b-7: und dieses neue Anliegen setzt sich in *V. 7b* weitläufig fort. So können V. 7aβb nicht ebenso ursprünglich sein wie V. 5b-7aα; sie sind als Erweiterung anzusehen.

Merkwürdig ist sodann, daß in V. 12 die Frau den König erneut um Redeerlaubnis bittet; damit wird der Gesprächsablauf ungeschickt unterbrochen, und nicht zuletzt geschieht die Anwendung des bisher von der Frau beim König Erreichten (V. 11b) auf diesen selbst, wie es dann in V. 13b der Fall ist, nicht mehr, wie notwendig, unmittelbar: Wenn die Frau ab V. 13 wirklich ihre eingeübte Rolle aufgibt und ihre Maske fallen läß [33]), dann kann das, soll es Wirkung haben, nur überraschend erfolgen; die Überraschung aber ist dahin, wenn wie in V. 12 umständlich darum gebeten wird, sie bieten zu dürfen. D.h. V. 12, genauer V. 12aβb (da V. 12aα als Einleitung zu V. 13b nötig ist!) muß ebenfalls aus dem ursprünglichen Text von 2 Sam. xiv 2-22 ausgeschieden werden. V. 12aβb hat deutlich einen höfisch-devoten Stil und stimmt darin zu V. 8f.

Schließlich zu V. 22. Wenn man den Vers liest, wundert man sich zunächst nicht, daß Joab, der Initiator des Auftritts der Frau (V. 2f.),

[31]) Für V. 13-17 gilt also nichts anderes als für V. 9-11, vgl. oben die n. 24.

[32]) Auch Boecker erblickt in V. 7aβ „einen Zusatz", „den wir nicht erwarten, der auch wieder eine gewisse Doppelung des Gedankens bringt" (p. 22) — ohne aber daraus zu folgern, daß diese Doppelung Zeichen für eine erweiternde Ergänzung sein könnte.

[33]) Mit Hoftijzer, p. 429: „After the king has carried out her wish, she confronts him with the consequences of his decision. By doing so she reveals that the case she presented to him was fictitious and meant as a kind of legal ‚trap', in other words she drops her mask."

David ganz überschwenglich dankt, daß er Absalom zurückkehren läßt; denn damit hat Joab sein Zeil erreicht. Störend empfindet man nur, daß Joab, der bei der Szene der Frau mit David in keiner Weise in Erscheinung getreten, sondern geschickt im Hintergrund geblieben war, nun doch noch „seine" Begegnung mit David hat und dabei in eigenen Worten sich selber dessen Sinneswandel zurechnet. Wie stimmt solch beflissenes Hervortreten zu der zuvor geübten strikten Zurückhaltung Joabs? Ja mehr noch: V. 22b sucht den Anschein zu erwecken, als ob David Joab zuliebe Absalom zurückholen lasse; nach V. 2f., 20 hingegen wird David durch Joabs List überrumpelt, so daß er, gebunden an die der Frau aus Tekoa gegebene Zusage, gar nicht mehr anders kann, als Absalom wieder zurückkehren zu lassen. War so Joab in V. 2f., 20 deutlich der David Überlegene, so ist das in V. 22b umgekehrt: die Überlegenheit liegt nun bei David. Damit widerspricht V. 22b ganz klar V. 2f., 20. Da sich aber V. 2f., 20 als Teil des Grundtextes der Einschaltung 2 Sam. xiv 2-22 erweisen, muß V. 22b ihnen gegenüber sekundär sein. Ohne V. 22b wäre ferner V. 22a ganz beziehungslos, d.h. V. 22a bedarf des V. 22b und muß darum ebenso sekundär sein.

Zum letzten: Weil zwischen V. 22a mit Ausnahme der Segenswendung und dem V. 4aβ eine fast wörtliche Parallelität besteht, gerät auch V. 4aβ in den starken Verdacht, Zusatz zu sein. Hinzu kommt, daß die Frau entgegen ihrem selbstbewußten Auftreten vor David im Grundbestand von 2 Sam. xiv 2-22, jedoch durchaus im Einklang mit V. 9, 12aβb und genau wie Joab in V. 22, sich in V. 4aβ gegenüber David höfisch-devot gibt. All das spricht für eine Herausnahme des V. 4aβ aus seinem Kontext. Mit der Entfernung dieses Versteils gewinnt V. 4 an dramatischer Unmittelbarkeit. Ist V. 4aβ sekundär, dann ist auch das wiederholte *wătto'mær* zu Beginn des V. 4b erklärt — eine Wiederaufnahme der gleichen Verbform in V. 4a nach Einfügung von V. 4aβ. Die allgemeine textkritische Verbesserung des *wătto'mær* in V. 4a ist demzufolge unnötig (gegen *BHS* z. St.). —

Zusammenfassend sei noch einmal der Umfang aller ermittelten Zusätze in 2 Sam. xiv 2-22 angegeben: V. 4aβ samt *wătto'mær* aus V. 4b, 7aβb, 8, 9. 11a samt *wăjjo'mær* aus V. 11b, 12aβb, 13a, 14, 16, 17, 22. [34]). Der Gesamttext von 2 Sam. xiv 2-22 ist nach Weglassen dieser Erweiterungen erheblich geschrumpft.

[34]) Delekat, p. 35, hat also etwas Richtiges gesehen, wenn er im Blick auf V. 9, 13 f., meint, sie seien aus dem Gang der Rede der Frau selber nicht zu ver-

Übersetzung der ursprünglichen vordtr Fassung von 2 Sam. xiv 2-22

2. Da sandte Joab nach Tekoa und ließ von dort eine kluge Frau holen; und er sprach zu ihr: Stelle dich doch trauernd, ziehe doch Trauerkleider an und salbe dich nicht mit Öl und benimm dich wie eine Frau, die nun schon lange Zeit um einen Toten trauert!
3. Dann gehe zum König hinein und rede mit ihm so und so! — und Joab legte ihr die Worte in den Mund.
4aαb*. So sprach die Frau aus Tekoa zum König: Hilf, o König!
5. Der König sprach zu ihr: Was hast du? Darauf sprach sie: Ach, ich bin eine Witwe, und mein Mann ist gestorben.
6. Deine Dienerin hatte aber zwei Söhne; die beiden gerieten auf dem Felde in Streit miteinander, und niemand war da, der schlichtete zwischen ihnen. ‚So schlug der eine den anderen' [s. *BH*] und tötete ihn.
7aα. Da erhob sich auf einmal die ganze Sippe gegen deine Dienerin, und man sprach: Gib den Mörder seines Bruders heraus, daß wir ihn töten für das Leben seines Bruders, den er umgebracht hat!
10. Der König sprach: Den, der mit dir geredet hat, ‚den bringe' [s. *BH*] zu mir, daß er dich hinfort nicht mehr antaste!
11b*. So wahr Jahwe lebt: es soll kein Haar deines Sohnes zur Erde fallen!
12aα. Darauf sprach die Frau:
13b. ‚Indem' der König dies ‚redet', ‚erweist er sich' [s. *BH*] als schuldbeladen, (darin,) daß der König nicht den von ihm Verstoßenen zurückkommen läßt!
15. Und nun: daß ich hergekommen bin, um mit dem König, meinem Herrn, dies Wort zu reden, (geschah,) weil mir die Bürger Angst machten; da dachte deine Dienerin: Ich will doch mit dem König reden; vielleicht wird der König das Wort seiner Magd ausführen!
18. Da hob der König an und sprach zu der Frau: Verhehle mir doch nichts, wonach ich dich jetzt frage! Und die Frau sprach: Möge doch mein Herr König reden!
19. Darauf sprach der König: Hat etwa Joab die Hand im Spiel auf dem allem? Die Frau antwortete und sprach: So wahr du lebst, mein Herr König: Wahrlich, niemand kann rechts oder links dem ausweichen, was irgend mein Herr König redet! Ja, dein Knecht Joab, der gab mir den Auftrag und der legte alle diese Worte in den Mund deiner Dienerin!
20. Um der Sache ein anderes Gesicht zu geben, hat dein Knecht Joab dies getan. Aber mein Herr besitzt Klugheit wie die Klugheit des Engels Gottes, daß er alles weiß, was auf Erden geschieht!
21. Da sprach der König zu Joab: So will ich denn diese Bitte erfüllen: geh nun, bringe den jungen Mann, den Absalom, zurück!

---

stehen. Aber der Schluß, diese Verse seien vom Erzähler der Rede „als versteckte Äußerung" seiner negativen Einstellung zum davidisch-salomonischen Königtum eingekleidet in die Worte der Frau aus Tekoa hinzugesetzt, ist offenbar nicht zu halten.

4. Die aufgezeigten Erweiterungen stehen allerdings nicht alle auf der gleichen literarischen Ebene. Vielmehr sind zwei Bearbeitungen: A. und B. zu unterscheiden: A. Verse mit der mehrfach erwähnten höfisch-devoten Art, nämlich V. 4aβ, 8, 9, 12aβb, 22; und B. Doppelungen des Grundtextes, wozu der den V. 7aα umdeutende V. 7aβb gehört, also V. 7aβb, 11a, 13a, 14, 16, 17 [35]). Bearbeitung A. mit V. 4aβ, 8, 9, 12aβb, 22 ist auch außerhalb von 2 Sam. xiv 2-22 nachweisbar, wie die Prüfung ihres Sprachgebrauchs ergeben wird. Bearbeitung B. mit V. 7aβb, 11a, 13a, 14, 16, 17 dagegen, die sich unmittelbar am ihr vorliegenden Grundtext ausrichtet, beschränkt sich auf 2 Sam. xiv 2-22; dabei wird V. 7aα durch V. 11a + 16; V. 13b durch V. 13a; V. 15a durch V. 16; V. 15b durch V. 17a; V. 20b durch V. 17bα verdoppelt, während V. 7aα zugleich inkongruent mit V. 7aβb ist.

Beide Bearbeitungen haben je ihren charakteristischen Sprachgebrauch. — Folgendes ist bezeichnend für Bearbeitung A.:

1. In *V. 4a*β steht der Ausdruck *wăttippol ʿăl ʾăppǽhā ʾărṣāh wăttištāḥû*. Die literarisch unspezifischen Vergleichsstellen sind 1 Sam. xx 41, xxv 23b, 41; 2 Sam. i 2b, xiv 33, xviii 28aβ, xxiv 20b; Hi. i 20b; vgl. 1 Sam. xxiv 9, xxviii 14. Maßgebend für die Einordnung der Wendung in 2 Sam. xiv 4aβ ist jedoch die schon länger bekannte Tatsache literarischer Übereinstimmungen zwischen 1 Sam. xxv und 2 Sam. xiv 4-20 [36]). Auf Einzelparallelen hat neuestens D.M. Gunn aufmerksam gemacht [37]). Er rückt 1 Sam. xxv 23b und 2 Sam. xiv 4aβ nebeneinander, ebenso wie 1 Sam. xxv 24aγ und 2 Sam. xiv 9aβ; 1 Sam. xxv 24b und 2 Sam. xiv 12aβb sowie 1 Sam. xxv 35b und 2 Sam. xiv 8b. Bei diesen engen Beziehungen kann kein Zufall herrschen, da die Belege aus 1 Sam. xxv in 2 Sam. xiv 4-20 ihre einzigen Parallelen im ganzen AT haben. Während aber 1 Sam. xxv einen originären Basistext aufzuweisen hat [38]), gibt es einen solchen in 2 Sam. xiv 4-20 nicht, denn diese Verse sind selber bereits Einschub in eine alte Textgrundlage. Die literarischen Übereinstimmungen von 1 Sam. xxv und 2 Sam. xiv 4-20 müssen dann auf An-

[35]) Aus der Unterscheidung der Bearbeitungen A. und B. ergeben sich redaktionsgeschichtliche Folgerungen, vgl. Teil III.

[36]) Vgl. dazu Veijola, p. 47, und n. 3.

[37]) D. M. Gunn, „Traditional Composition in the ‚Succession Narrative' ", *VT* 26 (1976), pp. 214-29; hier: pp. 221 f. Daß die von Gunn mit Recht aufgezeigten Parallelen auf „traditional stereotyping" (p. 222) deuteten, ist jedoch nicht einzusehen. — Die Beziehung speziell von 2 Sam. xiv 9 zu 1 Sam. xxv hat bereits Hoftijzer, pp. 425 f., 427 f. betont.

[38]) Vgl. dazu Veijola, pp. 47-51.

gleichung des letzteren an den erstgenannten Text beruhen. Hier wird jetzt entscheidend die Erkenntnis, daß der zu 2 Sam. xiv 4aβ parallele Versteil 1 Sam. xxv 23b dtr ist (im übrigen ist auch der zu 2 Sam. xiv 12aβb parallele Versteil 1 Sam. xxv 24b dtr). [39]). Aus der engen sprachlichen Zusammengehörigkeit beider Stellen geht hervor, daß auch 2 Sam. xiv 4aβ dtr sein muß (wie ebenfalls 2 Sam. xiv 12aβb aus verwandtem Grund als dtr anzusehen ist).

2. Zu *V. 9aβ* ist die einzige im Wortlaut nahekommende Parallele im AT 1 Sam. xxv 24aγ (dtr?) [40]). In dem letztgenannten Versteil nimmt ebenfalls eine kluge Frau die „Schuld" gegenüber David stellvertretend auf sich. Doch geht 2 Sam. xiv 9aβ insofern noch weiter, als hier die Schuldübernahme auch auf die Familie (*bêt*) der klugen Frau ausgedehnt wird; dies sicherlich im Kontrast zu dem *kissē*' des Königs in V. 9b. Im ganzen ist also der Versteil 2 Sam. xiv 9aβ im AT einmalig [41]). Da V. 9aβ von V. 9b nicht zu trennen ist, kommt für V. 9aβb insgesamt nur *eine* Zuweisung in Frage; ausschlaggebend ist dann, wie man V. 9b zu bestimmen hat, auch wenn 1 Sam. xxv 24aγ nicht dtr ist.

3. In *V. 9b* hat *kissē*' in der Bedeutung „Dynastie" mit 2 Sam. iii 10, vii 16; 1 Reg. i 37, 47, ii 33b, 45, ix 5 nur dtr Vergleichsstellen [42]); und die Unschuld (Stichwort *nāqî*) Davids und seiner Dynastie hebt sonst so direkt nur noch hervor 2 Sam. iii 28aβ (dtr). Dabei ist 2 Sam. iii 28aβ in Davids Mund geradezu dieselbe Aussage wie 2 Sam. xiv 9b im Munde der Frau aus Tekoa: und da dies die beiden einzigen Stellen im AT sind, die so offen Davids und seiner Dynastie Unschuld ausdrücken, sind die gewiß miteinander verbunden [43]). Nahe heran kommt an 2 Sam. iii 28aβ lediglich noch 1

---

[39]) Vgl. ibid. pp. 48, 50.

[40]) Veijola, pp. 47 f., 50, betrachtet 1 Sam. xxv 24a im ganzen als vordtr.

[41]) Mit Hoftijzer, p. 424. Die ibid. pp. 425-7 notierten *Sach*-parallelen zu 1 Sam. xxv 24a und 2 Sam. xiv 9aβ, nämlich Jud. x 10, 15; 1 Sam. xii 10, xv 24 f., 30, xxvi 21; 2 Sam. xii 13, xix 20 f., xxiv 10, 17 (die übrigen ibid. herangezogenen Belege sind m.E. nicht von Aufschluß) sind außer 2 Sam. xix 20 f. jedenfalls dtr.

[42]) Mit Veijola, p. 75, sind *alle* diese Stellen als dtr aufzufassen; darauf ist auch für 1 Reg. i 37, 47, ii 33b zu beharren, gegen E. Würthwein, *Die Bücher der Könige. 1. Könige 1-16*, (Göttingen, 1977), z. St.

[43]) Völlig zutreffend verzeichnet Hoftijzer, p. 424, n. 3, zu 2 Sam. xiv 9 die Parallele 2 Sam. iii 28, ohne indes schon sagen zu können, was dann Veijola, p. 75, n. 166 ausspricht: In 2 Sam. xiv 9 erinnere „die Betonung der Unschuld Davids und seines Königtums" „stark an DtrG" (vgl. dazu auch oben die n. 13). Hoftijzer lenkt überdies (ibid.), wieder aber ohne dabei an eine dtr Herkunft dieses Verses zu denken, mit vollem Recht die Aufmerksamkeit auf 1 Reg. ii 33; zu dieser Verweisstelle vgl. oben im Text den nächsten Satz.

Reg. ii 33b (ebenfalls dtr). Von diesen Seitenbelegen her ist 2 Sam. xiv 9b mit großer Sicherheit als dtr zu beurteilen. Dann gilt das aber auch für den von V. 9b nicht zu trennenden V. 9aβ. So dürfte mit der hier erreichbaren Gewißheit der *gesamte* Vers 2 Sam. xiv 9, der in seiner Art im AT einzig ist, dtr sein. Mit 2 Sam. iii 28 und 1 Reg. ii 33b gehört 2 Sam. xiv 9 im übrigen in eine Gruppe dtr Legitimationsworte für David und seine Dynastie.[44])

4. In *V. 22a* ist der Anfang *wăjjippol jô'āb 'æl-pānāw 'ărṣāh wăjjištăḥû* eine breit gestreute Formel, vgl. Gen. xliv 14; (Gen. l 18; Lev. ix 24; Num. xvi 22, xvii 10, xx 6;) Jos. v 14b, (vii, 10), Jud. xiii 20; 1 Sam. xxv 23b; 2 Sam. ix 6a; (1 Reg. xviii 7, 39;) Ruth ii 10a.

5. In *V. 22b* ist ebenso *māṣā' ḥēn beʿênê pelônî* eine Formel; sie ist indes wesentlich häufiger als die Formel in V. 22a [45]).

Spezifisch dtr sind die Formeln unter 4. und 5. der Sprache nach nicht. Das Bemerkenswerte an ihnen ist jedoch, daß das mit der Formel unter 4. umschriebene Verhalten *Joab* nachgesagt und daß ausgerechnet *ihm* die Formel unter 5. in den Mund gelegt wird. Eine derartige Ergebenheit in Tat und Wort wie nach V. 22 kennt man sonst von Joab gegenüber David überhaupt nicht; das wahre — eher schroffe! — Verhältnis beider zeigt 2 Sam. iii 24, xix 6-8. Also ist hier in V. 22 eine bewußte *Tendenz* am Werk, David mittels einer Huldigung hervorzuheben, wie das ja genau der Absicht auch des V. 4aβ entspricht. In den zu diesem Versteil herangezogenen Parallelen geht es darum, einen Höhergestellten auf Kosten eines Rangniederen aufzuwerten. Was aber ist es, das in V. 22 gerade *David* so sehr auszeichnet, daß es eine Huldigung Joabs hervorgerufen haben soll? Es ist offenbar Davids *Großmut*, die ihm erlaubt, dem Wunsche seines „Knechtes" Joab zu folgen und den verstoßenen Sohn zurückholen zu lassen. Diese Großmut nun hat David vor 2 Sam. xiv schon bewiesen, vgl. 1 Sam. xxiv 18, xxvi 21, und wird sie auch später üben, vgl. 2 Sam. ix 1, 7b, 10aβ, 11b, 13aβ, xxi 7: all das sind dtr Stellen [46])! Die Großmut Davids hervorzu-

---

[44]) Die Belege sind zusammengestellt bei Veijola, p. 132, n. 35 und 36; zu ihrer Legitimationsfunktion vgl. pp. 132 f.

[45]) Nach KBL³ 319a: Gen. vi 8, xviii 3, xix 19, xxx 27, xxxii 6, xxxiii 8, 10, 15, xxxiv 11, xxxix 4, xlvii 29, l 4; Ex. xxxiii 12 f., 16 f., xxxiv 9; Num. xi 11, 15, xxxii 5; Dtn. xxiv 1; Jud. vi 17; 1 Sam. xvi 22, xx 3, 29, xxv 8, xxvii 5; 2 Sam. xv 25, xvi 4; 1 Reg. xi 19; Prov. iii 4, xxviii 23; Rut. ii 2, 10b; Est. v 8, vii 3; vgl. Gen. xlvii 25; 1 Sam. i 18; Jer. xxxi 2; Rut. ii 13; Est. viii 5.

[46]) Zum dtr Bild vom großmütigen David und seiner Bedeutung für das dtr Davidbild im ganzen vgl. die Skizze bei Veijola, p. 130.

kehren, gerade auch durch seine sonstigen Gegenspieler, ist demnach ein augenfälliges Bestreben dtr Redaktion in 1/2 Sam.; es gehört zu dem generellen dtr Bemühen um Idealisierung Davids [47]), ganz ebenso wie die Betonung der Unschuld Davids und seiner Dynastie nach V. 9 [48]).

Auch wenn Bearbeitung A. keinen massiven dtr Sprachgebrauch besitzt, so verrät sie doch klar sprachlichen und gedanklichen dtr Einfluß. Sie ist dtr Interesse verpflichtet, genauer dem dtr idealisierenden Davidbild. Im Gegensatz zu Bearbeitung B. reicht Bearbeitung A. über den begrenzten Abschnitt 2 Sam. xiv 2-22 hinaus. Bearbeitung A. bringt in ihn das eigentlich davidbezogene Element hinein; sowohl im vorausliegenden Grundtext des Einschubs wie in Bearbeitung B. wird David viel nüchterner gezeichnet.

Wie steht es nun mit dem Sprachgebrauch von Bearbeitung B.?

1. In *V. 7aβ* hat *hišmîd* außerhalb der prophetischen Literatur und abgesehen von ganz jungen Belegen nur dtr Parallelen [49]). Das gleiche gilt für das *hišmîd* in *V. 11a* und *V. 16.*

2. Zu *V. 7b*: *kābāh* pi. erscheint in bildlichem Gebrauch nur noch an drei späten Stellen: 2 Sam. xxi 17b (dtr [50])); Jes. xlii 3; 2 Chr. xxix 7.

Seine einzige Parallele hat das Wort *găḥælæt* „Kohlenglut" in Jes. xlvii 14.

Die Wendung *śîm lipᵉlônî šēm ûšᵉʾērît* ist gebildet aus *śîm šᵉʾērît lᵉ*, was sonst nur noch Gen. xlv 7; vgl. Mi. iv 7 begegnet (*šᵉʾērît* „Nachkommenschaft" allein außerdem auch Jer. xi 23) und *šēm* „Nachruhm, Andenken", wozu es erst sehr späte weitere Belege gibt [51]). Dem Gesamtausdruck, der einmalig im AT ist, sehr nahe kommt mit *šēm ûšᵉʾār* der späte Halbvers Jes. xiv 22b; vgl. Zeph. i 4. Im übrigen ist *lᵉbiltî śîm...šēm ûšᵉʾērît* einfach das Gegenstück zu ...*wᵉʾim tašmîd ʾæt-šᵉmi* aus 1 Sam. xxiv 22 (dtr [52])).

Die Formel *ʿăl-pᵉnê hāʾᵃdāmāh* ist außerhalb des Tetrateuch (Gen.

---

47) Vgl. dazu ibid. den ganzen Abschnitt pp. 127-38.

48) Vgl. oben pp. 43f. und die n. 43 und 44.

49) Nach KBL 985a: Dtn. iv 3, vi 15, vii 4, 24, ix 20; 2 Sam. xxii 38; 1 Reg. xiii 34, xv 29, xvi 12; 2 Reg. x 17; ferner 1 Sam. xxiv 22; vgl. Dtn. i 27, ii 12, 21-23, ix 3, 8, 14, 19, 25, xxviii 48, 63, xxxi 3 f., Jos. ix 24, xi 14, 20, xxiii 15, xxiv 8; 2 Reg. xxi 9.

50) Gegen Veijola, pp. 118 f.

51) Es sind dies Hi. xviii 17; Jes. lvi 5, lxvi 22; Prov. x 7; vgl. Jos. vii 9; Ez. xxxix 13; Zech. xiii 2.

52) Nach Veijola, pp. 90-93 ist 1 Sam. xxiv 18-23a insgesamt dtr.

iv 14; vi 7 J) und außer in Jer. xxviii 16, xxxv 7 sowie Zeph. i 2 f. (dtr?) stets dtr oder nachdtr [53]).

3. In *V. 11a* ist zākar mit Jahwe als Objekt zum Zwecke der starken Mahnung gebraucht und hat nur dtr oder andere junge Parallelen [54]).

Der formelhafte Ausdruck *jăhwe ʾælohækā* ebendort ist wie auch in *V. 17bβ* die typisch dtn/dtr Gottesbezeichnung.

Der individuelle *goʾēl hăddām* nach *V. 11a* und *V. 16* als Verfolger eines Mörders anstelle des Kollektivs der Sippe tritt erstmals Dtn. xix 6, 12; Jos. xx 3, 5, 9 (dtr) auf.

Das Verb *šāḥăt* pi. intr. hat nur die beiden dtr Vergleichsstellen Ex. xxxii 7 und Dtn. ix 12.

4. Zu *V. 13a*: *ʿămm ʾælohîm* ist gleich mit *ʿămm jăhwe* [55]). Hat der König, wie hier, die Verantwortung für den *ʿămm jăhwe*, so ist dieser Ausdruck dtr, wie die Parallelen eindeutig beweisen [56]).

5. Zu *V. 14*: *ḥāšăb măḥašābôt* ist entweder dtr oder noch später anderwärts belegt [57]).

Das Verb *dāḥăḥ* ni. kommt sonst nur noch in dem echt jer. Vers Jer. xxiii 12 vor.

6. Zu *V. 16*: *năḥalăt ʾælohîm* ist gleich mit *năḥalăt jăhwe* und be-

---

[53]) Dtr: Dtn. vi 15, vii 6, xiv 2; 1 Sam. xx 15; 1 Reg. viii 40, ix 7, xiii 34, xvii 14, xviii 1; Am. ix 8; Jer. viii 2, xvi 4aβ, xxv 26. Daß die Formel in Am. ix 8 dtr sein muß, geht aus ihrer Übereinstimmung mit 1 Reg. xiii 34 hervor. Zur dtr Herkunft von Jer. viii 2 vgl. W. Thiel, *Die deuteronomistische Redaktion von Jeremia 1-25* (Neukirchen, 1973), pp. 128-34. Wenn Jer. xvi 4aβ, wie Thiel, p. 196 samt n. 8, selber angibt, nahezu wörtlich mit viii 2 gleich ist, besteht kein Grund, nicht auch xvi 4aβ für dtr zu halten. Jer. xxv wird bereits im „Grundstock des Kapitels" „als ein reiner D-Text anzusprechen sein" (p. 55), so daß Jer. xxv 26 als dtr gelten kann. (Auch Zeph. i 2f. fügt sich dtr Diktion ein!) — Nachdtr: Jes. xxiii 17 (vgl. O. Kaiser, *Der Prophet Jesaja. Kapitel 13-39* [Göttingen, 2. Aufl. 1976], p. 139); Jer. xxv 33 (vgl. Thiel, p. 196, n. 8); Ez. xxxviii 20.

[54]) Dtr: Dtn. viii 18; Jud. viii 34; vgl. Dtn. xxiv 9; anderweitig jung: Jes. lvii 11, lxiv 4; Jer. li 50; Ps. lxxviii 35; Zech. x 9. — Schottroff, p. 167, nimmt richtig Jud. viii 34; Jes. lvii 11, lxiv 4; Ps. lxxviii 35 mit 2 Sam. xiv 11 „sachlich zusammen", behauptet aber pp. 167f. zugleich zu Unrecht, 2 Sam. xiv 11 sei die „älteste Stelle". — Zur Sache vgl. pp. 166 ff. die informativen Ausführungen.

[55]) Dies nach N. Lohfink, „Beobachtungen zur Geschichte des Ausdrucks *ʿămm jăhwe*", Fs von Rad (München 1971), pp. 275-305; hier: p. 292, n. 66: „*ʿămm ʾælohîm* ist also Äquivalent zu normalem *ʿămm jăhwe*."

[56]) Diese sind 1 Sam. ix 16 f., x 1, (xii 14), xv 1, xxv 30; 2 Sam. iii 18, v 2, vi 21 aβ, vii 7 f., 10 f.; 1 Reg. i 35b, vi 13, viii 16, xiv 7, xvi 2; 2 Reg. ix 6b*, xx 5, alles dtr.

[57]) Dtr: Jer. xi 19 (hier wohl Zusatz in einem jer. Vers), xviii 18, xxix 11, xlix 20, 30, l 45 (vgl. Thiel, p. 216, n. 21) sowie Jer. xviii 11 (ibid., p. 95). — Noch jünger: Ez. xxxviii 10; Zech. viii 17; Dan. xi 25; Est. viii 3, ix 25.

zeichnet das auserwählte Volk [58]). Zu diesem Ausdruck gibt es mit zwei Ausnahmen nur dtr und nachdtr Vergleichsstellen [59]).

7. Zu *V. 17*: Die einzigen beiden Parallelen zu *m^enuḥāh* mit der psychologischen Bedeutung „Beruhigung" sind jung: Jer. xlv 3 und 1 Chr. xxii 9.

Die Formel *hăṭṭôb w^ehārā'* hat zahlreiche breit und unspezifisch gestreute Vergleichsbelege [60]).

Zu V. 17bβ bestehen mit einer Ausnahme erst eindeutig dtr Parallelen [61]).

Die Folgerung aus einer Übersicht über die spezifischen Sprachmerkmale der Bearbeitung B. mit ihren ganz geringen Tetrateuch- und Propheten-Vergleichsstellen, aber unverhältnismäßig vielen jungen allermeist dtr Parallelen kann nur sein, daß Bearbeitung B. sprachlich wie den angeschlagenen Themen und vertretenen Vorstellungen nach außerordentlich stark dtr bestimmt ist. Wie Bearbeitung A., so stellt sich also auch Bearbeitung B. als eine dtr Zufügung zum — selber ja vordtr! — Grundtext von 2 Sam. xiv 2-22 heraus. Das Hinzutreten der Bearbeitung B. führt zu einer deutlichen theologischen Prägung des ursprünglich von expliziter Theologie freien Abschnitts: durch den Appell an Jahwe gegenüber David (V. 11a); die Einbeziehung des Volkes (V. 13a) und des Erbbesitzes Gottes (V. 16); die Sentenz über die Flüchtigkeit des Menschenlebens und durch den Zuspruch der Gnade Gottes für den Verstoßenen (beides V. 14); schließlich den Wunsch, Jahwe möge mit David sein (V. 17bβ). Ohne Bearbeitung B. fehlte 2 Sam. xiv 2-22 jede direkte theologische Kommentierung seines vordtr Grundbestandes. —

Dieser von den dtr Bearbeitungen A. und B. befreite verbleibende alte vordtr Text von 2 Sam. xiv 2-22 ist klar gegliedert, hat einen

---

58) Aus der bei Lohfink, ibid. 292, n. 66 in Erinnerung gerufenen Tatsache: „Bekanntlich steht neben *'ămm jăhwe* häufig *năḥ^alăt jăhwe*" ist die Bedeutungsgleichheit von *'ămm ᵓ^ælohîm* und *năḥ^alăt ᵓ^ælohîm* zu erschließen, auch wenn Lohfink selber diese Folgerung nicht zieht. Das Nebeneinander und die Zuordnung von V. 13a und V. 16 zueinander ist ja doch ganz offenbar.

59) Dtr: Dtn. iv 20, ix 26, 29, xxxii 9; 1 Sam. x 1, xxvi 19; 2 Sam. xx 19bβ, xxi 3b; 1 Reg. viii 51, 53; vgl. 2 Reg. xxi 14. — Nachdtr: Jes. xix 25, xlvii 6; Mi. vii 14, 18; Ps. xxxiii 12, lxxviii 62, 71, xciv 5, cvi 5. Ausnahmen: Jer. xii 7; Ps. xxviii 9 (?).

60) Nämlich Gen. ii 9, 17, iii 5, 22; Dtn. i 39, xxx 15; 2 Sam. xix 36; 1 Reg. iii 9; Jes. v 20, vii 15f.; Am. v 14 f.; Mi. iii 2; Ps. lii 5; Eccl. xii 14.

61) Die Belege sind angeführt nach H. D. Preuß, „. . . ich will mit dir sein!", *ZAW* 80 (1968), pp. 139-73; hier: p. 146: Dtn. xx 1, 4, xxxi 8; Jos. i 9, 17, (xiv 12); Jud. vi 13 (alle dtr); 1 Sam. xvii 37(?), xx 13 (dtr); 1 Reg. i 37, viii 57 (dtr).

zügigen Handlungs- und Gesprächsablauf und ist dabei in dem, was die Frau sagt, vollkommen verständlich. Berücksichtigt man allein diese vordtr Fassung, so kann man Rede und Verhalten der Frau vor dem König wirklich klug nennen. Würthweins Kennzeichnung von 2 Sam. xiv 2-22 als weisheitlichen Einschub [62]) gilt also nach der vorgetragenen literarkritischen Analyse nur mehr für den vordtr Grundbestand dieses Einschubs. Erst die dtr Bearbeitungen A. und B. bewirken, daß die Frau streckenweise ein selbständiges Gespräch mit David zu führen scheint, indem sie deren Rede unangemessen ausweiten. So entsteht die Diskrepanz zwischen V. 2 f., 20, wonach Joab der Frau die Worte eingibt und sich ihrer derart als seines Sprachrohrs bedient, und dem jetzigen Umfang der Rede der Frau in V. 4 ff.

Daß Joab mit seinem Vorhaben, David umzustimmen, nicht selber bei diesem auftritt, sondern die beredte Frau aus Tekoa vorschickt, soll glauben machen, man habe es mit einer besonders geschickten List Joabs zu tun: *Sie* habe es vermocht, David zu seinem Sinneswandel zu bringen. Dieser List sei es nun zuzuschreiben, daß David den, wie der weitere Lauf der Dinge zeigen wird, verhängnisvollen Schritt zur Begnadigung Absaloms unternimmt. Damit hat der unbearbeitete Bestand von 2 Sam. xiv 2-22 jene joabfeindliche Tendenz gewonnen, die der von Würthwein aufgezeigten joabfeindlichen Überarbeitung der Thronfolgeerzählung überhaupt eigentümlich ist (p. 50).

III. *Folgerungen für die Redaktionsgeschichte von 2 Sam. xiv 2-22*

Die heute vorliegende Gestalt dieses Abschnitts ist in drei redaktionellen Vorgängen entstanden:

1. Vordtr wurde eine weisheitliche Anekdote [63]) zwischen die V. 1 und 23 von 2 Sam. xiv eingeschoben (vgl. ihren oben in der Übersetzung gebotenen Text).

2. Diese vordtr Einschaltung wurde durch die beiden dtr Bearbeitungen A. und B. erweitert. Weder A. noch B. bilden eine durchgehende zusammenhängende Einheit, sondern sind vielmehr eine Ansammlung unter sich unverbundener Zusätze. An beiden Bearbeitungen, weniger an A. als an B., fallen dabei die verhältnismäßig häufigen geprägten Ausdrücke und Wendungen auf.

---

[62]) Vgl. dazu oben die n. 7.

[63]) Nach Würthwein, p. 47, handelt es sich bei dem *gesamten* Einschub 2 Sam. xiv 2-22 um eine Anekdote. Diese Gattungsbezeichnung wird hier nur für den vordtr Bestand von 2 Sam. xiv 2-22 übernommen.

a) Zur Bearbeitung A.: Ihr ausschließlicher Zweck ist es, David gegenüber der klugen Frau und Joab nachdrücklich zur Geltung zu bringen. Bearbeitung A. hat die Tendenz, dadurch, daß sie die Frau und Joab vor dem König höfisch-devote Formen wahren läßt (V. 4aβ, 12aβb, 22), David über beide zu erheben; durch die Betonung der Unschuld Davids und seines „Thrones" (d.h. Königtums) (V. 9) deren Berührung mit dem Blutrachefall auszuschließen und so beide in einem idealisierten Bilde darzustellen; und durch die Segnung Davids sowie die Ergebenheitsbezeigung von seiten Joabs (V. 22) Davids Großmut herauszustellen, welche ihn dem Wunsche seines untergebenen „Knechtes" entsprechen läßt. Erhöhung Davids über andere; Idealisierung Davids und seines Königtums; Aufweis der Großmut Davids: all das ist kennzeichnend für eine nicht nur in 2 Sam. xiv 2-22, sondern in 1/2 Sam. durchgehend nachweisbare dtr Redaktion, die von Veijola, besonders in 1 Sam. xxv, ermittelt worden ist und die er mit DtrG gleichsetzt.

b) Zur Bearbeitung B.: Ihre Tendenz geht dahin, den Sohn, der in V. 7aβb, 11a fiktiv als der der Frau, in V. 13a, 14 aber als der Davids gilt (V. 16 greift wieder auf V. 11a zurück), zum Erben umzuwandeln und ferner das Volk (V. 13a) bzw. Erbteil (V. 16) Jahwes einzuführen. Während die vordtr Fassung von 2 Sam. xiv 2-22 darauf aus ist, daß der Vater um des Sohnes willen andern Sinnes werden muß, geht es der Bearbeitung B. darum, daß der König um des Erben und des Gottesvolkes willen seine Meinung zu ändern hat. D.h. jetzt soll der *Thronerbe* aus der Verbannung zurückgeholt werden. Damit aber geht es in Bearbeitung B. um *dynastische* Interessen! Diese wiederum berühren das Gottesvolk: Es darf nicht ohne Thronfolger sein [64]). Dieses alles wird dem König durch den beständigen Hinweis auf Jahwe bzw. Gott eindringlich vor Augen gestellt. So ist Bearbeitung B. eine betont *theologisch* argumentierende Neuinterpretation des vordtr Textes von 2 Sam. xiv 2-22 mit theokratisch-dynastischem Vorzeichen. —

Der mit jüngsten Schichten des Dtn. (iv 1-40, ix 7 ff.), den jüngsten Teilen von 1 Reg. viii, dtr Zusätzen zu Jer. und Dt.-Is. bekannte Sprachgebrauch der Bearbeitung B. weist sie auf eine Stufe nach dem

[64]) Für V. 13a hat zuerst Ehrlich (vgl. oben die n. 29), pp. 307 f., eine dynastische Interpretation vertreten (vgl. auch Hoftijzer, p. 430, der diese Deutung und weitere Vertreter referiert, ohne sich ihr selber anzuschließen). Diese Auffassung des V. 13a ist durchaus richtig, nur bemerkt sie noch nicht, daß V. 13a nicht zum Grundbestand von 2 Sam. xiv 2-22 gehört, sondern zu dessen Bearbeitung.

von Smend u.a. nachgewiesenen DtrN [65]). In 1/2 Sam. berührt sie sich nur mit wenigen sehr jungen Einzelstellen (1 Sam. x 1b, xxv 30, xxvi 19; 2 Sam. xxi 3b), ohne selbst in 1/2 Sam. vertreten zu sein. Da sie eine auslegende Kommentierung zu einem vorliegenden Textabschnitt ist, darf man sie als Ansatz eines Midrasch ansehen und DtrM nennen.

c) Während die Zusätze der Bearbeitung B. am szenischen Aufbau des vordtr Einschubs (s.o. unter 1.) nichts ändern, ergibt sich in diesem Aufbau durch die Zusätze der Bearbeitung A. eine erhebliche Verschiebung. Im vordtr Text von 2 Sam. xiv 2-22 besteht folgende szenische Gliederung:

1) V. 2-3: Einleitung
2) V. 4aαb*, 5-7aα, 10-11, 12aα, 13-14: Mittelstück
3) V. 15, 18-21: Abschluß.

Der Wendepunkt des Mittelstücks, an dem das Gespräch der klugen Frau mit David von dem fiktiven Fall und seiner Anwendung auf den König zum freien Dialog übergeht, liegt hier, klar durch *weʿättāh* markiert, in V. 15. Freilich wird das jetzt dadurch verdeckt, daß der der Bearbeitung B. zugehörige V. 16 wieder, obwohl die Frau in V. 13 schon „die Maske hat fallen lassen", hinter V. 13 zurückgreift (V. 16a ≙ V. 7aβb, 11a; V. 16b ≙ V. 13a). Bearbeitung A. hingegen legt den Wendepunkt des Mittelstücks auf V. 12, wie sie durch die erneute Bitte der Frau, reden zu dürfen, deutlich werden läßt. V. 12 steht nun genau in der Mitte zwischen den ersten zehn (V. 2-11) und den zweiten zehn (V. 13-22) Versen der gesamten Einschaltung 2 Sam. xiv 2-22 und zerlegt zugleich das vorgegebene Mittelstück (vgl. oben unter 2)) in zwei Teile. Der Wendepunkt, der in der vordtr und auch in der durch die Bearbeitung B. ergänzten vordtr Fassung von 2 Sam. xiv 2-22 *hinter* dem Fallenlassen der Maske der Frau in V. 13 lag, wird durch Bearbeitung A. mittels V. 12 *davor* gelegt.

d) Aus dieser geänderten Einteilung im Aufbau von 2 Sam. xiv 2-22 ist zu schließen, daß Bearbeitung A., indem sie die den Aufbau der vordtr Fassung unverändert lassende Bearbeitung B. voraussetzt,

[65]) Zuerst hat R. Smend, „Das Gesetz und die Völker. Ein Beitrag zur deuteronomistischen Redaktionsgeschichte", *Fs von Rad* (München, 1971), pp. 494-509, die dtr Redaktionsschicht DtrN festgestellt. Ihm sind gefolgt u.a. W. Dietrich, *Prophetie und Geschichte. Eine redaktionsgeschichtliche Untersuchung zum deuteronomistischen Geschichtswerk* (Göttingen, 1972), und T. Veijola (vgl. oben die n. 5).

jünger als diese sein muß und damit die späteste unter den drei in 2 Sam. xiv 2-22 vertretenen Redaktionsstufen darstellt. Bearbeitung B. war nach DtrN einzuordnen. Bearbeitung A. gehört einer von Veijola erkannten in 1/2 Sam. durchgehend anzutreffenden Redaktion an (vgl. oben unter a)). Veijola nennt sie DtrG. In 2 Sam. xiv 2-22 erweist sich diese Redaktion allerdings gegenüber der nach DtrN anzusetzenden Bearbeitung B. als jünger [66]).

Unsere Untersuchung setzte bei dem schon immer als schwierig empfundenen V. 9 ein und bezeichnete die mit diesem Vers sachlich verbundenen Textstücke als Bearbeitung A. Die übrigen Zusätze zur vordtr Gestalt von 2 Sam. xiv 2-22 konnten einer Bearbeitung B. zugewiesen werden. Daß mit der Benennung A. und B. keine chronologische Fixierung beabsichtigt war, wurde bereits betont [67]). In der Tat ergibt sich nun am Ende unserer Untersuchung, daß Bearbeitung B., die nach DtrN liegt, älter ist als Bearbeitung A.

3. Das redaktionsgeschichtliche Endergebnis lautet nunmehr: Nachdem der vordtr Bestand von 2 Sam. xiv 2-22 in die Thronfolgeerzählung eingeschaltet worden war (s.o. unter 1.), ist er seinerseits durch zwei verschiedene, jedoch jeweils dtr Redaktionen erweitert worden, die beide jünger sind als die jüngste bisher bekannte dtr Redaktionsschicht DtrN. Verhältnismäßig näher bei DtrN steht die Bearbeitung B.; sie bildet die 1. dtr und insgesamt 2. Redaktionsstufe von 2 Sam. xiv 2-22. DtrN verhältnismäßig ferner steht die Bearbeitung A.; sie bildet die 2. dtr und insgesamt 3. Redaktionsstufe von 2 Sam. xiv 2-22.

---

[66]) Von daher ist es m.E. fraglich, ob Veijolas Benennung „DtrG" für diejenige dtr Redaktion, die (übrigens als einzige) in 1/2 Sam. *durchgehend* begegnet, angemessen ist. Sicherlich ist sein DtrG nicht mit dem aus Reg. bekannten ältesten dtr Redaktor DtrG identisch.

[67]) Vgl. dazu oben die n. 35.

CHRONICLES, EZRA, AND NEHEMIAH: THEOLOGY AND LITERARY HISTORY

by

RODDY L. BRAUN

Arlington, Virginia

In recent years interest in the post-exilic period, and in the Chronicler's History, has accelerated rapidly. Viewpoints have appeared differing significantly from the "scholarly orthodoxy" of the first part of the twentieth century. To a degree these new views are the results of new data, such as the Wadi-ed-Daliyeh papyri, or mark the continuing results of textual and epigraphical studies relating to the Dead Sea Scrolls. But at another level they reflect continuing discontent with the current state of studies in this area, and have their basis in the desire to arrive at a more satisfactory understanding—literary, historical, and theological—of one of the most perplexing bodies of material in the Old Testament.

These new studies have already begun to occasion new emphases in the study of the Chronicler's theology. As early as W. Rudolph's commentary, less emphasis was being placed upon the position of the Levites in the book [1]). It is now rare to find the opinion voiced that the author was a Levite, perhaps even a member of the temple choir. There has been a renewed interest in matters relating to the monarchy, to the relationship between David and Solomon, to messianism and eschatology, and to the Chronicler's attitude toward foreigners in general and the north and Samaritans in particular. Through it all, however, retribution has continued to function as a convenient label under which many of the features unique to the Chronicler, in particular 2 Chron. x-xxxvi, may be grouped.

It is my understanding that, with the exception of the monarchy, some degree of consensus has been attained on these significant items so far as their occurrence in the two books of Chronicles is

---

[1]) *Chronikbücher* (Tübingen, 1954), pp. 13-16; "Problems of the Books of Chronicles", *VT* 4 (1954), pp. 401-9. As Rudolph has indicated, most of the passages commonly used to support the Chronicler's supposed dedication to the Levites are best considered later expansions.

concerned [2]). With new possibilities now at hand for considering the literary structure of Ezra-Nehemiah, and with literary and linguistic studies at something of a standstill [3]), I propose that we reinvestigate these area of primary concern in Chronicles and compare the results with Ezra-Nehemiah, hoping thereby to gain additional perspectives into the unity and extent of the Chronicler's History. I shall arrange the study under three headings: (1) Retribution; (2) Samaritans and Foreigners; and (3) Monarchy and Temple.

In considering the theology of Chronicles, I shall disregard portions of the books often considered later additions, such as 1 Chron. i-ix and xxiii-xxvii. Moreover, I shall consider only those portions of Chronicles which have no parallel in Samuel-Kings, both because of the textual difficulties inherent in such a study and because of the likelihood that the author's own thoughts would appear more clearly in portions of the work where he appears to be composing independently of known sources [4]).

I. *The Theology of Chronicles and Ezra-Nehemiah*

A. *Retribution*

Retribution has long been considered a major facet of the theology of Chronicles. However, insufficient attention has been given to the unique manner in which the Chronicler expresses the positive and negative aspects of this dogma. The message voiced repeatedly in Chronicles, intoduced already in David's programmatic speech to Solomon, is "If you seek him [Yahweh], he will be found by you;

---

[2]) Although R. Mosis, *Untersuchungen zur Theologie des chronistischen Geschichtswerkes* (Freiburg, 1973), pp. 201 f. *et passim*, has inveighed against a particular theory of individual retribution, in my opinion unsuccessfully.

[3]) Contrast, for example, the seemingly divergent results achieved on the basis of linguistic analysis by S. Japhet, "The Supposed Common Authorship of Chronicles and Ezra-Nehemiah Investigated Anew", *VT* 18 (1968), pp. 330-71, and H. G. M. Williamson, *Israel in the Books of Chronicles* (Cambridge, 1977), with those attained by Robert Polzin, *Late Biblical Hebrew: Toward an Historical Typology of Biblical Hebrew Prose* (Missoula, Montana, 1976), p. 159. The criticism of Japhet's work by Mosis (p. 215, note 23) is indicative of the kind of difficulties inherent in such a linguistic investigation. On other bases Williamson also diverges from the literary analysis of F. M. Cross, "A Reconstruction of the Judean Restoration", *JBL* 94 (1975), pp. 7-18 (= *Int* 29 [1975], pp. 187-203). Both Cross and S. Talmon, "Ezra and Nehemiah", *IDBS* (1976), pp. 317-28, have now returned to the" traditional" dating of Ezra *ca.* 458 B.C.

[4]) Cf. W. Lemke, "The Synoptic Problem in the Chronicler's History", *HTR* 58 (1965), pp. 349-63; R. Braun, "The Message of Chronicles: Rally 'Round the Temple' ", *CTM* 42 (1971), pp. 502-14, especially p. 504.

but if you forsake him, he will cast you off forever" (1 Chron. xxviii 9) [5]). The king and his people are faithful when they seek or rely upon Yahweh [6]). The blessing attendant upon such faithfulness is expressed in terms of numerous progeny, building operations, military armaments, victory in warfare, cultic reforms, religious instruction, tribute from the nations, honor and fear in the sight of the nations, and the direct conferring of prosperity and rest [7]). On the other hand, the faithless one forsakes (*'āzab*) Yahweh, his law, and his temple [8]), acts unfaithfully (*mā'al*) [9]), engages in foreign alliances [10]), and, most definitively, fails to give heed to Yahweh's prophets [11]). Such

---

[5]) Williamson, p. 67, has failed to notice this earlier expression of the doctrine, and found its basis instead in 2 Chron. vii 14.

[6]) For the Chronicler, *dāraš* attains a meaning far beyond the customary "to inquire of", signifying at times all that is involved in keeping the faith (cf. 2 Chron. xii 5, xv 2, xxiv 20). See J. Schumacher, "The Chronicler's Theology of History", *The Theologian* 13 (1957), p. 16, whose entire section on what he has termed "divine pragmatism" (pp. 15-18) is very sensitive to the Chronicler's message. For *šā'an*, see 2 Chron. xiii 18, xiv 10, xvi 7 f.

[7]) All but the last two of these categories are dealt with extensively by P. Welten, *Geschichte und Geschichtsdarstellung in den Chronikbüchern* (Neukirchen, 1973), pp. 9-186, who correctly notes that such notices appear only in that part of a king's reign evaluated positively by the Chronicler. Williamson's discussion of the division of the monarchy (pp. 97-109), as well as his valuable treatment of the Chronicler's presentation of the reigns of Ahaz and Hezekiah (pp. 114-25), could have been strengthened still further through the application of this insight. For the concept of rest (*m^enûḥāh, nûaḥ* hiphil) in Chronicles, see R. Braun, "Solomon, the Chosen Temple Builder: The Significance of I Chronicles 22, 28, and 29 for the Theology of Chronicles", *JBL* 95 (1976), pp. 581-90, especially pp. 582-86 and note 13.

[8]) Cf. 1 Chron. xxviii 9; 2 Chron. xxi 10, xxviii 6, xii 1, 5, xiii 9-12, xxiv 18, xxix 6 f., etc.

[9]) Some sixteen occurrences in Chronicles: cf. 2 Chron. xxviii 19, xxvi 16, 18, xxxiii 19, xxxvi 14, etc. In Ezra-Nehemiah this term regularly refers to intermarriage. See Williamson, p. 53.

[10]) Cf. 2 Chron. xvi 7-10, xix 1-3, xxv 1-10. The parallel with that concept of faithfulness found in the Jerusalem tradition is apparent.

[11]) See Rudolph, *Chronikbücher*, p. xx; Schumacher, p. 20; J. D. Newsome, Jr., "Toward a New Understanding of the Chronicler and His Purpose", *JBL* 94 (1975), pp. 201-17, especially pp. 203 f.; Williamson, p. 68. The definitive significance of the prophetic word in Chronicles has not yet been fully appreciated, however. Faithfulness to the prophetic message is paralleled with faithfulness to Yahweh himself (2 Chron. xx 20; cf. Exod. xiv 31), and rejection of the prophetic word always results in immediate punishment (xvi 10-12, xxiv 20-27, xxv 15, xxvi 18). But, most significantly, Judah's exile is traced directly to her disobedience to the prophetic admonition (2 Chron. xxxvi 15 f.). While G. von Rad's material on the Levitical sermon is in need of revision ("Die levitische Predigt in den Büchern der Chronik", *Festschrift Otto Procksch* [Leipzig, 1934], pp. 113-24 = *Gesammelte Studien zum Alten Testament* [Munich, 1958], pp. 248-61 = "The Levitical Sermon in I and II Chronicles", *The Problem of the Hexateuch and Other Essays* [Edinburgh,

faithlessness leads to the "wrath of the Lord", to war, defeat in battle, disease, conspiracy, and even sore feet [12]). Apart from those additions to his work directly related to the cult, it is difficult to find an addition which the Chronicler has made to his *Vorlage* which does not function in these terms.

However, the expected punishment can be partially averted or delayed by a positive response to the prophetic warning. This is apparent from 2 Chronicles xii, where Rehoboam and his princes repent (*kānaʿ* niphal) [13]) and confess God's righteousness. The result is that, although they will be servants to Shishak in order that they may know Yahweh's service and the sevice of the peoples of the lands (2 Chron. xii 8), God will give them "some deliverance" (*liplêṭāh*, *v*. 7) and will not destroy them completely (*v*. 12).

By contrast, the concept of retribution and the terms related to it in Chronicles are almost entirely lacking in Ezra-Nehemiah. Exceptions appear to be words common to many Old Testament traditions, such as *ʿāzab*, "forsake", or marks of priestly vocabulary, such as *māʿal*, "to act unfaithfully". The concept of reward and punishment is directly broached only in the prayers of Ezra ix and Nehemiah ix, both of which appear to be directly related to 2 Chronicles xii in that they too confess God's righteousness in inflicting punishment, refer to that punishment as servitude, and speak of a remnant [14]). Yet even here the differences in concept are apparent. In Ezra ix sin is intermarriage with the peoples of the land, an attitude never found in Chronicles [15]). Moreover, no punishment is cited. This is almost inconceivable in view of the Chronicler's characteristic treatment of apostasy. Instead the emphasis lies upon God's mercy, which has not permitted him to

London, and New York, 1966], pp. 267-80), Newsome has pointed to the absence of the prophetic discourse in Ezra-Nehemiah as one criterion for denying the authorship of these books to the author of Chronicles (pp. 210-12), and Williamson also refers to the absence of prophetic influence in Ezra-Nehemiah (p. 68).

[12]) For "the wrath of the Lord", see 2 Chron. xix 2, xxi 18, xxxii 26; war, 2 Chron. xvi 9, xxi 16; defeat, 2 Chron. xxiv 23 f., xxv 17-24, xxviii 6, 19, xxx 7; disease, 2 Chron. xvi 12, xxi 14, 18, xxvi 19; conspiracy, 2 Chron. xxiv 25, xxv 27; sore feet, 2 Chron. xvi 12.

[13]) Again, the term appears to have moved beyond the usual "to humble oneself" to a more theological concept of repentance; cf. 2 Chron. xv 4, xxx 6-9, xxxiii 12 f.

[14]) God's righteousness, 2 Chron. xii 6; Ezra ix 15; Neh. ix 33; servitude, 2 Chron. xii 8; Ezra ix 9; Neh. ix 36; remnant, 2 Chron. xii 7, 12; Ezra ix 8, 15; Neh. ix 31.

[15]) Cf. Newsome, pp. 205-7, although there is much within the article with which I would disagree; and Williamson, p. 53 (2), and pp. 60 f.

forsake his people in their servitude (*v.* 13). Ezra's fear is that continued intercourse with the people who practice certain unnamed abominations (Ezra ix 14, x 10) will lead to increased guilt, so that even the remnant will be destroyed (*v.* 14).

Nehemiah ix contains still another concept of sin and punishment. There is here no mention of intermarriage in the body of the prayer. Instead there is repeated reference to God's gracious acts in the past and to Israel's repeated sinning, such as we find it, for example, in Leviticus xxvi or Ezekiel. Interwoven with this is a cycle of sin, repentance, and deliverance after the Deuteronomistic model (Neh. ix 26-28), which concludes in disobedience to the law, refusal to repent, rejection of the message of the prophets, and final deliverance into the hand of the peoples of the lands (*vv.* 29-33). Nevertheless, even here the conclusion is that God did not make a "full end" of his people or forsake them (*v.* 31). The people confess God's righteousness in inflicting their present servitude upon them "since the days of the kings of Asshur" (*v.* 33). As a result, they make an agreement to keep God's law, not to marry the peoples of the land, and especially to support the temple with the required tithes and offerings (ix 38, x 28-31).

Thus the only connection between retribution in Chronicles and Ezra-Nehemiah lies in the associated areas of remnant, righteousness, and servitude. The divergent traditions present in the two prayers have long been recognized [16]). The similarities, striking as they may be, can be explained in other ways, and cannot offset the differences in concept and vocabulary.

B. *Samaritans and Foreigners*

A second area in which the contrast between the theology of Chronicles and that of Ezra-Nehemiah can be clearly seen is in their attitude toward the northern tribes, and in particular the Samaritans. James D. Purvis has demonstrated that the textual development of the Samaritan Pentateuch began much later than was formerly assumed, as late as the first century B.C. [17]), and R. J. Coggins [18]), James D.

[16]) See H. C. M. Vogt, *Studie zur nachexilischen Gemeinde in Esra-Nehemiah* (Werl i. W., 1966), pp. 4-8, and the standard introductions.

[17]) *The Samaritan Pentateuch and the Origin of the Samaritan Sect* (Cambridge, Mass., 1968).

[18]) *Samaritans and Jews: The Origins of Samaritanism Reconsidered* (Oxford and Atlanta, 1975), and most recently R. Pummer, "The Present State of Samaritan Studies: I", *JSS* 21 (1976), pp. 39-61; II, *JSS* 22 (1977), pp. 27-47.

Newsome (see n. 11), and Rudolph Mosis [19]) have called attention to passages in Chronicles which reflect a more positive attitude toward the north. In a brief study, "A Reconsideration of the Chronicler's Attitude Toward the North", *JBL* 96 (1977), pp. 59-62, I have attempted to present additional evidence of the writer's concern for the north. The Chronicler attributes to no less than six Judean kings military and religious activities in the north [20]). After the division of the kingdom the writer is constantly concerned to indicate acceptance of and participation in the Jerusalem cult by people from the north. Immediately after the division of the kingdom priests and Levites from the north take their stand with Rehoboam in Jerusalem, joined by representatives from all the tribes (2 Chron. xi 16). The participation of Yahwists from the north in the covenants of Asa and Hezekiah is explicitly noted (2 Chron. xv 9-15, 31). Prophets of Yahweh, such as Elijah and Oded, continue to function here, and the people of Samaria are said to have responded favorably to their warning and released their Judean captives, who are twice described as their kinsmen (2 Chron. xxviii 8, 11). Monies collected to defray Josiah's reformation are ascribed to Ephraim, Manasseh, and the remnant of Israel (2 Chron. xxxiv 9).

This attitude stands in marked contrast to that reflected in Ezra-Nehemiah. There a hostility toward the peoples of the land, who are to be sure never identified with the northern tribes, is of two types. First, there is a general opposition on the part of the peoples of the land to the erection of the temple (Ezra iv-vi; Neh. ii-vi). This opposition would appear to be largely of a political and economic nature and to originate with the Persian officials in the area. This fits well with the introduction to the Aramaic letter of Ezra iv 7-11, where the complainants are not descendants of the northern tribes, but are specifically called foreigners resettled in the land by one Osnappar, who is apparently to be identified with Asshurbanipal, c. 668-630 B.C. A second type of hostility appears in Ezra iv 1-4, where the adversaries of Judah and Benjamin, who are again identified with settlers imported by an Assyrian king, Esarhaddon (c. 676 B.C.), are refused

[19]) Note 2, especially pp. 169-72, 200 f., 224, 229, 232.

[20]) Asa, 2 Chron. xv 8; Jehoshaphat, 2 Chron. xix 4; Hezekiah, 2 Chron. xxxv 11; Josiah, 2 Chron. xxxiv 6; xxxiv 21 (contrast 2 Ki. xxii 13); Jehoram, 2 Chron. xxi 4; Ahaz, 2 Chron. xxviii. See Williamson, pp. 99 f., who rejects Japhet's attempt to see in these passages a regular pattern of territorial expansion. Japhet's dissertation, which has now been published as *The Ideology of the Book of Chronicles and its Place in Biblical Thought* (Jerusalem, 1977), was not available to me.

permission to help with the rebuilding of the temple, although professing worship of the God of the Jews. It is impossible to find anything of a similar nature in Chronicles [21]).

This note of hostility toward the peoples of the land reappears in Ezra vi 19-22, the account of the celebration of the Passover at the dedication of the temple, where, however, a conflation of concepts is apparent. The returning exiles are here said to be joined in their celebration by those who had *separated themselves* from the peoples of the land, thus introducing a third classification of people. A similar note occurs in Ezra ix and x and Nehemiah ix, x, and xiii. The problem now is intermarriage, however, based upon a Deuteronomic injunction (Ezra ix 10-15; cf. Deut. vii 1-3). Nehemiah ix also presents a mixed tradition. The introductory verses (*vv.* 1-2) indicate that the Jews separated themselves from the peoples of the lands, but the body of the prayer makes no reference to separation in this sense. Instead the peoples of the lands are those whom Yahweh had originally given into the hands of Israel (ix 24), but in whose servitude Israel now stands (ix 30; cf. ix 36). Nehemiah x mentions only briefly the agreement not to intermarry with the peoples of the land or to buy goods from them on the Sabbath (x 28-31).

Nehemiah xiii returns to the problem of mixed marriages, but under a different Deuteronomic injunction (Deut. xxiii 3-5) directed specifically against Ammonites and Moabites and extended here to include Ashdodites as well (Neh. xiii 1, 23). Tobiah the Ammonite is ejected from the temple (xiii 28 f.), and a grandson of Eliashib the high priest is physically removed from Nehemiah (?) because of his marriage into the family of Sanballat (xiii 28 f.) [22]). Further intermarriage is forbidden, with Solomon himself cited as an example of the dangers inherent in such a course of action [23]). The book ends with

---

[21]) Newsome, pp. 205-7; Coggins, pp. 13-81, includes a detailed study of the passages involved.

[22]) For recent developments in the study of the Sanballatids, see R. Klein, "Sanballat", *IDBS* (1976), pp. 781 f., and "Samaria Papyri", *IDBS* (1976), p. 772, and the bibliography there. Coggins is less positive in his appraisal of the new materials (pp. 101-15). That relationships between the Jews and the ruling parties of both Samaria and Trans-Jordan continued to be maintained throughout the fourth through the second centuries B.C. is now well documented; cf. V. Tcherikover, *Hellenistic Civilization and the Jews* (New York, 1970), pp. 117-43. Josephus relates that Joseph the Tobiad borrowed money from friends in Samaria to support his pro-Ptolemaic activities (Antiq. xii 168).

[23]) That such a statement could be made concerning Solomon, whom the author of 1 Chron. xxii-2 Chron. ix has gone to such lengths to present as without fault,

the statement, "Thus I cleansed them from everything foreign" (xiii 30).

Neither of these two types of hostility is apparent in the book of Chronicles. The differing concepts present in Ezra-Nehemiah would suggest that at least two, and possibly three, hands are present. Only in Ezra i-iii (omitting iii 3), vi 14-18 is it possible to find material relating to the rebuilding of the temple which is not overtly hostile to the peoples of the land. This hostility is also absent from Ezra vii and viii and Nehemiah viii, which differ radically from Ezra ix and x and Nehemiah xiii.

C. *Monarchy and Temple*

Older commentators have commonly pointed to the prominence of the Davidic hope in Chronicles [24]). This is not suprising when we consider both the amount of space which the writer has devoted to David and the writer's treatment of such passages as 2 Samuel vii (= 1 Chronicles xvii). Today such a view of the writer's "futuristic hopes" [25]) continues to be held by many, also among those who maintain the essential integrity of Chronicles-Ezra-Nehemiah. In general, however, recent studies have tended to move in one of two directions. First, many of those who accept the essential unity of the entire corpus have emphasized the contribution of the Davidic monarchs to Israel's temple and cult. Thus stated, the messianic and eschatological dimension of the work recedes to a greater or lesser degree. Rudolph views the theocracy as standing upon the single pillar of the temple (*Chronikbücher*, p. xxiii). Hans Engler "The Attitude of the Chronicler Toward the Davidic Monarchy" (Diss., Union Seminary, Richmond, 1972), pp. 29-61, has protested against the impossibility of such a "one-pillared" theocracy and attempted to demonstrate the predominate position accorded the king over against the high priest. In two earlier studies I have attempted to show the essential equality of David and Solomon in Chronicles and pointed to their work as a unity centered in the construction of the temple [26]). Otto

suggests strongly in itself a difference in authorship. R. Braun, "Solomonic Apologetic in Chronicles", *JBL* 92 (1973), pp. 503 f.; Williamson, pp. 60 f.

[24]) See Braun, "Solomonic Apologetic", pp. 503 f., notes 4-9, for a summary of the various positions held.

[25]) The phrase is W. F. Stinespring's, "Eschatology in Chronicles", *JBL* 80 (1961), p. 219. See also Newsome, p. 208.

[26]) "Solomonic Apologetic", "Solomon, the Chosen Temple Builder". H. G. M. Williamson's work, "The Accession of Solomon in the Books of Chronicles", *VT* 26 (1976), p. 357, has correctly observed that my article "Solomonic Apo-

Plöger believes the Chronicler actually wrote from an anti-eschatological perspective [27]), and Paul D. Hanson believes the victory of the priestly party has led to the absence of an eschatological dimension [28]).

Secondly, scholars such as Freedman, Cross, and Newsome have pointed to differing understandings of the monarchy in Chronicles and in Ezra-Nehemiah as evidence for the differing authorship of the books [29]).

It is likely that differences in viewpoint with regard to the significance of the monarchy in Chronicles will continue to abound. On the one hand, it can legitimately be argued that the great majority of the passages cited in support of the traditional messianic interpretation are passages which the writer has adopted from his *Vorlage*. Other passages commonly cited in this connection, such as the alterations introduced into 2 Samuel vii (cf. 1 Chronicles xvii) or the frequent use of such phrases as *ʿad ʿôlām* or *leʿôlām*, (Engler, pp. 16-18) are not as compelling as they might first appear when viewed against the Chronicler's method in dealing with his Deuteronomistic *Vorlage* as a whole. Newsome's view that the Chronicler has accorded additional status to certain Davidic monarchs, and particularly David, by viewing them as prophets (pp. 203f.) is opposed to that of Engler, who concludes that God revealed himself directly only to Solomon, but to others through prophets (pp. 19-22). All must admit that the Chronicler has little to say—and none of that positive—concerning the monarchy in his account of the last days of Jerusalem (2 Chronicles

---

logetic" tends to parallel rather than stress the complementary character of the work of David and Solomon, for which the author of Chronicles has used the relationship between Moses and Joshua as a model. In an older article which has not received the attention it deserves, O. Plöger has suggested that the Chronicler has attempted to place the activities of Ezra and Nehemiah in the same relationship to each other as those of David and Solomon through the use of the parallel prayers of Ezra ix and Nehemiah ix. Even if it should be impossible to maintain the unity of all three books, Ploger's suggestion may be of value for understanding the present arrangement of Ezra-Nehemiah and solving some of the chronological problems involved in the books ("Reden und Gebete im deuteronomistischen und chronistischen Geschichtswerk", in W. Schneemelcher [ed.], *Festschrift für Günther Dehn* [Neukirchen, 1957], pp. 35-49.

[27]) *Theocratie und Eschatologie* (Neukirchen, 1959), pp. 53 f. = *Theocracy and Eschatology* (Oxford, 1968), pp. 40 f.

[28]) *The Dawn of Apocalyptic* (Philadelphia, 1975), pp. 269-79, and "Apocalypticism", *IDBS* (1976), pp. 28-34. Williamson (*Israel*, pp. 132-40) concludes that the major concern of the author was the definition of community rather than debate over either eschatology or universalism and separatism.

[29]) D. N. Freedman, "The Chronicler's Purpose", *CBQ* 23 (1961), p. 440; Cross, pp. 17 f., Newsome, pp. 213 f.

xxxvi) [30]); on the other hand, the argumentation centered around the eternal character of the Davidic rule in 2 Chronicles xiii provides a strong counter-argument [31]).

Materials for a possible messianic interpretation of Ezra-Nehemiah are limited to Ezra i-iv. Even here, however, it is doubtful whether a view of the Davidic monarchy comparable to any of the diverse interpretations found in Chronicles is possible. Newsome (p. 214) has concluded that there is not the slightest shred of evidence for a royalist or messianic hope in Ezra-Nehemiah, nor is there any indication that Zerubbabel functioned in any capacity other than as the representative of the Persian court. Ezra i 8, 11 make Sheshbazzar, who is denoted as prince (*śar*) of Judah, responsible for the return of the temple vessels, and to this same individual the Aramaic letter of v 15 f. attributes both the return of the temple vessels and the laying of the temple's foundation. Ezra ii-iii, on the other hand, ascribe the laying of the foundation to Zerubbabel, who, working together with the priest Jeshua, erected an altar, reinaugurated the prescribed sacrifices, and, after the work had been interrupted by the peoples of the land (iv 1-4, 24), again took up the building of the temple at the urging of the prophets Haggai and Zechariah (v 1 f.). However, at the completion of the temple (vi 13-18, 19-22) neither Zerubbabel nor Jeshua (nor Sheshbazzar) is mentioned.

The paucity and diversity of this material may be seen to lead easily to diverse conclusions in which theological and literary judgements are closely related:

1) The minimal amount of attention given to the Davidic monarch even in the opening chapters of Ezra may suggest that here too the monarchy is viewed as having attained its goal in the erection of the temple, a conclusion suggested already in the Deuteronomistic account of 1 Ki. viii 54-56 [32]).

---

[30]) The same can be said, of course, for the Deuteronomistic Historian.

[31]) In addition to this passage and 1 Chron. xvii 13 f., Newsome (pp. 208-10) lists only 1 Chron. xii 39 f., xxii 9 f., xxviii 6 f., in support of the perpetuity of David's house. The first of these is indeed idealistic; to what degree, if any, it may be transferred to a future hope is debatable (*contra* Stinespring, p. 211). The remainder speak of the dynasty in direct relationship to the construction of the temple.

[32]) The fact that the Chronicler omitted these verses in his parallel treatment is no argument against their significance for him. He has also omitted 1 Ki. v 17-19 (Eng. v 3-5), of crucial importance in determining his theology of rest (Braun, "Solomon", pp. 582-6). I should also disagree with Williamson's argument ("The

2) The Chronicler's work did not include the rebuilding of the temple, either because he wrote before that event, as argued, for example, by Newsome (pp. 215 f.), or because it was not an integral part of his plan, as maintained by Williamson. Stated in such a manner, however, this view may be faulted for failing to give sufficient weight to the centrality of the temple throughout Chronicles.

3) The Chronicler's original history may have ended with the account of the laying of the temple's foundation (Ezra iii 13 = 1 Esdras v 65), as argued by Cross (p. 13). A second edition would have added the Ezra narrative, essentially in its 1 Esdras format, with Ezra v 1-vi 19 as its introduction. A third edition added the Nehemiah Memoirs, disrupting the order of the Ezra material in the process, as well as the genealogies of 1 Chronicles i-ix [33]).

4) The Chronicler's account also included the rebuilding and dedication of the temple, as argued by Freedman. The original ending of the history can no longer be determined, however, since it has been disturbed by the intrusion of Ezra iv 6-vi 18 [34]).

5) It is possible that material signifcant for the understanding of the Chronicler's conception of the monarchy and to some extent for the conclusion of his history is to be found in the writer's depiction of Cyrus. The Chronicler boldy states that it is Yahweh who has given all the kingdoms of the earth into Cyrus's hand and who has charged him to build the temple at Jerusalem (2 Chron. xxxvi 23; Ezra i 2-3). Is it possible that the Chronicler, like Second Isaiah (Isa. xlv 1, lv 3), has reinterpreted the "everlasting covenant" with David, and now views the Persian Cyrus as the founder of the rebuilt temple and the guarantor of Israel's existence in Palestine [35])?

Accession of Solomon", p. 354) that the Chronicler's omission of 1 Ki. ii 1-5 showed its lack of importance for him, although I should agree with his conclusion that the Chronicler's account of David and Solomon is directly dependent upon that Moses and Joshua. Cf. Braun, "Solomon", p. 187, and especially note 17.

[33]) Cross believes this final edition has also suppressed elements of the earlier editions which exalted Zerubbabel, including the wisdom tale still found in 1 Esd. iii 1-v 6 and the title "servant of the Lord" which occurs in 1 Esd. vi 27 but is absent from Ezra vi 7 (p. 14, and p. 13, note 54).

[34]) Freedman, "Purpose", p. 441. Freedman believes the Ezra material was added later by Ezra or his followers "because the stories dovetailed chronologically and because they diverged ideologically. The Ezra memoirs provide a badly needed new direction that complements the failed messianism of Chronicles" ("Son of Man, Can These Bones Lives?: The Exile", *Int.* 29 [1975], p. 183).

[35]) For this suggestion I am partially dependent upon Freedman, "Purpose" p. 439, who, however, cites only Isa. lv 6 and concludes that only Second Isaiah may have abandoned or transferred the traditional view of the Davidic hope. Cf.

II. *Conclusions and Literary History*

Chronicles differs from Ezra-Nehemiah in the concept and terms associated with the doctrine of retribution, in its attitude toward the surrounding inhabitants of the land, and at a minimum in its greater emphasis upon the Davidic monarchy. Since these concepts are so central to the Chronicler's theology, it would appear reasonable to conclude that the author of Chronicles is not responsible for at least a significant portion of Ezra-Nehemiah.

After saying this, however, it is necessary to add that in many cases portions of Ezra-Nehemiah show a continuing development of a tradition present in Chronicles, a development which at times extends to the use of a specific vocabulary and suggests immediate dependence upon the earlier work. By way of concepts we note the centrality of the temple in the initial chapters of Ezra and the manner in which its restoration is described. However, we have also seen the manner in which the author or redactor of the prayers in Ezra ix and Nehemiah ix has used elements of the Chronicler's retribution and remnant vocabulary, although adapting them to a new situation. We have also noted the continuing development of the Levitical temple personnel [36]).

Applied to specific portions of Ezra-Nehemiah, our study would suggest that the contents of Ezra i-iii and vi 14-18 lie closest to the thought world of the Chronicler. At the same time, there is a general parallel between the books of Ezra and Nehemiah themselves which is difficult to view as anything other than intentional. We have referred above to Plöger's suggestion that the activities of Ezra and Nehemiah have been paralleled with each other as have those of David and Solomon (see note 26). Ezra iv-vi are characterized by the political opposition of Persian officials in the land, as are also Nehemiah i-vii. At the same time, both Ezra iv and Ezra vi show obvious marks of redactional activity. Both Ezra vii-viii and Nehemiah viii approximate to Chronicles in tone, although there is additional emphasis upon the centrality of the law and the Book of the

---

also the interesting discussion in W. Th. In der Smitten, "Die Gründe für die Aufnahme der Nehemiaschrift in das chronistische Geschichtswerk", *BZ*, N.F. 16 (1972), pp. 213-6.

[36]) Much of the material related to the Levites in Chronicles should be assigned to a later hand. Ezra and Nehemiah, with its addition of the temple servants and the sons of Solomon's servants (cf. Ezra ii, 43, 55), continues this development still further. Cf. H. Gese, "Zur Geschichte der Kultsänger am zweiten Tempel", in O. Betz (ed.), *Abraham unser Vater* (Leiden, 1963), pp. 222-34.

Law (cf. Ezra vii 6, 10, 14, 21, 26, etc.). The note of hostility toward the peoples of the land and separation from them marks Ezra's prayer in Ezra ix and at least the framework of Nehemiah ix. This note of hostility is continued in Ezra x and Nehemiah x and xiii. The lists of Nehemiah xi-xii are difficult to relate directly to Chronicles, although such detail is reminiscent of later redactional activity in 1 Chronicles i-ix and xxiii-xxvii. The narrative of Nehemiah xii 22-47 has also been highly redacted.

Despite the clear signs of redactional activity in Ezra-Nehemiah (cf. Ezra iv, vi, ix; Nehemiah viii [?], ix, xii)—or perhaps rather because of it—the resulting parallels are obvious. Ezra i-vi and Nehemiah i-vii are concerned with the rebuilding of the temple and of the city walls respectively, both accomplished against the opposition of Persian officials. Ezra's return, and especially the provisions for the temple recorded in Artaxerxes' letter in Ezra vii, is reminiscent of the reading of the law and the celebration of Booths in Nehemiah viii. Although the prayers of both Ezra ix and Nehemiah ix are somewhat isolated in their present contexts, each introduces in its own way the problem of Israel's guilt, which is in each framework related to mixed marriages. Ezra x is an account of the removal of foreign wives, as is also Nehemiah x and xiii. The lists of Nehemiah xi, xii, and xiii 10-22 seem to point to what was for the final redactor the ultimate achievement of the post-exilic community—a full complement of priests, Levites, and gatekeepers occupying Jerusalem, with contributions and tithes for the temple pouring in (xii 44-47, xiii 10-14), the Sabbath faithfully observed (xiii 15-22), and God's people dwelling in isolated purity in the midst of the nations (xiii 30 f.).

That such later authors or redactors considered themselves as following faithfully in the train of the author of Chronicles is no doubt true. At the same time, the new problems which had risen both internally and externally sometimes called for solutions which, consciously or unconsciously, departed significantly from the theology of their model.

LES AVEUGLES ET BOITEUX JÉBUSITES

par

GILBERT BRUNET

Paris

La prise de la Jérusalem jébusite par David, qui, malgré un bon nombre d'études [1]), n'est pas encore élucidée, a pour seule source vraiment ancienne, trois versets du IIme livre de Samuel, que la *TOB* rend ainsi:

> (v 6) Le roi et ses hommes marchèrent sur Jérusalem contre le Jébusite qui habitait le pays. On dit à David: „Tu n'entreras ici qu'en écartant les aveugles et les boiteux". C'était pour dire: „David n'entrera pas ici".
>
> (7) David s'empara de la citadelle de Sion — c'est la cité de David.
>
> (8) David dit ce jour-là: „Quiconque veut frapper le Jébusite doit atteindre le canal! Quant aux boiteux et aux aveugles, ils dégoûtent David". C'est pourquoi l'on dit: „Aveugle et boiteux n'entreront pas dans la Maison".

Si ce texte est aussi énigmatique, c'est du fait de deux inconnues: le „canal", traduction discutable de l'hébr. *ṣinnôr*, et le rôle que jouent les aveugles et les boiteux. Pour le *ṣinnôr*, j'ai une hypothèse. Mais elle demande que soit éclaircie d'abord la question des aveugles et des boiteux. Je n'ai rien découvert personnellement à leur sujet, mais j'ai été éclairé par un rapprochement avec un texte hittite, fait, il y a déjà longtemps, par Yigael Yadin. C'est ce rapprochement et les conséquences à en tirer, que je voudrais exposer ici.

I

Les aveugles et boiteux reviennent ici à trois reprises:

— dans la phrase des Jébusites: „tu n'entreras pas ici, à moins que tu écartes les aveugles et les boiteux";

---

[1]) En particulier: L. H. Vincent, „Le Ṣinnôr dans la prise de Jérusalem", *RB* 33 (1924), pp. 357-70; G. Bressan, „L'Espugnazione di Sion . . . e il problema del Ṣinnôr", *Bib* 25 (1944), pp. 346-81; H. J. Stoebe, „Die Einnahme Jerusalems und der Ṣinnôr", *ZDPV* 73 (1957), pp. 73-99.

— à la fin du discours de David: „et les boiteux et les aveugles, l'âme de David les ‚hait' ";
— et dans le dicton qui conclut l'épisode: „aveugle ni boiteux n'entrera dans la Maison" [2]).

Remarquons d'abord que s'il n'y avait là qu'un *cliché*, si ces infirmes n'avaient d'existence que littéraire, ce ne serait pas un cliché absolument fixé. Car nous avons:

A B au pluriel, avec l'article,
B A au pluriel, aussi avec l'article,
et A B au singulier, sans article,

soit, les trois fois, trois formes différentes. On ne peut donc pas comparer à ces locutions, que, comme „le lait et le miel", on rencontre vingt fois, toujours sous la même forme.

Hors du passage, l'aveugle, *'iwwér*, se trouve 23 fois dans la Bible; le boiteux, *pisséaḥ*, 11 fois; et l'abstrait *'iwwârôn*, *aveuglement*, 2 fois. Le tout est réparti en 28 passages. Parmi eux, 9 considèrent l'aveugle ou le boiteux comme frappés d'infirmités qu'on déplore, mais aussi comme châtiés de ce qu'ont fait eux ou leurs pères [3]). Dix font de l'aveugle le symbole du malheur [4]), notamment, dans les parties exiliques du livre d'Isaïe, du malheur dont le prophète annonce la fin. Dans le Trito-Isaïe, deux passages symbolisent par la cécité l'aveuglement moral [5]). Et, par une curieuse figure où l'inclusion paradoxale du moins apte exprime l'universalité, l'énumération de Jer. xxxi, 8: „l'aveugle et le boiteux, la femme enceinte et l'accouchée", signifie seulement: „même les moins indiqués", c'est-à-dire „tout le monde"[6]).

Mais tous ces emplois ne doivent pas nous en faire oublier un autre. Car l'aveugle intervient dans une des plus terribles menaces de Deut. xxviii:

> (15) Si tu n'écoutes pas la voix de Iahvé, ton dieu . . . (28) Iahvé te frappera de folie, d'aveuglement, de stupidité . . . (29) tu seras tâtonnant en plein midi, comme tâtonne l'aveugle dans le noir . . .

---

[2]) Avec majuscule, puisqu'on admet qu'il s'agit du temple.

[3]) Ex. iv 11; Lev. xxi 18, xxii 22; Deut. xv 21; 2 Sam. ix 13, xix 27; Mal. i 8, 13; Pro. xxvi, 7. (Cette étrange conception s'applique même aux animaux).

[4]) Lev. xix 14; Deut. xxvii 18; Isa. xxix 18, xxxv 5-6, xlii 7, 16, 18-19, xliii 8; Ps. cxlvi 8; Job xxix 15.

[5]) Isa. lvi 10, lix 10.

[6]) De même, „les boiteux se livrent au pillage" (Isa. xxxiii 23) signifie „même les boiteux", donc tout le monde.

Menace que répétèrent Sophonie et l'un des Zacharie [7]), et que l'auteur des Lamentations crut voir réalisée sur ceux qui avaient „répandu le sang des justes" [8]):

> Ils ont titubé, aveugles, dans les rues,
> ils ont été souillés de sang . . .

La cécité conçue ainsi comme châtiment, ou employée comme menace de châtiment, mérite ici notre attention particulière. Car si la maxime: „Aveugle ni boiteux n'entrera dans la Maison" se réfère bien à des infirmes en tant que tels, les aveugles et boiteux qui étaient censés empêcher David de prendre Jérusalem, n'étaient pas tant des malheureux ou des maudits, que les *porteurs d'une menace*.

Relisons en effet le texte. „Tu n'entreras pas ici, *kî 'im-hèsîrkâ* les aveugles et les boiteux". Pour traduire mot à mot, deux questions:

— *kî 'im* est-il un adversatif [9]): „mais, au contraire", lat. „at", all. „sondern", ou est-il un exceptif [10]): „sauf si, à moins que?"
— et *hèsîrkâ*, hifil de *s w r*, est-il l'infinitif construit: „écarter, le fait d'écarter", avec pronom suff. de 2me pers., ou est-il le parfait: „il écarte?"

A *kî 'im* conviennent également les deux sens, bien que presque opposés [11]). A *hèsîrkâ* ne conviennent qu'assez mal les deux temps, car l'infinitif serait irrégulièrement vocalisé, et le parfait serait au singulier pour un sujet pluriel. Il y a donc, sans parler des corrections qui ont été proposées, quatre combinaisons possibles. Deux n'offrent guère de sens [12]), mais il faut choisir entre les deux autres:

— l'adversatif et le parfait: „tu n'entreras pas ici: au contraire, les aveugles et boiteux t'écartent", le pronom suffixe, qui représente David, étant le *régime* du verbe [13]);

---

[7]) Soph. i 17: „Ils marcheront comme des aveugles, parce qu'ils ont péché contre Iahvé". Zac. xii 4: „Je frapperai tous les peuples d'aveuglement" (bien qu'ici ce soit plutôt l'aveuglement mental, la folie: „quos vult perdere Juppiter dementat").

[8]) Thre. iv 14. Voir: G. Brunet, *Les Lamentations contre Jérémie* (Paris, 1968), p. 72.

[9]) G.K. 163a; Joüon 172c.

[10]) G.K. 163c; Joüon 173b.

[11]) Comparer: „les merles ne sont pas blancs, *mais* noirs" et: „les cygnes sont blancs, *sauf* les cygnes noir d'Australie".

[12]) Advers. et infin.: „tu n'entreras pas; au contraire tu écartes . . . " Except. et parf.: „tu n'entreras pas, sauf si les aveugles t'écartent".

[13]) La LXX: ὅτι ἀντέστησαν οἱ τυφλοί, sous-entend le pronom régime, mais met le verbe au pluriel, prenant ainsi pour sujet les aveugles. Elle est seule à le

— et l'exceptif suivi de l'infinitif construit: „tu n'entreras pas ici, sauf le fait pour toi d'écarter les aveugles", le pronom étant en fonction de „génitif subjectif" du verbe à forme impersonnelle („ton action d'ôter", disait Samuel Cahen), ce qui fait de David l'*agent* de l'action [14]).

Entre les deux, il faut sans doute choisir ce second mot-à-mot, car une vocalisation qu'on s'explique mal est plus admissible qu'une faute d'accord [15]). Il faut donc penser que David, pour prendre la ville, devait écarter les aveugles et les boiteux. Ce qui apparemment lui était impossible, puisque cette exigence équivalait à dire qu'il „n'entrerait pas". Ainsi, dans cette traduction comme dans l'autre, les aveugles et les boiteux *empêchent* de prendre Jérusalem!

Mais ce n'est généralement pas ainsi qu'on a compris la phrase. Pour Flavius Josèphe (*Ant.* VII, § 61), les Jébusites avaient placé des infirmes sur le rempart, pour proclamer, dans leur orgueil, que la ville n'avait pas besoin d'autres soldats, tant ses défenses étaient fortes. Le geste serait possible, mais, en l'absence de tout précédent, il est peu vraisemblable. Plus défendable est l'idée, que, sans avoir effectivement traîné quelques-uns de ces malheureux en vue des attaquants, on en avait *parlé* dans ce même sens de forfanterie. Cette opinion, professée par H. Ewald et Ed. Reuss, par Eugène Ledrain et E. Renan, par G. Maspero et Karl Budde, est encore la plus répandue. D'autres suppositions encore ont été faites, et qu'il serait trop long d'examiner ici: qu'„aveugles et boiteux" était une désignation injurieuse, soit des Jébusites, soit de certains des hommes de David; ou une façon des Jébusites, de dire qu'ils se battraient jusqu'au dernier [16]); ou un simple symbole des ennemis de David. Et ce ne sont pas les seules idées qu'on ait lancées. Mais toutes ne sont que l'explication par un sens

---

faire dans les versions anciennes. Malgré l'influence de la Vulg., l'idée est dominante dans les vers. modernes, depuis Luther (et en France, peut-être depuis M. de Genoude). Dans la tradition juive, c'était l'opinion d'Ibn Ezra.

[14]) Ainsi comprenaient les vers. anciennes autres que la LXX, soit: Symm., Vulg. (*nisi abstuleris caecos*), Targ., Syr. De même chez les modernes: Pagnino, Arias, Olivetan, *Authorized Version*, Sacy, Osterv., Sam. Cahen, Glaire, Allioli. L'opinion, de nos jours, bien que minoritaire, reste celle du grammairien Davidson et de versions comme *Rabb. Franç.*, *TOB*, *Revised Version*, New Engl. Bible, *Soncino*, M. Buber, H. Torczyner, *Pontificale*.

[15]) R. Kittel corrige *hèsîrkâ* en *hèsîrukâ* pour mettre le verbe au plur. comme le sujet. Mais son seul appui est le grec.

[16]) *TOB* (1975), note. Ce sens, détrôné par un meilleur, avait deux bons appuis bibliques: voir plus haut, et note 6.

figuré, d'un texte dont on ne s'explique pas le sens propre. Mieux valent encore, en un sens, les extravagantes explications du midrach [17]), qui imagine des automates représentant des aveugles et des boiteux, et tenant des barres de fer qui assomment les assaillants ...

C'est aussi du sens propre, mais d'une façon plus raisonnable, que Yigael Yadin a entendu donner la clé. Mais ses vues ont été exposées dans des pages [18]) où il défendait la thèse de son père [19]), suivant laquelle le *ṣinnôr* était un trident, thèse qui a rencontré beaucoup de scepticisme. Dans une tentative pour lui redonner vie, Yadin rappelait le rôle de l'aveugle et du sourd dans le serment hittite du départ en campagne. Les guerriers, disait-il, s'appuyant sur un document trouvé à Boghazköy, prêtaient serment de fidélité au roi, à la reine et au pays, et l'on faisait passer devant le front des troupes une femme aveugle et un homme sourd, en appelant sur ceux qui trahiraient leur serment, la cécité de l'aveugle et la surdité du sourd. On ne peut que s'étonner qu'un pareil rapprochement n'ait pas été plus exploité.

Le texte invoqué par Yadin semble peu récusable. Publié en 1924, il est à la portée de tous depuis 1950 dans le recueil bien connu de J. B. Pritchard [20]). Sans doute, on dispose sur lui depuis peu d'une étude plus récente [21]), et la citation de Yadin serait à modifier quelque peu, mais cela n'en diminue pas l'intérêt.

Le texte déchiffré commence par une phrase incomplète, qui est une malédiction, s'appuyant, semble-t-il, sur l'action symbolique d'un aveuglement. De quelque animal, on veut l'espérer, — mais rien ne nous l'assure:

> ... et il dit [22]) „... était frais et dispos, et pouvait voir le ciel. Et voyez: maintenant on l'a aveuglé sur le lieu du serment. (De même) celui qui rompra ce serment, et se conduira de façon déloyale envers le roi de Hatti ... les serments [23]) le saisiront, aveugleront sa troupe [24]),

[17]) On en trouvera d'amusantes listes dans: Sam. Cahen, *Bible* 7 (1836), 136; Dalman, *PJB* 11 (1915), pp. 40-41.

[18]) *The Art of Warfare in Biblical Lands* (Londres, 1963), pp. 267-70. Auparavant, communic. au *First World Congr. of Jewish Studies*, Summer 1947 (Jérusalem, 1952).

[19]) Le Prof. E. L. Sukenik, *JPOS* 8 (1928), pp. 12-16.

[20]) *ANET* (Princeton, 1950), p. 354. Auparavant: Joh. Friedrich, „Der hethitische Soldatereid", *ZAss*, NF 1 (1924), pp. 161-91.

[21]) Norb. Oettinger, *Die Militärischen Eide der Hethiter* (Wiesbaden, 1976).

[22]) Le texte n'est pas un récit, mais un rituel, c.à.d. un écrit de caractère normatif. Il dit tantôt *il*, tantôt *tu*, sans qu'on sache s'il s'agit d'un officiant unique ou de divers protagonistes.

[23]) C. à d. les dieux du serment.

[24]) Contrairement à ce que pensait Friedrich en 1924, le serment n'était sans doute pas exigé de tous les soldats, mais seulement des chefs. Hatti était une

et rendront sourds ses hommes. L'un ne verra plus l'autre, ni ne l'entendra plus . . . "

Après toutes sortes d'actions symboliques suivies de longues exécrations, vient le passage cité par Yadin [25]):

> On amène alors devant eux une femme aveugle et sourde, et tu leur dis: „Voyez, (voici) une femme aveugle et sourde. Eh bien, celui qui agira mal envers le roi et la reine, les serments le saisiront, d'homme ils le feront femme, et ils l'(aveugleront) comme un aveugle, et ils le (rendront sourd) comme un sourd!"

Le reste, mutilé, semble une prédiction d'extermination du parjure, lui, ses femmes, ses fils et sa race.

II

De ce texte impressionnant, on peut faire deux applications au bref discours des Jébusites: une application stricte — et qui va loin —, et une application plus lâche, mais qui est vraiment le moins qu'on puisse faire.

Le parallèle strict consiste à penser qu'il existait, entre les Jébusites d'une part, et David d'autre part, une *alliance* — c'est-à-dire un pacte de non-agression —, comportant les clauses pénales, comminations ou exécrations habituelles à l'époque [26]). Les Jébusites, en exhibant sur la muraille les témoins et instruments des serments échangés, ou simplement en en évoquant le souvenir, rappelaient à David qu'il ne pouvait pas attenter à leur ville sans les sanctions les plus terribles. On dit communément que la phrase jébusite était un défi à David: je ne crois pas. Je ne crois pas que les Jébusites provoquaient David, ni qu'ils croyaient qu'il y avait la moindre chance qu'il passe outre à leur sommation. Non: ils lui rappelaient que, raisonnablement, il ne pouvait pas se mettre sous le coup d'exécrations aussi solennelles, de malédictions aussi terribles, qu'il avait prononcées sur lui-même, pour l'impossible cas où il se parjurerait. Nul doute qu'ils avaient confiance au sortilège, et à la crainte qu'il inspirait. „Tu n'entreras pas chez nous de vive force" disaient-ils à David, „car tu ne peux pas écarter les garants et instruments des serments que tu as prêtés.

---

féodalité, et c'était des vassaux qu'on exigeait l'*hommage*, parce qu'on craignait leur révolte. La troupe se contentait de s'associer aux exécrations, en disant "Ainsi soit-il!" après chacune.

[25]) Oettinger, p. 13.

[26]) Voir p. ex. D. J. Wiseman, „The Vassal Treaties of Esarhaddon", *Iraq* 20 (1958), pp. 1-99, ou Dennis McCarthy, *Treaty and Covenant* (Rome, 1963).

Ces garants, ces puissants instruments, ils sont là. Tes hommes ne peuvent entrer dans la ville sans se heurter à eux, et le premier qui les touchera deviendra aveugle ou boiteux"!

Aucun texte, sans doute, mais seulement la tradition que reflète Flavius Josèphe, ne dit qu'on a effectivement exhibé ces témoins à action magique. Mais, exposés ou non à la vue des attaquants, c'était un fait qu'ils existaient. David ne pouvait, ni les écarter physiquement, ni faire qu'ils n'existent pas. Il les connaissait bien, et ce n'est pas pour rien, que, dans le texte, les aveugles et les boiteux sont déterminés par l'article. Ces porte-malheur étaient, pour David et ses hommes, une sorte de *mur moral*, plus infranchissable pour eux qu'un rempart.

Cette exégèse très près du texte surprendra peut-être certains. Vu la mentalité du temps, elle n'a pourtant rien que de normal. Elle a même pour elle, dans le cas présent, une raison particulière. La cité-Etat de Jérusalem, a remarqué Stoebe (pp. 79-81) avait subsisté facilement tant que la Palestine était dans la mouvance égyptienne, et que nul n'y était très puissant: mais au temps de David, elle était devenue une „impossibilité historique". Elle était trop petite pour des voisins trop gros . . . Le raisonnement semble juste. En tout cas c'est un fait, que Jérusalem est tombée. Mais seuls tombent les fruits mûrs, et il est bien probable, que dans les temps de faiblesse qui précédèrent sa chute, la Jérusalem jébusite n'avait trouvé d'autre moyen de se maintenir, que de passer des conventions de bon voisinage avec ses voisins. Et il n'y avait pas de pactes sans serments, pas plus en Orient que chez les Grecs. Un pacte entre Jérusalem et David, scellé par des serments avec exécrations, est donc tout à fait vraisemblable. Nous n'en aurons jamais la certitude, car si nous avons de beaux restes des traditions du peuple hébreu, nous n'avons rien des Jébusites ou autres Cananéens de l'an mil. Mais, à la lumière des traités du temps que nous connaissons, à la lumière du rituel hittite, la parole jébusite rapportée par la Bible donne fortement à penser qu'il y avait un traité, avec commination de cécité et de claudication pour le parjure.

Il se peut cependant que cette interprétation répugne à de certains esprits, ou qu'on estime qu'un pacte n'est qu'insuffisamment probable. Il faudrait alors adopter une hypothèse *minimale*. Si, en effet, on n'a pas la *preuve* d'un pacte, on ne peut écarter l'idée, que les Jébusites attendaient des aveugles et des boiteux en question, une protection *magique*. La cité-Etat de Jérusalem n'avait sans doute guère de force militaire, mais sa force était d'un autre ordre. C'était probablement déjà la ville de Sadoq et de Melkisédeq. Et c'était en tout cas la ville de ce Giḥon, attesté plus tard comme source sacrée, et dont l'étrange intermittence [27]) ne pouvait que sembler, à n'importe lequel des peuples de ce temps, la manifestation d'une force magique, ou de la volonté de quelque être divin. Même pour qui n'admet pas ici de pacte et de serments, il faut donc concevoir que la Jérusalem jébusite comptait pour sa défense sur des forces d'intimidation (dirai-je de *dissuasion*?) religieuses ou magiques; que les aveugles et les boiteux étaient les instruments de sorciers jébusites [28]) ou de quelque roi-prêtre; et qu'en vertu de cette „loi des semblables" qu'on retrouve partout dans la magie, ces malheureux, là aussi, servaient de *porte-malheur*. Comment ne craindrait-on pas celui que le doigt de Dieu a touché? Et qui sait ce que peut la malédiction d'un aveugle? Ainsi, dans cette hypothèse minimale, le rôle des aveugles et des boiteux s'explique à peu près comme dans l'autre.

De toute façon, donc, les aveugles et les boiteux doivent être regardés comme mentionnés au *v.* 6, non pas par dérision, non pas par figure de rhétorique, non pas même pour donner plus de relief à un défi, mais comme une *défense magique ou religieuse* de la Jérusalem jébusite. Défense crue parfaitement réelle par les Jébusites, et tout autant par leurs ennemis éventuels.

Reste à savoir comment David a pris Jérusalem malgré cette défense, à laquelle il croyait certainement comme les autres. Cela, c'est la question du *ṣinnôr*. Ce sera pour un autre article.

---

[27]) La source de Jérusalem (*gîḥôn*) débite par émissions plus ou moins fréquentes suivant la saison (1 à 4 par jour), mais qui durent toujours une quarantaine de minutes (J. Simons, *Jerusalem in the Old Testament* [Leiden, 1952], p. 163). C'est le temps qu'il faut à la poche d'eau pour se vider. Ces émissions sont précédées de bruit, et débutent avec violence. Avant qu'on ait compris la théorie du siphon, que pouvait-on penser d'un tel phénomène?

[28]) C'est l'idée de Yadin (p. 269). Il voit très bien la faiblesse des Jébusites, et pense qu'ils recouraient à la magie parce qu'ils ne pouvaient rien faire d'autre. Mais p. 270, il dit qu'ils ne croyaient pas que David oserait tenter un assaut „against the power of the OATH and the magic". Il envisage donc là, non seulement son hypothèse d'un sortilège unilatéral, mais aussi celle d'un *serment*.

DAVID ET LE *ṢINNÔR*

par

GILBERT BRUNET

Paris

Il faut maintenant l'admettre, la défense que la Jérusalem cananéenne [1]) opposait à David, était une défense *magique*, dont les aveugles et boiteux étaient les involontaires instruments [2]). Mais David prit cependant Jérusalem, et il reste à savoir comment.

Relisons 2 Sam.v 7-8, toujours dans la version de la *TOB*:

> (7) David s'empara de la citadelle de Sion — c'est la cité de David. (8) David dit ce jour-là: „Quiconque veut frapper le Jébusite doit atteindre le canal! Quant aux boiteux et aux aveugles, ils dégoûtent David". C'est pourquoi l'on dit: „Aveugle et boiteux n'entreront pas dans la Maison".

Texte parallèle, 1 Chron. xi 4-6 n'ajoutent guère qu'une assez suspecte *personnalisation* du récit, qui fait de Joab le valeureux exécutant des ordres de David. Josèphe (*Ant.* VII, § 61-64) ne fait qu'harmoniser et délayer ses deux sources.

Le mot-clé du passage, *ṣinnôr*, ci-dessus rendu par „canal", était compris dès l'Antiquité des façons les plus divergentes: „poignard" dans la Septante, „jaillissement" ou „filet d'eau" dans Aquila, „rempart" ou autre terme de fortification dans Symmaque, „bouclier" dans la Syriaque, et „tuyaux des terrasses" dans la Vulgate [3]). Et que comprenaient les Chroniques? nous n'en savons rien; elles n'ont pas repris le mot, sans doute parce qu'elles ne le comprenaient pas.

De ce mot, c'est un 6me sens qui prévaut aujourd'hui. On rend en effet *ṣinnôr* le plus souvent par „canal, aqueduc, watercourse,

---

[1]) Ou „Jébus", suivant une appellation traditionnelle, mais erronée (Vincent, „Jérusalem", *Suppl. au Dict. de la Bible* 4 (Paris, 1948), col. 898-9; J. Miller, „Jebus and Jerusalem", *ZDPV* 90 (1974), pp. 115-27).

[2]) Voir: G. Brunet, „Les Aveugles et Boiteux Jébusites", *supra*, pp. 65-72.

[3]) „Domatum fistulae". Les gouttières et tuyaux de descentes n'existant probablem. pas à l'époque, il faut penser à des „gargouilles," c. à d. à de courts tuyaux obliques déversant les eaux pluviales en avant du mur.

water shaft, Wasserleitung", etc.[4]), mots auxquels on fait signifier le souterrain de puisage découvert par l'archéologie [5]). Ce qui est curieux, car la traduction „canal" apparaît dès la Renaissance [6]), alors que ce n'est que depuis 1867 que le souterrain de puisage est connu [7]). Quoi qu'il en soit, il y a aujourd'hui une thèse majoritaire et quasi officielle de la prise de Jérusalem: l'entrée furtive par le souterrain d'un ou de quelques-uns des hommes de David, et leur intrusion soudaine dans la place, semant le désordre et la terreur ... Malgré le „puits de Warren", cheminée souterraine de 13 mètres à gravir avec équipement de combat, l'exploit ne serait pas matériellement impossible [8]). Mais il semble bien peu probable. Les versions dissidentes ne s'entendent pas entre elles, et ne sont pas plus crédibles [9]). Les plus prudents ne traduisent

---

[4]) Ainsi compris par 27 versions d'un choix de 42 versions encore lues aujourd'hui, de 11 langues et 5 familles spirituelles différentes, soit 64%.

[5]) Voir: H(ugues) V(incent), *Jérusalem sous terre* (Londres 1911), pp. 11-18; H. Vincent, *Jérusalem Antique* (Paris 1912), pp. 150-56 et pl. XVI; G.Dalman, „Zion, die Burg Jerusalems", *PJB* 11 (1915), pp. 65-7; A. G. Barrois, *Manuel d'Archéologie Biblique* 1 (Paris, 1939), pp. 228-31; Vincent, *Suppl. au Dict. de la Bible* 4 (1948), col. 909-10; J. Simons, *Jerusalem in the Old Testament* (Leiden, 1952), pp. 165-71; H. Vincent et M. A. Stève, *Jérusalem de l'Anc. Test.* 1 (Paris, 1954), pl. LXVI; K. M. Kenyon, *Jerusalem* (Londres, 1967), pp. 22-5, et pl. 4 et 5. Quelques mots dans G. Brunet, *Essai sur l'Isaïe de l'histoire* (Paris, 1975), p. 180.

[6]) Pagnino, 1528: „Quisquis percusserit Iebusæum et attigerit canales". Valera, 1602: „hasta las canales." Diodati, 1644: „fino al canale". David Martin, 1707: „et aura atteint le canal". Ostervald, 1744, a suivi.

[7]) Il a été découvert en 1867 par Ch. Warren, capit. du Génie britann. (plus tard général) au service du *Palestine Exploration Fund.* Mais sa connaissance exacte est due à Montague Parker, autre capit. du Génie britann., mais au service d'une espèce de syndicat de chercheurs de trésors. Il l'explora et en leva les plans de 1909 à 1911. (Sur cette étrange affaire, rien dans Vincent, esclave de la parole donnée; indications dans Dalman et J. Simons.) L'entreprise elle-même n'aboutit évidemment pas, et prit fin précipitamment, mais un archéologue qui se trouvait sur place, le dominicain Hugues Vincent, sut faire servir le travail de Parker à la connaissance désintéressée. Les seules fouilles intéressantes depuis lors sont les fouilles anglaises de 1961-62 (Kenyon, *Jerusalem*, pp. 24-7, et pl. 3 et 4).

[8]) L'ascension de la partie la plus difficile, le „puits de Warren", a été faite en 1867 par Warren, dont on a le journal, puis, en 1910, par le lieutenant anglais R. D***. On en a plusieurs récits par Vincent.

[9]) Sur la liste mentionnée note 4, cinq des minoritaires comprennent „gouttières" (comme la Vulg. mal comprise): J.-B. Glaire, *Authorized Version*, *Soncino*, M. Luther, F. von Allioli; trois, une „arme" ou le „trident" préconisé par E. L. Sukenik: *New English Bible*, *Pontif.*, H. Torczyner; trois, „rempart" ou partie du rempart: Sacy, A. Crampon, *Rabb. Franç.*; un, le „torrent" (où il faudra précipiter les boiteux et aveugles): *Synodale*; et un, le „cou" (des Jébusites qu'on sera à même de tuer, et qu'il faudra leur „toucher", pour bien montrer qu'on leur fait grâce): M. Buber.

pas [10]). Bref, c'est un véritable chaos. Et dans lequel un point primordial a été négligé, puisque personne — ou presque [11]) — ne s'est soucié de faire cadrer le sens du mot ici, avec les „çinnors de Dieu" du psaume [12]), qui sont visiblement de l'„eau qui fait du bruit", que ce soit „vagues, remous, cascades" ou „cataractes".

Ne faut-il donc voir dans le texte actuel qu'un texte mutilé, reste de deux légendes n'ayant rien d'historique? L'une, visant à expliquer un dicton sur les aveugles et les boiteux, et l'autre, parlant de *ṣinnôr* pour signifier quelque hypothétique action, qu'on regardait comme le type même de l'impossible? Ce serait peut-être là la sagesse. Mais se refuser à désespérer d'un texte n'est jamais interdit.

1. *Les deux verbes hikkâh et nâgaʿ*

La phrase des Jébusites indiquant sur quel genre de défense ils comptaient, à savoir une défense *magique*, la réponse de David doit logiquement dire par quel genre d'action il entendait en triompher. La *TOB* traduit cette réponse: *kol-makkéh yebusî*: „quiconque veut frapper le Jébusite"; *weyiggaʿ baṣṣinnôr*: „doit atteindre le canal". Acceptons cette syntaxe: une protase débutant par un participe, et une apodose introduite par un waw coordinatif. C'est le mouvement de pensée: „quiconque a fait ou fera telle chose, il fera, ou qu'il fasse, telle autre chose!" Mais „frapper" et „atteindre" sont-ils bien ici le sens des deux verbes?

Voyons d'abord le premier, ci-dessus traduit par *frapper*. Il se présente sous la forme *makkéh*, participe construit de *hikkâh*, hifil de *nâkâh*, inusité au qal. La traduction la plus courante de ce hifil est „frapper" [13]). Elle n'est pas fausse, et il n'est pas question d'ignorer tous les passages où *hikkâh* veut dire „frapper", et rien de plus, que ce soit le „qu'il tende la joue à celui qui le frappe" des Lamentations, ou Balaam tapant sur son ânesse pour la faire marcher droit, ou tels passages d'Ex.xxi. Mais la constatation s'impose cependant, que la plupart du temps, ou au moins très souvent, *hikkâh* signifie „frapper d'un coup fatal". C'est „abattre" bien plus

---

10) *Centenaire*, *Zürcher*.

11) Je ne connais comme exception qu'Arias Montano (Anvers, 1572). Il rend *baṣṣinnôr* par „in fistulam" dans le latin-calque de sa supra-linéaire (c. à d. qu'il se contente de mettre au sing. les „tuyaux" de la Vulg.). Mais, dans les éditions où il donne en marge les équivalents en bon latin, il note „cataractam" (sans „in").

12) Ps. xlii 8: „l'abîme au bruit de tes . . ." „Cataractes" est la traduction la plus courante, et la plus vraisemblable.

13) Lat. „percutere, ferire; all. „schlagen"; angl. „smite, strike".

que „battre", et, pour une armée ou un peuple, ce n'est plus „vaincre" ou „battre": c'est „écraser".

Suivons l'ordre de la concordance. Seule attestation au nifal: „Placez Urie en avant (...) et retirez-vous de derrière lui, pour qu'on le *descende*" (pardon du terme!) „et il sera mort!" (2 Sam. xi 15). Double attestation au poual: „Le lin et l'orge avaient été *abattus*" (par l'orage) „mais le blé et l'épeautre n'avaient pas été *abattus*, car ils sont tardifs" (Ex. ix 31-32). On traduit souvent par „frappés": mais l'orage frappe tout ce qu'il rencontre. La Bible ne se sert pas du poual de *nâkâh* pour dire que telles ou telles cultures ont été frappées ou non par l'orage, mais pour dire que certaines ont été „détruites", et d'autres, non.

Au hifil, qui nous intéresse plus directement, il faut comprendre de même en Ex. ix 25 que la grêle „abattit" ou „détruisit" toute herbe des champs; car si elle a brisé les arbres, elle a sûrement fait plus que „frapper" les récoltes. Dans la Xme plaie d'Egypte, „à minuit, Iahvé *frappa de mort* tout premier-né sur la terre d'Egypte" [14]). „Frappa" tout seul ne se comprend que parce que tout le monde connaît l'histoire; mais un public de culture chinoise ou hindoue ne comprendrait pas. Les peuples dont Israël s'est partagé le pays (Num. xxxii 4; Deut. iv 46) n'ont pas été seulement frappés, mais „écrasés" ... Sans passer en revue tous les emplois du verbe (il y en a 480), on a bien l'impression que ce n'est que dans une minorité d'entre eux, qu'il s'agit d'un coup quelconque, et que la plupart du temps, *hikkâh* signifie: „donner le coup fatal". Comment comprendre la chanson des femmes à la gloire de David, autrement que:

> Saül en a *abattu* des milliers,
> et David, des dizaines de mille?

Ce ne sont pas des ennemis à qui Saül ou David ont „donné des coups", mais qu'ils ont mis hors de combat.

„Quiconque veut frapper le Jébusite", traduit-on. Cela n'a pas grand sens. Tout le monde, à la guerre, veut frapper l'ennemi. Tout le monde, au combat, lui donne des coups, mais qui ne sont pas toujours des coups au but, ni décisifs. Si l'on réfléchit bien aux attestations de *hikkâh*, on se convaincra sans doute qu'il y a

---

[14]) Ex.xii 29. Cette Xme plaie, la „mort des premiers-nés" suivant l'expression française courante, est appelée par la haggada juive *makkat bekôrôt* (même racine que notre verbe): le „*massacre* des premiers-nés".

une forte présomption que ce n'est pas cela que signifie la phrase, mais, avec le sens le plus fort, le plus radical du verbe: „celui qui veut porter le coup décisif au Jébusite, l'*abattre*, celui-là, voilà ce qu'il doit faire!"

* * *

Nous voici au nœud du passage. Celui qui veut frapper d'un coup fatal les ennemis collectivement ou l'ennemi personnifié, celui-là, dit David, doit faire quelque chose au *ṣinnôr*, et cette action est exprimée par le verbe *weyigga*ʿ. Ce serait, nous dit-on, l'„atteindre". Est-ce bien là le plus probable?

*Weyigga*ʿ est l'inaccompli, précédé d'un waw coordinatif, de *nâga*ʿ: „toucher" [15]). Le sens „atteindre", assez voisin, n'aurait ici rien d'impossible. On n'en a toutefois qu'un seul exemple bien net en hébreu, celui des ailes des chérubins, qui, des deux côtés du sanctuaire, „touchaient" au mur, c'est-à-dire atteignaient le mur. Exemple probablement unique, et assez médiocre, car donnant un sens purement statique, et bien loin du vocabulaire guerrier habituel.

Or, de même que le verbe précédent, *nâga*ʿ a parfois aussi une valeur prégnante, un sens énergique, et qui conviendrait bien à un contexte militaire. Notre français „toucher" connaît aussi ce sens. Quand on lit: „au cours du premier bond, trois hommes furent touchés", on comprend bien que ce n'est pas par une douce main de femme. En hébreu, ce sens semble encore plus fréquent. L'exemple est dans tous les esprits, de l'ange luttant contre Jacob (Gen. xxxii 26), et le „touchant" au creux de la hanche. Autant dire qu'il le „frappa", et fort rudement, puisque Jacob en resta estropié. Mais ce n'est pas là le seul cas. Les Philistins se demandant si c'est le dieu de l'Arche qui les a accablés de maux, disent simplement (1 Sam. vi 9): „nous saurons" (dans tel cas) „que ce n'est pas sa main qui nous a *touchés*". Quand David répond à la femme de Téqoa (2 Sam. xiv 10): „celui qui t'en parlera, tu me l'amèneras, et il ne recommencera plus", il faut sans doute finir la phrase: „à t'*attaquer*", ou „à *s'en prendre* à toi". Si l'on traduisait: „à te toucher", personne ne comprendrait. Dans Zac. ii 12, „celui qui vous touche, touche la prunelle de mon œil" signifie bien: „celui qui vous *attaque*". En Ps. cv 15, le parallèle qu'ont repris les Chroniques:

---

[15]) Lat. „percutere"; all. „berühren"; angl. „touch".

ne touchez pas à mes oints,
et à mes prophètes ne faites pas de mal,

est synonymique quant aux verbes. Et dans l'affaire des Gabaonites, que les „princes" avaient épargnés, l'excuse (Jos.ix 19): „nous leur avons prêté serment par Iahvé, nous ne pouvons pas les toucher" signifie bien qu'on ne peut pas — et on le regrette — les „tuer". Ces cas sont loin d'être les seuls [16]), et l'octosyllabe du vieil Houbigant reste vrai:

*Naga*ʿ: *touche, atteint, fait blessure.*

Le plus indiqué semble donc ici de traduire: „Celui qui veut abattre le Jébusite, qu'il *s'en prenne* au *ṣinnôr*!"

D'une part, c'est conforme à l'idée de H. Vincent [17]), que le texte ne saurait être muet sur la façon dont fut réalisée la conquête. Ce qu'on peut, logiquement, attendre de notre phrase, c'est *la façon de prendre la ville*, bien plus que des consignes sur la conduite envers les vaincus. D'autre part, comprendre ainsi est penser, avec Wellhausen, Dalman et Albright entre autres [18]), que le *ṣinnôr* était ce qu'il fallait „toucher", au sens d'„atteindre" ou „mutiler". D'après les emplois de *nâga*ʿ *be*, c'est le plus vraisemblable. Ce qui était criticable chez eux, c'est leur idée que le *ṣinnôr* était une partie du corps des aveugles et des boiteux, ou des Jébusites pris individuellement alors que la phrase ne renferme aucun possessif. Or, aussi bien que des aveugles et des boiteux, aussi bien que du Jébusite, la phrase peut parler *de Jérusalem*, qu'il était question de prendre. Tout comme un être humain, une forteresse peut avoir son point faible, où il convient de l'attaquer. Le „talon d'Achille" d'une position n'est pas dans la botte de son commandant. Et le *ṣinnôr* n'a nul besoin d'être une partie du corps [19]): c'est une partie *de la forteresse.*

Ainsi, *s'en prendre* au *ṣinnôr* était le moyen trouvé par David de faire tomber l'acropole ennemie. Mais qu'était le *ṣinnôr*? Autrement dit, quel était le point faible de la Jérusalem jébusite?

---

[16]) Autres exemples: Gen. xxvi 11, xxxii 33; 1 Sam. x 26; 2 Sam. xxiii 7; Jer. xii 14; Eze. xvii 10; Job i 11, 19, v 19, xix 21; Pro. vi 29. Peut-être Gen. iii 2; Amos ix 5; Ps. civ 32, cxiv 5.

[17]) *RB* 33 (1924), p. 359.

[18]) G. Dalman, *PJB* 11 (1915), p. 43. W. F. Albright, *JPOS* 2 (1922), pp. 286-90.

[19]) Il n'y a donc pas à parler, comme Dalman, *PJB* 11, p. 43, du membre viril de ceux qui avaient nargué David.

2. *Le point faible du Jébusite*

On peut considérer comme acquis [20]) que le canal d'Ezéchias, ou de Siloé, creusé peu avant l'alerte assyrienne de 701, avait pour but de mettre Jérusalem à l'abri du manque d'eau en cas de siège; et que cet énorme travail se trouvait nécessaire parce que la galerie de puisage creusée par les Cananéens (et improprement appelée *ṣinnôr* depuis Vincent), n'était plus en service. Pour faire servir à nouveau (et pour perfectionner, car elle en avait besoin) cette installation inutilisée depuis près de trois siècles, on avait entrepris des travaux importants: les plans de Parker en portent la trace. Mais ils n'avaient pas abouti. En sorte que la source, le Giḥon, se déversait au VIIIme siècle dans un canal à flanc de colline, en dehors des murs, canal dont, en cas de siège, l'ennemi, dès le premier jour interdirait l'accès.

On pouvait se demander pourquoi la vieille galerie de puisage, si imparfait qu'en fût le principe par rapport à ce qu'on imagina à l'époque d'Isaïe, n'avait pas été maintenue en service. Etait-ce que, la guerre ne menaçant plus, on trouvait plus pratique, pour la vie de tous les jours, que l'eau s'écoule vers le sud, au flanc de la colline, dans un canal où tout le monde pouvait puiser? Etait-ce qu'après la conquête on avait systématiquement détruit tout ce qui était cananéen? Il se pouvait enfin que l'installation ait été endommagée par faits de guerre, et jamais rétablie.

Sur un possible fait de guerre, 2 Sam.v n'etait pas très éclairant, et les Chroniques étaient suspectes. Les plus nombreux rendaient *ṣinnôr* par „canal", mais on nous expliquait [21]) qu'il s'agissait plus exactement d'un tunnel, qui montait par paliers successifs de la source jusqu'à la ville. Or, d'après les plans de Parker reproduits par Vincent ou Simons, il apparaissait bien douteux que des hommes aient fait cet acrobatique parcours souterrain, et une fois dans la place, y aient engagé le combat. L'épisode historique restait donc une énigme.

Tout aussi mystérieux apparaissait le mot même de *ṣinnôr*. On peut en effet se l'expliquer de deux façons. D'après les *ṣanterôt* de Zac.iv 12, d'où sortent deux jets d'huile, comme d'après le sens de *ṣinnôr* en hébreu michnique, le sens primordial devrait être „tuyau", et l'on peut comprendre, à la rigueur, qu'on ait appelé de ce nom

---

[20]) G.Brunet, *Essai sur l'Isaïe de l'histoire*, pp. 168-83.

[21]) Ed.Dhorme, *la Bible* 1 (Paris, Pléiade, 1956), pp. 941-2.

une galerie tortueuse à dénivellations successives, où ce qui circulait n'était pas de l'eau, mais des porteurs d'outres, vides ou pleines. Toute galerie souterraine est, en un sens, un gros tuyau. Mais si l'on part du sens, non moins évident, des „çinnors de Dieu" du psaume xlii, qui ne peuvent être autre chose que de l'eau en mouvement, alors le nom de *ṣinnôr* ne convient plus à ce souterrain. Il ne peut convenir qu'à son étage inférieur, où il y avait de l'eau, et même, à strictement parler, qu'à cette *eau elle-même*, à quelque endroit où elle en mouvement violent. Or, à part la source, à laquelle on ne pouvait guère toucher (et qui avait un autre nom), il n'y avait qu'un seul endroit où l'eau était ainsi en mouvement: au *trop-plein*, soit que ce fût un orifice étroit d'où l'eau s'échappait en un *jet*, soit parce que l'eau s'écoulait en cascade sur la pente. *Ṣinnôr* signifiait donc:

— ou bien „tuyau", — mais alors, que comprendre dans le psaume?

— ou bien „eau en mouvement", „jet d'eau". Et en 2 Sam.v, „trop-plein", probablement avec le même double sens qu'en français, d'„eau en trop" qui s'écoule, et d'„orifice" la laissant passer.

Peut-être n'a-t-on pas assez remarqué que les galeries de puisage cananéennes ne sont pas toutes du même type. Certaines menaient à une nappe souterraine, soit dormante, soit alimentée par de simples suintements. C'est le cas des galeries de Gézer, de Mégiddo ou de Ḥaṣor [22]). D'autres menaient à une source d'une certaine abondance: c'était le cas à Gabaon, et aussi à Jérusalem [23]). Avec les galeries à source, on était peut-être plus sûr de ne jamais manquer d'eau. Mais, alors que les galeries à nappe étaient des espaces clos, sans autre communication avec l'extérieur que leur entrée normale, les galeries à source avaient forcément un trop-plein, par lequel sortait l'eau qu'on n'avait pas puisée à mesure qu'elle apparaissait. Ce trop-plein était nécessaire, et impossible à boucher. Car rien ne résiste à la pression de l'eau, et quand elle atteint une certaine force, si elle ne peut pas passer à un endroit, elle passe par un autre.

Donc, à Jérusalem, la galerie de puisage cananéenne, fort bien conçue — même si l'aqueduc du VIIIme siècle devait la surclasser définitivement — , comportait bien à son étage inférieur une nappe dans laquelle on puisait, mais cette nappe était alimentée par une

---

[22]) Gézer et Mégiddo: Barrois, *Man. d'Archéol. Biblique* 1 pp. 220-28. Ḥaṣor: *RB* 76 (1969), pp. 555-7.

[23]) Gabaon: Barrois, p. 220. Jérusalem: id., pp. 228-31, et ouvr. cités note 5.

source assez abondante, et, de surcroît, intermittente. Il lui fallait donc un trop-plein. Aujourd'hui, c'est le canal d'Ezéchias, qui se déverse dans le bassin de Siloé. Avant qu'il soit percé, l'eau en trop s'écoulait sur la pente de la colline. Passait-elle par un canal, ou formait-elle cascade jusqu'au Cédron? Sortait-elle de terre par un ortifice étroit, plus ou moins violemment, ou n'était-elle qu'un ruisseau s'écoulant d'une grotte? on peut en discuter. Une seule chose est sûre: puisqu'il y avait source, il y avait trop-plein.

Etant donné que la Jérusalem jébusite ne pouvait résister sans eau, c'était là son point faible. Car l'eau du Giḥon ne s'en allait sous terre jusqu'au bas du „puits de Warren" [24]), que parce que le seuil du trop-plein était plus haut que lui. Pas de beaucoup, quelques décimètres à peine [25]). Qu'on abaissât ce seuil de si peu que ce fût, et l'eau, au lieu d'aller à 25 mètres de là, au bas du puits de Warren, par où on la puisait, l'eau s'écoulerait tout naturellement, à quelques mètres de la source, vers l'extérieur. Et le puits souterrain des Jébusites serait à sec [26]).

„S'en prendre au *ṣinnôr*": que cela voulait-il dire? Le trop-plein était hors des murs. Personne n'y faisait probablement attention. On l'avait toujours vu comme il était, et l'on ne pensait pas qu'il pût être autrement. Mais si les hommes de David *s'en prenaient* au trop-plein? s'ils l'élargissaient et en abaissaient le seuil? Alors — et il suffisait de très peu —, l'eau dans laquelle puisaient les Jébusites s'écoulerait tout à coup sur la pente, et ensuite, la source ne débiterait plus que pour la pente. Les Jébusites n'auraient plus alors qu'à implorer qu'on les laisse sortir pour aller au point d'eau.

David serait ainsi le maître de situation. Et ce, sans avoir porté la main sur les Jébusites eux-mêmes, et donc sans rien avoir à craindre de ce que craignent les parjures.

3. *David et les infirmes*

C'est ce que va nous confirmer la fin du discours de David: *we'èt-happisḥîm we'èt-ha'iwrîm ŚN'W nèphèš dâwîd.*

---

[24]) H. Vincent, *Jérusalem de l'Anc. Test.* (Paris, 1954-56), pl. LXII et LXV.

[25]) Les questions de cotes de niveau sont délicates, et Vincent n'a donné les chiffres que pour le tunnel de Siloé (canal VIII). Néanmoins sa planche LXVI donne une élévation qui se prolonge en amont par d'autres canaux, jusqu'à la source, et au-delà jusqu'à la pente du Cédron. Elle montre bien que les cotes ne jouent que sur des centimètres ou des décimètres.

[26]) C'est un raisonnement très proche que fait H. J. Stoebe, *ZDPV* 73 (1957), en fin de son article.

Au premier abord, ces quelques mots sont peu compréhensibles. Ils parlent de „l'âme" de David (probablement David lui-même), et des boiteux et aveugles, avec *'èt*, qui peut être *nota objecti*, mais qui peut aussi marquer seulement l'emphase. Et entre les deux est une forme, qui fait question, du verbe *śâné'*, généralement rendu par *haïr*, et qu'en raison d'un qeré-ketib on peut prendre au passif aussi bien qu'à l'actif. En sorte qu'il faut se demander lequel des deux déteste l'autre.

Le ketib est *śân'û*: „ils détestent"; le qeré, *śenu'éy*: „détestés par"; et une autre lecture [27]), attestée à Qoumrân, est *śân'âh*: „elle déteste" (sujet: *nèphèš*, l'âme, fém.). Donc, d'aprés le ketib, les boiteux et aveugles détestent David, et d'après le qeré ou la tierce leçon, c'est David le sujet du verbe. Mais la grosse difficulté est le sens de ce verbe.

Pour la Septante, qu'a suivie la Vulgate [28]), les boiteux et aveugles appartenaient à la proposition précédente, dont le verbe est *yigga'*: les quelques mots parlant de haine pouvaient donc en être un déterminant [29]). Mais si l'on comprend que *ṣinnôr* est l'objet de *yigga'*, et non un complément d'instrument; que *baṣṣinnôr* et *'èt-happisḥîm* ne peuvent guère être conjoints par un *waw*; qu'on n'a pas le droit de créer une seconde proposition en ajoutant un second verbe; qu'il y a donc toutes chances que le *waw* en tête de nos quelques mots introduise une autre phrase; alors on se trouve devant une phrase, dont le seul rôle serait de dire que les boiteux et aveugles haïssent David, ou que David les hait. On se demande ce qu'elle viendrait faire [30]). Personne, à la guerre, n'a de bien bons sentiments pour ses ennemis. Et l'on a peine à croire que ce constat de haine, d'un côté ou de l'autre, soit bien le sens du texte [31]). Le sens „haïr"

[27]) Voir la *BHS*. C'était déjà une conjecture de R. Kittel, après K. Budde, H. Gressmann et d'autres.

[28]) La Vulgate dans ses meilleurs témoins. Dans l'édit. clémentine est un second verbe, „abstulisset" (en plus de „tetigisset", qui rend *yigga'*). D'où la trad. de Glaire: „et *enlèverait* les aveugles et les boiteux haïssant l'âme de David".

[29]) D'où des trad. comme celle de Dhorme: „Qu'il atteigne, par le Canal, les boiteux et les aveugles, ceux qui haïssent la personne de David!"

[30]) A moins de supposer une aposiopèse: „Quant aux boiteux et aveugles qui haïssent" (ou qui sont haïs) ... et des points de suspension lourds de tout ce qu'on ne dit pas. C'est l'explication de G. K. 167 a.

[31]) Sur 42 versions que j'ai examinées, seules évitent l'objection (en même temps que l'erreur de syntaxe de la LXX): E. Reuss: „ces *maudits* boiteux"; TOB: „ils *dégoûtent* David"; M. Buber: ordre d'épargner les boiteux et aveugles, car David ne les hait pas; *Pontif.*: la haine de David est pour ceux qui toucheront aux boiteux et aveugles; et trois qui n'ont pas traduit: *Centen.*, *Mared.*, *Capuchinha*.

du verbe apparaît donc suspect. Quant à ne pas trancher lequel déteste l'autre, et à se contenter d'énoncer qu'ils sont tous deux „ennemis" [32]), c'est encore plus faire parler l'auteur pour ne rien dire. Voyons donc d'abord si c'est bien de haine ou d'inimitié qu'il s'agit.

Le verbe *śânê'* est attesté 124 fois au qal. Et dans la grande majorité des cas, il n'y a pas de doute qu'il signifie bien „détester,haïr". Mais il a parfois un sens adouci, que notre mot „haïr" n'a jamais, parce que la haine est pour nous un sentiment *absolu*, et qu'une haine tempérée ou nuancée, n'est plus vraiment pour nous de la haine. C'est, pour *śânê'*, un second sens. Les dictionnaires commencent seulement à le distinguer [33]), et les versions sont plus en retard encore.

Ce sens est celui de mépriser quelqu'un ou de dédaigner quelque chose. Jéthro conseille à Moïse (Ex. xviii 21) de choisir des hommes „craignant Dieu, de confiance et *dédaignant* le gain" (*bâṣa'*, la part qu'on se taille). Même expression dans Pro. xxviii 13: „Qui *dédaigne* le gain prolonge ses jours". Et surtout, douze fois, le verbe *śânê'* caractérise la femme *dédaignée* de son mari [34]). Or, c'est évidemment celle à qui son mari en préfère une autre, souvent simplement parce qu'elle a vieilli, et non pas une femme à qui son mari veut du mal. Encore moins une femme objectivement odieuse. Des versions font dire à Léa (Gen. xxix 33): „Iahvé a entendu que j'étais *odieuse*". Mais en ce cas, Iahvé l'aurait punie; si au contraire il lui a donné une compensation, c'est qu'elle était *dédaignée*, et injustement. Et ce que Pro. xxx 21 trouvent intolérable, c'est, à côté de l'esclave qui devient roi, et de la servante qui hérite de sa maîtresse dans les faveurs du maître, la femme *dédaignée*, et en conséquence répudiée, et qui trouve un mari. Les Proverbes n'aiment pas les femmes divorcées qui font concurrence aux jeunes filles. Quant à la nuance *mépriser*, le verbe *śânê'* la présente aussi, au moins une fois (Judc. xiv 16), quand Dalila dit à Samson: „tu ne fais que me *mépriser*", car Samson, qui ne dédaigne pas ses charmes, la méprise trop pour lui confier ses secrets. En quoi l'on sait qu'il avait bien raison.

Au total, dans ces trois nuances, cela fait 15 attestations de *śânê'* au sens de „dédaigner" ou „mépriser". Il faut donc admettre qu'à

---

[32]) *Lille*, *Pirot-Clamer*, *Votre Bible*, *New American Bible*.

[33]) Il n'apparaissait guère dans les dictionn. de Gesenius et d'Oxford, mais correspond aux sens 2 et 4 du Koehler-Baumgartner.

[34]) Gen. xxix 31, 33; Deut. xxi 15-17 (4 fois), xxii 13, 16, xxiv 3; Judc. xv 2; Isa. lx 15; Pro. xxx 23.

côté de la haine, ce verbe peut parfaitement exprimer le „dédain" ou l'„indifférence: ne pas faire cas" de, „ ne pas se soucier" de, — et il y a plus énergique. Il est bien vraisemblable ici, en 2 Sam., d'abord que le sens du verbe est celui-là, et ensuite, que la bonne lecture est la leçon appuyée par Qoumrân, *śân'âh*, au singulier: „Quant aux boiteux et aveugles" porteurs de sortilèges, „David *ne s'en soucie pas*". Il s'en moque pas mal. Chacun exprimera ce dédain comme il voudra.

On comprend maintenant l'importance de la phrase. Les boiteux et aveugles, c'étaient eux qui liaient les mains à David, et qui l'empêchaient d'attaquer, de commander l'assaut. Mais là, donnant l'ordre de s'en prendre *au jet d'eau, au trop-plein de la source*, David n'attaquait pas! Il ne rompait pas son serment. Il ne faisait pas aux Jébusites un seul mort ni un seul blessé. Il les obligeait seulement, d'une façon intelligente et que personne ne prévoyait, à lui demander ses conditions et à solliciter sa clémence. Ce n'était pas la même chose. Les pouvoirs magiques des aveugles et des boiteux, il ne les mettait pas en doute, pas plus qu'il ne les bravait de front. Mais puisqu'il avait trouvé le moyen de faire tomber la ville sans rien avoir à craindre d'eux, il se *moquait pas mal* d'eux et de leurs sortilèges.

4. *Conclusions*

Il semble qu'on puisse rendre le texte complet comme suit:

> (6) Le roi et ses hommes marchèrent sur Jérusalem contre les Jébusites qui occupaient [35]) le pays. Ils dirent à David: „Tu n'entreras pas ici, à moins d'enlever des aveugles et les boiteux", c'est-à-dire „David n'entrera pas ici." (7) Mais David prit la forteresse de Sion (c'est la Cité de David). (8) David avait dit ce jour-là: „Qui veut abattre le Jébusite, qu'il s'en prenne au jet d'eau [36])! Quant aux boiteux et aux aveugles, David s'en moque pas mal!" C'est pour cela qu'on dit: „Aveugle ni boiteux n'entrent dans la Maison."

Ce récit appelle quelques commentaires.

1° La phrase adressée à David: „tu n'entreras pas ici ..." doit bien être mise, comme on fait d'ordinaire, dans la bouche des Jébusites. Sans doute, un sujet indéterminé ou le passif rendent correctement *wayyomèr*, et offrent l'avantage de cadrer avec toutes

---

[35]) *yôšéb*. Le verbe *yâšab* signifie bien „habiter", mais aussi, au sens militaire, „*occuper*": 1 Sam. xiii 16; 1 Reg. xi 16; jeu de mots en Jer. xlvi 19 entre *yôšèbèt* au sens militaire et *mé'éyn yôšéb* au sens ordinaire.

[36]) Ou „à la décharge", ou „au trop-plein", ou „au çinnor".

les hypothèses sur l'identité du locuteur. Mais la proximité de *yebusî* dans le texte, et l'adverbe *hénnâh*: ici, montrent bien que c'est le Jébusite qui parle. C'est, adressé à un voisin lié par un pacte de paix, le rappel du pacte et de sa sanction: la cécité ou l'infirmité promises à l'agresseur.

2° Que la parole de David: *kol-makkéh* etc. ait été prononcée ou non, elle nous donne „l'idée de manœuvre" du chef. „*S'en prendre* au jet d'eau", c'était attaquer à la pelle et à la pioche le trop-plein de la nappe souterraine, de manière à la vider. Le bas du „puits de Warren" serait ainsi mis à sec, et l'eau sortant de la source s'écoulerait par la suite à l'extérieur, sur la pente allant au Cédron. La ville, alors, sans eau, n'aurait plus qu'à se rendre. Moyen imparable de faire capituler la forteresse, tout en ne l'attaquant pas par les armes.

On ne sait si la manœuvre a été effectivement exécutée, ou seulement commencée, ou s'il a suffi de sa menace par une équipe à pied d'œuvre. Nous savons qu'au temps d'Isaïe et d'Achaz, l'eau s'écoulait directement dans un canal extérieur, alors qu'à l'époque cananéenne la galerie de puisage était en service. Mais quand et par qui le çinnor a-t-il été *saboté*? Apparemment par les hommes de David, pour faire capituler la ville. Mais ce peut être aussi plus tard, pour un motif que nous ignorons.

3° Entre le sarcasme de David à l'adresse des infirmes et la sentence les excluant du Temple, il n'y a pas de rapport logique. Que, dans un cas très particulier, David ait été l'objet d'une menace dont des infirmes étaient les instruments, ne prouvait évidemment rien contre les infirmes en général. Mais la parole „David s'en moque pas mal" exprimée à l'aide du verbe *śâné'*, pouvait très bien s'entendre: „David déteste les infirmes", — et les infirmes en général. C'est sûrement en ce sens qu'on a compris cette parole, quand on en a rapproché la sentence finale, et quand les deux phrases, celle de David et la sentence, ont été ajoutées au texte [37]).

Quant à savoir si les infirmes ont été réellement exclus du Temple, et ce qu'on a pensé de la cruelle sentence à leur sujet, c'est évidemment une tout autre affaire.

4° Le plus important est enfin, que, dans l'histoire de l'accession de David, qui fut sanglante, la prise de Jérusalem a été une victoire

[37]) Tout le monde est d'accord pour voir un ajout dans le *v.* 8, qui revient en arrière (ce pour quoi le *wayyomèr* qui l'ouvre est généralem. traduit par un plus-que-parfait).

sans combat. Sans doute, on ne sait quel fut le sort des vaincus, et l'on discute si l'oracle de Zac. ix disant qu'Eqron sera „comme un Jébusite", était une promesse d'accueil bienveillant ou une menace de servitude. Mais que la Ville ait été prise sans combat aide à comprendre bien des choses. Car cette Jérusalem, ville sainte du yahvisme, et d'où est sortie la grandeur d'Israël, nous savons qu'elle retenait bien des éléments originairement étrangers au yahvisme et à la tradition des Hébreux conquérants: Sadoq, Melkisédeq Elyôn le Très-Haut ... Le schisme de Jéroboam est sans doute en partie une réaction contre elle, et pour cette raison. Et les Samaritains ne l'ont jamais appelée que *Jébis* ou *Jébus*, ne voulant voir en elle que la ville des Jébusites. Il y eut là en effet une conjonction, ou au moins des emprunts, qui étonnent. Nous en comprendrons mieux la possibilité, sachant que David et ses hommes n'ont pas pris Jérusalem de vive force comme le disent les Chroniques, mais qu'ils s'en sont rendus maîtres par un trait surprenant d'intelligence technique, et sans avoir eu à faire couler le sang.

THE DESTRUCTION OF THE SHILOH SANCTUARY AND JEREMIAH VII 12, 14

by

JOHN DAY

Durham

In Jer. vii 12, 14 (cf. xxvi 6, 9), in the prophet's famous Temple speech, Yahweh draws attention to the ruined sanctuary at Shiloh and declares that because of the people's wickedness the Temple at Jerusalem will suffer a like fate. At what date did the Shiloh sanctuary undergo the destruction here alluded to? Until quite recently it was almost universally assumed that Shiloh was destroyed by the Philistines following their massive victory over the Israelites and their capture of the Ark at the battle of Aphek, ca. 1050 B.C. (1 Sam. iv) [1]. The archaeological excavations at Shiloh were held to support the destruction of the town at that date [2]. However, the Danish re-evaluation of the excavations at Shiloh published in 1969 concluded that what had been taken as evidence of an 11th century B.C. destruction in fact related to the 8th century B.C.[3], and furthermore, S. Holm-Nielsen [4] who led the renewed Danish excavations, J. van Rossum [5] and R. A. Pearce [6] have argued that the biblical data give no particular warrant for assuming an 11th century B.C. destruction. The purpose of the present article is to argue that, on the contrary, the balance of the evidence still favours the opinion that the Shiloh sanctuary was destroyed in the 11th century B.C.

---

[1]) Amongst the many works which could be cited in favour of this view, cf. M. Noth, *Geschichte Israels* (Göttingen, ²1954), p. 154 (Eng. tr., *The History of Israel* [London, ²1960], pp. 166-7); O. Eissfeldt, "Silo und Jerusalem", *SVT* 4 (1957), p. 138; R. de Vaux, *Les Institutions de l'Ancien Testament* II (Paris, 1960), p. 136 (Eng. tr., *Ancient Israel* [London, ²1965], p. 304). The few dissenting voices include F. Buhl, *Geographie des alten Palästina* (Leipzig, 1896), p. 178, and J. N. Schofield in H. H. Rowley and M. Black (ed.), *Peake's Commentary on the Bible* (London, 1962), p. 314, § 269g.

[2]) Cf. H. Kjaer, "The excavation of Shiloh 1929", *JPOS* 10 (1930), p. 105.

[3]) M.-L. Buhl in M.-L. Buhl and S. Holm-Nielsen, *Shiloh, the Danish excavations at Tall Sailun, Palestine, in 1926, 1929, 1932, and 1963* (Copenhagen, 1969), p. 34.

[4]) In Buhl and Holm-Nielsen, pp. 56-9.

[5]) "Wanneer is Silo verwoest?", *NedTT* 24 (1970), pp. 321-32.

[6]) "Shiloh and Jer. VII 12, 14 & 15", *VT* 23 (1973), pp. 105-8.

and that the clearest indication of this is provided by the implications of the Deuteronomistic language employed in Jer. vii 12, 14.

First, briefly, the question of the archaeological evidence. The Danish excavator of Shiloh, H. Kjaer, argued for a mid 11th century B.C. destruction of Shiloh on the basis of a number of large "collared-rim" jars associated with the destruction of House A in the western sector of the town (see n. 2). Such "collared-rim" jars are a typical feature of certain Early Iron I sites [7]). M.-L. Buhl, however, who undertook a re-evaluation of the earlier excavations, argued that the "collared-rim" jars at Shiloh pointed rather to an 8th century B.C. destruction of House A, and in support she compared certain Early Iron II "collared-rim" jars from Hazor [8]). At this point it is important to note that Buhl has been criticized by the Israeli archaeologist Y. Shiloh [9]), who has pointed out that the Early Iron II "collared-rim" jars from Hazor are considerably smaller than the "collared-rim" jars of the Early Iron I period as well as having the collar in a somewhat different place, and it is to be noted that the "collared-rim" jars from Shiloh resemble those from other Early Iron I sites rather than those from Hazor of Early Iron II. In addition, he holds that none of the additional undisturbed sherds from House A belongs to Early Iron II (Buhl and Holm-Nielsen, plate 14), pointing out in particular the absence of any burnished ware. It thus appears that a serious question mark has to be raised against Buhl's denial that there is any archaeological evidence attesting a destruction of Shiloh in the 11th century B.C. However, even if it should be demonstrated that there was no destruction of Shiloh in the 11th century B.C., this would not prove that the Shiloh *sanctuary* was not destroyed then. Only the discovery of a temple at Shiloh which had not been destroyed in the 11th century would prove that. This is a point which has perhaps not been sufficiently borne in mind in discussions of this subject.

We turn, therefore, to the biblical data. The most significant piece of evidence in this regard, in my opinion, is Jer. vii 12-14. There Yahweh declares: "Go now to my place that was in Shiloh,

---

7) Cf. R. Amiran, *Ancient Pottery of the Holy Land* (Jerusalem, 1969), pp. 232 f., pl. 77.

8) Y. Yadin et al., *Hazor* I (Jerusalem, 1958), pl. LXII: 3; II (1960), pl. LXXXIX: 7-9; III-IV (1961), pl. CLXXXV: 19, CLXXXVI: 2-3.

9) In a review of M.-L. Buhl and S. Holm-Nielsen in *IEJ* 21 (1971), pp. 68-9; idem, in *Eretz Shomron, The 13th Archaeological Convention* (Jerusalem, 1973), pp. 10-18 (in Hebrew).

where I caused my name to dwell at first, and see what I did to it because of the wickedness of my people Israel. And now, because you have done all these things, says the Lord, and I spoke to you persistently but you did not listen, and called you but you did not answer, therefore I will do to the house which is called by my name and in which you trust, and to the place which I gave to you and your fathers, as I did to Shiloh." It is very significant that Shiloh is here called "the place ... where I caused my name to dwell at first" (*v.* 12). This is a very clear instance of the use of Deuteronomistic language, whose presence in Jeremiah has been increasingly noted in recent years [10]). For the particular expression "the place ... where I caused my name to dwell" one may compare Deut. xii 11, xiv 23, xvi 2, 6, 11, xxvi 2 (also note Deut. xii 5, 21, xiv 24; 1 Kings ix 3, xi 36, xiv 21; 2 Kings xxi 4, 7) [11]). Now, according to the Deuteronomists there was only one legitimate place where Yahweh caused his name to dwell (cf. Deut. xii 14) [12]) and from the 10th century B.C. onwards this was Jerusalem, specifically its Temple (cf. 1 Kings ix 3, xi 36, xiv 21; 2 Kings xxi 4, 7). In view of this, the reference in Jer. vii 12 to the destruction of Shiloh, the place where Yahweh caused his name to dwell, cannot refer to an 8th century destruction but only one prior to the building of the Jerusalem Temple in the 10th century B.C.[13]).

It is illegitimate to seek to avoid this conclusion by arguing that the destruction of Shiloh in Jer. vii 12, 14 might have occurred in the 8th century B.C., several centuries after it had ceased being the place

---

[10]) Cf. E. W. Nicholson, *Preaching to the Exiles* (Oxford, 1970); W. Thiel, *Die deuteronomistische Redaktion von Jeremia 1-25* (Neukirchen, 1973).

[11]) On this "name theology", cf. G. von Rad, *Deuteronomiumstudien* (Göttingen, 1947), pp. 25-30 (Eng. tr., *Studies in Deuteronomy* [London, 1953], pp. 37-44). Also, note R. de Vaux, "Le lieu que Yahvé a choisi pour y établir son nom", *Das ferne und nahe Wort. Festschrift für Leonhard Rost, BZAW* 105 (Berlin, 1967), pp. 219-28.

[12]) Cf. E. W. Nicholson, *Deuteronomy and Tradition* (Oxford, 1967), pp. 53-5, for a discussion rejecting the occasional attempts to avoid this conclusion.

[13]) It is probable that the Deuteronomists believed in a cultic succession in which the Shiloh sanctuary was regarded as the first dwelling-place of Yahweh's name in Palestine until its destruction, after which its place was taken by Jerusalem. (Cf. Jer. vii 12, where Shiloh is "the place.... where I caused my name to dwell *at first*".) Cf. R. E. Clements, "Deuteronomy and the Jerusalem cult tradition", *VT* 15 (1965), p. 312, who cites this as one reason why Deuteronomy constantly refers to the legitimate cult place as "the place which the Lord your God will choose, to make his name dwell there" or the like, rather than explicitly mentioning Jerusalem by name, another reason being to avoid the anachronism involved in placing the name of Jerusalem on the lips of Moses.

where Yahweh caused his name to dwell, for in that case the whole force of the parallel with the coming destruction of the Temple at Jerusalem, here referred to as the place "which is called by my name" (Jer. vii 14; cf. 1 Kings viii 43), would be lost. Furthermore Shiloh in the 8th century B.C. was a place of little or no religious significance, as the absence of references to it in the prophets indicates, and so it would be difficult to explain why Jeremiah or the Deuteronomistic redactor should pick on an 8th century B.C. destruction of Shiloh *in particular* as an object lesson for Jerusalem, whereas a destruction of Shiloh in the 11th century B.C. would be theologically extremely meaningful, since at that time Shiloh was the place where Yahweh caused his name to dwell and was therefore on a par with the status of Jerusalem in the time of Jeremiah when it was called by Yahweh's name. Hence the total invalidity of Holm-Nielsen's claim that "it is improbable that Jeremiah, who lived about the year 600 B.C., in an urgent warning to his contemporaries should have pointed to a destruction of the sanctuary of Yahweh in Shiloh which had occurred approximately 450 years earlier" (p. 58) [14]).

Moreover, the theologically piercing nature of a comparison with Shiloh's fate in the 11th century B.C. to a Jerusalem audience is all the more evident in view of the fact that Ps. lxxviii reveals that the Jerusalem cult made special play of the fact that Yahweh had rejected the Ephraimites with their sanctuary at Shiloh and that the role of that sanctuary had been appropriated by Jerusalem. In *vv.* 59-64 we read, "God heard and was enraged and utterly rejected Israel. He forsook his dwelling at Shiloh, the tent where he dwelt amongst men, and gave up his power to captivity, his glory to the hand of the foe. He abandoned his people to the sword and was enraged with his heritage. Fire consumed their young men, and their maidens had no marriage song. Their priests fell by the sword, and their widows made no lamentation." The most natural view is that the verses quoted here refer to the events associated with the battle of Aphek in ca. 1050 B.C. (1 Sam. iv) and that the rejection of Shiloh is the same event as the destruction of Shiloh alluded to in Jer. vii 12, 14. Van Rossum, however, argues (p. 327) that an early date for Yahweh's

---

[14]) It may furthermore be pointed out that the above conclusion is not offset by the fact that Jer. vii 15 goes on to allude to the exile of the Northern Kingdom in the 8th century B.C. This event serves as a reinforcement of the earlier judgment on the sanctuary rather than indicating that both events are to be dated to the same time.

abandonment of Shiloh does not necessarily follow from the fact that it is described (*v.* 60) prior to the election of David (*v.* 70) since the Psalm is not always in chronological order (e.g. *vv.* 17-31 are chronologically later than *vv.* 40-51). Whilst it is true that the Psalm is not always in chronological order, it is difficult to believe that the rejection of Shiloh pertains to the 8th century B.C., a view which van Rossum apparently espouses. There is no reference in the Psalm to the exile of the Israelites to Assyria — the omission of which is inexplicable if it had occurred, since it would have strengthened the Psalmist's claim that God had rejected Ephraim [15]) — and it is difficult to see why Shiloh (rather than, say, Samaria or Bethel) should be singled out for special mention since, as its absence of mention in the prophets testifies, Shiloh was of little or no religious significance in the 8th century B.C. Furthermore, it is significant that the verses following the reference to the abandonment of Shiloh are concerned with the battle of Aphek—*v.* 61 refers to the loss of the Ark (cf. 1 Sam. iv 21-2, where the departure of Yahweh's glory is associated with the loss of the Ark) and *v.* 64 with its allusion to the death of the priests surely reflects the death of Hophni and Phinehas (1 Sam. iv 11). In view of all this, the events alluded to in Ps. lxxviii 59-64 must relate to the 11th and not the 8th century B.C. Pearce (p. 106), whilst accepting that this is the case with *vv.* 59-61, unnaturally holds that *vv.* 62-4 are a later gloss on the Philistine domination and do not refer to any specific event, overlooking the probable reference to the death of Hophni and Phinehas in *v.* 64 when he states that "these verses lack corresponding events in 1 Sam." Pearce also holds that *vv.* 60-61 do not imply the destruction of the Shiloh sanctuary but only the loss of the Ark. Whilst this is possible, it is equally possible that the reference does imply its destruction, especially when we recall that the comparable allusion to the departure of Yahweh's glory from the Jerusalem Temple in Ezek. xi 22-3 (cf. xliii 2-5) is clearly a sign of its imminent destruction.

As has frequently been noted previously [16]), the destruction of the Shiloh sanctuary ca. 1050 B.C. provides us with a ready reason

[15]) In view of the complete absence of any reference to the downfall of the Northern Kingdom in Ps. lxxviii, I am inclined to hold that the "Deuteronomisms" which have been detected in it indicate that Ps. lxxviii is amongst the prototypes of the Deuteronomic school, rather than that it has been subjected to a late Deuteronomistic redaction. Similarly, M. Weinfeld, *Deuteronomy and the Deuteronomic School* (Oxford, 1972), p. 365.

[16]) Cf. K. Budde, *Die Bücher Samuel* (Tübingen and Leipzig, 1902), p. 30.

for the fact that only a few decades later the descendants of Eli are at Nob and no longer at Shiloh (1 Sam. xxi 1 ff., xxii 9 ff.), that the Ark never returned to Shiloh but remained at Kiriath-jearim for twenty years prior to its removal to Jerusalem (1 Sam. vii 2), and that the sanctuary at Shiloh suddenly and permanently disappears from the pages of the Old Testament. The reasons brought forward to account for these facts by those who deny that the Shiloh sanctuary was destroyed in the 11th century B.C. tend to be inadequate. Thus Pearce (p. 106) notes (following E. Nielsen) the close relationship existing between Shiloh and Benjamin as a motive for the removal of the Elide priesthood from Shiloh to the Benjamite town of Nob, which he says would be even more understandable if Nob is to be identified with the great high place of Gibeon. However, apart from the fact that there is no particular reason to identify Nob with Gibeon or its high place [17]), the close relationship between Shiloh and Benjamin would explain why, if the priests of Shiloh had to move, they would move to a sanctuary in Benjamin, but it does not itself provide a sufficient ground for why they actually chose to move. As for the fact that the Ark was not returned to Shiloh after its loss to the Philistines—curious if the shrine at Shiloh still existed—van Rossum (p. 325) merely refers to the fact that under David Jerusalem took the place of Shiloh. However, this is totally inadequate as an explanation as it fails to account for the period of about twenty years when the Ark was at Kiriath-jearim (cf. 1 Sam. vii 2)—prior to the capture of Jerusalem and the removal of the Ark there. As for the sudden and permanent disappearance of Shiloh from the pages of the Old Testament, Pearce writes that "Attention naturally moves from the 'empty' shrine, with its disquieting memory of Yahweh's abandonment of the Ark and people, to the nationalist border sanctuaries. Bethel, Gilgal and Dan are the religious expressions of the new political reality and separatism. Even Shechem is eclipsed" (p. 107). However, it is difficult to believe that the matter can be so easily disposed of, since the more it is pleaded that though continuing to exist the Shiloh sanctuary dwindled in importance, the harder it becomes to explain why it should be the destruction of an 8th century Shiloh sanctuary *in particular* to which Jeremiah appeals as an object lesson against Jerusalem (Jer. vii 12, 14, xxvi 6, 9), whereas, as was noted above, a threatened

[17]) Rather it is more natural to suppose that it is identical with the Nob alluded to in Is. x 32, which, the context shows, was very near Jerusalem.

comparison with the destruction of 11th century Shiloh, the precursor of Jerusalem in significance, is fully understandable.

Although it is strongly maintained here that the Shiloh sanctuary was destroyed ca. 1050 B.C., it is clear that the town Shiloh—whether or not it too was destroyed at that time—continued to exist during the succeeding centuries. The re-evaluation of the Danish excavations at Shiloh makes it certain that Shiloh continued to exist throughout Early Iron II and this is further borne out by the references to Ahijah the Shilonite in 1 Kings xi 29, xii 15, xiv 2, 4 and xv 29 and the allusion to the pilgrims from Shiloh (amongst other places) in Jer. xli 5. However, the continued existence of the town is not the same as the continued existence of the sanctuary. Furthermore, it may here be noted that the fact that Jeroboam chose as his sanctuaries Dan and Bethel (the latter not far removed from Shiloh) rather than Shiloh suggests that no sanctuary was available there [18]).

One passage which has been used by Pearce (p. 107) and van Rossum (pp. 328-30) to support the view that the sanctuary at Shiloh was destroyed in the 8th and not the 11th century B.C. is Judg. xviii 31, "So they set up Micah's graven image which he had made, and it was there all the time that the house of God was at Shiloh", following on *v*. 30 where we read, "And the Danites set up the graven image for themselves; and Jonathan the son of Gershom, son of Moses, and his sons were priests to the tribe of the Danites until the day of the captivity of the land." *V*. 30 surely refers to the persistence of the Danite priesthood until the exile of the Northern Kingdom, i.e. most probably 733 B.C. or possibly 721 B.C. *V*. 31 does not necessarily imply that the sanctuary at Dan existed only as long as the house of God was at Shiloh *and no longer* [19]). The Hebrew text certainly allows one to hold that the sanctuary at Dan could have

---

[18]) At this point it is appropriate to mention the interesting but unprovable thesis of A. Caquot, "Aḥiyya de Silo et Jéroboam 1er", *Semitica* 11 (1961), pp. 17-27, that the real reason why Ahijah the Shilonite initially supported Jeroboam's rebellion but subsequently rejected him—distorted by Deuteronomistic redaction in 1 Kings xi and xiv—is that, as a Shilonite, he naturally resented the claim of Jerusalem to have superseded Shiloh and would have hoped for the restoration of the Shilonite sanctuary, but he turned against Jeroboam because he chose Bethel and Dan instead.

[19]) Thus, although *vv*. 30 and 31 may well be from different hands, M. Noth, "The background of Judges 18-19", in B. W. Anderson and W. Harrelson (ed.), *Israel's Prophetic Heritage* (London, 1962), p. 83, who accepts that the Shiloh sanctuary was destroyed in the 11th century B.C., is wrong in maintaining that the dates given in these two verses are irreconcilable.

persisted even after the house of God was at Shiloh. In fact, it may even be argued that the latter is more likely, since the whole point of the reference to Shiloh here is surely that it represents the legitimate shrine of the period (cf. 1 Sam. 1 ff.) set over against the shrine at Dan, which the account in Judg. xvii-xviii clearly regards as illegitimate and apostate. Judg. xviii 31 is saying that all the time the legitimate sanctuary was at Shiloh, the apostate shrine existed at Dan. Since Shiloh was no longer regarded as the site of the legitimate shrine after the 11th century B.C., it is difficult to believe that "all the time that the house of God was at Shiloh" extends down to the 8th century B.C., for then the point of *v.* 31 would no longer be a contrast between a legitimate and an illegitimate shrine and the reason why Shiloh of all sanctuaries should come in for particular comparison here becomes difficult to explain. Consequently, Judg. xviii 31 cannot be used as an argument in favour of the continuance of the Shiloh sanctuary down to the 8th century B.C.

In conclusion, then, it may be argued that the arguments which have been adduced in favour of the destruction of the Shiloh sanctuary in the 8th century B.C. are invalid and that the balance of the evidence still favours the view that it was destroyed in the 11th century B.C., in spite of certain recent claims to the contrary. The clearest indication of this emerges from Jer. vii 12, 14. Certain other biblical passages tend to suggest that it is likely, whilst the archaeological evidence leaves the way open for such a conclusion.

THE ISRAELITE TRIBES IN JUDGES

by

BARNABAS LINDARS
Manchester

Martin Noth's theory of an Israelite Amphictyony, *Das System der Zwölf Stämme Israels* (Stuttgart, 1930), has had a good innings in Old Testament study, but is heavily under fire today. It has never been without critics [1]). Now, with the work of A. D. H. Mayes, *Israel in the Period of the Judges* (London, 1974), and C. H. J. de Geus, *The Tribes of Israel: an investigation into some of the presuppositions of Martin Noth's Amphictyony hypothesis* (Assen/Amsterdam, 1976), its defeat may be said to be complete. This means that we have to look afresh at the Book of Judges, to see what the Israelite tribes were really like before the monarchy was established.

It is obvious that the subject is too large for comprehensive treatment in a single article, and that it will be necessary to be selective. In what follows attention will be drawn to three important lists in Judges, which provide information about the tribes in the period. The first is the list of the Minor Judges (x 1-5, xii 7-15). It will be shown that such information as may be gleaned from the list is significant for an understanding of the nature of the tribes, but does not support a theory of inter-tribal organization. The second is the list in the composite first chapter of the book, which ostensibly shows the state of the tribes at the beginning of the period, but in fact gives a useful picture of the position at the very end of it. The third is the

---

[1]) One of the earliest critics was O. Eissfeldt, "Der geschichtliche Hintergrund der Erzählung von Gibeas Schandtat (Richter 19-21)", in A. Weiser (ed.), *Festschrift Georg Beer* (Stuttgart, 1935), pp. 19-40 (= *Kleine Schriften* II [Tübingen, 1963], pp. 64-80). An important critique of the theory as a whole was given by J. Hoftijzer, "Enige opmerkingen rond het Israëlitische 12-stammensysteem", *NThT* (1959-60), pp. 241-63. The recent chorus of criticism was largely stimulated by G. Fohrer, "Altes Testament—"Amphiktyonie" und "Bund"?", *ThLZ* 91 (1966), Sp. 801-16, 893-904 (= *BZAW* 115 [1969], pp. 84-119). These doubts about the theory are reflected in recent histories of Israel, cf. R. de Vaux, *Histoire ancienne d'Israël: la Période des Juges* (Paris, 1973); S. Herrmann, *Geschichte Israels in alttestamentlicher Zeit* (Munich, 1973; E.T., London, 1975); J. H. Hayes and J. M. Miller (ed.), *Israelite and Judaean History* (London, 1977).

list in the Song of Deborah in chapter v. This reveals a fluid situation, in which the tribes are in process of development and are not yet permanently settled. Finally an attempt will be made to discover the basis of unity among the tribes in this period.

I. *The Minor Judges*

The Minor Judges make a good starting point, because they have been taken to be amphictyonic officers having a pan-Israelite status, and the information about them is certainly very ancient. But it must be said at once that this is a case where the theory has influenced the interpretation. In fact the theory of the Amphictyony has had an extraordinary effect on the interpretation of Judges as a whole. Though supposedly supported by the evidence of Judges [2]), it has been taken too readily to be the key to its problems, as can be seen in the recent commentaries of John Gray, *Joshua, Judges and Ruth* (London and Edinburgh, 1967), and Robert Boling, *Judges* (Garden City, 1975). It has been long agreed that Judges is a collection of traditions of tribal exploits, worked over with a new introduction by the Deuteronomic historian, and that it is he who has imposed upon the book its pan-Israelite interpretation. Take away his framework, and the amphictyonic impression disappears. The tribes do not at all behave as if they were an Amphictyony conforming to the pattern of Noth's *System*. But the theory presupposes pan-Israelite institutions, including a central sanctuary, periodic assemblies of representatives of all the tribes, mutual obligations in the wars of Yahweh, and the personal supervision of a chief of all the tribes known as the Judge. Consequently the critic who accepts this theory is tempted to read into the early sources precisely the sort of interpretation presupposed by the Deuteronomic historian, so that what he takes away with one hand he puts back with the other. And when facts are few and far between he is always liable to use his amphictyonic imagination to fill in the gaps.

An example may be given from Gray's comment on one of the

---

[2]) Noth, *System*, Exkurs IV, argued that Jud. xix-xxi, in spite of much reshaping, gives evidence for the actual working of the Amphictyony. In fact the pan-Israelite features of the story are better explained as due to rationalization of events which originally had only local significance. The process is comparable to the idealization of the tribal system in Jos. xxii. The weaknesses of Noth's analysis of these chapters were already pointed out in the article of Eissfeldt mentioned above.

Minor Judges. Ibzan of Bethlehem [3]) judged Israel for seven years, according to Jud. xii 8-10. He had thirty sons and thirty daughters, and married them all to partners outside his clan. Gray observes: "Ibzan's policy of exogamy for his numerous family was probably designed to increase his influence as judge of the sacral confederacy by as wide a connection as possible" (p. 341). But it can scarcely be supposed that all the sixty weddings took place in the seven years in which Ibzan was judge. In fact, as no tribe is mentioned, exogamy outside the *mišpāḥāh* is probably intended, which at this period would be the population of the town or district. The marriages are thus more likely to have taken place over a longer period, and to have helped Ibzan to establish his personal ascendancy widely among the clans, but not necessarily beyond the confines of his tribe.

This conclusion is supported by the work of de Geus (pp. 133-9), who has shown that the tribal structure of old Israel is primarily a matter of kinship and marriage. The "father's house" (extended family) is obviously the basic unit, but is too restricted for the needs of a settled society. Hence the clan (*mišpāḥāh*) is the endogamous unit, which is usually limited topographically to relatively enclosed areas by the rough terrain. The Samaria ostraca have proved that the clan names continued to be attached to these places well into the eighth century. The larger group of the tribe is a voluntary association of clans cutting across natural barriers, extending the range of intermarriage. As the name (*šēḇeṭ* or *maṭṭeh*) implies, the tribe was presided over by a chief who holds the staff of office (cf. Jud. v. 2, 9, 14). This need not have been a permanent office.

Thus, whatever be the historical value of the editorial notes that each man "judged Israel" for a modest, but varying, number of years, the actual information provided about them relates to their local position, not to a pan-Israelite status. The same is obviously true of Jair the Gileadite (Jud. x 3-5). Gilead is here a geographical designation, and Jair is remembered for his success in building up a local unity in the thirty villages known as the Havvoth-Jair [4]).

Jephthah is particularly interesting from this point of view, because his exploit has been inserted from the other source at the point where

[3]) Bethlehem in Zebulun (= *Beit Laḥm*, 7 miles west of Nazareth) may be meant, cf. Jos. xix 15. This is favoured by the absence of Judean traditions in Judges, and by the fact that Bethlehem in Judah is specified as such in xvii 8, xix 1.

[4]) Cf. Num. xxxii 41, where the inclusion of these villages in what later became Manassite territory has been rationalized by making Jair a son of Manasseh.

he is mentioned in the list of the Minor Judges (Jud. x 6-xii 6). He is thus the one member of the list who is the subject of a tradition preserved independently. But the tradition does nothing to remove the impression that the Minor Judges were only local leaders. Jephthah's qualities of leadership were recognized in the locality. The oath of the chieftains at Mizpah in Gilead (xi 11) was necessitated by the ill-treatment which he had previously received at their hands. But there is not the slightest hint that this was a matter of conferring inter-tribal status upon him at a central sanctuary. Here again amphictyonic presuppositions easily lead to false conclusions. Gray's comment shows only too clearly the tension between the given facts and the amphictyonic interpretation: "Mizpah was thus a central sanctuary of various Israelite groups worshipping Yahweh east of Jordan, which gave the agreement its validity. All this implies a more regular office in the case of Jephthah than in that of any other judge, and indeed is reminiscent of the regularization of Saul's kingly office at the central sanctuary of Gilgal" (p. 333). But this is not the case at all. It was a local matter at a local sanctuary, and it took place before the action which established his ascendancy.

Thus the statement in the list of the Minor Judges that "Jephthah judged Israel six years" (xii 7) is not to be connected with the oath at Mizpah, but with the results of his continuing eminence after his success against the Ammonites. As Mayes has pointed out, the specification of a limited number of years indicates appointment to a recognized office, though not necessarily to the office of tribal chief, or even as the sole holder of the office of judge (cf. Deut. xvii 9, xix 17). If the verb is taken in its strict meaning to denote a judicial function, the most likely model is Samuel, whose eminence in judicial matters was recognised comparatively widely among the Israelite clans, even cutting across tribal boundaries (1 Sam. vii 15-17). Significantly *špṭ* never has a tribe as object. It seems likely that the list of the Minor Judges was the source from which the Deuteronomic editor compiled the concluding notes to the hero stories in the narrative source, taking advantage of the range of meaning afforded by the verb, which can mean to rule as well as to judge (cf. Mayes, pp. 55-67).

To sum up, the Minor Judges give an indication of the basis of the tribal structure as a society founded on kinship. The judges are men of eminence in a locality, sometimes achieving this position through military prowess. As they are judges for varying numbers of years, it may be supposed that they only received formal appointment within the tribe late in life, so that age and maturity must be added to their other qualifications. Though pre-eminent judges may have been recognized beyond the limits of their own tribe, there is no indication of a pan-Israelite status.

II. *The Tribes in Judges i*

The picture of Israelite tribal life which we have gained so far has a timeless character, and it might be supposed that there was very little change over a long period. This may be true from the point of view of social structure, but it is certainly not true as regards political organization. The first chapter of Judges presupposes that all the tribes had their proper areas covering the whole land, like the counties of England, apart from pockets of resistance presented by the unconquered Canaanite cities. But this is not the impression that is given by the stories of the narrative source. This may be illustrated from a further feature of the story of Jephthah. In xii 1-6 the men of Ephraim express their jealousy following his success against the Ammonites. But their taunt that the Gileadites are "fugitives in the midst of Ephraim and Manasseh" (*vs.* 4) betrays confusion, with its false implication that Ephraim extends to the region of Gilead east of the Jordan, and the whole statement does not fit the actual terms of the story [5]). Manasseh does not figure in the story at all, so that it must be concluded that the mention of it here (as also in xi 29) [6]) is an insertion to bring the position into line with the later tribal designations. There is no indication in the older material of Judges that Manasseh had territory east of the Jordan. The story is about Gilead, which does not figure in any of the twelve-tribe lists at all [7]), and is not mentioned in Jud. i.

Thus, even if there was a tribal confederacy at this period, it was not identical with any form of it that can be deduced from the tribal lists on which Noth's theory was based. Noth argued that the tribal

---

5) The words *kî ʾāmᵉrû pᵉlîṭê ʾeprayim* in xii 4 seem to be an accidental insertion from the next verse, where they make good sense, and the rest of the sentence has been added in an attempt to clarify them. The whole sentence is missing from the original LXX.

6) This verse also shows signs of corruption, and can scarcely be regarded as an original part of the story. The hand of the editor can be seen in the verbal allusion to iii 10 and the anticipation of verse 32, and the addition of the verse is to be attributed to the inclusion of verses 12-28, which are based on an extraneous source (so Moore, Gray).

7) There are no secure grounds for the identification of Gilead with Gad; cf. Hoftijzer, pp. 245-9; de Geus, pp. 108-11.

system could only have arisen during the period of the Judges, because the unified kingdom under David (if not already under Saul) marked its end. In fact the story of Jephthah presupposes no such thing as a sacral confederacy, though it does illustrate the demand for a strong leader in the face of an enemy. If the unification of Israel was mainly brought about by the need to band together against the strength of the Philistines, there is no need to assume the interposition of a tribal confederacy. In such circumstances the movement towards tribal unity is likely to pass directly from local leadership to kingship [8]). It is thus doubtful if it is appropriate to speak of a confederacy of the tribes at all, implying some kind of military league, quite apart from the difficulty of identifying a group of twelve (or six) tribes as a coherent unit in this period. It thus begins to look as if the tribal lists are the result of a rationalization of a more complex and confused state of affairs, worked out subsequently. So far as they have an historical basis at all, this would seem to be derived from the tribal positions which obtained when Israel settled down under David, after the Philistines had been suppressed and the lingering allegiance to the house of Saul was ended.

If this is correct, it becomes a serious possibility that the number twelve belongs to the rationalization in David's time, so that the lists of twelve cannot certainly be taken back earlier. As is well known, both ten and twelve were widely used in the ancient Near East as numbers denoting wholeness. The sanctuaries at Gilgal and Shechem had twelve stones, and cultic use of them to represent tribal participants may have helped to fix twelve as the "complete" number of Israelite tribes. From this point of view it is reasonable to argue that the unity of Israel was expressed in the cult long before it was realized in any political institutions.

It follows from this that the Blessing of Jacob (Gen. xlix), which Noth took to be the oldest of the tribal lists, cannot be taken back earlier than the time of David with any assurance, although it undoubtedly contains some much older individual items. The same is true of the Blessing of Moses (Deut. xxxiii) [9]). The list of tribal

[8]) The transition can be seen in the local kingship of Gideon and Abimelech (Jud. viii 22-ix 6) and in the rise of Saul, quite in the style of the Judges, in 1 Sam. xi, cf. B. Lindars, "Gideon and Kingship", *JTS*, N.S. 16, 1965, pp. 315-26.

[9]) De Geus, p. 116, maintains that Deut. xxxiii is an older collection than Gen. xlix, though the individual items in it are not so ancient, on the grounds that it is not really a collection of twelve. The individual items are traced back to settlement traditions, of varying date and provenance, by H.-J. Zobel, *Stammesspruch und Geschichte*, *BZAW* 95 (1965).

boundaries in Jos. xiii-xix also contains some old individual items, but even if the list as a whole is not to be dated as late as has often been maintained, it is not safe to rely on it for the geographical positions of the tribes before the time of David.

The same caveat must be made with regard to the information in Jud. i. In any case the evidence of this chapter has to be used with caution. It is a pastiche of old material, mostly derived from Joshua, and was added by the final editor to smooth the transition from one book to the other. But it does include some items not found in Joshua, so that a debt to other sources cannot be excluded. Its value for our present purpose is that it has some interesting links with the Blessing of Jacob. This suggests that it can be taken as a kind of summary of the state of the tribes at the end of the Judges period.

First, the section on Judah, besides repeating legends of the non-Israelite clans, speaks of Simeon as Judah's brother. This is reminiscent of Gen. xlix 5-7, where we read: "Simeon and Levi are brothers; weapons of violence are their swords . . . I will divide them in Jacob and scatter them in Israel". The implication that Levi might have been a landed tribe remains puzzling, but need not concern us now. The important thing is that both Simeon and Levi at this time are landless tribes. This agrees with Jud. i in suggesting that Simeon, though ethnically akin to Judah (if that is the implication of "brother" here) was subordinate to Judah by the time that it linked up with the northern tribes to form David's kingdom.

Secondly, in Jud. i 22-26 we are told that the house of Joseph captured Bethel [10]). This is usually taken to refer to the original tribe of Joseph, before it was divided into Ephraim and Manasseh. Dc Geus strenuously denies this, on the grounds that the house of Joseph is a designation which appears only in literature of the time of David and afterwards. Thus Shimei the Benjamite claims to be the first of the house of Joseph to welcome David's return after the death of Absalom (2 Sam. xix 20). As the contrast is with the tribe of Judah, the house of Joseph is here clearly a designation for the former dominion of Saul. Again, in 1 Kings xi 28 Jeroboam is put in charge of the house of Joseph in Solomon's levy. This area of responsibility is probably identical with the first of Solomon's administrative dis-

[10]) Zobel, pp. 107-11, suggests that the tradition originally concerned Benjamin, but that the city was subsequently lost to the Ephraimites. The suggestion belongs to a theory of an early attempt on the part of Benjamin to gain the hegemony in Ephraim, for which there is little positive evidence.

tricts, called simply Ephraim in 1 Kings iv 8, which included Jeroboam's home town Zeredah. It is thus in some way equivalent to Ephraim, though it is clearly a genealogical name whereas Ephraim is geographical. It is thus possible that the house of Joseph was an aggressive clan which became the predominant clan in Ephraim, though there is not sufficient evidence to be certain of this. But it explains why the Blessing of Jacob, which is genealogically based, eulogizes Joseph without reference to Ephraim and Manasseh (Gen. xlix 22-26). The extension of reference to include Manasseh as well as Ephraim, which might seem to be merely a device to make the list of tribes fit the required number of twelve [11]), can then be seen to arise for a quite different reason precisely at this time. For, if the use of the ethnic name Joseph was common for Ephraim at the time of the beginnings of tribal unification under Saul, it would be natural for his administration at Mizpah in Benjamin to regard Manasseh as a kind of extension of Ephraim (just as the Assyrian records speak of Israel as the Hatti-land). Hence it is not surprising to find that Ephraim, which continued to be the preferred designation, is used to denote both Ephraim and Manasseh in the description of Ishbosheth's kingdom in 2 Sam. ii 9 [12]). Of course this usage is still apparent in the eighth century, when the northern kingdom is normally referred to as Ephraim.

Thirdly, the list of unconquered Canaanite cities in Jud. i 27-33, which belongs to a different literary stratum from the preceding paragraph on the house of Joseph, includes not only information on Manasseh and Ephraim, derived from Jos. xvi 10 (Ephraim) and xvii 11-13 (Manasseh), but also similar items in connection with Zebulun, Asher and Naphtali. This information again reflects conditions in the time of Solomon, under whom many of these cities (e.g. Gezer) were resettled. The impetus to make an inventory of these cities is clearly not separable from the need to list the tribal holdings. Such lists would certainly be required for Solomon's administration, even though his

---

[11]) Cf. Deut. xxxiii 13-17, which is a similar eulogy of Joseph, but ends: "Such are the ten thousands of Ephraim and the thousands of Manasseh".

[12]) He is said to be king "over Gilead and the Ashurites and Jezreel and Ephraim and Benjamin and all Israel". The description is geographical rather than ethnic, and "all Israel" is an inclusive designation of the places already mentioned, and does not necessarily imply any further territory. The obviously corrupt *hā-ʾᵃšûrî* is best emended to refer to Gesher (north of Gilead) with Syriac and Vulgate, rather than to Asher with Targum. The Philistine victories over Saul had cut off the northern tribes altogether.

system of districts to some extent disregards tribal boundaries, possibly making use of the old Canaanite city-states for practical reasons [13]). But there is no mention in Jud. i of Issachar, Gad and Reuben. The last two are accounted for by the fact that their territory was in Transjordan. But this does not apply to Issachar, so that its omission is surprising. But it may well be that there were no unconquered cities in Issachar's lot. This may also seem surprising, but for the answer we must wait until we have considered the tribal list in Jud. v.

Fourthly, there is a further surprise in the brief notice on Dan (i 34). Here the old position of the Danites [14]), west of Mt. Ephraim, is referred to, but the pressure is not from the Philistines, but from the Amorites. But the information in this verse is scarcely reliable, as it is a memory of the former occupation of this territory, which was still referred to as Dan (cf. Jos. xix 40-48), though the Danites had long since migrated north. When this territory was recovered it formed the second of Solomon's districts, and was presumably counted as part of Ephraim. Hence in Jud. i 35 the Amorite cities in this region are said to be reduced by the house of Joseph. Once more these verses contribute to the picture of the Israelite tribes at the time of transition at the end of the Judges period and the beginning of the monarchy.

III. *The Tribes in the Song of Deborah*

The Song of Deborah has always been a threat to the Amphictyony theory, because the ten tribes mentioned in it cannot be related to any of the tribal lists in a formal way, and the tribes appear to recognise no such mutual obligations as the theory presupposes. Noth (*System*, pp. 5 f., 36) was well aware of this, but argued that the list in Jud. v has no bearing on the twelve-tribe system, on the grounds that (a) the poet mentions only those tribes which either took part in the battle or might have been expected to do so, and (b) the tribal designations are geographical rather than ethnic in the main. Both

---

[13]) Cf. A. Alt, "Israels Gaue unter Salomo", *Alttestamentliche Studien Rudolf Kittel zum* 60. *Geburtstag dargebracht* (Leipzig, 1913) pp. 1-19 (= *KS* II [Munich, 1953], pp. 76-90).

[14]) The name may be connected with the Danuna, mentioned along with the Philistines and other sea peoples in a text of Ramses III (W. F. Edgerton and J. A. Wilson, *Historical Records of Ramses III* [Chicago, 1936]; *ANET*, p. 262). But the identification is difficult, because they must have become circumcised and integrated into Israelite society some time before the Song of Deborah, and this would only be possible on a very late date for the battle.

these observations are correct, but the conclusion to which they point is that a genealogical system of the tribes had not been constructed at this stage (cf. de Geus, p. 111). In fact the evidence of the Song of Deborah for the state of the tribes in the period of the Judges is of prime importance, because it has not been subjected to the rationalizing process which lies behind the other lists. It gives a very different picture from Jud. i.

Ten tribes are listed in a sort of roll-call in Jud. v 14-18. In the last of these verses Zebulun and Naphtali appear as the heroes of the battle. As these are the only two tribes to be mentioned in the prose account of Jud. iv, it has been argued that the other verses do not refer to a mustering for war, but to a call for tribal representatives to attend a subsequent pan-Israelite cultic assembly at which Yahweh's prowess in the battle was acclaimed [15]). But this must be dismissed as another figment of the amphictyonic imagination. The natural interpretation is that the reference is to a call to join in the offensive against the Canaanites who controlled the valley of Jezreel. There is no hint of a sacral obligation to do so. If *vs.* 18 is excluded as the beginning of the description of the battle, then the list gives, first, the tribes which responded to the call, Ephraim, Benjamin, Machir, Zebulun and Issachar, and then those which refused, Reuben, Gilead, Dan and Asher. The omission of Naphtali from the first group is strange, but it can be explained if Barak himself belonged to Naphtali, as is asserted in iv 6 [16]). The same verse of the prose account also implies that Naphtali holds Mt. Tabor, though it is included in Issachar in the later boundary lists. This information is consistent with the implications of the poem, where it is said that Barak's army "marched down" (v 13).

We have here a first indication that the Israelite tribes had not yet penetrated the Galilean uplands, though Naphtali had a footing on the east side of the valley, where it is shut in by Tabor and Moreh. There is then much to be said for the old view of Steuernagel and Burney that the contingents came from the south [17]). This obviously

[15]) Cf. A. Weiser, "Das Deboralied: eine gattungs- und traditionsgeschichtliche Studien", *ZAW* 71 (1959), pp. 67-97.

[16]) The statement that his home was at Kadesh in Naphtali may be accepted, if the reference is to Khirbet Qadisa, SW of the Sea of Galilee. But the narrator probably took it to mean the better known Kadesh north of Hazor, which helps to explain the introduction of the Jabin material in this chapter (derived from Jos. xi).

[17]) C. Steuernagel, *Die Einwanderung der israelitischen Stämme in Kanaan* (Berlin, 1901); C. F. Burney, *Israel's Settlement in Canaan* (London, 1918).

applies to Ephraim and Benjamin, which are the first to be commended for their response (14ab). It should be noted that the preposition "from" with Ephraim implies that the name is used in a geographical sense, so that it means the tribe consisting of the clans centred on Mt. Ephraim, whereas Benjamin is clearly an ethnic name [18]). The same preposition is used with Machir and Zebulun (14cd), so that it is reasonable to infer that these also are geographical designations, though neither of them is attested as a place name [19]). Machir should not be identified with Manasseh, which seems to be too insignificant for mention at this period. But it may have been settled in the region later known as Manasseh, and only subsequently crossed over the Jordan to the region of Gilead [20]). This is borne out by Jos. xvii 1, where Machir is said to be the eldest son of Manasseh and the father of Gilead, which furnishes an interesting illustration of the transformation of historical geography into genealogical theory. For it represents the subordination of the Gileadite clans to the Machirites when they crossed the Jordan, and the subsequent subordination of them to Manasseh at the end of the Judges period.

Zebulun may also have been in the central mountain region to the north of Mt. Ephraim, presumably to the west of Machir [21]). As a topographical name it could well denote "height". The fact that the tribe had not yet settled in Galilee is suggested by the old proverb on Zebulun preserved in the Blessing of Jacob (Gen. xlix 13). For here it is said to be "at the shore of the sea" (*ḥôp yammîm*, i.e. the Mediterranean), which seems to refer to the coastal region between the mouth of the Kishon and Acco. The very same phrase is used of Asher in Jud. v 16c. This suggests that Zebulun pressed to the coast after the battle, before moving to the Galilean uplands behind the Phoenician cities [22]).

---

[18]) The phrase *ʾaḥᵃreyḵā binyāmîn* is generally held to be a traditional battle-cry, attested also in Hos. v 8 (where, however, it is often emended on the basis of LXX; the text is accepted by Rudolf and Elliger).

[19]) This seems better than Zobel's theory that Machir is to be connected with *mkr* = to sell, implying mercenary service.

[20]) Cf. de Geus, p. 77; Hoftijzer, p. 243.

[21]) It has been suggested on the strength of Jud. xii 12 that Zebulun was as far south as Aijalon, but the fact that Aijalon is virtually identical with Elon makes this a very insecure basis of evidence.

[22]) There may be a taunt at Zebulun's territorial ambitions in Gen. xlix 13c, where it is said that its border would be at Sidon. Zobel agrees that Zebulun reached the coast after the battle, though he holds that it had already settled in Galilee as a result of the fall of Hazor in the thirteenth century. But this means that we have to assume that, unable to hold the coastal region, it drew back to where it was before.

The last tribe to be commended in the roll-call is Issachar (15abc) [23]. The words do not suggest a geographical designation. In fact Issachar is an elusive tribe. If Naphtali held Mt. Tabor at this time, we must assume that Issachar was not yet settled in the territory assigned to it in the boundary lists (Jos. xix 17-23), which also figures in Solomon's administrative districts (1 Kings iv 14). The story of Gideon may be expected to give us some help, because it belongs to a time between the battle of the Kishon and the rise of Saul. Here we find that Manasseh has risen to prominence as a tribe embodying the clans of the north central region, as in the later lists. After the success of Gideon against the Midianites at the Well of Harod, the local tribes rallied to his support (Jud. vii 23). But those which are named are only Naphtali, Asher and "all Manasseh" (i.e. the other clans of Manasseh besides the Abiezrites). The omission of Zebulun can be accounted for if it was pushing towards the coast. But the omission of Issachar is strange, if it was settled in the valley of Jezreel at this time. It is for this reason that I find it impossible to accept the common view, held for instance by Zobel, that Issachar had been already settled in Jezreel earlier, but had been subject to Sisera until his hold over the valley was broken by the battle of the Kishon. If this had been so, the success of the battle would have put Issachar into the best possible position to help Gideon in the rout of the Midianites.

It looks, then, as if Issachar was not settled in Jezreel in the time of Gideon, even though it had taken part in the battle of the Kishon some time earlier. This can be explained if the name Issachar really does imply mercenary service, as is often supposed, so that the tribe was not seeking territory of its own at this stage. If *kēn bārāq* in v 15 means "faithful to Barak", it could reflect a degree of personal loyalty unusual in those whose military allegiance is a way of earning a living. As this is the oldest reference to Issachar, it is possible that its association with Barak in this crucial battle marked its acceptance as an Israelite tribe, though not really of Israelite stock.

The first mention of Issachar as a landed tribe comes in the Blessing of Jacob, where the tribe has accepted a situation of ease, "crouching between the sheepfolds" (*bên ham-mišpeṯayim*). Once more, the very same phrase is used in Deborah's Song, but applied to Reuben (v 16)[24].

---

[23]) Numerous critics read Naphtali for Issachar in 15b, but this has no textual authority, and is unnecessary, as we have seen.

[24]) The word occurs only in these two places, but *šepattayim* in Ps. lxviii 14 is probably the same word (also in Ezek. xl 43, unless *śepāṭām* be read with the

It is tempting to see a geographical reference in this problematical phrase, just as in the case of Zebulun and Asher. This, then, would be comparable to Shephelah, which is a topographical word regularly applied to denote a particular region. Thus the transference of the proverb from Reuben to Issachar would be caused by Issachar's settlement on land which had been formerly occupied by Reuben. There are in any case sufficient indications that Reuben had once been settled in the central mountain region, though much further south. The tradition of Reuben's crime at Migdal Eder (Gen. xxxv 21 f.), which is probably referred to in the Blessing of Jacob (Gen. xlix 4), and the Stone of Bohan son of Reuben on the north boundary of Judah (Jos. xv 6, xviii 17), both imply this. Moreover, the persistence of the tradition that Reuben was Jacob's firstborn, in spite of the tribe's virtual disappearance after crossing to its traditional position in Transjordan, suggests that it had once been a powerful clan. But neither the south nor the region south of Gilead in Transjordan really suits the requirements of the Song of Deborah. It is thus not impossible that Reuben, as a pastoral tribe, moved north along the mountain range to a position on the north-eastern slopes of Gilboa, which were the site of Issachar's first settlement later on. Expansion here would be difficult, because of the continuing power of Beth-shean (i 27), so that Reuben (like Machir) moved over to Gilead, and Issachar eventually settled in the former territory of Zebulun and Naphtali in the valley of Jezreel [25]). Thus the proverb of Gen. xlix 15, making a pun on the name Issachar, reverses the facts, for it attests the emergence of Issachar as a landed tribe at the end of the Judges period, after its long years of servitude are over. As it acceded to territory originally freed by the battle of the Kishon, we can see now

versions), and is variously translated "panniers [of an ass]", "hearth-stones" or "sheepfolds" (cf. the review of Zobel by J. A. Emerton, *JTS*, N.S.19 [1968], p. 245 f.). Though there can be no certainty about the meaning of the word, the dual after *byn*, and the verbs used with it (*škb* and *rbṣ*), suggest a topographical reference, or special feature of farming.

[25]) In the Blessing of Moses (Deut. xxxiii 18f), Issachar is coupled with Zebulun, and the two tribes control an important mountain sanctuary, identified by many scholars with Mt. Tabor (cf. O. Eissfeldt, "Der Gott des Tabor und seine Verbreitung", *ARW* 31 [1934], pp. 14-41 = *KS* II [Tübingen, 1963], pp. 29-54). Our argument does not support the view that Tabor was the central shrine of a northern Amphictyony of six tribes, but there is no difficulty in supposing that Zebulun and Issachar promoted Tabor as a centre of pilgrimage during the eleventh century. If Issachar was in process of settlement, its territory would have overlapped that of Zebulun in this area.

why there were no unconquered Canaanite cities in its region in the situation presupposed by the first chapter.

Returning to the Song of Deborah, we pass on to the group of tribes which failed to respond to the call to arms. Reuben has already been dealt with. Next comes Gilead (17a), and the reason is that Gilead is the region across the Jordan, where there was no threat from the Canaanite cities [26]). Finally Dan (17b) and Asher (17cd) also failed, being too far to the west along the coast. Though attempts have been made to evade the impression that Dan was on the coast at this time [27]), it can be accepted if the Danites have already moved from the western Shephelah on account of Philistine pressure, and are in the Plain of Sharon, before eventually making their way to the far north at a later date [28]). Asher may also have moved by way of the Plain of Sharon to the coastal region around Acco, retaining its position in spite of the subsequent attempt of Zebulun to gain a foothold there.

IV. *Conclusions*

Though it is inevitable that many of the above suggestions are speculative, being derived from scraps of information which are impossible to interpret with certainty, a convincing general picture emerges from the evidence. The picture is one of movement, the tribes dispersing from the main central mountain region around Mt. Ephraim. There is a similar process in the south, where the tribe of Judah is establishing hegemony over a number of ethnic groups, in-

[26]) Some editors wish to transpose the curse on Meroz (*vs.* 23) to this point, but it is more likely that Meroz was a small clan or township near to the site of the battle, which failed to assist in cutting off the flight of Sisera. The name is unknown from other sources, and there is no way of telling whether it was a Canaanite (Alt), Israelite (Grether), or Hebrew but not Israelite (Gray) settlement.

[27]) The phrase *yāgûr ʾᵒniyyôṯ* is not very informative, but seems acceptable when compared with Gen. xlix 13, where *lᵉḥôp̱ ʾᵒniyyôṯ* is parallel to *lᵉḥôp̱ yammîm* in the blessing of Zebulun. Older critics emend the text to get rid of the nautical connection, but Gray has suggested that *ʾᵒniyyôṯ* is an adverb cognate with Arabic *ʾāna* = to be at ease, comparing a similar phrase in the Legend of Krt; but his elucidation of the Krt passage is by no means certain.

[28]) The tendentious narrative of Jud. xvii-xviii cannot be regarded as a reliable account of the migration of Dan, even if it is correct in claiming that the tribe's cult image and Levitical priesthood were derived from Micah's household in Ephraim (cf. M. Noth, "The Background of Judges 17-18", in B. W. Anderson and W. Harrelson [ed.], *Israel's Prophetic Heritage* [London, 1962], pp. 68-85). The presence of the Tjekker at Dor at this period would prevent permanent settlement in the Plain of Sharon (cf. The Journey of Wen-Amon, *ANET*, pp. 25-9).

cluding the Israelite tribe of Simeon. How far this process had gone by the time of Deborah it is impossible to say. But in the north we can see the expansion of the Ephraimite clans, headed by the house of Joseph, and presumably the rise of Manasseh follows a similar pattern, though this is more obscure. The dispersal of other tribes in the area was no doubt partly due to pressure from Ephraim and Manasseh, but is better regarded as a general movement of expansion and territorial acquisition. This was facilitated by the collapse of opposition in the north and east. As far as the east is concerned, the story of Ehud (Jud. iii 12-30) shows that expansion across the Jordan was scarcely possible in the earlier part of the period, because there was a Moabite bridgehead across the Jordan in his time as well as Ammonite and Amalekite pressure. Thus the suggestion above, that Reuben moved north before taking up its position in the southern part of Transjordan, which can only be very tentative, is supported by the difficulties of expansion eastwards earlier. By the time of Deborah, however, Israelites were settled on the east bank further north in Gilead. The expansion north beyond Jezreel, on the other hand, can be attributed to the resounding victory of the battle of the Kishon, undertaken by Barak of Naphtali at the instigation of Deborah, which was notable for the degree of tribal co-operation achieved, and no doubt owed its success to this. The Israelite penetration of the Galilean hills would on this view belong to the end of the twelfth and the beginning of the eleventh century, which agrees with the dating of the earliest Iron Age settlements at Hazor [29]).

Though Barak's success depended on co-operation, there is very little sign of it elsewhere. If the tribes do join together, it is usually for mopping up after the success of a local leader, when they hope to prevent further trouble from the enemy, and presumably to cash in on the spoils (Jud. iii 27, vii 23 ff., xii 1-6). Moreover the individual tribes do not seem to have any internal cohesion. De Geus is unable

---

[29]) Hazor was destroyed about 1230 B.C. There was an Iron I settlement, without permanent buildings, in the twelfth century, and another unfortified settlement in the eleventh. Similar Iron Age settlements belong to this time in other parts of upper Galilee. Cf. Y. Yadin, "Hazor", in D. W. Thomas (ed.), *Archaeology and Old Testament Study* (Oxford, 1967), pp. 258 f.; *Hazor* (London and Jerusalem, 1975). Whether the twelfth century settlement was a consequence of the battle of the Kishon depends on the date of the battle, which has been estimated to be 1200 (J. Garstang), 1125 (W. F. Albright), or 1100 (H. Wheeler Robinson). Of course the view put forward in this paper does not allow the conclusion that the destruction of 1230 was actually due to Joshua (Jos. xi 1-11).

to find any political entity to which the designation tribe can be given. The tribes from this point of view are rather groups of clans banded together for military purposes. That is why the tribal names are mainly geographical rather than ethnic. Indeed the variation between geographical and ethnic names shows how haphazard was the evolution of the tribes. Some, like Ephraim and Gilead, answer well to the description of a group of clans banded together. Others, like Manasseh and Judah, are individual clans which have established hegemony over a wide region. Others, like Benjamin and like Dan after its migration, are small clusters of clans which have retained their independence. The tribes in Judges are evolving unities of clans. As we have seen in connection with the Minor Judges, the tribe is best regarded as a regional unit of clans, providing a wider circle for intermarriage. As this requires a real or supposed basis of consanguinity, they have a genuine collective self-consciousness as an ethnic unit. Family matters require judicial officers recognized by the whole tribe, and they look to the leadership of an outstanding warrior in time of war. It is thus only to be expected that the growth of a national self-consciousness will be expressed in the formation of a genealogical system, embracing all the tribes in one family. Geographical names become the personal names of eponymous ancestors, and the twelve-tribe system is formed.

Such unity as does exist during the period of the Judges must, then, be seen in the sense of belonging together which the Israelites had over against other peoples occupying the same region—Canaanites, Philistines, Amorites, Amalekites, Moabites, Ammonites—all of whom are foreigners from an Israelite point of view, and outside the approved circle for intermarriage (cf. Jud. viii 31, xiv 1-3). Basic to this sense of unity are two things, both of which appear very clearly in the Song of Deborah. First, there is, as we should expect, a real ethnic basis in the consciousness of belonging to Israel. Not all the clans were ethnically related, of course, but the social system required that they should claim kinship, and a sufficient number of them were so related as to ensure that the designation Israel was universally accepted as their collective description. The name is to be connected with the El shrines of central Palestine, and this fits the importance of Ephraim for the origins of the tribes [30]).

---

[30]) For this reason it seems necessary to assume that the origins of Israel are separate from the introduction of Yahwism. The Merneptah Stele (*c.* 1218 B.C.) is consistent with the view that Israel first became identifiable as a people in this area.

Secondly, the Israelites acknowledge Yahweh as their only, or at least their principal, God. No defined obligations to one another, however, are implied in the covenant with Yahweh. Nor does the common religion necessarily include pan-Israelite cultic gatherings at a central sanctuary. No such gathering is ever heard of in the Book of Judges. Deborah's Song was certainly intended for recitation at a Yahwistic assembly, but the fact that it mentions ten tribes does not prove that representatives from them all were expected to be present. Because Yahweh is the God of Israel, not just of a particular tribe, there is a sense in which all religious gatherings involve the whole people, without the necessity of an institutional organization including formal representation. As there was no single central sanctuary, the pilgrimage feasts could not provide the opportunity for representation of all the tribes at once. Such meetings are likely to have been extremely rare events, when urgent necessity compelled common action [31]), and even then are scarcely likely to have succeeded in bringing together *all* the tribes, at any rate during the period of dispersal and expansion in the time of the Judges. How Yahwism became the religion of Israel is a question which belongs to an earlier period, along with the thorny problem of the origins of Israel. I will only say that the evidence of Judges, such as it is, supports the old idea that it was the landless Levites who brought Yahwism to Israel, together with the Exodus traditions [32]). Thus in xvii 13 Micah the Ephraimite says, "Now I know that Yahweh will prosper me, because I have a Levite as priest". Later we discover that this priest was "Jonathan the son of Gershom, son of Moses" (xviii 30) [33]).

However that may be, the main point of this article has been to expose the fluid nature of the tribes in the time of the Judges. The

[31]) Cf. 1 Sam. xi 7. The covenant ceremony at Shechem (Jos. xxiv) may well preserve the memory of the adoption of Yahwism by the clans on Mt. Ephraim, before the dispersion in the Judges period. For the importance of Shechem in the ancient traditions of Israel, cf. H. Seebass, *Der Erzvater Israel und die Einführung der Jahweverehrung in Kanaan*, *BZAW* 98 (1966).

[32]) De Geus, p. 119, is favourable to this view.

[33]) As Noth points out, this information comes as an afterthought, and cannot be regarded as part of the original source. But it is not to be lightly set aside for this reason, as it is most unlikely that the Deuteronomic historian or a later interpolator would be pleased to include this pedigree of the priests of the shrine of Dan. The Massoretic tradition reads Manasseh for Moses, no doubt wishing to class Jonathan with the wicked king Manasseh of Judah, but that Moses was known to be the true reading is shown by the fact that many manuscripts have *nûn suspensum*, and some actually read Moses, and this is supported by the original LXX and Syrohexapla.

tribes are in process of formation, and this includes decline as well as development. They are at the same time expanding territorially, and this means that they are far more concerned with their own welfare than with obligations of mutual support. Their common identity as the people of Israel and worshippers of Yahweh was no doubt strongly felt, but was not expressed in pan-Israelite institutions. There was no tribal *system*—much less an Amphictyony—in the days of the Judges. The credit for inventing the system must go, first, to those in the time of David and Solomon who were responsible for the national cult, for the army, and for secular administration, and who thus crystallized the actual state of the tribes at the time, and secondly to the national historians, culminating in the Deuteronomic historian, who read it back into the ancient traditions of Israel.

JONATHAN AT THE FEAST

A NOTE ON THE TEXT OF 1 SAMUEL XX 25 [1])

by

B. A. MASTIN

Bangor, North Wales

The Revised Version translates 1 Sam. xx 25, "And the king sat upon his seat, as at other times, even upon the seat by the wall; and Jonathan stood up (*wayyāqom yᵉhônāṯān*), and Abner sat by Saul's side: but David's place was empty." However, it is commonly supposed that *wayyāqom* does not offer good sense, and the most popular solution to this apparent difficulty is to read *wayᵉqaddēm* instead (e.g. *BH*[3] *in loc.*). As far as I am aware, this emendation was first proposed by O. Thenius (*Die Bücher Samuels* [Leipzig, 1842], p. 86). The purpose of this article is to examine what the Hebrew text of this verse says about Jonathan, and it will be convenient to begin by setting out the evidence provided by the versions. The range of meaning which the verb *qûm* may have in Hebrew will then be considered, and it will be asked how the versions which read *wayyāqom* understood it. The reasons for objecting to *wayyāqom* and for reading *wayᵉqaddēm* will be discussed next, and attempts to handle the problems involved will be reviewed. Finally, a new suggestion will be advanced.

I

The LXX renders "and he [Saul] went before Jonathan (καὶ προέφθασεν τὸν Ἰωναθάν), and Abner sat beside Saul (A: and he sat and Abner sat facing him beside Saul)", with which may be compared Lucian's καὶ προέφθασεν αὐτὸν Ἰωναθάν, found in 19, 56, 82, 93, 108 and 127 (A. E. Brooke, N. McLean and H. St J. Thackeray [ed.], *The Old Testament in Greek* II, 1 [Cambridge, 1927], p. 70; cf. P. de Lagarde [ed.], *Librorum Veteris Testamenti Canonicorum pars prior* [Göttingen, 1883], p. 283). However, Symmachus has παρέστη δέ (F. Field, *Origenis Hexaplorum quae supersunt* I [Oxford, 1871-75], p. 523). The Old Latin was translated from a Greek reading in part

1) An abbreviated form of this article was read as a short communication at the Sixth International Congress on Biblical Studies held at Oxford in April 1978.

identical with the one attributed to Lucian by Lagarde but before Lucian's time, though it continues the verse differently: "et praecessit eum Ionathan et sedit, et Abner erat ad latus Saul" (C. Vercellone, *Variae Lectiones Vulgatae Latinae Bibliorum* II [Rome, 1862-64], p. 276). By contrast the Vulgate (ed. R. Weber et al. [Stuttgart, ²1975], I, p. 399) offers the interpretation, "cumque sedisset rex super cathedram suam. . . surrexit Ionathan et sedit Abner ex latere Saul", though some authorities insert "et" before "Abner" (Vercellone, p. 274). The Targum (ed. A. Sperber [Leiden, 1959], p. 138) uses the cognate verb *qām* for *wayyāqom*, while the Peshiṭta has *wqm ywntn w'stmk w'bnyr ʿl gnb šw'l/š'wl* (so the editions of B. Walton [London, 1653-57], II, and S. Lee [London, 1823-26], the Urmia edition [1852], the Mosul edition [1887-91] and A. M. Ceriani, *Translatio Syra Pescitto Veteris Testamenti ex Codice Ambrosiano Sec. Fere VI photolithographice edita* [Milan, 1876-83]). The Arabic, according to the translation in Walton's Polyglot, II, says, "tum discubuit post eum Jonathan a dextera regis, et Abner discubuit a sinistra Saulis." Similarly Josephus, *Ant.*, vi § 235, states that Jonathan and Abner sat one each side of Saul, but does not mention that Jonathan previously stood up.

II

There is general agreement that in Hebrew *qûm* signifies both "to arise" and "to stand", the latter meaning being used in a figurative way (cf., e.g., Amos vii 2, 5; 1 Sam. xxiv 21; Job viii 15; Num. xxx 5; Jer. xliv 28 f.; 1 Sam. iv 15; and see further *BDB s.v.* qal 7). In cognate languages verbs which can have the literal sense "to stand" are derived from this root. This is so in Ugaritic, and *CTA* 2. I. 21 will be discussed in section V below. It has been thought that *qm* also denotes "to stand" in *CTA* 2. I. 31 [2]) and 10. II. 17 [3]), but in neither case is this certain. Clear instances of *qm* = "stand" are found in Aramaic (Dan. ii 31, iii 3, vii 10, 16; cf. *Jahrbuch für Kleinasiatische Forschung* 1 [1950-51], p. 203, line 4), in Syriac (Exod. xxxiv 2; Luke vii 38; P. de Lagarde, *Bibliothecae Syriacae* [Göttingen, 1892], p. 65, note to Exod. xiv 7), and in Samaritan (J. Macdonald [ed.], *Memar Marqah* I [Berlin, 1963], p. 17, line 6; p. 38, line 29; p. 135,

[2]) A. Goetze, in *Studia Orientalia Ioanni Pedersen . . . Dicata* (Copenhagen, 1953), p. 119.

[3]) So C. H. Gordon, according to G. R. Driver, *Canaanite Myths and Legends* (Edinburgh, 1956), p. 117, n. 9. However, Driver translates *wyqm* here "and rose", while C. H. Gordon (*Ugaritic Literature* [Rome, 1949], p. 50) has "in her presence he proceeds to arise" for the line.

line 30; cf. II, pp. 23, 60, 221). Neither *BDB*, F. Zorell, *Lexicon Hebraicum... Veteris Testamenti* (Rome, 1946-54), nor *KB* identifies this sense for *qûm* in Hebrew, but the possibility that such a usage exists cannot be excluded, and the assumption of some scholars that there is an example of it in 2 Sam. xii 17 may be justified. Here the RSV translates *wayyāqūmû ẓiqnê bêṯô ʿālāw lahᵃqîmô min-hāʾāreṣ*, "and the elders of his house stood beside him, to raise him from the ground" [4]).

In 1 Sam. xx 25 *wayyāqom* was read by the Vulgate, the Peshiṭta, the Targum, and, probably, Symmachus. The Vulgate's "surrex it" and the Peshiṭta's *wqm ywntn wʾstmk wʾbnyr* both support "and he arose", but it is not possible to tell from the context what the Targum intended to convey by *qām*. However, παρέστη δέ in Symmachus may well reflect an understanding of *wayyāqom* as "and he stood". At Dan. vii 10 both the LXX and "Theodotion" have παρειστήκεισαν for the Massoretic Text's *yᵉqûmûn*, and at Sirach li 2, where the term describes the writer's adversaries, the LXX's καὶ ἔναντι τῶν παρεστηκότων corresponds to the Hebrew *ngd qmy*. The only other verse in which παριστάναι could be equivalent to *qûm* is Job xxix 8, where, however, Symmachus has παρίσταντο as against the two verbs *qāmû ʿāmāḏû* of the Massoretic Text. The reading of Symmachus at 1 Sam. xx 25 seems to imply a Hebrew text *wayyāqom* which was taken to mean "and he stood", and, though Dan. vii 10 is the sole passage which can be cited as a parallel, it is not easy to find a satisfactory alternative explanation of the evidence. Thus, "to arise" and "to stand" should both be considered as possible denotations of *qûm* in this verse. The former is supported by the Vulgate and the Peshiṭta, and it is likely that the latter is supported by Symmachus.

L. H. Brockington holds that "it is just possible that [*wayyāqom*], based on a Syr. cognate, could mean 'was present' " [5]), and this is the interpretation of the New English Bible. This theory will be examined in section IV below.

III

The objection to reading *wayyāqom* in 1 Sam. xx 25 is that, whether it means "and he arose" or "and he stood", Jonathan's action is

---

[4]) Cf. earlier H. P. Smith, *A Critical and Exegetical Commentary on the Books of Samuel* (Edinburgh, 1899), p. 325.

[5]) In M. Black and H. H. Rowley (ed.), *Peake's Commentary on the Bible* (London, Edinburgh, etc., 1962), p. 327.

hard to understand. "And Jonathan arose" is incomprehensible (Thenius, p. 86), and "why Jonathan should stand while the others sit is not clear" (Smith, p. 193).

Two reasons are given for reading *way^e qaddēm*. First, the LXX and Lucian have προέφθασεν. Elsewhere in the LXX προφθάνειν translates a Hebrew word sixteen times, and is used once for the hiph'il of *rûṣ* (Ps. lxvii 32) and on fifteen occasions for the pi'el of *qdm* (2 Reigns xxii 6, 19; 4 Reigns xix 32; Job xxx 27; Ps. xvi 13, xvii 6, 19, xx 4, lviii 11, lxvii 26, lxxxvii 14, xciv 2, cxviii 147, 148; Jon. iv 2). Therefore προέφθασεν points to *way^e qaddēm*. But the second reason, that "Jonathan was in front of him" is implied by the statement in verse 33 that Saul picked up (or, according to the unemended text, hurled) his spear to kill Jonathan [6]), can safely be ignored, since it is gratuitous to suppose that Saul could have tried to attack Jonathan only if they were sitting opposite each other.

Because προέφθασεν in the LXX and Lucian does not make sense, it is reasonable to suppose that it is a mechanical rendering of the pi'el of *qdm*. Thus it is hard to escape the conclusion that a Hebrew manuscript which read *wyqdm* lies behind the reading of the LXX. Moreover, *ye hônāṯān* is understood as the object of the verb by the LXX (as distinct from the Old Latin and the Lucianic recension, which supply "him" as object), though it would be more natural to take it as the subject. Since προφθάνειν is found in nineteen other places in the Old Testament and is followed by an accusative fourteen times (including all three instances of the word in Reigns) it might have seemed appropriate to regard the name Jonathan as accusative in this verse. But even if τὸν Ἰωναθάν is due to some other cause, this idiosyncracy confirms the character of the LXX's translation here.

IV

If, then, there are strong grounds for holding that *wyqdm* was the reading of a Hebrew manuscript or manuscripts, it must be asked whether it has a better claim to be original than *wayyāqom*. It is not possible to deduce anything from the Targum or Symmachus, but the interpretations of the other versions which read *wayyāqom* do not show that it offers good sense. The variation in the tenses of the verbs in the Vulgate indicates that Jonathan was thought to have stood up after Saul had seated himself, presumably so that Abner

[6]) P. R. Ackroyd, *The First Book of Samuel* (Cambridge, 1971), p. 167.

could sit beside Saul, but it is far from clear either why Jonathan should have done this or what he did next. However, the Peshiṭta, in which the conjunction *w* is prefixed to *'bnyr*, says that Jonathan stood up and then sat down again. The Old Latin and variant readings in the Vulgate and the LXX may be compared. But, while a *waw* before *'aḇnēr* might have been omitted from the Hebrew text by accident, there is no obvious reason why this should have happened, and it is at least as possible that "and" was added before "Abner" to make a difficult verse more intelligible. Even so, Jonathan's behaviour remains perplexing. It is not necessary to review all the interpretations which have been advanced by modern scholarship, such as C. F. Keil's opinion that the Massoretic Text relates how "Jonathan beim Eintreten Abners von seinem Sitze neben Saul aufstand und diesen Platz Abnern einräumte" [7]) or Thenius's theory (p. 86) that *wayᵉqaddēm* signifies that, whereas "gewöhnlich mochten *Jonath.* und *Dav.* zu beiden Seiten *Sauls*, *Abner* diesem gegenüber sitzen, diessmal *wollte Jonath.* nicht *neben* dem Vater sitzen." It is most natural to take the Massoretic Text as a description of what was customary in which the detail of the scene is stated in full, and J. Wellhausen rightly observes, "die Pointe beruht darauf, dass, während im Allgemeinen Alles an der Tafel hergeht *kᵉpa'am bᵉpa'am*, eben dadurch die Eine Veränderung fühlbar wird" [8]). The noteworthy thing was David's absence, and the question is whether *wayyāqom* gives an accurate picture of Jonathan's part in a normal feast.

P. A. H. de Boer (*OTS* 6 [1949], pp. 28 f.) argues that "the Hebrew text tries to link this verse closely with the preceding scene in the field and therefore reads *wayyāqom*." But H. J. Stoebe correctly characterizes this as a "freilich wenig deutliche Verbindung" [9]), and it is also hardly conceivable that such a statement should have been inserted in what would otherwise be a coherent narrative. Thus de Boer's defence of the Massoretic Text is unconvincing.

At the text-critical level, the issue is whether *wyqm* or *wyqdm* can be accounted for as a straightforward corruption. It has been claimed that the *daleth* in an original *wyqdm* was taken to be a *waw*, presumably because the manuscript was damaged or the letter badly written, and that this was then either understood as a vowel letter for short

---

7) *Die Bücher Samuels* (Leipzig, 1864), p. 156.
8) *Der Text der Bücher Samuelis* (Göttingen, 1871), pp. 118 f.
9) *Das Erste Buch Samuelis* (Gütersloh, 1973), p. 377, note c to xx 25.

o or deleted as a mistake [10]). This hypothesis is tenable, though it is just as likely that a *daleth* was left out by accident. Yet on the other hand at a time before final and medial *mem* were distinguished *wyqm* could have become *wyqdm* under the influence of the sequence *wypqd mqwm* later in the verse. Even if "*scriptio continua* was not a practice of early Hebrew scribes" (A. R. Millard, *JSS* 15 [1970], p. 14), it is necessary to suppose only that a manuscript in which these words were written closely together was being used. Manuscripts in which the words were not all clearly separated perhaps contributed to some of the instances of what is generally agreed to be faulty word-division in the Old Testament, such as Amos vi 12 (but cf. also H. W. Wolff, *Dodekapropheton* 2. *Joel und Amos* [Neukirchen-Vluyn, 1969], p. 330 on this passage). Thus each reading can be explained satisfactorily as a corruption of the other, and the priority of either can be established only on the basis of its suitability to the context.

However, there are difficulties if *wayeqaddēm* is read. S. R. Driver, who regards this as the true reading, thinks that "the relative position of those at the table is described, and Jonathan *was in front*, opposite to Saul: the seat opposite to Abner was vacant" [11]). He continues, "true, *qiddēm* commonly denotes *to come* or *go in front*; but not perhaps necessarily, and the use of the word here would closely resemble that in Ψ. 68, 26 *qiddemû šārîm* the singers *were in front*." It is important to stress that there is no precise parallel in the Old Testament to what *wayeqaddēm* is assumed to signify in 1 Sam. xx 25. In addition, Wellhausen (p. 119) notes that "man vermisst...ein auf Saul bezügliches Suffix in *wayeqaddēm*", and, although by itself this would not carry much weight, it is another indication that "to be in front" may be a forced interpretation of *qiddēm*.

Perhaps such considerations were in the mind of H. W. Hertzberg, who comments, "MT unverständlich.... Das vermutete *wajeḳaddēm* der LXX ist auch nicht besser; es wird lediglich für diese Stelle mit 'und J. setzte sich gegenüber' wiedergegeben. Vielleicht lautete der ursprüngliche Text *ûlephānāu meḳōm*; das mag früh unleserlich geworden und nur die vier Buchstaben *wjḳm* mochten übriggeblieben sein" [12]). But, though Hertzberg's conjectural restoration is undeniably ingenious, it has a precarious basis. The reconstructed text

---

10) Wellhausen, pp. 18, 119; A. Klostermann, *Die Bücher Samuelis und der Könige* (Nördlingen, 1887), p. 90.

11) *Notes on the Hebrew Text . . . of the Books of Samuel* (Oxford, ²1913), p. 169.

12) *Die Samuelbücher* (Göttingen, 1956), p. 133, n. 6.

which he argues may have become illegible contains ten letters (or nine, if the *ô* of *m*ᵉ*qôm* was written defectively). Not only is this considerably more than the four required to give *wyqm*, but two of these four letters are narrow. Further, there would have been a gap of three letters between the legible *waw* and *yodh*, and a gap of two letters between the *yodh* and the *qoph*. Therefore a scribe using a manuscript which had been damaged in this way might reasonably have been expected to know that something longer had once been written. It would be strange if, in these circumstances, he constructed a word from four letters which he would hardly have believed should be taken together. The improbability becomes all the greater if Hertzberg's view that *wayyāqom* is unintelligible here is correct, and, equally, if he is wrong the versions suggest that the word might well not have been intelligible to the scribe whose activity is postulated. While this scribe might not have thought it necessary to consult another manuscript which was intact, assuming that one was available, if he was unable to arrive at a reading which satisfied fully the data provided by the manuscript which he was copying, a more sensitive treatment of the text than is envisaged by Hertzberg would be expected. Hertzberg also fails to show how the reading of the LXX could have originated, but an explanation of this which would be consistent with his theory has been given above. Yet, although he rightly recognizes that *way*ᵉ*qaddēm*, like *wayyāqom*, is not without its difficulties, his attempt to go beyond the readings of the Massoretic Text and the LXX is unconvincing.

W. Caspari deletes *wayyāqom*, "aus dem sich nichts entwickelt", as arising from dittography of *haqqîr*, *y*ᵉ*hônāṯān* being later added as subject (*Die Samuelbücher* [Leipzig, 1926], p. 262). But it would be odd if Jonathan were left out of the description of the meal while Abner was included, and *hqyr* and *wyqm* are so dissimilar it is not easy to see why *wayyāqom* should have originated from *hqyr*, especially if it is meaningless. Thus this hypothesis also is to be rejected.

It was noted in section II above that *wayyāqom* has been taken to mean "and he was present". The merit of this suggestion is that, if it is correct, the Massoretic Text makes sense. But, in view of the detailed information provided about the places occupied by Saul and Abner, it would be more natural for something less general than this to be said about Jonathan. "And he was present", which receives no support from any of the versions, would therefore lose all plausibility if a case could be made for either "and he arose" or "and he stood".

V

The reading *wayyāqom* will now be re-examined in the light of the probability that *qûm* can mean "to stand". The Ugaritic phrase *bʿl qm ʿl ʾil* (*CTA* 2. I. 21) is normally translated, "Baal was standing beside El". Though U. Oldenburg, who admits that this rendering is possible, prefers "Baʿal was rising against El" [13]), J. C. de Moor cogently objects that there is nothing in the context to warrant such a translation [14]). This clause may offer an instructive parallel to *wayyāqom*, though it must first be asked why Baal is standing. F. M. Cross, who is concerned primarily to defend the translation "Baʿl stands by (enthroned) ʾĒl", observes, "This idiomatic use of *ʿl* with a verb of 'standing' is well known, applying to the courtiers (heavenly or earthly) standing by a seated monarch or judge (divine or human). Cf. 1 Kings 22: 19; Zech. 4: 14 (both of council of Yahweh; cf. Isa. 6: 2), and Exod. 18: 13, 14 (Moses sitting in judgment)" [15]). "Courtiers" may not be the correct term to use in connection with Exod. xviii 13 f., but, this apart, while the soundness of the translation need not be doubted, what Cross says is insufficient to account for the fact that Baal alone was standing while the rest of the gods were sitting (lines 20 f., cf. 23-29). C. H. Gordon states that "the gods were seated for banqueting when Baal spied the messengers coming. The gods, anticipating the unpleasant message, bent their heads in sadness, but Baal, showing the courage befitting the king-to-be, took his stand by El" [16]). By contrast M. H. Pope, who mentions this as one of two alternatives which he seems to consider equally plausible, claims that Baal may have been hoping that El would protect him [17]). The latter suggestion is unlikely in view of Baal's fighting words in lines 24-28, and neither position reckons seriously with *hlm* immediately after *bʿl qm ʿl ʾil* (line 21). Presumably *ʾap ʾilm l⟨l⟩ḥ* [*m*] *yṯb bn qdš lṯrm bʿl qm ʿl ʾil* (lines 20 f., following Herdner) describes the gods feasting while Yam's messengers were on their way (lines 19 f.) and *hlm* introduces the next stage in the drama: *hlm ʾilm tphhm tphn mlʾak ym tʿdt ṯpṭ* [*nhr*] (lines 21 f., following

13) *The Conflict between El and Baʿal in Canaanite Religion* (Leiden, 1969), p. 135 and n. 3.

14) *The Seasonal Pattern in the Ugaritic Myth of Baʿlu* (Neukirchen-Vluyn, 1971), p. 130. I am grateful to Dr John Day for drawing my attention to the importance of this book and of that by P. J. van Zijl (n. 18 below) for the study of this text.

15) *Canaanite Myth and Hebrew Epic* (Cambridge, Mass., 1973), p. 37 and n. 147.

16) *Before the Bible* (London, 1962), p. 179.

17) *El in the Ugaritic Texts*, *SVT* 2 (Leiden, 1955), p. 28.

Herdner). Thus it is more natural to take *bʿl qm ʿl ʾil* with what precedes.

One of the two hypotheses which P. J. van Zijl seems to think equally possible would bypass these objections. He writes, "from the broken portion at the beginning [of *CTA* 2. I] it appears that Baal rejects the kingship of Yam and refuses to pay tribute.... From the context...one gains the impression" that all the gods were "expectant.... When the gods prepared to dine, Baal went and stood in the vicinity of El in order to be ready for any action that he indirectly expected from Yam" [18]). But there is nothing in the text to support this interpretation, and, as the story unfolds, it is not clear why it should be an advantage for Baal to stand beside El. Presumably this would be the focal point of the *pḫr mʿd* from which it would be easiest to harangue the assembled gods when Yam's embassy was sighted, and it is the place to which the ambassadors come (lines 30-33), but there is no surprise attack: the question is whether the gods will accede to Yam's demands. Whatever untoward events were imminent, it is more satisfactory to hold that Baal participated in the feast in the usual way until Yam's messengers were seen.

C. Virolleaud's opinion that Baal "va chercher refuge auprès de son père...El" [19]) may be compared. Virolleaud supposed that the two enemies had not yet fought, but that, because Astarte would aid Yam, Baal "sans doute ne se sent pas le plus fort, n'ayant point Anat à ses côtés." Later he modified this by leaving out the reference to Anat, who, he claimed, was not mentioned anywhere in this text [20]), though Herdner (p. 8, n. 4) considers that *[ymnh ʿn]t* should be restored at the beginning of line 40. However, according to R. Dussaud, "on voit [Yam] demander à Astarté de frapper Baʿal et de lui briser la tête.... L'intervention d'Astarté amène la défaite de Baʿal qui s'enfuit auprès du dieu El" [21]). But the badly damaged lines at the top of *CTA* 2. I, which are the basis for this thesis about the relationship between Astarte and Yam, can be understood in several different ways, and it would be unwise to insist on any one interpretation.

---

[18]) *Baal. A Study of Texts in Connexion with Baal in the Ugaritic Epics* (Neukirchen-Vluyn, 1972), pp. 23, 26.

[19]) "Le Dieu de la Mer dans la Mythologie de Ras Shamra", *Comptes Rendus des Séances de l'Académie des Inscriptions et Belles-Lettres* (1946), p. 501.

[20]) *Légendes de Babylone et de Canaan* (Paris, 1949), p. 76. Cf. idem, "Le Dieu de la Mer", p. 500.

[21]) "Astarté, Pontos et Baʿal", *Comptes Rendus des Séances de l'Académie des Inscriptions et Belles-Lettres* (1947), pp. 208, 211.

Pace Dussaud, the mutilated remains of the Astarte Papyrus (on which see A. H. Gardiner, in *Studies presented to F. Ll. Griffith* [London and Oxford, 1932], pp. 74-85) do not suggest that Astarte would have assisted Yam, even if G. Posener's conclusion that the two documents are quite distinct [22]) is wrong. Virolleaud observes that "Yâm reste sur ses positions, tandis que Baal...se retire" and is found immediately afterwards at the Assembly of the Gods, but, if the actual combat has not begun, the intention could just as well be to portray Baal's defiance in contrast to the attitude of the other gods (lines 23-28, and perhaps also lines 38-40), or El's reaction to what Yam asks (lines 36 f.). Even if *dtqh* in lines 18 and 34 means "whom you protect", this would not necessarily imply that Baal was present at the *pḫr m'd* because he felt in need of protection. What H. L. Ginsberg (*JCS* 2 [1948], p. 143) calls "a lurid picture of Yamm's heyday" shows the rest of the gods in terror of Yam (lines 23 f.), while Baal alone is ready to resist (line 28). Indeed, the fragmentary lines at the top of *CTA* 2. I could indicate that the gods expected Baal to act as their champion against Yam, though, because of the incomplete condition of the tablet, this argument should not be pressed. Even so it is most straightforward to conclude that lines 20 f. recount what happened ordinarily when the gods dined.

The second theory which is advanced by both Pope (p. 28) and van Zijl (p. 26) is that Baal is standing by El to minister to him. This explanation is accepted by a number of other scholars who do not record alternative possibilities [23]). Pope comments (p. 28, n. 17), "note the subservient position of Kumarbi before he dethroned Anu", and this Hittite myth provides two significant parallels to the Ugaritic phrase under discussion. It tells how "once in the olden days Alalus was king in heaven. (As long as) Alalus was seated on the throne, the mighty Anus, first among the gods, was standing before him. He would sink at his feet and set the drinking cup in his hand." Then Alalus was deposed by Anus, and "Anus took his seat upon the throne. (As long as) Anus was seated upon the throne, the mighty Kumarbis would give him his food. He would sink at his feet and set the drinking cup in his hand." Subsequently Anus in

[22]) "La Légende Égyptienne de la Mer Insatiable", *Annuaire de l'Institut de Philologie et d'Histoire Orientales et Slaves* 13 (1953), pp. 461-478.

[23]) H. L. Ginsberg, in *ANET*, p. 130; O. Kaiser, *Die Mythische Bedeutung des Meeres in Ägypten, Ugarit und Israel* (Berlin, 1959), p. 62; and R. J. Clifford, *The Cosmic Mountain in Canaan and the Old Testament* (Cambridge, Mass., 1972), p. 47.

his turn was deposed by Kumarbis (*ANET*, p. 120). The precise relationship between Baal and El at Ras Shamra is much disputed, but it is plausible to regard El as a patriarchal figure (Cross, pp. 42 f.), while Baal is an important god. El is the god at whose feet Yam's messengers either do or should bow down (lines 30 f.), and he is superior to Baal because the demand for Baal's surrender is addressed to him and he agrees to hand Baal over to Yam (lines 16-19, 33-37). If Anus waited on Alalus and Kumarbis on Anus, it would not be strange to find Baal waiting on El. Thus not only are there good reasons for rejecting the other proposals which have been examined and for treating *bʿl qm ʿl ʾil* as part of a description of the gods feasting normally, but also, because of the Hittite material to which Pope refers, it is intelligible that Baal should stand to serve El.

One would expect the procedures of the heavenly court to reflect those of an earthly court, and, if there is Hittite evidence for the chief god being served by the god who ranks immediately beneath him and if, as is probable, Baal stood to serve El, Jonathan, who is the most prominent of Saul's sons in 1 Samuel and whom Saul wishes to succeed him on the throne (1 Sam. xx 31), may have stood to serve his father. It is generally assumed that the Ugaritic epics provide reliable information about aspects of Canaanite religion in the Israelite period, and they may also mention a feature of court life which could have been taken over by the Israelites when the monarchy was introduced. Court ceremonial tends to be conservative, and, whatever the exact character of Saul's rule, it represented an attempt to establish dynastic kingship. Therefore a practice attested elsewhere only in non-Israelite stories about the gods could have been found at Saul's court.

It might be objected that *wayyāqom yᵉhônāṯān mēʿim haššulḥān* (1 Sam. xx 34) suggests that Jonathan was seated at the table. But in other passages which are in any way similar the prepositions used after *qûm* are *mēʿal* (Judg. iii 20) and *min* (Jon. iii 6) of rising from a *kissēʾ* and *min* of rising from a *mištēh hayyayin* (Esth. vii 7). Further, *BDB* (p. 769a) lists all the passages in which it considers *mēʿim* is followed by a word denoting a place. Excluding Job xxviii 4, where the text is probably corrupt, they are: *wayyôṣēʾ yôsēp̄ ʾōṯām mēʿim birkāw* (Gen. xlviii 12), *mēʿim mizbᵉḥî tiqqāḥennû* (Exod. xxi 14), *wᵉʾîš lōʾ-ʾaḵrîṯ lᵉḵā mēʿim mizbᵉḥî* (1 Sam. ii 33), and *hinnēh-ʿām yôrᵉḏîm mēʿim ṭabbûr hāʾāreṣ* (Judg. ix 37). In the light of these examples *wayyāqom yᵉhônāṯān mēʿim haššulḥān* may be translated "and Jonathan left the table" and need mean no more than that he had participated in the feast.

Thus, if *wayyāqom* is rendered "and he took his stand", it may reveal a forgotten feature of Saul's court. The Massoretic Text then offers good sense and may be retained.

VI

The argument of the article may be summarised as follows. Three meanings have been suggested for *qûm* in 1 Sam. xx 25, "to arise", "to stand" and "to be present". "To arise" is supported by the Vulgate and the Peshiṭta, and "to stand" is probably supported by Symmachus. It is commonly thought that *wayyāqom* must be incorrect because neither "and he arose" nor "and he stood" seems to offer good sense, and the most popular solution to this difficulty is to read *way^e^qaddēm* instead. The evidence of the LXX points to such a reading, though there are good grounds for doubting whether *qiddēm* could have had the sense which is commonly attributed to it here. Equally, the other theories which have been examined, including the belief that *wayyāqom* may signify "and he was present", all have weaknesses. However, in the light of the Ugaritic parallel which has been adduced it is no longer necessary to question the Massoretic Text, which describes how Jonathan may well have behaved at a feast at Saul's court. Therefore *wayyāqom* should be retained, and the clause is to be translated "and Jonathan took his stand".

WAS THE *ŠĀLÎŠ* THE THIRD MAN IN THE CHARIOT? [1]

by

B. A. MASTIN

Bangor, North Wales

BDB records three Hebrew words *šālîš*. It gives "adjutant or officer" as the English equivalent of the third of these, and says that the term is "best explained as *third* man (in chariot)". This interpretation is widely accepted, though *BDB* notes that it is not held by some scholars, and other, more recent names could be added to those which are listed. In this article it will first be asked to what extent non-biblical evidence indicates how many men are likely to have formed part of an Israelite chariot's crew. The usage of the Old Testament will then be examined, and the interpretation of *šālîš* in antiquity will be reviewed. Next two verses which may supply relevant information, theories that *šālîš* is a loan-word, and hypotheses which link it to military practice in the ancient Near East will be considered. Finally, attempts to elucidate its etymology will be discussed, and it will be asked how the word may most satisfactorily be understood.

I

It will be convenient to begin by examining information from extra-biblical sources about the number of men carried by a chariot,

---

[1]) I am indebted to Dr C. E. Chaffin, Professor J. N. Coldstream, Dr J. H. Crouwel, Professor J. A. Emerton, Professor O. R. Gurney, the Hon. Mrs V. Hankey, Dr K. A. Kitchen, Professor W. G. Lambert, Mr A. R. Millard, Professor J. S. Pym and Professor M. Wilcox for their kindness in readily offering assistance on a number of points connected with this article, which was read in a shortened form at the summer meeting of the Society for Old Testament Study held at St Andrews in July 1978. The following abbreviations are used:

ANEP = J. B. Pritchard (ed.), *The Ancient Near East in Pictures relating to the Old Testament* (Princeton, 1954).

ANET = J. B. Pritchard (ed.), *Ancient Near Eastern Texts relating to the Old Testament* (Princeton, ²1955).

BDB = F. Brown, S. R. Driver and C. A. Briggs, *A Hebrew and English Lexicon of the Old Testament* (Oxford, 1907, reprinted with corrections 1953, 1957).

NEB = *The New English Bible. The Old Testament* (Oxford and Cambridge, 1970).

Yadin = Y. Yadin, *The Art of Warfare in Biblical Lands in the Light of Archaeological Discovery* (London, 1963).

since it is often supposed that Hittite and Palestinian chariots were manned by a shield-bearer in addition to the driver and the warrior and are to be distinguished from Egyptian chariots, which had a crew of two [2]).

A. R. Schulman states that Egyptian reliefs of the New Kingdom (*c.* 1550-1070 B.C.) "never show more than a two man crew operating the chariot". The driver "had some sort of a command authority. Likewise he had the more difficult responsibility of managing the chariot during the fight, while the second man had only to keep his mind on doing the fighting and protecting the driver" [3]). I am grateful to Dr K. A. Kitchen for informing me that no war-scenes (or other scenes) in temples or tombs (or from any other monuments) that illustrate Egyptian usage on chariot-manning after the New Kingdom are known, and that there is no textual evidence bearing on this point. Thus in the present state of our knowledge it is impossible to establish whether Egyptian chariots continued to have a crew of two.

The belief that the Hittite chariot carried three men is based on Egyptian reliefs showing the Battle of Kadesh, which took place *c.* 1286 B.C., and on the description of this battle by an Egyptian scribe found in both Papyrus Sallier III and inscriptions on the walls of Egyptian temples [4]). But this account of the battle "was intended, from the start, no less than the Reliefs, to be inscribed on a temple wall", and both sources of information were designed to complement each other [5]). Thus they do not provide independent evidence about Hittite practice. Cf. Yadin, pp. 88, 104 f., 107 ff., 236-9 for reproductions of representative reliefs; it should be noted that some of the Hittite chariots contain only two men (Yadin, pp. 104 f., 107 ff., 237). No information is available from Hittite sources about the size of a war-chariot's crew in this period.

---

[2]) E.g., R. de Vaux, *Les Institutions de l'Ancien Testament* I (Paris, 1958), p. 188; M. Noth, *Das zweite Buch Mose* (Göttingen, 1959), p. 89.

[3]) *Military Rank, Title and Organization in the Egyptian New Kingdom* (Berlin, 1964), pp. 67 f. The first quotation is from p. 67, the second from p. 68. Cf. Yadin, pp. 334 f., for a drawing of a relief from the reign of Ramesses III (*c.* 1183-1152 B.C.) which shows the Egyptian chariot in action. Here, as elsewhere (cf. Schulman, p. 67), the crew of two does not follow the standard practice described above.

[4]) J. H. Breasted, *Ancient Records of Egypt*, III (Chicago, 1906), pp. 140 f.; A. Gardiner, *The Kadesh Inscriptions of Ramesses II* (Oxford, 1960), pp. 8 f.

[5]) Ibid., pp. 46-53. The quotation is from p. 53.

An Egyptian relief at Medinet Habu from the reign of Ramesses III (*c.* 1183-1152 B.C.) depicts chariots belonging to Sea Peoples with a crew of three (Yadin, p. 336, *Medinet Habu* I [Chicago, 1930], Plate 34; but cf. W. Wreszinski, *Atlas zur Altaegyptischen Kulturgeschichte* II [Leipzig, 1935], Tafeln 113 and 114, where the additional headdress in the drawing of Tafel 114 is perhaps a misinterpretation of what may be damage to the stone). Though these chariots are commonly said to be Philistine, this is not certain: the warriors on the chariots are identified by their clothing (and especially their headgear), but the dress of the Peleset cannot be distinguished from that of some of the other Sea Peoples. However, the *p^elištîm* of the Old Testament should perhaps not be equated with the Peleset but may well also include other Sea Peoples, and in any case the groups which Ramesses fought seem subsequently to have been allowed to settle in Palestine. Thus it might be natural to conclude that the Israelites would have come into contact with chariots which carried three men. Further, without entering into the thorny question of Philistine origins [6]), it may be significant that some of the Sea Peoples fought at Kadesh, where the Sherden were on the Egyptian side and the Lukka formed part of the Hittite army. The practice of the army repulsed by Ramesses III, if it has been correctly understood, provides further support for use of the three-man chariot in the general area from which the Hittite army at Kadesh was drawn.

Nevertheless, although, as far as I am aware, biblical specialists have always taken the third man in the Hittite chariots at Kadesh to be the shield-bearer, A. R. Schulman (p. 39) notes the possibility that he was a footsoldier called the "runner" who was being carried into battle on the chariot but who "dismounted and fought on foot when the need arose". I am indebted to Dr J. H. Crouwel, who emphasizes that the Medinet Habu relief does not show the Sea Peoples drawn up in battle array, for the suggestion that the chariots of the Sea Peoples are similarly depicted transporting warriors who actually fought dismounted. However, if these theories are correct both Hittite practice at Kadesh and the practice of the Sea Peoples are irrelevant to any discussion of the *šālîš* as a permanent member of a chariot's crew. It is sound method to give maximum weight to such

---

[6]) Cf. T. C. Mitchell, in D. W. Thomas (ed.), *Archaeology and Old Testament Study* (Oxford, 1967), pp. 410-13, 422 ff.; K. A. Kitchen, in D. J. Wiseman (ed.), *Peoples of Old Testament Times* (Oxford, 1973), pp. 54-60, 70-74; and N. K. Sandars, *The Sea Peoples* (London, 1978), especially chapter 7.

evidence as there is for chariots with a crew of three, but it must be noted that there is no certainty that chariots were manned in this way by either the Hittites or the Sea Peoples.

G. A. Wainwright (*VT* 9 [1959], p. 78, n. 5) refers to E. Gjerstad and others, *The Swedish Cyprus Expedition* II (Stockholm, 1935), Plates 234 and 235 and pp. 711, 714, 740, 741, 766 and 789, for model chariots from Ayia Irini which he thinks indicate that "at the beginning of the Iron Age, say about 1125 B.C., the custom of driving three men in a chariot was introduced into Cyprus in the Cypro-Geometric Period", though "the custom was not the same as that of the Hittites and Philistines for the chariots were four-horsed, not two-horsed as the others had been". However, according to the Swedish chronology, the earliest Iron Age stratum at this site should not be dated before the seventh century B.C. Professor J. N. Coldstream has kindly allowed me to consult him on this subject, and he tells me that these models must be at least 400 years later than the Sea Peoples, even if the eighth century date suggested by J. Birmingham (*AJA* 67 [1963], p. 20) is adopted. He also observes that even at Ayia Irini chariots carrying three men are by no means in the majority. In view of their lateness he doubts whether they have any obvious bearing on the Hittites or the Sea Peoples.

J. Garstang said that the absence of the shield-bearer from the hunting scenes depicted on some Neo-Hittite sculptures is self-explanatory [7]), but when he wrote only one relief showing a Neo-Hittite war-chariot was known. It comes from Zinjirli and is dated by Garstang to perhaps the tenth century B.C., by J. B. Pritchard (*ANEP*, p. 269) to perhaps the eighth century, and by T. A. Madhloom (*The Chronology of Neo-Assyrian Art* [London, 1970], p. 28) to the ninth century; the chariot carries two men, and a fallen enemy lies under the horse (which represents a team of two horses) to which it is harnessed [8]). Neo-Hittite war-chariots with a crew of two are represented on orthostats of similar design from the ninth century B.C. at Tell Halaf and Carchemish (Yadin, pp. 366 f.; L. Woolley and R. D. Barnett, *Carchemish* III [London, 1952], Plates B. 41 and 42) [9]). The Carchemish chariot shows "a decided Assyrian

[7]) *The Land of the Hittites* (London, 1910), p. 364.

[8]) Ibid., pp. 278 ff., 297; *ANEP*, p. 53.

[9]) Yadin, p. 366, dates the Tell Halaf orthostat to the tenth century B.C., and W. F. Albright, *BASOR* 119 (1950), p. 26, places it in the second half of that century, with the first quarter of the ninth century as a *terminus ad quem* (*Anatolian Studies* 6 [1956], pp. 75-85); also idem, in S. S. Weinberg (ed.), *The Aegean and the*

influence" (Yadin, p. 366), but earlier this important Hittite centre had sent a contingent to fight at Kadesh. Moreover, Yadin (pp. 186 f.) draws attention to the close similarities between the charioteers shown hunting in an Egyptian wall painting of *c.* 1430 B.C. and on a Ugaritic gold patera also published in *ANEP* (p. 56), which states (p. 270) that it is "from 'Ugarit Récent 2' (1450-1365, according to excavator)"; both men are alone. Ugarit also fought on the Hittite side at Kadesh. Thus it is not safe to assume that chariots were manned in a uniform way in Syria-Palestine over a long period. Indeed, although Papyrus Sallier III tells how each Hittite chariot at Kadesh contained two mercenaries and one Hittite while the parallel hieroglyphic texts speak simply of three-man crews [10]), it may be asked whether the large Hittite army did not display greater diversity than this. O. R. Gurney points out that "with regard to the clothing and armament of the Hittite infantry there is a strange discrepancy between the Egyptian reliefs and their own monuments", and thinks the explanation of this "probably lies in the heterogeneous nature of the Hittite confederacy" [11]). Equally, it is conceivable that some of its chariots had a crew of two, but that the unfamiliar, heavy chariots bearing three men made a special impression on the Egyptians.

Further, a relief commemorating Ramesses II's capture of the town of Deper in Amurru three years after the Battle of Kadesh shows its defenders "dressed as Hittites and protected by the Hittite 'waisted' figure-eight shields" (Yadin, p. 229) or by rectangular shields like, for example, those of the Asiatics portrayed (Yadin, p.

Near East (Locust Valley, New York, 1956), pp. 150-53. But cf. *ANEP*, pp. 261, 268. It is published in *ANEP* on p. 50. Woolley and Barnett (pp. 242, 245) date the reliefs from Carchemish to the reign of Katuwas, which they place in the early part of the ninth century B.C., though W. F. Albright (*The Aegean and the Near East*, p. 160) prefers "not later than about 900 B.C." T. A. Madhloom (p. 28) dates both the Tell Halaf and the Carchemish reliefs to the ninth century. I am grateful to Professor J. N. Coldstream for informing me that M. E. L. Mallowan (*Anatolian Studies* 23 [1972], pp. 63-85) also dates the Carchemish reliefs to the ninth century, and to Mr A. R. Millard for drawing my attention to M. E. L. Mallowan's dating of the Tell Halaf reliefs to the last quarter of the ninth century (*Nimrud and its Remains* [London, 1966], I, pp. 134 f., 331 f.).

[10]) J. H. Breasted, p. 140 and n. b. See also n. 4 above.

[11]) *The Hittites* (Harmondsworth, Baltimore and Ringwood, ^{2}1954, 1969), pp. 106-8. J. G. Macqueen, *The Hittites and their Contemporaries in Asia Minor* (London, 1975), p. 99, says that "the principal offensive weapon of the Hittite infantryman seems to have varied according to the nature of the terrain", but, even if this was the case, it does not account for all the differences noted by Gurney. Cf. Macqueen, pp. 102 f., for a defence of the view that our two sources of information about the dress of Hittite infantry cannot readily be reconciled.

193; *ANEP*, p. 103) on the exterior of the chariot of Tuthmosis IV (*c*. 1412-1403 B.C.). Two enemy chariots are depicted in the relief, though neither is on the part that is reproduced by Yadin; cf. the drawing in H. Gressmann, *Altorientalische Bilder zum Alten Testament* (Berlin and Leipzig, ²1927), Tafel XLVI, and the photograph in *ANEP*, p. 111, which, however, does not include half of the chariot which is underneath Ramesses's horses. Both chariots contain two men. One of the men in the chariot fleeing before Ramesses is wounded and both men are hanging dead out of the other chariot. The horseman in the relief is more plausibly accounted for as a scout than as a charioteer escaping from the battle on horseback [12]), though if he were a charioteer it is unlikely that he would belong to either of the chariots which are under discussion (W. Wreszinski, Tafel 109). It could be argued that a third man had already fallen from these chariots, but it is more straightforward to suppose that they carried a crew of two. This conclusion is supported by the fact that one of the men in the former chariot holds a shield while the other has the reins tied round his waist and fights with bow and arrow. The same is true of the two wounded men in a Canaanite chariot shown in a relief from Karnak depicting an attack by Ramesses II's immediate predecessor Sethos I on Kadesh (W. S. Smith, *The Art and Architecture of Ancient Egypt* [Harmondsworth, Baltimore and Mitcham, 1958], p. 223, *ANEP*, p. 106). Attack, defence and management of the chariot are carried out by the two men, and there is no need to postulate the existence of a third man who is no longer in the chariot. See W. Wreszinski, Tafeln 107 and 53 for these reliefs, and Tafeln 36, 45 and 47 (reign of Sethos I) and 55a, 56 and 77 (reign of Ramesses II) for other reliefs showing chariots with a crew of two from this area. Thus Egyptian descriptions of the Battle of Kadesh do not establish how chariots were manned throughout Syria-Palestine at that time.

In any case the chariot was introduced into Israel no earlier than the reign of David [13]), and Yadin's assumption (p. 285) that the Israelite and Neo-Hittite chariots were identical may well be justified.

---

[12]) A. R. Schulman, "Egyptian Representations of Horsemen and Riding in the New Kingdom", *JNES* 16 (1957), p. 268.

[13]) Cf. Yadin, p. 285, for the view that chariots formed part of David's army. In addition to the considerations which Yadin advances there is the further point that the Canaanite city-states which had previously retained their independence were absorbed into Israel in David's reign. The use of chariots by the Canaanites is given as a reason for their military strength at an earlier period (cf. Josh. xvii 16, 18; Judg. i 19, iv 3), so it is not surprising that David had at least a small chariot corps.

An Assyrian relief from the reign of Sennacherib (704-681 B.C.) shows an empty Judaean chariot which is similar to the chariots of Sargon and Sennacherib (Yadin, pp. 299, 301, 430, 432 f.), but this illustrates the period of the wars with Assyria and is too late to serve as evidence for the reigns of David or Solomon. No other archaeological material which gives direct information about the type of chariot used in Israel or Judah is known. Thus extra-biblical data are insufficient to determine whether the early Israelite chariot carried three men or two. The most that can be said is that, if the Sea Peoples used chariots with a crew of three it is highly probable that the Israelites would have known such chariots, though there was no standard Hittite-Palestinian practice of manning chariots in this way.

It may be added that reliefs from the north-west palace of Asshur-naṣir-pal II (884-860 B.C.) at Kalakh show Assyrian chariots holding two men. There is a third man in the king's chariot, and some other chariots have a crew of three (E. A. W. Budge [ed.], *Assyrian Sculptures in the British Museum. Reign of Ashur-nasir-pal, 885-860 B.C.* [London, 1914], Plate XVI; R. D. Barnett and M. Falkner, *The Sculptures of Aššur-naṣir-apli II (883-859 B.C.)* ... [London, 1962], Plate CXVI). By the reign of Sargon II (721-705 B.C.) a crew of three was normal (Yadin, pp. 298 f., 382 f., 386 f., 420 f.). In the reign of Asshur-naṣir-pal I (*c.* 1049-1031 B.C.) the Assyrian war-chariot contained two men (A. Salonen, *Die Landfahrzeuge des Alten Mesopotamien* [Helsinki, 1951], Tafel XXVII). But, apart from meagre information from the reign of Tukulti-Ninurta II (888-884 B.C.), there is no evidence for Assyrian practice in the century and a half before the reign of Asshur-naṣir-pal II, and it is uncertain when a third man first appeared in the Assyrian chariot.

II

It must now be asked to what extent the usage of the Old Testament helps establish whether *šālîš* ever meant "the third man in a chariot". Prov. xxii 20 need not be discussed here. *BDB*, p. 1026a, says that the Qᵉrê *šālîšîm* is an impossible reading, but, even if it were to represent the original text, the word would presumably mean "noble sayings", "excellent sayings", or something similar [14]). However, 2

[14]) Cf. C. H. Toy, *A Critical and Exegetical Commentary on the Book of Proverbs* (Edinburgh, 1899), p. 423. B. Gemser, *Sprüche Salomos* (Tübingen, ²1963), p. 84, and W. McKane, *Proverbs* (London, 1970), p. 372, tentatively suggest "Kernsprüche" and "key-sayings" respectively. None of these scholars wishes to read the Qᵉrê.

Kings vii 2, 17, 19 mentions an unnamed *šālîš* "on whose hand the king leaned", who is put in charge of the gate of Samaria after a siege, 2 Kings ix 25 tells how Jehu gave a special commission to his *šālîš* Bidkar, and 2 Kings xv 25 states that Pekah, Pekahiah's *šālîš*, conspired against his master and succeeded him on the throne. In each case the *šālîš* is an officer of high rank. Though C. F. Burney thinks the word to be "of unknown meaning", he notes that 2 Kings ix 25 is one of several passages whose contexts could suggest that the *šālîšîm* "may have been a class of warriors usually connected with chariots "[15]). But the fact that Bidkar was Jehu's *šālîš* at the time of the story being related is not necessarily to be interpreted in the light of what 2 Kings ix 25 also says about both Jehu and Bidkar in Ahab's reign. Equally, even if Jehu and Bidkar were *šālîšîm* at this earlier period, it would hardly be surprising to find important officers in the king's retinue. Yet, whatever the true reading in the second half of the verse, it would be possible to use the information provided there in a cumulative argument which relied more heavily on other evidence to show that the *šālîšîm* were normally associated with chariots.

Burney also cites 1 Kings ix 22, which the Revised Version translates, "But of the children of Israel did Solomon make no bondservants: but they were the men of war, and his servants (*wa*ʿ*ăḇāḏāw*), and his princes (*wᵉśārāw*), and his captains (*wᵉšālīšāw*), and rulers of his chariots and of his horsemen (*wᵉśārê riḵbô ûpārāšāw*)". However, as Burney recognizes, the fact that the *šālîšîm* are mentioned next to the *śārê riḵbô* is insufficient to demonstrate that they were chariot-warriors. The Revised Version renders the parallel passage 2 Chr. viii 9, "But of the children of Israel did Solomon make no servants for his work; but they were men of war, and chief of his captains (*wᵉśārê šālîšāw*), and rulers of his chariots and of his horsemen (*wᵉśārê riḵbô ûpārāšāw*)". J. Gray holds that *wᵉśārê šālīšāw* should be read instead of *wᵉśārāw wᵉšālīšāw* in 1 Kings ix 22 (*I and II Kings* [London, ²1970], p. 242, n. h). If this emendation is accepted the phrases *śārê šālīšāw* and *śārê riḵbô* would stand side by side, and it would be less likely that the *šālîšîm* of this verse are to be connected with chariotry. A similar conclusion is required by the Massoretic Text of 2 Chr. viii 9. Nevertheless, it is also possible to make a plausible case for the view that *wᵉśārāw wᵉšālīšāw* is to be read in 2 Chr. viii 9 as well as 1 Kings ix 22 (cf. W. Rudolph, *Chronikbücher* [Tübingen, 1955],

15) *Notes on the Hebrew Text of the Books of Kings* (Oxford, 1903), pp. 139 f.

p. 218). Because it is far from certain whether either theory of textual corruption is correct or whether the Massoretic Text is original in both places, it would be unwise to rely on an argument based on the reading *śārê šālīšāw*. However, 1 Kings ix 22 illustrates the assertion that the Israelites were not subjected to forced labour by naming other tasks which they are said to have performed for Solomon, and the intention is presumably to accumulate terms which describe what freeborn Israelites might legitimately have been expected to do. They could be officials or soldiers, but the context does not indicate more precisely what *šālîš* meant. The most that can be claimed is that this verse could corroborate other evidence for linking the *šālîšîm* with chariotry. That material in lists should be used with caution is confirmed by Sefîre III 4 f., 9 f., 13, in which some degree of exactness is to be expected since the text is a treaty [16]). Here there is divergence from a common basic pattern, and in particular *srsy* in line 5 is replaced by *ngdy/ngry* in line 10 and *'bdy* in line 13. But it would be wrong to infer that these words are necessarily synonyms; rather, like *pqdy* (lines 4, 10, 13) they refer to men belonging to the official or military classes.

According to Burney, in 2 Kings x 25 *šālīšîm* is "coupled with *rāṣîm* 'foot-runners' as though in contradistinction". But here *rāṣîm* has the technical meaning "members of the royal body-guard" (cf. *BDB*, p. 930b), and the point may simply be that the *šālīšîm* were not part of it. An alternative suggestion which might be advanced is that in 2 Kings x 25 the *šālīšîm* were the captains of the body-guard, but this is unlikely since 1 Kings xiv 27 = 2 Chr. xii 10 speaks of the *śārê hārāṣîm* (cf. 2 Kings xi 4). It is of interest that, when Absalom and Adonijah attempt to seize the throne, each prepares "fifty men to run (*rāṣîm*) before him" (2 Sam. xv 1; 1 Kings i 5), while the *rāṣîm* and *šālīšîm* used by Jehu on this occasion total 80 (2 Kings x 24; cf. *BHS* for the reading). The presence of only a small number of *šālīšîm* would be consistent with, but does not require, the view that they were officers of some kind. Further, Bidkar is said to be Jehu's *šālîš* (2 Kings ix 25), and so, at least in this period, while someone could be the *šālîš* of an important person (or perhaps only of the king),

[16]) Cf. H. Donner and W. Röllig, *Kanaanäische und Aramäische Inschriften* (Wiesbaden, [2]1966-69), I, p. 44, for the text, and II, p. 268, for the reading *ngdy/ngry* in line 10, on which see further J. A. Fitzmyer, *The Aramaic Inscriptions of Sefîre* (Rome, 1967), pp. 112 f., and J. C. L. Gibson, *Textbook of Syrian Semitic Inscriptions* II (Oxford, 1975), p. 54.

there was also a class of *šālîšîm*. The English word "lieutenant" (by which the *NEB* translates *šālîš* in both 2 Kings ix 25 and x 25) may be compared. *The Oxford English Dictionary* gives as one definition for it "an officer civil or military who acts for a superior", but it can also denote a military rank. In any event, whatever the merit of this analogy, there is little in 2 Kings x 25 to associate the *šālîšîm* with chariotry.

That such a link could exist is established by Exod. xiv 7, which the Revised Version renders, "and he [Pharaoh] took six hundred chosen chariots, and all the chariots of Egypt, and captains over all of them (*wešālīšīm ʿal-kullô*)". *BDB*, pp. 481 f., records an idiomatic use of *kōl* with the 3 m.s. suffix "understood as referring to the *mass* of things or persons meant", so that what is literally "*the whole of it*, is equivalent to *all of them*, *every one*". Thus here *ʿal-kullô* signifies "upon *the whole of it* (the *rekeb* collectively) = *all of them*", and each chariot would have carried a *šālîš*. The alternative is to suppose that the *šālīšīm* were in charge of all the chariotry (cf. *BDB*, *s.v.* *ʿal* II. 3). In that case they would be officers and the verse states that the Egyptian army went out in full battle array. But if, as is not impossible, *ʿal-kullô* means "on every chariot", it is less easy to see what the writer wished to convey. As A. Dillmann pertinently observes, "wäre *šālīšīm* die Benennung der gewöhnlichen Wagenkämpfer, so wäre die Bemerkung *wešālīšīm ʿal-kulô* (*sic*) sinnlos, weil selbstverständlich" [17]). M. Noth (*Das zweite Buch Mose*, p. 89) holds that in this phrase "wird gesagt, dass auch die 'dritten Männer' auf allen Streitwagen waren", following "die hethitisch-palästinische Weise, nach der noch ein 'dritter Mann' als Adjutant und Schildträger des Streitwagenkämpfers sich auf dem Streitwagen zu befinden pflegte". It has been argued above that extra-biblical data are insufficient to demonstrate that there was a standard Hittite-Palestinian way of manning chariots, but, since it is not known whether Egyptian chariots continued to have a crew of two after the New Kingdom, an Israelite writing at a later date might be describing contemporary Egyptian practice. Equally, it could have been assumed that Egyptian chariots contained three men because this was the case with chariots elsewhere, for example perhaps among the Philistines. Just as an Egyptian account of the Battle of Kadesh draws attention to the presence of a third man on the Hittite chariots, if the Israelite chariot held only

[17]) *Die Bücher Exodus und Leviticus* (Leipzig, 1880), p. 146.

two men, the intention could have been to stress the size of the force pursuing the Israelites by mentioning the additional member of an Egyptian chariot's crew. But if the Israelite chariot carried three men it is not clear why it seemed necessary to say that this was also true of the Egyptian chariot. Noth supposes that *wešālīšīm ʿal-kullô* shows that the crews of the chariots were complete, but this would surely have been taken for granted. On the other hand, P. Haupt (see n. 40 below) suggests it may have been thought that the Egyptian chariots "were exceptionally well manned for the pursuit of the Israelites". His view that, when the clause was composed, the Egyptian chariot was known to contain only two men can be neither disproved nor verified, but, if he is right, it is not easy to understand the inclusion of this statement when it was known that Egyptian practice was different. Moreover, if the *šālîš* was originally the "aide and shield-bearer", it must be explained how the word came to denote the higher status of "officer". It might be replied that it was once a title given specifically to the royal aide (cf. p. 153 below), but then its use of a man found on every Egyptian chariot would be unintelligible if Exod. xiv 7, which is JE, should be placed early in the monarchic period. In addition, this hypothesis is by no means the same as that advanced by Noth, and, if the *šālîš* was originally the royal aide, Noth's standpoint must be abandoned. Though Haupt observes that those who rode in the king's chariot would have been of high rank, there is no explicit evidence that any *šālîš* accompanied the king in his chariot. Furthermore, if *šālîš* signifies "the third man on a chariot" and if some *šālîšîm* were important because they were associated with the king, it would be natural for a distinction to be drawn between these men and the generality of the *šālîšîm*. But the Old Testament does not do this, for even 2 Kings vii 2, 17, ix 25, xv 25 do not indicate that *haššālîš ʾašer-hammelek̲* (cf. *BHS*) *nišʿān ʿal-yād̲ô* or Bidkar or Pekah belonged to a different class from the other *šālîšîm*. Thus the problem cannot be resolved along these lines either. Noth also maintains that in 1 Kings ix 22 *šālîš* means "Streitwagenmitkämpfer", not "eigentlich Streitwagenkämpfer" [18]). Yet it is odd that the shield-bearer should be singled out: if a category of chariot soldiers (as distinct from the *śārê rik̲bô*) is included in the list, it might be expected that the warrior would have been named. Noth's position is weakened if "Streitwagenmitkämpfer" is not a legitimate rendering of *šālîš* in 1 Kings ix

[18]) *Könige* I (Neukirchen-Vluyn, 1968), p. 217.

22, though this is not decisive for the interpretation of Exod. xiv 7. However, his theory is to be rejected both because it is difficult to understand the development from "shield-bearer" to "officer" and because the presence of a third man on the Egyptian chariot would be worth recording only if the Israelite chariot had a crew of two. In that case there would have been no Israelite *šālîšîm*, if *šālîš* is correctly defined by Noth. In addition Dillmann (p. 147) rightly objects that if the intention were to say "'und 3fache Bemannung darauf', so wäre der Ausdruck zu kurz und würde *mibḥar šālīšāw* [Exod.] 15, 4 sich nicht erklären". This conclusion is supported by the two main arguments directed against Noth above, one of which becomes even more telling when it is a question of showing how the term for a particular way of fighting in chariots came to describe an officer.

By contrast, B. Baentsch starts from his source-analysis of Exod. xiv 7. He considers that the verse belongs to E apart from the phrase "and all the chariots of Egypt", which either comes from J or is the "Zusatz des Red., dem die 600 Wagen noch nicht genug waren". It must then be asked why E states expressly that there were *šālīšīm* on all 600 *rekeb bāḥûr*. B. Baentsch's answer is that "da nun das Wort [*šālîš*] sonst im AT immer eine bestimmte Art von Elitesoldaten, Officiere, Adjutanten oder Leibgardisten oder dergl. bezeichnet ..., so wird man auch hier wohl an eine Elitetruppe zu denken haben, wie sie sich für die Elitewagen gehörte" [19]). But if this is so, whether one should think of the combination of J and E material or of an addition by a redactor, the work has been done clumsily and unintelligently since it would have made more sense to add "and all the chariots of Egypt" at the end of the verse. The view that the *šālīšīm* of Exod. xiv 7 are officers may well be correct, but, as the text stands, the suffix in *ʿal-kullô* refers to "all the chariots of Egypt", and an explanation which accounts for this would be more satisfactory. If the *šālîš* is taken to be the driver, who, as was noted in section I of this article, "had some sort of a command authority" in the New Kingdom, *wešālīšīm ʿal-kullô* is redundant. Instead, the fact that officers were on all the Egyptian chariots may have been mentioned without attention being paid to the precise military role of the *šālîš* on this occasion, the aim being to emphasize the greatness of Yahweh's victory over Pharaoh, his picked chariots, and all the chariots of Egypt, each of which carried a man of some importance. This hypothesis is consistent with the general usage of the Old Testament, in which

[19]) *Exodus-Leviticus-Numeri* (Göttingen, 1903), p. 122.

šālîš designates an officer wherever its exact meaning can be determined, and escapes the difficulties encountered by the suggestions which have been reviewed. Thus, if *ʿal-kullô* indicates that every chariot had its *šālîš*, it is most likely that there was no special relationship between the *šālīšīm* and chariotry. Officers would in any case fight in chariots, and the exaggeration of this verse is introduced deliberately for thematic reasons.

In Exod. xv 4 *markeḇōṯ parʿōh weḥêlô* and *ûmiḇḥar šālīšāw* are parallel. The first half of the verse may be overloaded, and if, as W. F. Albright holds, *markeḇōṯ parʿōh* and *parʿōh weḥêlô* are ancient variants between which it is impossible to choose [20]), the *šālîšîm*, though soldiers, were not necessarily connected explicitly with chariots in the original poem. Unless this ended at xv 12 or *yōšeḇê pelāšeṯ* (xv 14) is an anachronism, before it was composed the Israelites would presumably have come into contact with Philistine chariots which carried a crew of three (but cf. pp. 127 f. above). However, S. R. Driver rightly points out that "the expression, 'the choice of his *shālīshim*,' would seem to suggest some more select and distinguished body than those who took only the *third* place in the chariots" [21]). The opinion that the *šālîš* is the "aide and shield-bearer" here is therefore implausible because of the context, quite apart from the other considerations which were advanced when Exod. xiv 7 was discussed above.

Much later Ezek. xxiii 23 speaks of the *šālīšîm* riding on horses—unless *sûsîm* denotes "chariots" here [22])—and in Ezek. xxiii 15, 23 they seem to be men of high rank.

Finally, in 1 Chr. xi 11 Jashoboam, and in 1 Chr. xii 19 Amasai, are said to be *rōʾš haššālîšîm* (Qerê) or *rōʾš haššelôšîm* (Kethîbh). It is not necessary to establish the true reading either in these verses or in 2 Sam. xxiii 8 (// 1 Chr. xi 11), on which see further S. R. Driver, *Notes on the Hebrew Text ... of the Books of Samuel* (Oxford, ²1913), p. 364. At most these passages could show that *šālîš* can have a military connotation, but in any event *šālîšîm* are found in the army elsewhere in the Old Testament.

20) In F. M. Cross, Jr., and D. N. Freedman, "The Song of Miriam", *JNES* 14 (1955), p. 244; cf. F. M. Cross, *Canaanite Myth and Hebrew Epic* (Cambridge, Mass., 1973), p. 127, n. 54.

21) *The Book of Exodus* (Cambridge, 1911), p. 116.

22) Cf. K. Galling, "Der Ehrenname Elisas und die Entrückung Elias", *ZThK* 53 (1956), p. 133, n. 2, commenting on *rōḵeḇê sûsîm* in Ezek. xxiii 6, 12. Although Galling does not refer to Ezek. xxiii 23, the repetitive style of this chapter suggests that the phrase has an identical meaning in all three places. I hope to discuss this understanding of *sûsîm* in a later article.

To sum up: apart from Prov. xxii 20, every occurrence of *šālîš* in the Old Testament could refer to an officer. Sometimes the *šālîš* appears to be an adjutant (2 Kings vii 2, 17, 19, ix 25), but it is not possible to specify the range of meaning which the word has. 1 Kings ix 22, 2 Kings ix 25, and, less probably, 2 Kings x 25, could provide some support for, but in no way require, the conclusion that the *šālîšîm* were normally associated with chariots. That such a link could exist is attested by Exod. xiv 7 and (at least in its present form) Exod. xv 4, but in each case the *šālîš* can hardly be the "aide and shield-bearer", nor can the term describe the practice of manning a chariot with a crew of three. Equally, *šālīšīm* in Exod. xiv 7 cannot denote "chariot-warriors". Because it is late the explicit statement in Ezek. xxiii 23 that the *šālīšîm* ride on horses is not germane to the purposes of this article. Indeed, even if this verse says that the *šālīšîm* ride in chariots, in the light of Exod. xiv 7, xv 4 it would not be possible to claim that *šālîš* is a technical term for someone who fights in a chariot. Exod. xiv 7 is JE, and Exod. xv 4, whatever its exact date, is unlikely to have been written after the reign of Solomon. Thus these passages, both of which may well be early and which are also the only places where there is no doubt that the *šālîšîm* and chariotry are mentioned together, are evidence that the *šālîšîm* were not a class of warriors connected with chariots. The theory that *šālîš* had such a sense is opposed to what can be gleaned from the usage of the Old Testament.

III

The interpretation of *šālîš* in antiquity must now be considered.

At Exod. xv 4 the LXX renders *šālīšāw* by ἀναβάτας τριστάτας, though in the Syro-Hexaplar ἀναβάτας is marked with the obelus and παλλικ . . . is read instead of it by a corrector of Codex Ambrosianus (A. E. Brooke and N. McLean, *The Old Testament in Greek*, I. II [Cambridge, 1909], p. 203). The LXX translates eight of the remaining occurrences of *šālîš* by τριστάτης (Exod. xiv 7 ; 2 Kings vii 2, 17, 19, ix 25, x 25 [bis], xv 25), which is also used by Symmachus at Ezek. xxiii 15, 23, and is a variant reading in the LXX at Ezek. xxiii 23. But δυνατός is found at 2 Chr. viii 9, and τρισσός at 1 Kings ix 22 [23]) ; Ezek. xxiii 15, 23. Aquila and Theodotion have τρισσός at Exod. xiv 7 ; 1 Kings ix 22 and Ezek. xxiii 15 respectively,

[23]) τρισσός is a correction made by the original scribe of A, and τρεῖς υἱοί is a variant reading; cf. A. E. Brooke, N. McLean and H. St J. Thackeray, *The Old Testament in Greek* II. II (Cambridge, 1930), p. 243.

Aquila σκυλευτής at Ezek. xxiii 15, 23, and Symmachus ἀνὰ τρεῖς at Exod. xiv 7. Here and elsewhere in this section verses in which *šālîš* is not represented will not be listed. τριστάτης is not yet known in secular writers unless the claim in the Scholia in Homeri Odysseam 3. 324 (ed. W. Dindorf [Oxford, 1855], I, p. 152) that τριστάται signifies the three men who stood on an Egyptian chariot falls into this category [24]), and Professor Max Wilcox has suggested to me that the word may have been coined to represent *šālîš* in Greek. In any case it would be hazardous to rely too heavily on the usage of ecclesiastical authors [25]), who may have learnt the term from the Bible. That there was no unanimity about its meaning is certain, for Origen records five possibilities. Among these is the statement ἄλλοι δέ φασιν, ὡς εἰς τὰς χεῖρας τῶν πολεμίων ἅρματα ἐποίουν μεγάλα, ὥστε καὶ τρεῖς χωρεῖν, ἵνα ὁ μὲν εἷς ἡνιοχεῖ, οἱ δὲ δύο πολεμοῦσιν (*Selecta in Exodum*, 14 :7, Migne, *PG*, 12, col. 288). This opinion is repeated in marginal notes to the Syro-Hexaplar (P. de Lagarde, *Bibliothecae Syriacae* [Göttingen, 1892], p. 230, cf. p. 65 ; A. M. Ceriani, *Monumenta Sacra et Profana* II [Milan, 1863], p. 215). The Mekilta offers four interpretations of *šālîš*, but comes no nearer to the theory just cited than the following saying, which is ascribed to R. Simeon ben Gamaliel [26]) : "Das ist der dritte, der für den Streitwagen hinzugefügt wurde : Vorher waren es nur zwei, welche den Streitwagen zum Laufen brachten, Pharao aber fügte zu ihnen einen hinzu, um das Verfolgen hinter den Israeliten zu beschleunigen" (trans. J. Winter and A. Wünsche, *Mechiltha* [Leipzig, 1909], p. 87 ; text in M. Friedmann [ed.], *Mechilta de-Rabbi Ismaël* [Vienna, 1870], p. 27a, ad Exod. xiv 7). Friedmann emends *ẓh hšlyšy šʿl hmrkbh* into *ẓh hšlyšy šhwsyp ʿl hmrkbh*, the alternative being to render with, for example, J. Z. Lauterbach (*Mekilta de-Rabbi Ishmael* I [Philadelphia, 1933], p. 202), "it refers to the third man on the chariot". Yet it is not clear why placing a third man on every chariot would make the pursuit more rapid, and the Targum of Pseudo-Jonathan gives as the relevant part of Exod. xiv 7, "and he [Pharaoh] added a third mule to each chariot, that they might pull (it) and pursue swiftly" (text in M. Ginsburger, *Pseudo-Jonathan*

[24]) Cf. H. G. Liddell and R. Scott, *A Greek-English Lexicon*, revised by H. S. Jones (Oxford, 1940); *Supplement*, ed. E. A. Barber (Oxford, 1968), *s.v.*

[25]) See G. W. H. Lampe, *A Patristic Greek Lexicon* (Oxford, 1961), *s.v.*, for references.

[26]) According to W. Bacher, *Die Agada der Tannaiten* II (Strassburg, 1890), p. 333, this is R. Simeon ben Gamaliel II (*c.* A.D. 80-120).

[Berlin, 1903], p. 122). Because the passage from the Mekilta both makes more sense if it speaks of an animal harnessed to the chariot and is similar in detail to the exposition of Exod. xiv 7 in the Targum of Pseudo-Jonathan, it is likely that it should be understood in the light of the fuller information about the identity of "the third" which appears in this latter source. In that case it is not safe to suppose with N. R. M. de Lange that the tradition about chariots with a crew of three preserved by Origen is also found in the Mekilta [27]). However, in Ep. 190, written in A.D. 374, Basil comments Ἅρματα ἀναβάτας τριστάτας [cf. Exod. xv 4 LXX] ἔχοντα οἶδεν ἡ Γραφή, διὰ τὸ τῶν λοιπῶν ἁρμάτων δύο εἶναι τοὺς ἐπιβάτας, τόν τε ἡνίοχον καὶ τὸν ὁπλίτην· τὰ δὲ τοῦ Φαραὼ δύο μὲν εἶχε τοὺς πολεμοῦντας, ἕνα δὲ τὸν τὰς ἡνίας τῶν ἵππων ἔχοντα (Migne, *PG*, 32, col. 701). I am grateful to Dr C. E. Chaffin for pointing out to me that Basil may well be dependent on Origen's *Selecta in Exodum*. If this is so, what is presumably Basil's reply to an unknown question asked by Amphilochius indicates only which of the opinions listed by Origen he prefers. By contrast, Jerome thinks that this view is wrong (*Commentaria in Hiezechielem*, *Corpus Christianorum*, *Series Latina*, 75 [Turnhout, 1964], p. 312; cf. *Commentaria in Danielem*, *Corpus Christianorum*, *Series Latina*, 75A [Turnhout, 1964], p. 824), and his position will be described below. Though at least three fathers know that τριστάτης was held by some to denote "one of three warriors in a chariot" it would be unwise to lay much weight on this fact, both because Origen and Jerome are acquainted with more than one explanation of the term and because the interpretation which is being discussed, like that of *šālîš* quoted above from the Mekilta and the Targum of Pseudo-Jonathan, could be an inference from the context of Exod. xiv 7, xv 4. Further, it is striking that the LXX does not use τριστάτης in four verses where it might have been expected to do so, but has δυνατός or τρισσός instead. Though E. A. Barber, *s.v.* τρισσός, argues on the basis of Aquila's reading at Exod. xiv 7 *alibi* that this latter word and τριστάτης could on occasion be synonyms, it is hazardous to rely on so idiosyncratic a version for lexicographical information. The most that can be said is that Aquila considered τρισσός a suitable equivalent for *šālîš* in these verses.

---

27) *Origen and the Jews* (Cambridge, 1976), p. 130. For the purposes of the present article it is not necessary to consider further whether explanations of τριστάτης/*šālîš* are shared by Origen and the Mekilta.

The Vulgate (ed. R. Weber, Stuttgart, ²1975) normally translates by "dux" (Exod. xiv 7; 1 Kings ix 22; 2 Kings vii 2, 17, 19, ix 25, x 25 [bis], xv 25; Ezek. xxiii 15), but at 2 Chr. viii 9 *wᵉśārê šālîšāw* is rendered "duces primi". "Principes" is found at Exod. xv 4, "principes principum" at Ezek. xxiii 23. In his *Commentaria in Hiezechielem*, loc. cit., Jerome defends the correctness of "principes principum" and is emphatic that "tristatae" (*sic*) does not signify "ternos stratores" but "nomen est apud Hebraeos secundi gradus post regiam dignitatem." Thus his rendering of Ezek. xxiii 23 is designed to convey a precise understanding of the word, and this may well be his intention throughout the Vulgate.

The Peshiṭta [28]) translates uniformly by *gabrâ* (Exod. xiv 7; Ezek. xxiii 15, 23) or *ga(n)bārâ*, the intensive form of the same word (Exod. xv 4; 1 Kings ix 22; 2 Kings vii 2, 17, 19, ix 25, x 25 [bis], xv 25). Similarly the Targum [29]) uses *gibbārāʾ* (Exod. xiv 7, xv 4; 1 Kings ix 22; 2 Kings vii 2, 17, 19, ix 25, x 25 [bis], xv 25; Ezek. xxiii 15, 23; 1 Chr. xii 19 [representing the Qᵉrê]; 2 Chr. viii 9). Though *mašrîṭāʾ* is found at both 2 Sam. xxiii 8, where the Massoretic Text reads *haššālīšî*, and the parallel passage 1 Chr. xi 11, where the Qᵉrê *haššālîšîm* is rendered, these verses have undergone midrashic expansion and at 2 Sam. xxiii 8 and perhaps also 1 Chr. xi 11 *gibbārayyāʾ* may be the true equivalent. Codex Neofiti I (ed. A. Díez Macho, Madrid, 1970) has *špr ʿwlymw gbrwy dprʿh* for *mibḥar šālīšāw* at Exod. xv 4 (cf. Targum Pseudo-Jonathan's *šypr ʿwlymy gbrwy*), but reads *rbrbnyn* for *šālīšîm* at Exod. xiv 7, with *pwlymrkyn* as a marginal gloss. The Mekilta (loc. cit.) gives *gibbôrîm* as one possible meaning of *šālîšîm*, comparing Ezek. xxiii 23, and the choice of *gabrâ/ga(n)bārâ* and *gibbārāʾ* may be related to this tradition. Further, if Codex Neofiti I "is an eclectic compilation consisting primarily of early Palestinian material" and in Exod. xv that "contained in *Mekiltaʾ* is closest", it may be preferable to suppose, against É. Levine [30]), who does not note that this manuscript and the Targum of Pseudo-Jonathan both

[28]) *The Old Testament in Syriac*, Part I, fascicle 1 (Leiden, 1977), and Part II, fascicle 4 (Leiden, 1976), was consulted for Exodus and Kings, and A. M. Ceriani, *Translatio Syra Pescitto Veteris Testamenti ex Codice Ambrosiano Sec. Fere VI photolithographice edita* (Milan, 1876-83), was used for the remainder of the Old Testament. See the Leiden edition of Kings, pp. cviii, cxi and 104, for the *v.l. gabrâ* at 1 Kings ix 22; 2 Kings vii 2, 19.

[29]) A. Sperber (ed.), *The Bible in Aramaic* (Leiden, 1959-68). R. Le Déaut and J. Robert, *Targum des Chroniques* (Rome, 1971), was also consulted.

[30]) "*Neofiti* 1: A Study of Exodus 15", *Biblica* 54 (1973), p. 309. The immediately preceding quotations are from p. 325.

have a double translation of *šālīšāw*, that *ʿwlymw*/*ʿwlymy* forms part of an attempt to convey a technical sense which *šālîš* was thought to possess.

The Samaritan Pentateuch Targum (ed. A. Brüll, Frankfurt a. M., 1873-76, pp. 80, 82), renders *tlyttym* at Exod. xiv 7 and *tlytʾhw* at Exod. xv 4, while *tlytyn* is attested for Exod. xiv 7 by Memar Marqah (ed. and trans. J. Macdonald, Berlin, 1963, vol. I, p. 27, but cf. II, p. 42, n. 148, where the word is printed *tlyʾyn*). Macdonald translates "officers" and refers to the Arabic version, which uses a term denoting "generals, leaders" (II, p. 42 and n. 148).

Even if *šālîš* originally described someone connected with chariotry it may not do so in Ezek. xxiii 23, and if the meaning of the word had changed this might explain in part why the exegesis discussed above is so varied. Equally, the existence of diversity of opinion is not of itself an argument against the correctness of any of the views expressed, though caution should be exercised in relying on these authorities as support for a particular theory. If on other grounds there is reason to suppose that the *šālîš* was one of three men who rode on the chariot, this conclusion could be corroborated by some of the evidence assembled in this section. But in antiquity it was only one of several competing interpretations, each of which has its own logic, and it may be based on no more data than are available to us from other sources.

IV

It is convenient to examine next two verses which may supply relevant information.

First, if in 1 Kings x 29 *mimmiṣrayim* should be emended into *mimmuṣrî*, Solomon would have obtained his chariots from a place which, whatever its precise location, was in the general area from which the Hittite army at Kadesh was drawn. I. Benzinger (*Hebräische Archäologie* [Leipzig, ³1927], p. 303) accepts this emendation and concludes that the Israelite chariot, like the Hittite, would therefore have carried three men. However, there is no certainty that the Hittites manned their chariots with a crew of three (cf. pp. 127 f. above). Moreover, it is not yet established that *mimmuṣrî* is the true reading here, though this possibility is by no means to be excluded [31]). Fur-

[31]) Cf. A. Šanda, *Die Bücher der Könige*, I (Münster i. Westf., 1911), pp. 292-5. I hope to return to this question in a later article.

ther, in view of what was said in section I above about the Neo-Hittite and early Assyrian chariot, it cannot be assumed that chariots which came from Muṣri in Solomon's reign would have had a crew of three.

Secondly, according to A. Alt "ist etwa aus 2 K 7 17 *haššālîš ʾšer-nišʿān ʿal-yādô* zu ersehen, daß der Adjutant des Wagenkämpfers, der als 'Dritter' neben dem Wagenlenker im Wagen steht, die Aufgabe hat, bei der Wendung des Wagens den Kämpfer zu stützen und so zu ermöglichen, daß dieser sich schußbereit halten kann" [32]). It is true that a chariot provided a highly unstable platform from which to shoot, but the phrase quoted from 2 Kings vii appears to be the sole basis for Alt's suggestion. 2 Kings vii 17 refers back to 2 Kings vii 2, where *haššālîš ʾašer-hammeleḵ* (cf. *BHS*) *nišʿān ʿal-yāḏô* has accompanied the king to Elisha's house. A similar expression is used in 2 Kings v 18 of Naaman and the king of Syria when the latter worships in the temple of his god. It is therefore certain that the function of an important officer in attendance on the king is being described, and it is hardly conceivable that the *śar-ṣeḇāʾ meleḵ-ʾarām* (2 Kings v 1) steadied his master in battle. Even if the *šālîš* was the "royal aide and shield-bearer" in 2 Kings vii, since 2 Kings v 18, vii 2, 17 are the only places where *nišʿan ʿal-yāḏ* is found, a connection between this formula and the technique of fighting in chariots is unlikely.

Thus the possible mention of Muṣri in 1 Kings x 29 would be consistent with the view that the Israelite chariot had a crew of three but in no way requires this, while Alt's attempt to find a task of the "third man on a chariot" indicated in 2 Kings vii is implausible.

V

Theories that *šālîš* is a loan-word must now be reviewed.

A. Cowley (*JTS* 21 [1919-20], pp. 326 f.) and A. Jirku (*ZAW* 39 [1921], pp. 151 f.) claimed, apparently independently, that *šālîš* = Hittite *šalliš*. Cowley's thesis was that the passages in which *šālîš* occurs show that the *šālîš* was an important officer, with which *šalliš*, "a title of high distinction", may readily be compared. Jirku denied that the *šālîš* was the "third man in a chariot" because then a word like *šelîšî* would be expected "ähnlich, wie sich in Assyrien ein Beamtentitel šalšu 'Der Dritte' nachweisen lässt". However, *šalliš* "etwas wie 'gross, mächtig' bedeutet. Eine solche Bedeutung würde dem

[32]) In W. Zimmerli, *Ezechiel* I (Neukirchen-Vluyn, 1969), p. 531.

šālîš im AT vollauf gerecht werden". R. Tournay's objection (*RB* 65 [1958], p. 342) that "le *š* final ne fait pas partie du radical" since *šalliš* is the nominative of *šalli* is far from conclusive. There are all sorts of oddities in the history of loanwords and it would be difficult to justify a hard and fast rule that the nominative case-ending could not be included. However, H. Donner (*ZAW* 73 [1961], p. 275) says that, because the *lamedh* in *šālîš* is not doubled, *šālîš* and *šalliš* cannot be related. Further, C. Rabin (*Orientalia*, n.s. 32 [1963], p. 133) pertinently observes that "the borrowing of a Hittite word of such general meaning to denote what seems to be a definite type or definite types of officer is rather strange". I am grateful to Professor O. R. Gurney for informing me that *šalliš* is simply a common adjective signifying "great, large" which even the Hittites themselves seem not to have used with the sense "great man, grandee".

Instead, E. Laroche (in R. Tournay, *RB* 65 [1958], p. 342 and n. 1) suggests tentatively that *šālîš* and Hittite *šalašḫaš* may be "un emprunt indépendant du sémitique et du hittite à un mot 'hourrite' se rapportant au vocabulaire du cheval et du char". Professor O. R. Gurney has kindly drawn my attention to L. Jakob-Rost's proposal that *šalašḫaš* means "Stallbursche" (*Mitteilungen des Instituts für Orientforschung* 11 [1965], p. 210). Professor Gurney tells me that the *šalašḫaš* certainly seems to be connected with horses, but that he seems not to ride on the chariot; whatever his precise function may have been, he is some sort of menial. Thus this hypothesis also is not compelling.

P. C. Craigie (*VT* 20 [1970], p. 85) thinks that *šālîš* "may be a nominal adaptation of Egyptian *srs*, 'to have command of (a corps)'. Evidence for the use of the Egyptian word comes from an eighteenth dynasty text. The Hebrew *l* would be a regular equivalent of Egyptian *r*. The equivalence *š* (Hebrew) = *s* (Egyptian) is more complex, but is justified by the equation of cognates *ḥšb* (Hebrew) = *ḥsb* (Egyptian). The meaning would be 'corps commander' or more simply 'officer (of high rank)'". Craigie refers to R. O. Faulkner, *A Concise Dictionary of Middle Egyptian* (Oxford, 1962), p. 237, for Egyptian *srs*, and to A. H. Gardiner, *Egyptian Grammar* (London, 1957), p. 27, for the equation of *l* and *r*. I am grateful to Dr K. A. Kitchen for his kindness in supplying me with the following observations about Craigie's position. First, the Egyptian verb *srs(ỉ)* has the main meaning "to awaken", "to command (a corps)" being a secondary and isolated case. R. O. Faulkner gives the main meaning and then the other, but the much fuller lexical evidence in A. Erman and H.

Grapow, *Wörterbuch der Aegyptischen Sprache* IV (Leipzig, 1930), pp. 200 f., makes clear that this verb, which is attested from the Pyramid Age to the Ptolemies, normally signifies "to awaken", the sole exception recorded being the one eighteenth dynasty reference noted by Craigie. Hence, semantically, Craigie's view, which derives a noun from a verb and uses a fleeting secondary nuance, is not strongly based. Secondly, while Egyptian *s* 〉 Hebrew *š* is possible, it is not without problems, since more usually Egyptian *s* 〉 *samekh* in true loan-words, as opposed to cognates. Similarly *r* 〉 *l* is again possible, but *srs* is the *s*-causative from a simplex (and very common) verb *r(ỉ)s*, "to be vigilant, awake(n)", which appears in Coptic as *roeis*, with *r*, not *l*. Thus, while a Hebrew *šlš* and an Egyptian *srs* could in theory be connected, Craigie's attempt to link *šālîš* with *srs* is far from fully convincing.

Ugaritic *ṯlṯ* in *ṯlṯ sswm mrkbt* (A. Herdner, *Corpus des tablettes en cunéiformes alphabétiques* ... [Paris, 1963], 14. III. 128, 140; VI. 285 f., and, with restoration of the text, 14. II. 55 f.; V. 252 f.; VI. 271 f.) is associated by H. L. Ginsberg with "the Heb. *šālīš*, meaning something like 'captain of chariotry,' of Exod 14: 7; 15: 4". He writes, "it has seemed pointless to me to render [*ṯlṯ*] by 'three' or 'teams of three' unless and until evidence is produced for chariots being drawn by teams of three horses in pre-Greek antiquity ... Rather than a singular absolute, it may be a plural construct; in which case render *ṯlṯ sswm* by 'horse-keepers,' or the like" (*The Legend of King Keret* [New Haven, 1946], p. 36). He translates "a groom" (p. 15, etc.), which, like "horse-keepers", is hardly a sense that can be obtained by comparing a word held to denote "captain of chariotry". However, Y. Sukenik (*JCS* 2 [1948], pp. 11 f.) has shown that it would not be incorrect for three horses to be mentioned together with a chariot. His argument from the size of what have been identified as stables in Stratum IV at Megiddo may not be pressed [33]), there is no unanimity about the significance of the numbers given in connection with Solomon's chariotry, and T. A. Madhloom (pp. 15 ff.) believes that "the representation of three horses in the chariots of Ashurnaṣirpal II is a simplification of four" (though this position is implicitly rejected by M. A. Littauer and J. H. Crouwel, *Archäologischer Anzeiger*, 1977, p. 5),

---

[33]) Cf. J. B. Pritchard, "The Megiddo Stables: A Reassessment", in J. A. Sanders (ed.), *Near Eastern Archaeology in the Twentieth Century* (Garden City, 1970), pp. 268-76, who argues persuasively that these buildings were not stables, though by no means all scholars agree (e.g. Y. Yadin, *Hazor* [London, 1972], p. 150, n. 3).

but Odyssey iv 590 (cf. C. H. Gordon, *JBL* 70 [1951], p. 160) and Iliad xvi 152, 471 should be added to the three remaining items which Sukenik mentions. Ginsberg subsequently translated *ṯlṯ sswm mrkbt* "one-third of the chariot-steeds" (*ANET*, pp. 143 f.), but the only point which need be considered here is that his original objections were met by Sukenik. Though J. C. L. Gibson renders "triads of horses (and) chariots" (*Canaanite Myths and Legends* [Edinburgh, ²1978], p. 83, etc.), he offers as an alternative "a third man, horses and a chariot" (p. 83, n. 7). Nevertheless, this interpretation of *ṯlṯ* rests on the assumption that *šālîš* has a similar meaning in Hebrew, and therefore it cannot help establish who the *šālîš* was. Craigie (loc. cit.) strangely says, "More recent suggestions [than Cowley's] have indicated the possibility of [*šālîš*] indicating 'three horses', by analogy with Ugaritic *ṯlṯm* (*sic*) *sswm mrkbt*, meaning 'three horses and a chariot'". But the authorities to which he refers take *ṯlṯ* in this phrase to be the numeral "three", and it is difficult to understand how *ṯlṯ* without *sswm* could denote "three horses". The term *ṯlṯ* seems to add nothing to the present discussion.

Accadian *šalšu* is frequently cited as a parallel to *šālîš*. For example, G. A. Cooke thinks "the etymology of *shâlîshîm* suggests *the third* in rank", but adds that the term "may have been borrowed from Akk., at any rate *šalšâa* = 'third in rank' may be compared" [34]). *šalšu* is the ordinary word for "third", and W. von Soden says that *lúšal-šú* means "2. Vertreter im Amt" (*Akkadisches Handwörterbuch* [Wiesbaden, 1959-], p. 1150). It is disputed whether *šalšu* can also signify "the third man on a chariot" or whether *tašlīšu*, which is certainly used in this sense, is the correct reading of this group; cf. A. Salonen, *Hippologica Accadica* (Helsinki, 1955), pp. 213 f., 216. Mr A. R. Millard has kindly drawn my attention to von Soden's entry *s.v.* *tašlīšu* (p. 1339). He defines the word as "3. Mann auf dem Kampfwagen" and observes that it was given the lexical equivalent *kizû*, "groom, personal attendant" by scribes in antiquity. However, *šālîš* is sufficiently unlike *šalšu* for this hypothesis that it is a loanword to be excluded. If it could be shown on other grounds that the *šālîš* is the "third man on a chariot", *tašlīšu* could be adduced as a corresponding title in Accadian, together perhaps with *šalšu*. Equally, if the *šālîš* is an officer, *šalšu* can have a similar denotation in Accadian. Yet, though *šālîš* and *šalšu* are presumably derived ultimately

[34]) *A Critical and Exegetical Commentary on the Book of Ezekiel* (Edinburgh, 1936), pp. 251, 260.

from the same root, if *šālîš* means "officer" it would be wrong to suppose that it is necessarily the precise equivalent of *šalšu*. The Hebrew word for "third" is *šelîšî*, not *šālîš*. Further, in Accadian there was a *šanû* as well as a *šalšu*, and these are found, for example, as second and third in rank in a city corporation [35]). But the *šalšu* seems to have been originally the man who came after the *šanû*, and it is difficult to trace a comparable development in Hebrew. *Mišneh* can be used to designate a minister as second in rank (2 Chr. xxviii 7; Esther x 3, cf. 1 Sam. xxiii 17), and it might perhaps be argued that the *šālîšîm* were a class of officers which came after the *mišneh*, just as in 2 Chr. xxxi 12 f. one Levite who is *nāgîḏ* and another who is *mišneh* are placed over ten *peqîḏîm*. But *šālîš* and *mišneh* never appear in the same context, and it would be strange if the relatively common term *šālîš* were to be explained by reference to an expression which is used in the required sense only three times in the Old Testament [36]), especially since 2 Chr. xxviii 7 and Esther x 3 are late while in 1 Sam. xxiii 17 it is not certain that *mišneh* is a formal title. It is better to recognize that both *šālîš* and *šalšu* have their own history. Thus Accadian usage cannot establish who the *šālîš* was, though it indicates that another Semitic language had at least one word for the third man on a chariot derived from the root with which *šālîš* is commonly associated. But it is not possible to equate *šalšu* and *šālîš* if the latter is an officer since allowance must be made for differences as well as similarities when the words are compared.

According to C. Rabin (*Orientalia*, n.s. 32 [1963], p. 133), N. H. Tur-Sinai, in E. Ben Yehudah, *Thesaurus Totius Hebraitatis*, XIV, ed. Tur-Sinai, p. 7163b, n. 1, says that *šālîš* is "a loan-translation from Akkadian *šalšu* which, besides meaning a certain high official, also means the third man on a war chariot, thus accounting for the use of Heb. *šališ* in Ex. xiv, 7." But it has been argued above that *šālîš* in Exod. xiv 7 does not signify "the third man on a chariot", and, as has just been observed, it is not universally agreed that *šalšu* has this denotation. Further, if *šālîš* = "officer" is a loan translation, a native Hebrew term has been given a new sense because it is used to render Accadian *šalšu*. But the only other known Hebrew words *šālîš* desig-

---

[35]) C. H. W. Johns, *Assyrian Deeds and Documents* II (Cambridge, 1901), pp. 114f.

[36]) Gen. xli 43 and 2 Chr. xxxv 24, in both of which *mirkeḇeṯ/rekeḇ hammišneh* *ʾašer-lô* is translated by the *NEB* "his viceroy's chariot", might be added, though the use of *ʾašer-lô* perhaps suggests that in this phrase *mišneh* refers to the chariot and not to the person who rode in it (cf. *GK* § 129h, and *KB*³, p. 614).

nate a measure (Isa. xl 12; Ps. lxxx 6) and a musical instrument (1 Sam. xviii 6), and neither lends itself to reinterpretation in this way. Moreover, the Hebrew equivalent of *šalšu* is *šᵉlîšî*, not *šālîš*. Thus this suggestion is unconvincing.

To sum up: *šālîš* is not a borrowing of Hittite *šalliš* or Accadian *šalšu* or a nominal adaptation of Egyptian *srs*, nor does it share a common origin with Hittite *šalašḫaš*, nor is it illuminated by Ugaritic *ṯlṯ*. Further, though there may be some parallel material in Accadian, this does not help determine the meaning of *šālîš*.

VI

C. H. Gordon notes that "military commanders were grouped in threes" in Homer (Iliad ii 563-7, 819-23; xii 86-104; Odyssey xiv 470 f.), and he thinks that this was also true of David's army (cf. 2 Sam. xxiii // 1 Chr. xi). Kebriones and Asius are called τρίτος (Iliad xii 91, 95), and Gordon argues that "this use of 'third' clarifies the Hebrew word *šālîš*, 'officer', derived from the numeral *šālôš*, '3.' Each East Mediterranean military contingent had three officers" [37]). But τρίτος (Iliad xii 91, 95; Odyssey xiv 471) and τρίτατος (Iliad ii 565) refer to the third member of a group of officers, not to each and every member of a group of three officers. The corresponding Hebrew term is *šᵉlîšî*, and the Homeric usage cited by Gordon is not parallel to *šālîš*. However, it may still be asked whether this title is related to an Israelite practice of putting three men in charge of a unit. It is certain from 2 Sam. xxiii 9 that at least one group of three heroes followed David, and 2 Sam. xxiii 13-17 recounts an exploit of three different men, but it is difficult to establish more than this from the lists on which Gordon relies [38]). Moreover, apart from 2 Sam. xxiii 8 // 1 Chr. xi 11 and 1 Chr. xii 19 there is no mention of *šālîšîm* among David's troops, and the text is uncertain in these verses. The *šālîš* may well be an officer, but the view that the term should be linked with the way in which David's army was commanded is based on insufficient evidence.

Since David was once a vassal of Achish of Gath and also used Philistine mercenary troops, it is likely that he "learned much about

[37]) "Homer and Bible", *HUCA* 26 (1955), p. 83; idem, *Before the Bible* (London, 1962), pp. 16 f.

[38]) Cf. S. R. Driver, *Notes on the Hebrew Text . . . of the Books of Samuel*, pp. 367 ff., for the view that 2 Sam. xxiii 18 f., 22 f. do not assign Abishai and Benaiah to a group of three worthies. By contrast, Gordon finds "clear examples" of "triads of officers" in these verses as well (*Before the Bible*, p. 17).

the art of war from his Philistine associations" [39]). But it is not known how the Philistine army was led, and what is needed is definite information about the practice of the Israelites or of peoples who may have influenced them. In this connection G. A. Wainwright (*VT* 9 [1959], p. 78) develops Gordon's basic theme in a different way, stating that "we read of Hector and Polydamas and Kebriones in their chariot" (Iliad xii 88-91), while "the Philistines fought three men in a chariot". He concludes that "it is no doubt this custom of the Philistines that introduced into Hebrew the curious military title *šalîš* (*sic*) which seems to be applied to chariot-warriors (Ex. xiv 7), hence indicating three men to the chariot". But, first, Wainwright misunderstands Iliad xii 88-91, for these three men are not in a chariot, as, for example, Iliad xii 65-85, 91 f. makes clear. Secondly, elsewhere in Homer chariots carry only two men (cf. Iliad v 159 f., 608 f., xi 91-147, 748 f.). It follows that Wainwright is wrong to use this material when he attempts "to connect the Philistines with Dardanians and originally at some time with the Troad". Further, thirdly, if the argument of section II above is sound, the usage of the Old Testament suggests that *šālîš* does not denote "chariot-warrior". While the Israelites may have known chariots which contained a crew of three, Wainwright has not shown that such a practice was taken over by them from the Philistines, and his contention that it is also found in Homer is incorrect.

It is entirely possible that *šālîš* is a technical military term, but the theories advanced by Gordon and Wainwright are unconvincing.

VII

In an article which has become the classic presentation of this position, P. Haupt claims that *šālîš* is "certainly not a foreign word but a genuine Hebrew term" coined to describe "*the third man* on the chariot, *i.e.*, the *armor-bearer* or *shield-bearer*" [40]). Haupt refers to C. Siegfried and B. Stade, *Hebräisches Wörterbuch zum Alten Testamente* (Leipzig, 1893), *s.v.*, for this hypothesis. As has already been noted, "one of three warriors in a chariot" is an interpretation of τριστάτης which was current in the early church. This opinion might be used to corroborate Haupt's conclusion, but, for reasons given in section III

[39]) Gordon, *Before the Bible*, p. 18.

[40]) "The Hebrew Term *šālîš*", *Beiträge zur Assyriologie* 4 (Leipzig, Baltimore and London, 1902), pp. 583-7; cf. idem, *JBL* 21 (1902), pp. 74-7.

above, by itself it is not sufficient to show that there is a presumption that he is right. Further, Haupt relies on Egyptian reliefs which depict Hittite chariots carrying three men to establish how chariots were manned in Asia, but, whatever the precise significance of this data (cf. pp. 127 f. above), there was no standard Hittite-Palestinian practice of manning chariots with a crew of three. In addition, apart from the understanding of τριστάτης which has just been mentioned, which in any case differs to some extent from Haupt's theory, no evidence points to "the third man on a chariot" as the denotation of *šālîš*, and indeed, as has been argued in section II of this article, the usage of the Old Testament indicates that it did not mean this. Thus, if *šālîš* is to be connected with the root *šlš* = "three", this must be done in some other way.

However, there is at least one proposal which does not trace the word to this root. C. Rabin (*Orientalia*, n.s. 32 [1963], pp. 133 f.) holds that "the Hebrew *šališ* is not a high official at all, but a rather lowly one", for he is "mentioned together with the 'runners'" (2 Kings x 25) and "Jehu, when still a military officer, has his own *šališ*" (2 Kings ix 25). Also, if *śārê šālīšāw* is restored in 1 Kings ix 22 after 2 Chr. viii 9, the *šālîšîm* are lower in rank than the *'aḇᵉḏê hammeleḵ*. "Where they are mentioned, they accept orders rather than exercize delegated authority." Though Rabin considers that *šālîš* may mean "the third man on a chariot" and be "a loan-translation from Akkadian *šalšu*" (cf. pp. 147 f. above), he thinks "it might be worth while examining a possible Semitic derivation for *šališ* = servant. This is Mishnaic Hebrew *šališ* 'trustee', which seems to have survived in Syrian Arabic *šālaš* 'to make a persistent effort', Damascene *šāleš*! 'have a try!', Lebanese *šělěš* 'patient, persistent'. These words go with Arabic *salis* 'soft, submissive', thus establishing a Semitic *šlš* apart from *ṯlṯ*, the root of the word for 'three'". He finds this second root *šlš* "also reflected—with a change of liquids not unusual near sibilants—in Syriac, Aramaic, and Mishnaic Hebrew *šammeš* 'to serve'". The only question which need be asked here is whether it is plausible to associate *šālîš* with such a root, though it may be remarked that M. Jastrow, *A Dictionary of the Targumim* ... (London and New York, 1903), p. 1584b, associates *šālîš* meaning "trustee" with the root *šlš* = "three". Rabin is commenting on the theory that *šālîš* = Hittite *šalliš*, and according to this the *šālîš* is an important officer. Whatever the merits of the rest of his case (cf. p. 144 above), at this point his objections are far from conclusive. Since the "runners" of 2 Kings x 25 are members of the royal body-guard, officers who fight beside them would not necessarily be of low rank. Jehu is already king in 2 Kings ix 25, but, even if he had his own *šālîš* when he was still one of the *śārê haḥayil* (2 Kings ix 5), this adjutant could not legitimately be described as "rather lowly". Because the reading is uncertain, it would be unwise to rely on the emended text of 1 Kings ix 22. A measure of authority is delegated to the *šālîš* of 2 Kings vii 17, and in the army all officers receive orders as well as give them (cf. Matt. viii 9 = Luke vii 8). Moreover, at times the *šālîš* seems to be of relatively high rank (2 Kings vii 2, 17, 19, xv 25; Ezek. xxiii 15, 23). Rabin lays undue stress on the subordinate position of the *šālîš*, and his explanation is therefore unlikely to be correct.

By contrast A. Marzal (*Biblica* 44 [1963], pp. 343-51) connects *šālîš* with Ugaritic *ṯlṯ* meaning "bronze" or "copper", and supposes that the *šālîš* was an important person who wore body-armour made from this metal. Though *ṯlṯ* can be linked with the root *šlš* = "three" (cf. C. Virolleaud, *Syria* 30 [1953], p. 194), if this is the etymology of the word it has no bearing on its subsequent history. Marzal compares the Greek term χαλκός, which can signify both "copper" and things made of copper, including weapons, and argues that *šālîš* came to stand by synecdoche for a man wearing armour made of copper or bronze. A similar (but not identical) development in French which Marzal does not mention may be noted. The noun "cuirasse" is formed from "cuir" or is a borrowing of Old Provençal *coirassa*, which "est issu du lat. tardif *coriacea* (*vestis*) '(vêtement) de cuir' ", derived from *corium*, which is found in French as "cuir", and a soldier wearing a cuirasse came to be known as a "cuirassier" (cf. É. Littré, *Dictionnaire de la Langue Française* I [Paris and London, 1881], p. 925, and P. Imbs, *Trésor de la Langue Française* VI [Paris, 1978], pp. 579 f.). It might at least be conceivable that the *šālîš* should have acquired his name in a corresponding way. Marzal incautiously suggests that the *šālîš* may originally have been the second in command, but there is no evidence for this and his hypothesis requires no more than that at one time important officers, and they alone, should have worn this sort of armour. If "the Sea Peoples do not seem to have had any special interest in iron production" (N. K. Sandars, p. 177), 1 Sam. xiii 19-22 underlines the difficulties encountered by Saul's followers when they faced a better equipped enemy. Saul himself appears to have had a *širyôn* (1 Sam. xvii 38, but cf. A. E. Brooke, N. McLean and H. St J. Thackeray, *The Old Testament in Greek* II. I

[Cambridge, 1927], p. 59, and *BHS* ad loc. for the omission of this feature by some authorities, and P. A. H. de Boer, *OTS* 1 [1942], p. 96, who considers that *wayyalbēš 'ōṯô širyôn* was left out because it was regarded as superfluous). Armour similar to Goliath's *širyôn qaśqaśśîm* (1 Sam. xvii 5) may well have been worn by the Israelite leaders but not by their men. But Goliath's *širyôn* is said to have been made of *neḥōšeṯ*, as were both Goliath's and Saul's helmets (1 Sam. xvii 5, 38), and, unless Marzal is right in thinking that Ezekiel was aware that the title *šālîš* was associated with a metal or that the *šālīšîm* of 1 Sam. xviii 6 were so called because they were musical instruments made from *šālîš*, there is no hint in the Hebrew preserved in the Old Testament that a metal was known by this name in Israel. The absence of any clear indication that *šālîš* or, indeed, any word from a root *šlš* was ever used in Hebrew to describe a metal is a weakness in this thesis. The objection might be met by claiming that, when the Israelites first obtained the coat of mail, the name which it already had entered the Hebrew language. Yet, secondly, Marzal's argument depends on there having been a period when only prominent Israelites wore armour. It is true that data are sparse for the early part of Israel's history, but Marzal's position would be more secure if he could show that *šālîš* once denoted "cuirass" in Hebrew, as *širyôn* unquestionably did. Such information as we have about the Hebrew terms for both copper or bronze and the coat of mail creates a presumption that Marzal is wrong.

In principle *šālîš* could be derived from a root which is at present unknown, but from antiquity onwards attempts have been made to relate it to the root *šlš* = "three", and this approach deserves serious consideration. However, it must be admitted that it is much easier to find fault with the theories of others than to develop a more satisfactory alternative of one's own. For example, Jerome gives as one possible interpretation of "et tertius in regno meo erit" (Dan. v 7), "unus ex tribus principibus quos alibi 'tristatas' legimus" (*Commentaria in Danielem*, loc. cit.), while he justifies his understanding of this word in Ezek. xxiii 23 by saying that τριστάτης "nomen est apud Hebraeos secundi gradus post regiam dignitatem, de quibus scriptum est: *Verumtamen ad tres primos non peruenit*, qui principes equitum peditumque erant et tributorum, quos nos magistratus utriusque militiae et praefectos annonarii tituli nominamus" (*Commentaria in Hiezechielem*, loc. cit.). But it is generally agreed that 2 Sam. xxiii 19 = 1 Chr. xi 21 does not refer to a second triad of worthies (cf. n. 38 above), and because of this Jerome's explanation must be rejected. Again, in modern times R. Kraetzschmar (*Das Buch Ezechiel* [Göttingen, 1900], p. 190) holds that, unless *šālîš* is a loan-word, it may well stand for "'der Dritte' im militär. Range, vgl. unser früheres Premier-, Seconde [-Leutnant]". But this is implausible since the Hebrew for "third" is *šᵉlîšî*, not *šālîš*. Dillmann (p. 147) observes, "dem Wortsinn nach scheint *šālîš* 'Mann dritten Grades' zu bedeuten", but it is far from easy to demonstrate in what sense the *šālîš* occupied the third place. J. A. Montgomery claims that the expression "is etymologically 'thirdling,' that is the third in the royal chariot, along with the king and charioteer, the bearer of the shield and bodyguard, the title then developing into a general court honour" [41]). But this view would be tenable only if Exod. xiv 7, xv 4 and 1 Kings ix 22 were late, and the date of these verses is disputed. It is also necessary for Montgomery to assume that the king's chariot carried a third man in Israel, as unquestionably happened in Assyria from the reign of Asshurnaṣir-pal II (884-860 B.C.). However, there is no evidence that this either was or was not an Israelite practice. Thus Montgomery's hypothesis has a precarious basis.

The usage of the Old Testament establishes that the *šālîš* was an officer who was at least on occasion of relatively high rank, but only three individual *šālîšîm* are mentioned. Two of these are adjutants (2 Kings vii 2, 17, 19, ix 25), and it is therefore likely that Pekah was also an adjutant (2 Kings xv 25) [42]), though certainty about this is unattainable. Otherwise the *šālîšîm* always appear as a class. When Jehu exterminates the worshippers of Baal (2 Kings x 18-28) he uses his body-guard and the *šālîšîm*, so it would not be surprising if they stood in a close relationship to the king. The point should not be pressed, but in Exod. xiv 7, xv 4 the Pharaoh and Egyptian *šālîšîm* are mentioned in the same context. A number of *qāṭîl* formations such as *nāgîḏ*, *nāśî'*, *pāqîḏ* and *qāṣîn* are titles of officials, and it is possible that the *šālîšîm* were officers who were attached to the king's person. In that case they may have been called men "of the third rank" because they came after both the king and his senior officers, that is, those who held posts such as are listed in 1 Kings iv 2-6. While the function of the *šālîšîm* may not be defined with any greater precision than is allowed by the explicit statements of the Old Testament about

[41]) *A Critical and Exegetical Commentary on the Books of Kings*, ed. H. S. Gehman (Edinburgh, 1951), p. 210.

[42]) For a different opinion, see H. J. Cook, *VT* 14 (1964), pp. 124 ff.

their role, it is legitimate to suggest that the designation *šālîš* may have been given to the king's adjutant because he was "of the third rank".

The argument of this article may be summarized as follows. The extra-biblical evidence for the way in which chariots were manned in the ancient Near East provides no support for the belief that there was a standard Hittite-Palestinian practice of using chariots with a crew of three, though the Israelites may have known such chariots. Apart from Prov. xxii 20, every occurrence of *šālîš* in the Old Testament could refer to an officer, and Exod. xiv 7, xv 4 are evidence that the *šālîšîm* were not a class of warriors connected with chariots. In antiquity *šālîš* was interpreted in a variety of ways, and at best such data could corroborate an understanding of the word reached on other grounds. 1 Kings x 29 and 2 Kings vii 17 do not contain relevant information. Theories that have been examined which relate *šālîš* to Hittite, Egyptian, Ugaritic and Accadian terms are not convincing. The hypotheses of Gordon and Wainwright which link *šālîš* with military practice, Haupt's view that it is a native Hebrew term coined to describe the third man in the chariot, Rabin's derivation of it from a second root *šlš*, and Marzal's proposal that it should be associated with Ugaritic *ṯlṯ* denoting "copper" or "bronze", are all unsatisfactory. Though it is not easy to explain the relationship of *šālîš* to the root *šlš* = "three", it may be conjectured that the king's adjutant was given this designation because he was "of the third rank".

NARRATIVE STRUCTURE AND TECHNIQUE IN THE DEBORAH-BARAK STORY (JUDGES IV 4-22[1]))

by

D. F. MURRAY

Southampton

The eclipse of attention and interest within Old Testament scholarship, which has been the fate of the Deborah-Barak prose narrative in Jdg. iv, was only in part due to the obvious and undoubted literary merits of the poem on the same theme in chapter v. In larger measure it was the result of a characteristic preoccupation with historical questions, coupled with an assumption of the close chronological connection of the poem with the events it narrates. This led, by means of an over-hasty comparison of the two "versions", to an almost uniformly negative evaluation of the prose story as an inferior, and probably derivative, historical source[2]). I should like to redress the balance somewhat, not by indulging in negative evaluation of the poem, but by suggesting a more fruitful, and certainly more appropriate, way to approach the prose narrative[3]). This will

---

[1]) The following article was read in first draft to the research students' seminar of the Department of Biblical Studies of Sheffield University in February 1976, and excerpts of a second draft to the Winter Meeting of the Society for Old Testament Study, December 1976. I am grateful to all who made comments and suggestions.

[2]) Cf. e.g. J. Wellhausen, *Prolegomena zur Geschichte Israels* (Berlin, [6]1905), pp. 236-8, ET *Prolegomena to the History of Israel* (Edinburgh, 1885), pp. 240-42; G. A. Cooke, *The History and Song of Deborah* (Oxford, 1892), pp. 1 ff.; and such recent works as H. W. Hertzberg, *Josua, Richter, Ruth* (Göttingen, [2]1959); and J. Gray, *Joshua, Judges, Ruth* (London, 1967), Introduction, pp. 216-20. In this respect, W. Richter, *Traditionsgeschichtliche Untersuchungen zum Richterbuch* (Bonn, [2]1966), pp. 29-112, is an exemplary exception.

[3]) It might have been circumspect, in view of the lack of precision of the term "structure" and its cognates in present usage, to have avoided them altogether, but a more suitable set of terms has not presented itself. As a preliminary orientation for the reader, let me say that I do not refer to the kind of structuralism practised by C. Lévi-Strauss and Edmund Leach, but have in mind rather "... the application of principles derived from certain movements within linguistics to ... units of speech greater than the sentence, such as narrative" (R. Jacobson, "The Structuralists and the Bible", *Interpretation* 28 [1974], p. 146), which enable the critic, through repeated readings, "to perceive the shape of the work he seeks to interpret" (R. C. Culley, "Structural Analysis: Is it Done with Mirrors?",

have its own implications for the comparison and historical evaluation of the two chapters, but my concern will be, not with such a comparison, but with the logically prior consideration of the prose narrative as an entity in its own right.

The first section of the article will seek to elucidate the narrative structure of the story, the second section will discuss the way in which the unity of the story and its purpose have been realized by skilful use of narrative devices, and the final section will seek to draw out some of the implications of my study, both for the particular text before us, and for the general issues it raises.

I

The narrative introduction[4]), *vv.* 4f., serves the function of introducing the character who initiates the action of the piece, Deborah, and of providing appropriate background information about her. The action itself does not begin until *v.* 6, and thus *vv.* 4f. are to a degree comparable in function with the prologue of classical drama, in which the author provides his audience with necessary background information before the action proper gets under way.

The plot movement, then, is initiated by 6, where we are apparently to understand that Deborah is at her home, according to the "prologue" between Bethel and Ramah (*v.* 5). This locale is maintained throughout the exchange between Deborah and Barak, until a removal to Kedesh is made explicit by 9b. This locale is then maintained in 10a (*qdšh*), and is not explicitly changed until 11, where both locale and subject are different. Thus one would assume that Kedesh remains the locale for the whole of 10. However, this is rendered some-

---

Interpretation 28 [1974], p. 168), and "on the basis of close textual analysis" to demonstrate "the inherent framework from evidence in the text itself" (R. Knierim, "Old Testament Form Criticism Reconsidered", *Interpretation* 27 [1973], p. 461).

[4]) There is a problem in regarding *v.* 4 as the beginning of the narrative. On the one hand, discourse coherence requires that the mention of Sisera in 7 should have been previously prepared, as also that of Harosheth-haggoyim 13 (cf. the preparation for the mention of Wady Kishon in 13 by its mention in 7); but such previous mention occurs only in 2 f. On the other hand, great difficulties arise in seeking to begin the narrative earlier than 4, (with J. S. Ackerman, "Prophecy and Warfare in Early Israel: A Study of the Deborah-Barak Story", *BASOR* 220 [1975], p. 11), not least because 1-3 as a unit constitute a distinct and stereotyped framework introduction, from which formal narrative elements cannot readily be disengaged. There is thus no obvious solution to this difficulty. In any case, it would not affect my discussion to any major extent, and need not be pursued here.

what problematic by 12, where it is reported to Sisera that the forces of Barak are at Mt Tabor. It may be that we have here a case of narrative ellipsis, whereby the actual movement of Barak's forces from Kedesh to Mt. Tabor is not expressly narrated, but left to be inferred. On the other hand, there is some reason to think that the twofold use of *ʿlh* in 10 may imply Mt Tabor.[5]).

Whatever the precise explanation of the scenic locale in *v.* 10, *v.* 11 clearly effects a momentary change of scene to the nearby[6]) camp of Heber the Kenite at Elon-bezaanannim. With 12 we are transported to the enemy stronghold, which (if we did not already know) we may deduce from 13 is Harosheth-haggoyim, and from there to the battle-scene by the Kishon in 13b. *V.* 14 then switches back to the Israelites at their battle-launching post on Mt Tabor, and brings them into the thick of the battle, which is narrated in 14bf. *V.* 16 takes us along with the victorious Israelites in their headlong pursuit of the fleeing Canaanites back to Harosheth-haggoyim, but 17 abruptly whisks us away to the tent of Jael, wife of Heber. The action takes place initially outside the tent, 18a, but 18b effects a smooth transition to the interior, through Sisera's response to Jael's invitation to enter. This leads up to the murder of Sisera, which takes place inside (21). A degree of abruptness results from the sudden appearance of Barak outside the tent in 22a, but we are clearly still on the inside looking out with Jael, and move outside with her in 22b. The final movement into the interior in 22b, parallelling that of Sisera in 18b, is smoothly effected in the same way, by Barak's response to Jael's invitation.

Thus there are some eleven scene-changes in the course of unfolding the plot of this story. However, closer examination shows that most of these changes take place smoothly and preparedly, in the orderly unfolding of the plot. So. e.g. the change from Deborah's home to Kedesh narrated by 9b, has already been signalled by her

[5]) Note that *ʿlh* of Deborah in 10b contrasts with *hlk* in 9b; and that *ʿlh* is used with specification of Mt Tabor in the report of *v.* 12. Might there have been loss of *hr tbwr* at the end of 10b, by a kind of haplography between the consonantally very similar words *dbwrh* (10b), and *wḥbr* (11a)? In favour of this possibility is the parallelism it would create between 10b and 12b, and that such verbal parallelism is a feature of this narrator's technique will appear from subsequent discussion.

[6]) Without going into a discussion of the difficult question of the topography of this chapter, suffice it to say that the fact that *ʾt qdš* in 11 is added to *ʾlwn bṣʿnym* as an indication of the latter's locale (decidedly not the other way around, as R. G. Boling, *Judges* (Garden City, New York, 1975), p. 97, *ad loc.* would have it) must indicate its identity with the Kedesh mentioned in the preceding verses.

words to Barak in 9a; or again, the audience's expectation of the change from Mt Tabor to the battle-site in 14b is sufficiently prepared by Deborah's words in 14a, and actually incorporated into the narrative by 14b. However, four of the eleven are changes of scene which involve a higher degree of discontinuity with what has immediately preceded than do the remainder.

The first of these is the "cut" from the Israelites at Kedesh (or Mt Tabor?) in 10 to Heber's encampment in 11. This is quite unexpected at this point, since the only other agents in the plot which the narrative has so far indicated, and whose appearance on the scene at some stage in the narrative is therefore anticipated by the audience, is Sisera and his army. Thus this change of scene is as abrupt as it can be.

The second occurs between 11 and 12, where we as suddenly find ourselves at the stronghold of Sisera as we did at the encampment of Heber, hardly a moment before. Admittedly, the message to Sisera telling of Barak's battle preparations in 12 forms a connecting link but not, be it noted, with 11[7]), but with 10: we listeners or readers do not go directly with the spy on his journey from Kedesh (Mt Tabor) to Harosheth-haggoyim. Instead we have been diverted via Elon-bezaanannim, and arrive at Harosheth to find Sisera already making battle preparations in 13.

A further abrupt change takes place between 16 and 17: in place of the victorious Israelite rout of Sisera's army towards Harosheth, we are suddenly confronted with Sisera in headlong flight, lighting upon[8]) Jael's tent as a haven of refuge. This scene has, it is true, been

---

[7]) Boling, if I understand aright his cryptically laconic comment on 12a, "Most of them had defected", links 12 directly with 11 and apparently supplies some such subject as "Heber's people" for *wygydw*. This interpretation has obvious attractions, such as the closer integration of 11 into its immediate context, and, at a wider level, the added irony it would import into the story by making the husband Heber and the wife Jael work towards contrary ends. But, on the one hand, it is doubtful whether 11 supplies a plural subject for the plural verb of 12, and, on the other, this verb is quite frequent in the indefinite third person plural. Moreover it is not quite obvious that Heber's company (assuming he had such) would have been in a position to inform Sisera about Barak's battle preparations, if, as on Boling's view, they were encamped near Kedesh in North Galilee, well removed from the scene of Barak's activities.

[8]) It is not clear from 17a whether Sisera knowingly makes for Jael's tent, or merely happens across it in his flight. 17b tends to suggest the former alternative, though its explanation could be proleptically directed towards the reception accorded him by Jael; or it could serve both purposes. In any casc, 17b brings in the extraneous figure of Jabin, and its explanatory value depends on the pre-

thrice adumbrated (9aβ, 11, 15b), but in so veiled a manner that its actual occurrence at this point is hardly the less unexpected.

Finally, 22 has a sufficient degree of discontinuity to make it stand out from the immediately preceding narrative. The action unfolded in its brief compass is an organic, and thus inevitable, working out of the story's theme, but is not an ineluctable element of the plot (cf. the narrative poem's use of an entirely different final scene, Jdg. v 28-30).

Analysis of the plot-structure of the story in terms of its scene-changes, then, shows these four to be disjunctive. They represent nodal points in the development of the plot, where one stage of the narrative reaches a point of rest, and a further development is initiated from another direction. Thus, with *v.*10 the Israelite preparations for battle are in hand, but for the battle actually to take place it is necessary for the Canaanites to respond in kind, as 12ff. narrates. 16 completes the battle episode, but 17 initiates a fresh development in the plot with the fateful meeting of Sisera and Jael. Finally, the sudden appearance of Barak at the scene of the murder brings the narrative to its true dénouement: the ironic juxtaposition of victor and vanquished.

The indications of this aspect of our analysis are that the Deborah-Barak story falls naturally into four connected episodes: *vv.*6-10 Deborah's initiative and Israelite preparations for battle; *vv.*12-16 Sisera's response, battle, rout of Canaanite forces; *vv.*17-21 Sisera's escape and death at the hands of Jael; *v.*22 Barak's confrontation with his enemy and the woman who defeated him. 11, on the other hand, hardly constitutes an episode in its own right, since it presents us, not with plot-unfolding action, but rather with a brief tableau-scene depicting concomitant circumstances. The relevance of these concomitant circumstances does not appear until the third episode, and thus the positioning of the scene here is proleptic. Our analysis at this point suggests that this scene falls between episodes one and two, without belonging to either. However, I shall shortly bring forward formal considerations which point to its beginning the second episode.

---

supposition of a friendly connection between Jabin and Sisera which is only otherwise attested in the narrative in 7aα, in a phrase which occurs also in the framework introduction. Jabin clearly has no integral function in this narrative, and 17b seems to me a secondary attempt to provide an explanation, whose lack was felt, for the meeting of Sisera and Jael.

So far my discussion has made use of one aspect of narrative, namely, its capacity for interior visual depiction of a train of events, and its practical converse, namely that this series must have points of lesser continuity, analogous in some degree to the scene-changes and act-divisions of drama. However, narrative is essentially a linguistic art, and must realize its structure by purely linguistic means, unlike drama, which can avail itself of visual and temporal discontinuities as well (changes of scenery and costume etc; lapse of real time[9]) between scenes and acts). That narrative has therefore developed formal linguistic means to signalize to the listener or reader important nodal points in its structure is only to be expected.

The significance of this for Hebrew narrative has been briefly discussed by W. Richter[10]), and, along apparently quite independent lines, in an important recent study of the Hebrew sentence by F. I. Andersen[11]). Andersen in particular draws attention to the significant function of the Hebrew circumstantial clause as an episode marker (pp. 78-82). Thus, according to Andersen, they may be used to begin or end episodes, or, if circumstantial to an episode as a whole, they are usually inserted parenthetically between episodes. Andersen does not refer to our pericope at all in his study, nonetheless an analysis of the discourse functions of the circumstantial clauses which it contains not only offers additional instances of some of his general conclusions on the discourse functions of circumstantial clauses, but, more significantly in the present context, to results which exactly coincide with the outline structural analysis I have generated in terms of scene-changes.

The pericope contains in all ten circumstantial clauses:—4a, 4b, 5a, 11a, 16a, 17a, 21bα, 22aα, 22bβ, 22bγ. In our present connection 21bα (*whw'-nrdm*) and 22bγ (*whytd brqtw*) may be eliminated from further discussion, since they function at sentence- rather than episode-level[12]), adding a particular circumstance in explanation

[9]) To some extent this is open to narrative also in an oral storytelling situation, where pauses can be inserted by the narrator. Moreover, even in the situation of the writer or reader, the use of serialization (as practised by Dickens among others) can serve the same purpose to a degree, but at the cost of close continuity.

[10]) pp. 354-75; cf. esp. 355, 357 f., 364-6. Richter's discussion is restricted to the prose material in Jdg. iii-ix, and his conclusions are dependent on his preceding analysis of this material.

[11]) *The Sentence in Biblical Hebrew* (The Hague, 1974); the chapter on circumstantial clauses, pp. 77-91.

[12]) *contra* Richter, p. 357: the phrase is parenthetic, and does not effectively break the flow of WP (waw + prefix conjugation) verbs.

or amplification of the immediately preceding clauses, 21a, and 22bβ, respectively.

The string 4a, 4b, 5a is clearly episode-initial by its position. Indeed, these verses correspond in form to other examples of Hebrew narrative openings[13]), thus illustrating the discourse-initial function of the circumstantial clause.

11a, with its continuative clause 11b, also fits the formal schema of a narrative introduction, giving the appearance of beginning a new narrative thread, with the introduction of a new *dramatis persona*[14]) Formally, then, 11a begins a new episode, and the circumstantial clause, which breaks the sequence of WP clauses, marks the episode-boundary.

16 is a circumstantial sentence, consisting of a circumstantial clause, *wbrq rdp ʾḥry hrkb . . . ʿd ḥršt hgwym*, which is continued by a WP construction, *wypl kl-mḥnh sysrʾ . . . wᵉgōmer*. This serves to narrate an action which was partly concomitant with the final clause of the previous verse, *wyrd sysrʾ mʿl hmrkbh wyns brglyw* 15b, and thus appropriately breaks the flow of WP verbs with inversion of subject and verb in the first clause, before this narrative thread is carried to a point of rest with the WP clause. The opening of 17, *wsysrʾ ns brglyw ʾl-ʾhl yʿl . . . wᵉgōmer*, is resumptive of the narrative thread, temporarily left suspended at the end of 15b, and again appropriately breaks the flow of WP verbs with inversion of subject and verb in a circumstantial clause, before the narrative flow resumes with WP verbs (here not until 18, owing to the interposition of an explanatory clause, 17b). Clearly, then, 16 serves formally to conclude one episode, and 17a to begin another.

22aα and 22bβ,γ are less clear-cut as episode-markers, since the *wᵉhinnê*-clauses have the function of calling attention[15]) to a striking and important development, and thus have their justification irrespective of formal structural considerations. Nonetheless, this need

---

[13]) For a brief discussion, see Richter, pp. 12 f., and to the exx. there cited add Gen. xvi 1 f., which resembles our passage in tacking on two additional circumstantial clauses to the lead-clause.

[14]) For this function of an episode-initial circumstantial clause, cf. Andersen, p. 79, para. 5.1.1.

[15]) Andersen, pp. 94 ff., designates clauses introduced by *hinnê* as "surprise clauses", but, as pointed out by J. Barr in his review of Andersen's book *JTS*, NS 27 (1976), p. 152 f., this is but one of a variety of functions fulfilled by clauses so introduced. Perhaps Andersen would have done better to use the same tag for the clauses as he has for the particle, i.e. deictic-exclamatory.

not exclude such a function, and it is precisely the fact that 22a effects the (largely) unforeseen entrance of Barak upon this scene that warrants the use of the deictic-exclamatory *wᵉhinnê*-clause: i.e. it is episode-initial of an episode which could not certainly have been anticipated. 22bβ (+ 22bγ) then concludes the action of the narrative in a vivid tableau, creating a lingering impression of the scene which expresses the full essence of the narrator's theme.

It can thus be seen that, by their discourse function, the circumstantial clauses in 4a (4b, 5a), 11a, 16a, 17a, 22a are episode-bounding, and that the resultant episodes (4-10, 11-16, 17-21, 22) correspond exactly with those we have already arrived at through analysis of scene-changes.

This coincidence in results of two independent formal analyses of the pericope, one in terms of scene-changes (plot-structure), the other in terms of discourse structure, to my mind provides convincing evidence for two related conclusions. Firstly, that what we have arrived at is not merely a convenient, but arbitrary, structural outline, one of many possible and equally valid structural analyses[16]), but rather as near as possible the basic structural framework employed by the narrator. Secondly, that because this basic structure is signalised to the hearer or reader by the means I have discussed, it is part of the built-in interpretative "grid", and as such is of prime importance to the understanding of the story. It is an essential indication of the relationship between narrative events (plot) and the significance which the narrator sees in them (theme)[17]). But before we can

---

[16]) I do not doubt the validity of B. Nathhorst's statement (*Formal or Structural Studies of Traditional Tales* [Stockholm, ²1970], p. 31) "... that structural analysis is a way of dealing with a material, a method, and that one and the same material can be structurally analysed in not only one, four or a thousand different ways but in an infinite number of different ways". At the linguistic level alone one could analyse the phonological, the phonemic, or the syntactic structure of a text, to name but a few possibilities. But, in Nathhorst's terms, the goal which my analysis has set itself is that of attempting to discover the narrative structure which, making the trivial but necessary assumption that the piece is not a random collocation of words, the author has built into the narrative and signalised to the hearer or reader by the use of "recurrent units" and "relational qualities". I take it that there can be only one such structure, though many imperfect critical realizations of it.

[17]) This seems to me a more satisfactory formulation than that of B. O. Long, "2 Kings III and Genres of Prophetic Narrative", *VT* 23 (1973), p. 338: "After all, structure is an *important* key to what is *essential content* and what is not" (my italics). What is to be deemed essential or not is subject to infinite variation according to one's point of view: all critical inquiry proceeds on the basis of the selection of all, and only, *relevant* facts. But after all (to parody Long), all content

properly pursue this lead, we must develop our structural analysis further by examining the structure of the individual episodes.

A closer look at the individual episodes reveals a common pattern in their structure which consists of four major elements (see schematic summary). Each opens with a relatively static scene devoid of any plot-developing action[18]), and expressed linguistically by means of circumstantial clauses. In each case, apart from the second episode, this "tableau" serves to set the scene for the ensuing action. In the case of the second episode, the "tableau" which begins it has a proleptic function with regard to the third episode, and we shall postpone discussion of the reasons for this until the next section, on narrative technique. However, we may point out here that already our discussion has brought to light one justification for its position at the beginning of the second episode, namely structural balance. That this is not the only function of its positioning we shall see later.

The second element is an action which, as it were, breaks the stasis of the "tableau" and initiates the unfolding of that part of the plot which the episode contains. In each case it is expressed by a WP verb, which is the first of a series which continues unbroken until the end of the episode is reached, where again circumstantial clauses appear in all except the first episode. Thus the action of the episode grows out of this initiating action with a certain inevitability: Deborah summons Barak to hear Yahweh's commission and the outcome is preparations for battle; Sisera is informed of Barak's preparations and the outcome is his own preparations leading to war; Jael comes out to meet first Sisera, and then Barak, and each meeting is fraught with fateful consequences.

The elements *Speech* and *Response* are clearly closely related, and most easily considered together. Between them, they constitute the major part of each episode, but the proportions, and the way they are used, vary. Indeed, in the first episode the element *Response* consists itself predominantly of counter-speech, and only finally

---

is essential to a text's structure, since this is what both constitutes its unique givenness, and articulates its unique meaning.

[18]) Each of the clauses or sentences which form the "tableau" use verbs of action, but the action is depicted not as in process of happening, but rather as constituting an existing state out of which develops a particular segment of the plot. This is well illustrated by the twofold reference to Sisera's fleeing, in 15b where it is narrated as part of the action; and 17a, where it is narrated as part of the antecedent circumstances. On this function of nominal-sentences cf. Richter, pp. 361-4, esp. 364.

issues in action at the end of the episode. This imparts a relatively static quality to this first episode, in comparison with the subsequent ones, which contributes, by way of contrast, to their greater tension and excitement. Moreover, it serves the essential function of giving an initial exposition of motifs fundamental to the narrative[19]).

The second episode perceptibly accelerates the speed with which the plot unfolds, quickly bringing one narrative thread to a point of conclusion. The role of speech is reduced to a minimum, the maximum of action is packed into a brief narrative compass. Not only are a large number of events briefly recorded, but the narrative space accorded them is disproportionate to the length of time they would have occupied in the real world, in comparison with the other episodes. Thus the battle and rout of Sisera's forces would certainly have taken far longer than the whole of the incident at Jael's tent, yet are narrated in a mere six lines of *BHS* text (*vv.* 14-16) as against eleven for the Jael incident (*vv.* 17-22). Moreover, of these six, one and a half are devoted to Deborah's summons to battle.

This high degree of compression is not necessarily the result of a lack of narrative skill[20])—why should the manifest skill of our narrator desert him here? Nor need it be the reflex of a non-narrative interest i.e. a didactic, or theological one[21]). An explanation which accords far better with the structure of the pericope as a whole is

---

[19]) Richter, p. 60, rightly perceives that this episode points beyond itself to what follows, but nevertheless quite inappropriately demands that it should show almost every one of a number of specified features, in order to be classed as narrative. But this is quite simply to mistake the part for the whole: one might as well take the exposition section of a movement in sonata form, and deny that it is sonata form because it has no development section or recapitulation. Indeed, taken alone, it is not; but the exposition section nonetheless has a formal structure of its own, which is appropriate to this particular *kleine Einheit* as a unit of a larger structure. So too our initial episode, which is not a narrative in itself, but the opening episode of a narrative. Yet of the eight examples of the "narrative-*Gattung*" which Richter finds in Jdg. iii-ix, including iv 17a, 18-21, he is forced to say of all except one (iii 15b-26) that they are lacking an initial exposition (cf. pp. 384-9). It hardly seems wholly consistent to disqualify iv, 4a. 6-9 as 'narrative' for being a good exposition section rather than a self-contained narrative, and yet allow this *Gattung* to seven *kleine Einheiten* which, on Richter's own showing, are lacking one of its fundamental elements.

[20]) So L. Alonso Schökel, "Erzählkunst im Buche der Richter", *Bibl.* 42 (1961), p. 162, following A. Schulz, *Erzählungskunst in den Samuel-büchern*, *Bibl. Zeitfr.* XI 6-7 (1923), p. 44, who finds a general inability of Hebrew narrators to handle battle-scenes.

[21]) So Richter, pp. 54-6; and, following him, F. Stolz, *Jahwes und Israels Kriege* (Zürich, 1972), pp. 103 f.

that the climax of the story does not lie here, but further on[22]). The battle and rout is but a necessary stage in the working out of the plot: in fact, a plot-complicating, rather than plot-unravelling, stage, since it is the very fact of Sisera's escape from Barak's hands at the battle, that leads on to the third and fourth episodes. The particular formulaic phrases used here to narrate the battle-scene[23]) *may* have been chosen for their theological overtones[24]), but they clearly provide the narrator with a convenient device to take the narrative as quickly as possible through this stage and on to its climactic phase.

The third episode makes use of the same basic pattern of *Speech* and *Response*, but in a way that differs from both the preceding episodes. The opening of the third episode having created a high degree of narrative tension, the speed of the plot-dénouement is deliberately retarded by the use of a less-dense narrative style. The narrator introduces circumstantial detail, "trivial" incidents which at once give a vivid reality to the action, and postpone the anticipated climax. Greater narrative space is again devoted to speech, but in contrast to the first episode, this speech is not given in large static blocks, but in short sharp bursts. Further, these brief segments of direct speech do not result in dialogue, as in the first episode. There is no

---

[22]) So against Alonso Schökel, p. 162: "So kommen wir zum Höhepunkt der Handlung"; and "Für den glaubenden Israeliten erreicht die Handlung hier den Gipfel". The latter statement *may*, of course, be true, irrespective of whether this was the narrator's intention; but if it is true, it involves a negative judgement on the narrator's skill, since the climax would then have been reached well before the story's end, and not where, on my understanding, the narrator intended.

[23]) For a well-informed discussion of examples of patterned narrative, including battle-scenes, in Hebrew prose, see D. M. Gunn, "Narrative Patterns and Oral Traditions in Judges and Samuel," *VT* 24 (1974), pp. 286-317, who sees in them evidence of oral prose composition. However, Gunn does not discuss our present passage, nor any others of a similar "Holy-War" patterning.

[24]) This is not the place to enter into a discussion of the origins, formulation, and transmission of traditions of "Holy-" or "Yahweh-War". What is of concern here is the fact that, even if the formulaic expressions used here are evidence of "Yahweh-War" conceptions, this does not *eo ipso* prove that this narrative, in whole or in part, originated in a (putative) group of Holy War Traditionists. Certainly no less to be reckoned with is the possibility that a narrator, not himself a "Holy War traditionist" in any specific sense, nor having any specific didactic-theological intention, may yet avail himself of its stereotyped terminology for narrative purposes, either out of sheer convenience; or because it reflects his own conceptions. But this hardly establishes it as a major concern of the narrative. On the contrary, my argument is that, put into its proper context in the narrative as a whole, the narration of the battle-scene is seen to be deliberately low-key, and eminently to serve its function in that context. It is a mistake to seek for its intention in isolation.

verbal reply to any of the commands or requests in this episode, even where such would normally be expected in the real world, as e.g. when Sisera requested Jael to stand guard: the only response is immediate action. By this means is achieved a close nexus of speech and action, the closest of any episode, bar the brief fourth. This imparts a tightness of construction to this episode which contributes to its climactic tension, and also serves to focus the listener's or reader's attention on the important relationship between speech and action in this story.

The brief fourth episode again reduces speech to a minimum, but a minimum of concentrated effectiveness: the speaker, her words, and the response they elicit are all deeply significant, as we shall later see. Here the speed of dénouement is all-important, culminating in a final tableau which leaves a vivid impress of the narrative's resolution on the audience's mind.

These four elements of the episode-structure are thus clearly plot-functional, accomplishing, by a skilful adjustment of their balance, a tense and suspenseful variation in the forward momentum of the story. Additionally, they are so used as to give a parallel, but not rigidly uniform, structure to each episode, thereby reflecting in the surface-structure the deep-structure unity of theme. It is all the more significant to have observed this in this story, where the fact that no one central character is present more or less throughout the piece, has often been felt as a flaw in its unity[25]).

II

The narrator chooses to begin his story with Deborah. This seems obvious enough, given that it is Deborah's summons to Barak which initiates the whole train of events incorporated in the plot. However, a moment's reflection is sufficient for us to perceive that he might easily have started by introducing Barak, and brought in Deborah in a more subsidiary way, to give the oracle [26]). So why begin with

---

[25]) Cf. Richter, p. 44, who argues from this, and his claim that the changes in central characters are accompanied by quite new foci of interest (*ganz neue Schwerpunkte*), to the conclusion that "Diese Tendenzveränderung . . . kann kaum einem Verfasser zugeschrieben werden". That the points which Richter alleges in favour of *Tendenzveränderung*, which are essentially concerned with the changes in prominence from Deborah to Barak to Jael, on the contrary do manifest "der Kompositionswille eines Verfassers" I hope to show in what follows.

[26]) Purely *exempli gratia* one might give the following as a possible, if trivial, alternative opening: *wbrq bn ʾbynʿm ʾyš gbwr ḥyl* (. . .) *wyhy dbr YHWH ldbwrh ʾšh nbyʾh wtšlḥ wtqrʾ lbrq wᵉgōmer*.

Deborah, according her a prominence which is denied Barak? It may be nothing more than the constraint of tradition, which gave to Deborah the pre-eminent role, and one may point to the poem of chapter five for confirmation of this. But that comparison turns out to be two-edged, for it soon becomes apparent that, whilst in the poem Deborah is accorded greater prominence than Barak, Barak does not suffer such eclipse there as he appears to do in the opening of this narrative. Whether the present form of the introduction to the narrative is all of one piece with the rest of the narrative is a difficult question to decide [27]), but what is clear is that the position assigned to Deborah by the narrative's opening is bound to arouse the expectation of the audience that the role she will play in the narrative will accord with this prominence. The fulfilment of this expectation is immediately put in train by Deborah's mediation to Barak of the word of Yahweh. However, a tension as soon arises, since this very word of Yahweh mediated by Deborah the prophetess [28]) confers on Barak the function of executor of Yahweh's *mišpāṭ*. This role of Barak was also presumably a basic element in the tradition, and thus a not easily dispensable feature of the story (cf. chap. v). But our narrator turns it to good account for the development of his theme precisely at this point, as a kind of παρὰ προσδοκίαν [29]): having begun the narrative

[27]) A decision is not essential here; for a discussion cf. Richter, pp. 37-42. On the question of Deborah's home, it is to be noted that if one seeks to solve the difficulties of *v.* 5a by treating it as a (mistaken) editorial gloss, this succeeds only in creating the further difficulty that Deborah would then summon Barak from his home, which is specifically identified in *v.* 6a, to come to her at her home, for which a specific identification would then be lacking. This would surely strike the listener or reader as odd and is therefore not likely to have been the case: some specification of Deborah's home seems to be necessary.

[28]) The conception of Deborah as prophetess is frequently regarded as anachronistic (Richter, p. 63, seems to imply this; F. Stolz *Jahwes und Israels Kriege*, pp. 102, 173, expressly states it); however, on this see now J. S. Ackerman (see n. 4 above), pp. 5-13. I do not find Ackerman's main thesis, that the Deborah-Barak story combines the two genres of "call" and "summons to battle", convincing (on one aspect of his argument cf. n. 4 above), but the evidence he adduces on the connection between prophecy and warfare in Israel and related areas (e.g. Mari) backs up the authenticity of the presentation of Deborah's role here.

[29]) This term is current in Hellenic studies for a comic device particularly favoured by Aristophanes, whereby the unexpected is suddenly substituted for the expected: cf. W. B. Stanford *Aristophanes*: *The Frogs* (London, 1958), p. xxxv, who quotes the Wildean example, a "face once seen never . . . remembered". My use of the tag here does not necessarily imply humour, certainly not of the highly jocular Aristophanic kind, but is intended as a convenient label for the device of "contrary-to-expectation". That there is, however, an element of ironic, even sardonic, humour involved, will emerge as we proceed.

with Deborah cast in the leading role, he now undercuts his exposition by assigning executive action to Barak. Moreover, the narrator here brilliantly begins to play upon the prepossessions of the listener or reader, namely that decisive action is a man's province, to develop an ironic counterpoint between his audience's instinctive reading of the story and his own reflected view.

Firstly, from this point the story-line develops basically around the actions of the men: Barak insists (*v.* 8) on Deborah's accompanying him in the preparations for battle [30]), which he carries out (*v.* 10); Heber pitches camp at Elon Bezaanannim (*v.* 11); Sisera gets a report of Barak's preparations (*v.* 12), and makes his own (*v.* 13); Barak engages in battle (*vv.* 14b, 15a) (admittedly at the prophetess's summons (*v.* 14a)), and inflicts a decisive defeat on his enemies (*v.* 16); Sisera escapes to the tent of Jael (*vv.* 15b, 17a) and requests succour and concealment at her hands (*vv.* 19a, 20), a request with which she has already shown a readiness to comply (*v.* 18); Barak arrives at Jael's tent in pursuit of Sisera (*v.* 22). Secondly, in accord with this is a feature of the basic structure: if the first episode begins with a tableau in which the woman is the central figure, each of the following episode-initial tableaux focusses instead upon a man: Heber (*v.* 11), Sisera (*v.* 17a), and Barak (*v.* 22aα). Thus these features of the narrative tend to suggest that it is the men who play the decisive roles in this story, an ostensible reading in which, as already said, the audience is reinforced by its own social mores.

Throughout the narrative, but especially in its central section, the author uses the plot-action of the men in an ironic play of Barak against Sisera, in which there is a subtle interplay between the surface contrast but underlying similarity of their roles. This complex web of motifs is realized by means of a series of plays on words and

---

[30]) The question whether the LXX addition to Barak's words in *v.* 8, reflecting a Hebrew *Vorlage* something like *ky lʾ ydʿty ʾt ywm ʾšr hṣlyḥ mlʾk YHWH ʾty*, is original or not gains added significance, if the function of prophetic figures in Israelite warfare is as Ackerman argues (cf. *v.* 14). Moreover, his suggestion that there is a deliberate play on *lʾ ydʿty* in *v.* 8 and *dʿ* (= γίνωσκε) in *ʾps dʿ ky* in *v.* 9 LXX is attractive, in view of the numerous other examples of such plays on words we cite below. However, his claim (following R. G. Boling, p. 96) that the syntax of *ʾps ky* in *v.* 9 demands a verb following *ʾps* cannot be upheld: cf. Num. xiii 28; Dt. xv 4; Amos ix 8, for similar usages of *ʾps ky*. Could it be that the LXX text of *vv.* 8 f. represents, not a version of MT glossed in order to alleviate the condemnation of Barak implicit in the latter, as is usually claimed, but a true variant version? In that case, the shorter MT could have resulted from the narrator's desire to tighten up the text by eliminating excess verbiage, or a desire to heighten the implicit condemnation of Barak's hesitancy.

syntactical parallelisms [31]), which are found both within and between the episodes.

The first clear example is provided by *vv.* 10 and 13, where the same verb is used to narrate the military preparations of both Barak and Sisera: *wyzʿq brq ʾt zbwln* .... (*v.* 10a); *wyzʿq sysrʾ ʾt kl rkbw* ... (*v.* 13a). Not only is the syntax as similar as it can well be, but each notice occupies the same position in its sentence. Moreover, it should not fail to be observed that in each case this is the first action predicated of the respective leaders [32]).

This parallel action of the two leaders has already been foreshadowed by an earlier play on the verb *mšk* in *vv.* 6 f. In this case the syntax of the verb is not the same in both instances: in *v.* 6b it is used absolutely, without expressed object, but in *v.* 7a an explicit object is given. But commentators have failed to notice that there is also a significant lack of parallelism in subject and implicit or explicit object. In *v.* 6b *wmškt* has Barak as its subject, and the ten thousand men from Naphtali and Zebulun, mentioned immediately subsequently, as its implicit object. However, *wmškty* (*v.* 7a) has Yahweh for subject, with Sisera and his forces as its expressed object. Thus in the foreshadowing, what Barak is to do is paralleled, not with what Sisera, but with what Yahweh, will do. This parity of Barak's action with Yahweh's imports an element of the favoured hero into the initial characterization of Barak, whereas Sisera's subjection to Yahweh casts him as a polar opposite. The expectations thus raised by this verbal parallelism are drawn into a subtle interplay of fulfilment and belying, belying and fulfilment, in the further development of the narrative. Yet in terms of substantive action, the verbs imply the same in each case: Barak and Sisera will each marshal their forces, both at the instigation of Yahweh, the one directly, in response to a

---

31) For what follows cf. the perceptive discussion of this pericope by L. Alonso Schökel (see n. 20 above), pp. 160-67, esp. 167. In general it may be said, however, that my discussion develops further the question of the narrative function of the stylistic devices which his article admirably covers.

32) The significance of this in the present (unique) text is completely lost on Richter, who can only see a (general) formula (*Formel*) which must be pigeonholed according to the strictest form-critical methods, as properly applicable only to the calling-up of the Israelite citizen-army. Consequently, of its use in iv 13 of the enemy Sisera (cf. x 17; 2 Kings iii 21) he can only say "Hier wird eine ungenaue und abgeblasste Übertragung vorliegen" (p. 51); and of its use in iv 10, that the fact that we here come up against a formula is significant, since "eine Erzählung wird auf eine solche weitgehend verzichten, da der Fluss der Erzählung dem Erzähler wichtiger ist". It is not clear to me why the use of a formula should be so inimical to narrative flow.

prophetic summons, the other indirectly. *wyz'q* in *vv.* 10 and 13 then clearly brings out this inherent parity of roles of the two leaders, at the same time avoiding further explicit reference to Yahweh's role. Here we have the seeds for a fruitful thematic development.

It is notable in the parallel expressions, both of *vv.* 6 f. and of *vv.* 10 and 13, that the object of *mšk* and *z'q* in the first instances respectively consists of people only, men of the tribes of Zebulun and Naphtali who constitute the whole of Barak's military resources; in the second instances, however, Sisera's men are indeed part of the compound object of the verb, but they are pushed into the background by the 900 iron chariots, which fill the syntactical place of honour. This contrast between Sisera's invincible mobility and Barak's pedestrian vulnerability allows the narrator to make further use of parallel and contrasted expressions to ironic effect. In *v.* 10aβ *wy'l brglyw 'śrt 'lpy 'yš*, *brglyw* is quite properly interpreted as "at his [*scil.* Barak's] heels", i.e. "under his command". However, already the prominent position given to Sisera's chariots in the oracle, *v.* 7, is likely, by contrast, to impart to the expression here resonance of its other common meaning, "on foot". This resonance is reinforced by the even more emphatic reference to Sisera's chariots in *v.* 13, and becomes the dominant note when the expression is twice repeated in parallel phrases of Sisera, in *vv.* 15b and 17a:

15b *wyns brglyw*
17a *wsysr' ns brglyw.*

Moreover, it is probably not unintentional, in view of this ironically emphasized pedestrianization of Sisera, that we have an additional contrast between *'lh* and *yrd.* In *v.* 10 Barak's troops "go up" Mt Tabor "at his heels" *brglyw* (*eo ipso* Barak himself also goes up "on foot"), in order to gain the tactical advantage of high ground; in *v.* 15b Sisera "goes down" from his chariot and flees "on foot" *brglyw*, thereby abandoning the symbol of his tactical superiority. It is worth noting that this play on *brglyw* is carried through from episodes one (*v.* 10), and two (*v.* 15b), into episode three by means of the reprise in *v.* 17a. Sisera's descent from his post of command at the head of 900 iron chariots, in order to become a solitary foot-slogger fleeing for his life, is fraught with unlooked-for consequences, which arise directly out of this self-imposed "going down and fleeing". Thereby the anti-heroic polarity latent in his initial presentation realizes its full potential in episode three.

There is a further play on the verb *yrd,* which sets up another ironic contrast between Barak and Sisera. *V.* 14b narrates Barak's attack in terms of a "coming down" from Mt Tabor, *wyrd brq mhr tbwr.* Not far removed, and coming at the corresponding point in its sentence, is the closely-parallel expression of Sisera's "dismounting" from his chariot, *wyrd sysrʾ mʿl hmrkbh* (*v.* 15b). In addition to the contrast brought out by the use of *brglyw* on the one hand with *ʿlh* in *v.* 10a, and on the other with *yrd* in *v.* 15b, there is a further contrast in the two uses of *yrd*: Barak "comes down" to (ostensibly) glorious victory, Sisera to shameful flight. But this very parallel intensifies the irony; for Sisera's descent to flight effects at the least a postponement of Barak's glory, since the enemy *par excellence* thereby eludes his grasp. Thus is set in train the tragic belying of Barak's heroic role.

At this stage in the narrative the fateful parallel in true position between Barak and Sisera has become apparent, and the irony of their essentially similar destiny is now heavily underscored by the use of further syntactical and verbal parallelisms.

The two circumstantial clauses, *vv.* 16a and 17a, which marked the boundary between the second and third episodes, are carefully phrased to make a balanced contrast between the actions of Barak and Sisera:

16a *wbrq rdp ʾḥry hrkb wʾḥry hmḥnh ʿd ḥršt hgwym*
17a *wsyrsʾ ns brglyw ʾl ʾhl yʿl ʾšt ḥbr hqyny*

Again, the syntax is as similar as possible, and the similarity is emphasized by both clauses appearing at the beginning of their respective sentences. This means that the sets of contrasts between *rdp/ns*, *ʾḥry hrkb/brglyw*, *ʿd ḥršt hgwym/ʾl ʾhl yʿl* cannot fail to have been intended. Barak pursues whilst Sisera flees: Barak vaingloriously pursues the now insignificant chariotry to an abandoned fortress; Sisera ingloriously flees on foot to the tent of a tinker's wife. Yet, though outwardly so contrasted, each is inexorably effecting for himself the loss of the very thing he so desperately seeks.

Despite the misdirection of Barak's pursuit in 16a, he does arrive, albeit belatedly, at the tent of Jael, *v.* 22aα. This clause thus resumes that part of the narrative thread which had been left at a half-close in *v.* 16. However, *v.* 22aα does not back-track with the use of suffix-tense verbs [33]), as in *vv.* 16a, 17a, but draws the suspended thread to-

[33]) So *nās* in *v.* 17a should be interpreted, paralleling MT's (correct) *rāḏap* in *v.* 16a: "(Meanwhile) Barak had pursued ... (meanwhile) Sisera had fled"; cf. L. Alonso Schökel, p. 163.

gether with the main thread at a point coetaneous with that which the narrative has just reached. Hence the participle is used here, with the signification of action in progress reinforced by the use of *hinnê*. These differences apart, *v.* 22aα is closely parallel to *v.* 16a, but with one further significant and, in the context deeply ironic, difference:

16a *wbrq rdp ʾḥry hrkb wʾḥry hmḥnh*
22aα *whnh brq rdp ʾt sysrʾ*

It is not now the joint pursuit by the hero and his army of the routed and leaderless forces of the enemy in hopes of the glory of victory, but the lonely pursuit of a solitary foe, alas! in vain. For already he has fallen—to the hand of a woman.

The essential oneness in destiny of Barak and Sisera is strongly emphasized at this point by a parallelism between the arrival of each at the tent of Jael:

17a *wsysrʾ ns brglyw ʾl ʾhl yʿl* . . . 18a *wtṣʾ yʿl lqrʾt sysrʾ wtʾmr ʾlyw swrh ʾdny swrh ʾly ʾl tyrʾ wysr ʾlyh hʾhlh.*
22 *whnh brq rdp ʾt sysrʾ wtṣʾ yʿl lqrʾtw wtʾmr lw lk wʾrʾk* . . . *wybʾ ʾlyh.*

Jael comes out to meet Barak, as she had Sisera, to invite, or rather command, him to enter the tent, as she had Sisera: thus each is brought face to face with the *ʾiššâ* all unbeknown, and thus in entering each is confronted with the loss of the prize he seeks. The unity of situation is highlighted through the verbal similarity, but the reprise in *v.* 22 is the terser and more compact, pressing forward to the final denouement.

An internal parallel in *v.* 22 further brings out the ironic destinies of Barak and Sisera in the dénouement:

22aα *whnh brq rdp ʾt sysrʾ*;
22bβ *whnh sysrʾ npl mt.*

While Barak yet pursues, Sisera lies dead where he has fallen. Even the word *nōp̄ēl*, common though it is in this usage, sets off an ironic resonance with the only other occurrence of the verb in the narrative, *v.* 16b, where it is used of Barak's complete slaughter of Sisera's troops (also a standard usage): *wypl kl mḥnh sysrʾ lpy ḥrb*. There Sisera's whole army lies felled by the swords of Barak and his troops; here Sisera lies alone, felled—by the hand of a woman.

Finally, the irony of Barak's fate is brilliantly expressed in a reprise that spans the narrative, and draws together the four characters:

6bβ *lk wmškt bhr tbwr wlḥqt ʿmk ʿśrt ʾlpym ʾyš*
22aγδ *lk wʾrʾk ʾt hʾyš ʾšr ʾth mbqš*

Barak is twice summoned with the same imperative by a woman, but with what different prospects! Then to be the doer of deeds matching Yahweh's own (*wmškt* ... *wmškty*); now to be but a spectator of a woman's; then at the head of a multitude to gain glorious victory over a multitude; now alone to see his solitary foe in abject defeat; then the heroic leader, parleying with a woman, and getting his way; now mutely obedient, like a vanquished foe, at a woman's behest. Note the contrasted verbs immediately following the imperative: in the former instance Deborah makes Barak the subject, and the ten thousand men the object; in the latter, Jael makes herself the subject and both Barak and Sisera the objects. Could anything be more eloquent and at the same time as economic? No doubt there is also an ironic resonance between the ten thousand men that Barak is to take in *v.* 6, and the one man he now seeks in vain.

Thus in the surface structure of the story Barak and Sisera are at opposite poles; and at this level they can be said to suffer different fates. Barak gains a victory over the forces of Sisera, and Sisera himself loses his life in the aftermath of the battle. But the deep structure of the narrative, the level of the author's theme, shows Barak and Sisera to be united in a tragic fate: ignominious subjection to the effective power of a woman.

In the bringing about of this fate, Deborah and Jael play different roles; but here too the surface disparity is transcended so as to unite the women in complementary functions. We have already considered the way in which the narrator chose to focus attention on Deborah at the narrative's opening, only immediately to divert attention to Barak and his anticipated role, by means of Deborah's oracle. However, that Barak, for all his bluster (*v.* 8), is not really in control of the situation, is carefully though not obtrusively indicated. The real initiative lies with Deborah, who not only impels Barak to prepare for battle, but (it is implied) has it in her power to check him, by refusing to comply with his ultimatum. Barak's parleying, arising out of his reluctance to act on his own initiative, has delayed action in this episode, but Deborah's very positive response *hlk ʾlk ʿmk* (*v.* 9a) is quickly realised in decisive action, *wtqm dbwrh wtlk ʿm brq qdšh* (*v.* 9b), where the pleonastic expression serves to emphasise Deborah's initiative. It is not until *v.* 10 (*wyzʿq* . . .) that Barak *does* anything, but from this point on he comes into his own in the narrative, and

Deborah begins to slip into the background: this is one function, in comparison with *v.* 9b, of the much more incidental notice of her accompanying Barak in *v.* 10b. On the other hand, this notice serves to emphasize by repetition the fact of her sticking close to Barak throughout the battle preparations, in fulfilment of her undertaking *hlk ʾlk ʿmk* in *v.* 9a [34]). But the emphasizing of this notion has an important function in relation to Deborah's words in 9a, to which we shall return.

Barak's conviction that to him is vouchsafed decisive action takes its rise from Deborah's opening summons *vv.* 6 f, especially its closing words, *wnttyhw bydk*, the so-called "committal formula" (*Übergabe-/Übereignungs-formel*) [35]). As a conventional assurance of victory, this formula is unlikely especially to engage the listener's or reader's attention at this point. But it gains resonance as a result of a twofold repetition within a relatively short space of narrative (*vv.* 9aβ, 14aα). So far as the expression here gives rise to expectations of the outcome of the plot, these are to the effect that Barak seems likely to defeat Sisera and his forces in battle. So far as this more or less eventuates, we have in *v.* 7 a foreshadowing device, which alerts the listener or reader to what is coming. This creates its own kind of narrative suspense, as the listener or reader awaits its eventuality [36]). However, the audience's expectations are not precisely fulfilled, and "not precisely" is the essential. For the committal-formula of *v.* 7 is so expressed as to be both a true and a false foreshadowing. The third person singular verbal suffix in *wnttyhw* is synecdochic: in

[34]) Richter, p. 46, perceives the difference of emphasis between *vv.* 9b and 10b, but, as a result of his atomistic approach, sees this as evidence of a lacuna(*Hiatus*) between *vv.* 9 and 10, corresponding to a claimed difference of purpose (*Tendenz*) between *vv.* 4a, 6-9 and 10, 12-16.

[35]) On this formula and its connection with "Holy-War", see Richter, pp. 21-4, 182-5; F. Stolz, p. 21 f., who concludes: "Es handelt sich also nicht um eine Formel, die einen exklusiven Sitz in einer allfälligen Schilderung 'heiligen Krieges' hätte, sondern um eine allgemein verwendbare Redewendung".

[36]) This feature has been discussed in detail for classical epic by G. E. Duckworth *Foreshadowing and Suspense in the Epics of Homer, Apollonius and Vergil* (Princeton, 1933), where he shows that, to ancient prepossessions if not to modern, such foreshadowings were not destructive but rather creative of narrative suspense and interest. It is a reasonable assumption, unless it can be shown otherwise, that the ancient Hebrews would have shared this attitude. On this basis alone, Richter's "deshalb" in "... dass der Gottesbefehl und dessen Verheissung (*v.* 6b.7) das Ergebnis vorwegnehmen und deshalb keine Spannung aufkommen lassen" (p. 60) is unjustified; but even were it justified, this would not make this feature evidence of a nonnarrative genre. However, as I shall go on to demonstrate, even Richter's premise is not true as it stands.

the preceding part of the verse, Yahweh has undertaken to "draw out" Sisera *and* his forces ("his chariots and his troops") to battle. Consequently, the verbal suffix, though singular, must be understood to include his forces along with Sisera. Nonetheless, the singular suffix focusses on Sisera, as the significant enemy, and it is precisely not Sisera who is committed to Barak's hands. Thus, far from destroying narrative suspense, the committal-formula actually helps create it, by arousing false expectations as to the outcome.

The first repetition of the committal-formula [37]) follows closely on its first occurrence: *ky byd 'šh ymkr YHWH 't sysr'* (*v.* 9aβ). But clearly this is a highly differentiated repetition, in which hardly a word exactly corresponds with the initial form. This in itself emphasizes both forms by contrast; but additional emphasis results from the use of inversion, whereby the *byd* NN component is brought from final to initial position, and the object moves from the less prominent penultimate, to the more prominent final, position [38]). Accordingly, what strikes the listener's or reader's attention most in this version of the formula is the change from *bydk*, (*v.* 7b) to *byd 'šh* (*v.* 9aβ). The way for this change is prepared by the preceding exceptive clause (*'ps ky l' thyh tp'rtk ... wegōmer*), for which the following *kî* clause, containing the new form of committal-formula, provides an explanation, which itself turns upon that very change. What would an audience take this alteration of the committal-formula to signify, and, perhaps more importantly, what would they suppose Barak to have understood?

In the immediate context Deborah's words *need* have no further implication than that, by his insistence on her accompanying him to

[37]) Richter, pp. 21 ff., does not include any discussion of the connection between his *Übereignungsformel* using *ntn* and the six examples (Jdg. ii 14, iii 8, iv 2, 9, x 7; 1 Sam. xii 9) of a parallel formula using *mkr*; nor on p. 60 on iv 9, although here he cites the other five examples.

[38]) The formula has no fixed word-order. Besides the frequent order: verb, subject, object, *byd* NN (cf. *vv.* 7 and 14), other orders occur: e.g. verb, subject, *byd* NN, object, a frequent form with compound objects for obvious reasons, e.g. Dt. ii 24; Josh. vi 2, viii 1; verb, object as verbal suffix, subject, *byd* NN: this seems merely to be a variation on the standard form necessitated by the use of a verbal suffix for the object, but a substantive for the subject, e.g. Dt. xxi 10; Josh. x 19; Jdg. xi 32. However, the instances of inversion are much rarer, and were probably chosen for emphasis. I have noted Num. xxi 34 = Dt. iii 2; Josh. x 8. It is worth noting that of the five other examples of the formula using *mkr*, all are of the form verb, object (as verbal suffix; 1 Sam. xii 9 detached pronoun), subject (not Jdg. x 7; 1 Sam. xii 9, where verb forms have subject anaphora), *byd* NN; with this cf. Jdg. ii 14, vi 1, xiii 1; 2 Kings xiii 3, xvii 20 for similar forms with *ntn*, all in Deuteronomistic contexts.

the battle, Barak has deprived himself of the glory, which will redound to Deborah's honour rather than his own. There is no necessary implication that Barak will not himself be the victor over his enemy, but only that his dependence upon a woman will deprive him of the credit for it [39]. A serious enough implication perhaps, from Barak's point of view, but the narrative gives no indication that he has seen even this much in Deborah's words. Certain it is that throughout the narrative Barak betrays no suspicion of any more sinister import, and that, until the very last moment, he acts as if the deed is still his for the doing.

But the audience? Much depends in the first place on whether or not they are familiar with this version of the story. If they are, then they will share the author's ironic stance *vis-à-vis* Barak (and Deborah?) [40], appreciate the subtlety of the foreshadowing of things to come, and await with expectation their working out. If they are not, and I think we must reckon with the fact that there would always be those who did not know—for what narrator does not relish a virgin audience?—the foreshadowing and irony are there still, but for such an audience they are but darkling hints. Hints which the speed of narration [41] barely allows the listener or reader to perceive, let alone reflect upon. For such an audience the foreshadowing and irony are to be perceived in retrospect, when the course of events brings full realization of what was but a bare suspicion. With such an audience the narrator is able to interpose an ironic distance between himself and them, dropping hints, tantalizing with flashes of the truth, leaving them in suspense until the final moments bring home the inevitability of the outcome.

The indefinite form of reference in this version of the committal-formula, *byd ʾšh*, in the context of the causal clause of which it forms part, crystallizes the essence of the changed situation which necessi-

[39]) As evidence of the partial eclipse of Barak by Deborah in the tradition, one may cite the poem of chap. v.

[40]) Of course, Deborah, as prophetess, could be understood to be in the secret, and thus herself taking an ironic stance *vis-à-vis* Barak.

[41]) One must not neglect here the fact that oral narration would allow the use of significant pauses, voice inflections, even facial expressions, gestures and other non-verbal devices in delivery. But even if this story was primarily oral, it is difficult for us to take such possibilities into account in our discussion, other than by making a general concession that their use may have alerted the audience to what the narrator was doing, more than appears simply from the written text. But it remains problematic to my mind to demonstrate that this story was clearly intended for oral narration.

tates a change in the divine undertaking: Barak, the man, the military leader, cedes effective leadership to a woman; consequently that woman will gain the glory. However, the ambiguity inherent in the indefinite form allows the narrator to play upon the two possibilities, namely that Deborah is referring to herself, or to another, without as it were committing himself at this stage to either. Nonetheless, the possibility that Deborah is referring to herself is highlighted by the insistent way (*v.* 10b as emphatic repetition of 9b) we are made aware that she goes along with Barak: Deborah, it is true, now retreats into the background behind Barak, but remains nevertheless very much on stage.

The possibility that Deborah is the *'iššâ* is further strengthened when, suddenly back on centre-stage at the scene of battle itself, Deborah repeats the committal-formula: *ntn YHWH 't sysr' bydk* (*v.* 14aβ). But, curiously, she has reverted to the original form of the undertaking, as in *v.* 7b: is it that Barak then will gain the prize after all? The repetition of the formula here also serves to particularize the object of the undertaking, *'t sysr'*. For, though in principle still synecdochic in reference, by reason of greater separation from mention of his forces (*v.* 13a) than obtained in *v.* 7, *'t sysr'* here in *v.* 14 has a predominantly individual reference. Moreover, this individual reference is immediately underlined in *v.* 15a, where Sisera is enumerated separately from the rest of his forces. But the expectation, so carefully fostered at this point in the narrative, that Sisera is after all to fall to the hand of Barak, is suddenly but quietly belied by the almost unobtrusive narration of Sisera's flight from the battlefield, 15b. This unobtrusiveness is heightened by *v.* 16's immediate return to Barak's victorious rout of Sisera's forces, thus drawing the listener's or reader's attention for the moment away from Sisera and his fate. Thereby the narrator has created uncertainty about the eventual outcome: has Sisera escaped Barak's hands, or will he yet catch up with him? Is it that Deborah has yet a role to play in all this?

It is only with the resumptive narration of Sisera's escape in *v.* 17a, with its additional information of the goal of Sisera's flight, that the true significance of Deborah's *byd 'šh* becomes apparent; and with it comes the realization that Sisera has, all unwitting, been the instrument of his own fate. Thus the indefinite *byd 'šh* not only foreshadows the denouement of the plot, but also the theme of the narrative: the subjection, at once self-imposed but divinely-ordered, of presumed authority-bearing men to presumed subservient women. There is a sense in which both Deborah and Jael are the *ʾiššâ* of *v*. 9: Deborah, by "subjugating" Barak, effectively achieves the victory over Sisera's forces; Jael, by achieving the victory over Sisera, effectively subjugates Barak.

In the light of this, the use, in the second version of the committal-formula, of *mkr*, with its connotations, when used of people, of slavery and subservience [42]), hardly appears to be simply accidental, or governed merely by a desire for elegant variation. For its telling juxtaposition with the *byd ʾšh* in inversion foreshadows the crushing ignominy of the proud leader's fate. The heavy note of irony which it sounds is in tune with that already sounded for Barak by *hlk* in the immediately preceding exceptive clause: *hdrk ʾšr ʾth hlk*. For though one of the most frequently occurring of Hebrew verbs, and all but unavoidable in this particular phrase, there is an ineluctable resonance

[42]) Cf. Gen. xxxvii 27 f., 36; Ex. xxi 7 f., 16; Amos ii 6, etc. That *mkr* here is an example of late (so K. Budde *KHAT* and W. Nowack *HAT*) Deuteronomistic usage (so Richter, p. 60) seems to me much less certain than these writers assume. It is true that *mkr* occurs elsewhere in Judges only in the stereotyped formula of the editorial passages, *wymkrm YHWH* (omitted in x 7) *byd* NN ii 14, iii 8, iv 2, x 7. But whilst these passages have in common with the present passage that they all use *mkr* instead ot *ntn* in the "committal-formula", there are significant differences. The most important of these is that all the clearly editorial examples are of a syntactically highly stereotyped kind, different from the present example (see note 38 above), which moreover occur uniformly in the context of the "anti-Holy War" statement typical of the editorial sections of Judges, of Israel's committal by Yahweh into the hands of her enemies. Thus the present usage is unique in Judges in syntactical form, in occurring in a narrative rather than an editorial context, and in a normal "Holy War" usage of the committal-formula, rather than the editorial "anti-Holy War" usage. Further, apart from the six passages cited in n. 38 above, *mkr* does not occur elsewhere in the committal-formula, contrary to the misleading impression given by M. Weinfeld, "The Period of the Conquest and the Judges", *VT* 17 (1967), p. 108. None of the passages he cites (Dt. xxviii 68; 1 Kings xxi 20, 25; 2 Kings xvii 17) is a version of the committal-formula: none has the element *byd* NN; none has YHWH for subject; on the contrary all use the hithpael of *mkr* reflexively, and the hithpael of this verb does not otherwise occur; finally, only Dt. xxviii 68 refers to a selling (of oneself) to an enemy (*lʾybyk*, not *byd ʾybyk*), and thus has any real resemblance to the passages in Judges; the Kings passages make use of the quite different notion of "to sell oneself to do evil". Whether or not W. Beyerlin ("Gattung und Herkunft des Rahmens im Richterbuch", in E. Würthwein and O. Kaiser [ed.], *Tradition und Situation* [Göttingen, 1963], pp. 1-29) is right in his contention of the largely pre-Deuteronomic origin of the Judges framework material (including the *mkr* formula), it cannot be claimed that *mkr* is a clearly late or characteristically Deuteronomic or Deuteronomistic word. In sum then, the *mkr*-formula in Jdg. iv 9 could be of deuteronomistic origin, but the evidence for this is far from certain. Indeed it is at least as arguable that the more petrified formula in the four editorial passages (and in 1 Sam. xii 9) has taken its rise from the original adaptation of the committal-formula in the narrative passage before us.

with its six-fold repetition in the dozen words immediately preceding the exceptive clause [43]); and beyond that to Deborah's initial summons, *lk wmškt* (*v.* 6b). This resonance will contribute a note of heavy irony to Jael's summons in *v.* 22, as we have seen. By this temporizing, and all unwitting, Barak has taken a path different from that he was commissioned to take, with all its fateful consequences.

The brief scene (*v.* 11) which begins the second episode has caused difficulty, by reason of its positioning at this point in the narrative on the one hand, and the role it assigns to Heber the Kenite, on the other. If we leave aside for the moment the question of Heber's relevance to the narrative, it is possible to suggest a number of important narrative considerations which may have prompted the narrator to place this brief scene here.

Purely from consideration of the "mechanics" of narrative it is difficult to see where else it could well be placed. Its most obvious plot-function is to provide some explanation of how it is that, in fleeing from the battlefield, Sisera comes upon the tent of Jael the Kenite. For this reason the more prosaic and logical have desiderated a placing of the verse much closer to *v.* 17 [44]). What has not entered into their calculations is precisely the consideration which would weigh most heavily with a skilled narrator: where to place this in the narrative so that he gains most and loses least? Clearly not in the vicinity of *v.* 17a. I have already indicated how tight is the structure of *vv.* 16, 17a, 18 [45]), the bridge between the second and third episodes: this balance would be upset by the addition of *v.* 11. Moreover, the conjunction of the flight of Sisera from the battlefield to Jael's tent with Barak's pursuit of Sisera's forces in another direction, has built

[43]) One might point out in passing that this element of insistent repetition, present in the MT version of *vv.* 8 f., would be weakened by the LXX addition to *v.* 8. This would provide an additional reason for regarding the MT as the better version.

[44]) Cf. K. Wiese, *Zur Literarkritik des Buches Richters* (Stuttgart, 1926), p. 16: "Die Bemerkung, die *v.* 11 macht, wäre höchstens hinter *v.* 17 sinnvoll". Richter's view (p. 58), that *vv.* 11, 17b constitute a single, independent traditionary unit, only exacerbates his failure to give an adequate account of why *v.* 11 should have been so far separated from its logical and substantive connection.

[45]) *V.* 17b may well be intrusive: at any rate, Jabin has no clear organic connection with the action of the narrative. The explanation has been provided in order to fill out a narrative ellipsis; namely, why did Sisera go to Jael's tent? How did Jael know (as she apparently did) who he was? My understanding is that *v.* 11 provides the possibility of a sufficient answer to both these questions, but that in any case the tightness of structure and compression so characteristic of Hebrew narrative dispensed with a detailed exposition of such peripheral questions.

the narrative up to a high point of tension which would be immeasurably weakened by the introduction here of this static explanatory flashback [46]. But if not here, where else? Only the bridge between the first and second episodes offers itself as a possible alternative. And indeed there is not lacking a point of connection here, namely in the proximity of Heber's encampment to Kedesh, where Barak is mustering his troops.

Furthermore, there are positive advantages in such a placing. It conveniently occupies a gap in narrative time, between Barak's setting in train preparations for battle, narrated in *v.* 10, and Sisera's receiving a report of them, V. 12 [47]. Moreover, in so doing it postpones the appearance of the enemy Sisera, keenly anticipated by the audience as a result of the first episode. The suspense thus created is intensified by the way in which *v.* 11, with its stylized opening, introduces a new thread as though beginning a fresh narrative. Yet that new thread is immediately left hanging and the old thread taken up again in *v.* 12. The effect of this is to arouse intense curiosity as to the relevance of Heber's encampment to Barak and Sisera, which further contributes to narrative suspense, as the listener or reader waits for some hint. In this connection it is worth noting how the narrator maintains that suspense as long as possible by deliberately suppressing, at the first mention of Sisera's flight from the battlefield (*v.* 15b), any mention of the direction of his flight. The suspicion that his flight will take him in the direction of Heber's encampment may suggest itself to the astute listener or reader, especially as a result of the juxtaposition between Heber and Sisera already created by *v.* 12 following hard upon *v.* 11.

However, that suspicion is not quite the full truth, and this brings us to consider the second difficulty of *v.* 11; what has Heber to do with all this? The answer is very little directly, and for this reason many have sought to link Heber with Jabin (cf. *v.* 17b), as belonging to a secondary strand of narrative, originally distinct from a Jael-strand [48].

[46]) So already G. F. Moore, *Judges* (Edinburgh, 1895), p. 118.

[47]) Cf. L. Alonso Schökel, p. 161.

[48]) The view that Heber belongs to a Jabin-strand in the story which has only secondarily been linked to the Jael-strand through a fictive marriage-relationship is so widespread as to need no special citation. As an hypothesis about the origins of the traditions underlying the narrative, this seems to me possible, though not very probable, since it rests on assumptions about topographical discrepancies, about the connection of Jabin with Heber, and of both with the text, which are themselves dubious. The former question is too involved to raise here, and I hope to deal with it in some detail elsewhere. As to the latter, I cannot see that the two

Notwithstanding, since in the narrative before us Heber and Jael belong together, can one make any reasonable suggestions why *v.* 11 mentions Heber, and not Jael? These are actually two distinct, though related, questions, and it is probably easier to tackle the latter first.

We have already seen how, by the time Sisera actually enters the narrative in person in *v.* 12, that entrance is eagerly awaited because well-prepared for in the first episode. It comes as no surprise, merely as the fulfilment of an expectation regarded as certain. *V.* 11, on the other hand, prepares the way for the eventual entrance of Jael, without so much as intimating that any such person exists. When she does appear on the scene in *v.* 17, surprise is the essential element. This heightens the impact of the denouement of the plot, since only with her unannounced appearance does the possibility of the *ʾiššâ* of 9aβ being other than Deborah really enter the horizon of the narrative.

---

minor references to Jabin within *vv.* 4-22, namely the phrase in *v.* 7 and the clause in *v.* 17b, can be taken as evidence of an isolable Jabin strand in the narrative. This is wholly out of proportion to the evidence, which is more simply accounted for as explanatory additions. Far from it being clear that *v.* 17b is independent evidence of a tradition of treaty relations between Heber and Jabin (Richter, p. 58), it is as likely that this was itself a "deduction" made from the otherwise puzzling fact of Sisera's apparently making directly for Jael's tent (Heber's encampment) and Jael's apparent recognition of him, by someone to whom the connection between Sisera and Jabin was an accepted fact. This "deduction" was then added to the text to provide an explicit explanation for Sisera's and Jael's behaviour. I find Richter's argument peculiarly tortuous here. Arguing for the close connection of *v.* 11 with *v.* 17b, on the basis that *v.* 11 is intended as a preparation for 17b, not 17a, because it mentions Heber and not Jael (so already Budde *KHAT*), he then quietly assumes that Jael had already been identified as "wife" of Heber the Kenite in the text before the addition of *vv.* 11, 17b, and that this was what gave the impetus for the editor to add the note about Heber. But what this view regrettably ignores is the fact that *v.* 17b is indisputably an explanatory clause attached to *v.* 17a: yet Richter gives no account of how his traditionist thought that *vv.* (11), 17b provided an explanation for *v.* 17a, nor is it clear how it could have on Richter's view. The fact that *v.* 17b is an explanatory clause to *v.* 17a (or more generally, to the context *vv.* 17a, 18 ff.) entails that *v.* 11, if a preparation for *v.* 17b, is mediately a preparation for *vv.* 17a, 18 ff. also. Moreover, as I have already argued, *v.* 17b, to have any explanatory potential for the context, must presuppose that the connection of Sisera with Jabin has already been made. But on Richter's view this connection is the *result* of the addition of *vv.* 11, 17b to the text. Finally, if, as Richter assumes, Jael was already identified as the husband of Heber the Kenite in the text before the addition of *vv.* 11, 17b, then why assume that this marriage tradition is false, and on the other hand assume the correctness of the "tradition" in *v.* 17b of a treaty-relationship between Heber and Jabin? The independent evidence for the one tradition seems no greater than the other; on the other hand, it is easier to see how a secondary explanation about peaceful relations between Heber and Jabin can have arisen, than a secondary connection of Heber and Jael, which still remains to be accounted for on Richter's view.

The impact of this surprise forces on the listener or reader the realization of the horrible outcome of the meeting of Jael and Sisera, and holds him fascinated to the end. Moreover, it heightens appreciation of the narrator's theme, by withholding the possibility of its full realization until the climactic moments of the narrative.

If the avoiding of any mention of Jael until the moment of her appearance is of such clear narrative advantage on the one hand, yet some kind of preparation for that appearance a necessity on the other, then it is difficult to see how that preparation could be as economically achieved as it is through mention of her husband, Heber the Kenite. For that allows the narrator to make the connection between *v.* 11 and *v.* 17 at the cost of three words, *'št ḥbr hqyny* in *v.* 17aβ, at a point in the narrative where excess verbiage would be ruinous. Moreover, in the form in which the notice is given in *v.* 11, it could hardly avoid mention of Heber, since presumably the decision to move camp would belong to the male head of the household.

Lest the more ingenious reader should counter the preceding argument by formulating a version of *v.* 11 which omits reference to Heber, yet serves the same narrative functions, let me hasten to add that again there are positive advantages in the specific mention of Heber. Firstly, if the avoidance of reference to Jael until the moment of her appearance contributes an element of surprise to the denouement, the fact that thereby Heber the Kenite is shown to have (or to be likely to have) no independent function adds to this surprise by παρὰ προσδοκίαν, and in so doing heavily underlines the function of the woman Jael, Heber's wife. This in its turn intensifies the irony of the narrator's theme. By placing Heber in the limelight at the beginning of episode two, in the act of moving his camp, the narrator is playing upon his audience's prepossessions as to the normal role of the man, in order to arouse false expectations about the role of *this* man in *this* story. These false expectations are fostered in the course of episode two by the way in which the action is largely dominated by the men, Barak and Sisera. However, a degree of ironic counterbalance is achieved by the disproportionate narrative space devoted to Deborah's summons to battle: i.e. the action of the men is but the reflex of the woman's effecting word. Thus the realization, when it comes at the beginning of episode three, that Jael is the *'iššâ*, is at the same time the realization that she, and not her husband, her lord and master, will take the decisive action: Sisera is committed into her hands, not his.

Thus both the placing of *v.* 11 and its focusing on Heber and not Jael are not due to chance or redactional ineptitude, but effectively subserve the working out of the plot and the theme of the narrative, as well as its structural balance.

The climactic episodes make the most of this skilful narration by a masterly display of compressed irony. Jael initiates the action of the third episode by coming out to meet Sisera, urging him to turn aside into her tent (*v.* 18). Her assurance *'l tyr'*, redolent as it must be in this narrative of the assurance-of-victory formula, has sardonic overtones in the context of Sisera's flight. Having complied with her summons (no parleying here!) and any lingering suspicions being allayed by Jael's covering him over, as though to hide him, the initiative apparently passes to Sisera, who first requests a drink (*hšqyny n'*, *v.* 19), then commands Jael to stand guard (*'md*, *v.* 20) [49]). The terms of his command are full of significance, with its twofold *'yš* and final *'yn* (cf. Alonso Schökel, p. 164). The narrative has distilled out the quintessential situation, foreshadowed by the committal-formulae: the confrontation is, not now of two leaders at the head of vast armies, but of two men in the presence of a woman; and one word put with dreadful irony into the mouth of Sisera who so cravenly abandoned his position of leadership, adumbrates the impending fate of them both: *'ayin*. This word at the same time throws into relief the emptiness of Sisera's assertion of authority over Jael. For eliding any verbal expression of submission or compliance on Jael's part, the narrator expresses her position of dominance by an immediate response in action, a deed which grimly actualizes Sisera's final word. But in its way this word no less expresses the fate of Barak. For, contrary to Sisera's expectation, the man, when he comes, does not so much as utter a syllable: he, too, is as good as *'ayin* in the presence of the triumphant woman, whose hand has, with one stroke, brought ignominy and shame to those whose right was glory and honour. Thus, in a final tableau, which balances the narrative's initial focus on the woman Deborah, is graphically depicted the ironic subjection of men of action to subservient woman.

---

[49]) The repointing of this masculine imperative to an infinitive absolute may be correct. But it is worth considering whether the reading of MT may not be correct, since it would again contribute a note of ironic humour here: Sisera now passes from addressing Jael with polite request to commanding her as though she were one of his own troops (hence the *masculine* imperative).

III

When we make all due allowance for the dangers of over-explanation inherent in this kind of study, the conclusion seems nonetheless unavoidable that the story of Deborah and Barak in Jdg. iv 4-22 is a unified narrative which displays a very high degree of technical competence and artistic finish. There is hardly an element in the story which cannot be shown to subserve the unfolding of the plot and out-working of the narrator's theme, and to do so in a way which cannot but elicit our admiration for the author's skill and discernment. This itself makes probable certain further conclusions as to the nature and purpose of this narrative.

Firstly, such a narrative positively demands the controlling intelligence of an author. The weaving of a web of such complex inter-relationships and subtle nuances can hardly have resulted merely from the haphazard conglomeration of disparate traditionary units, or the constant overlayings of centuries of folk narration. This is not to deny that the pericope may involve originally separate traditions, or that it is firmly anchored in oral folk narrative: for all we know, Jael may have had nothing to do with Barak, or with Sisera for that matter, and may have come to be linked with one or both only in the course of folk narration. What I hope to have demonstrated is that *in this narrative* Jael is inextricably bound up with both, that this is indeed crucial to the effectiveness of the story. If so, speculation about a Jael-narrative which originally had nothing to do with a Deborah-Barak narrative is completely without evidence, for clearly *this* Jael-episode cannot conceivably be separated from *this* Deborah-Barak story, and neither affords any positive evidence that there ever was such a separation [50]).

Secondly, if my exposition has led to an interpretation of the story which has reasonable correspondence with the author's own, it follows that the narrator has an essentially literary rather than historical or quasi-historical interest. It has long been recognized that the pur-

[50]) It is a major defect of Richter's discussion that he gives no satisfactory account of how the pericope comes to be in its present form. It is, for example, not at all obvious why the Holy War traditionists, to whom, on Richter's view, Barak's battle against Sisera was the focal point, should have bothered with the Jael-Sisera narrative. On the contrary, to have Sisera escape from Barak and be killed by a non-Israelite woman appears to be the very opposite of what would best serve their theological-didactic purpose. Moreover, if they retained the Jael story as Richter assumes they did, then why did they not give this an explicit theological colouring?

pose of the narrative in *vv.* 4-22 cannot originally have been that of bearing out the historical understanding reflected in the framework passages, *vv.* 1-3, 23 f., and my discussion serves only to support such a judgement. But the rejected reading of the Deuteronomist has by and large been replaced by another, which for all its apparent recognition of the nature of ancient literary forms, still sees the text in historical terms, as essentially some kind of "historical report" [51]) of the battle of Barak against Sisera, of which we have a more reliable (as supposed) account in Jdg. v. Whilst such a view is understandable enough in the light of 18th and 19th century preoccupation with the historical, which inevitably led to a premature assessment of texts under historical categories, it is nonetheless misconceived, and can lead to conclusions which are grotesque in their inappropriateness [52]). The narrator is not concerned to give a report of any kind; nor is he primarily concerned with history as such: his concern is to narrate a story which appeared to him to comment with telling irony on the roles of two men and two women, and thus on the relationship of men and women in general.

Thirdly, one is led to question the appropriateness of the widely-used designations "saga" and, more precisely, "hero-saga" [53]), at least to this particular pericope in the book of Judges. If my estimation of its nature and purpose is substantially correct, then these are not easily compatible with those of a "hero-saga" as generally understood. The story as it stands is hardly a folk account of the glorious victory of Israel over the forces of Sisera. Nor is it obviously a dramatic presentation of the prowess under Yahweh of Barak or

---

[51]) Cf. e.g. K. Budde, *Die Bücher Richter und Samuel* (Giessen, 1890), pp. 105 f. where *Geschichtserzählung* and *Bericht* (twice) are used of chap. iv; and H. W. Hertzberg, p. 173, "dramatisch erzählten Bericht": *Bericht* is used as a standing designation of chap. iv.

[52]) In addition to the example cited in the text below, cf. the entirely gratuitous way in which chap. iv is assimilated to chap. v by Burney's comment on iv 14: "*hath not Yahweh gone forth before thee*? The scene gains much in vividness if we may suppose (with Thomson, *LB.* p. 436) that Deborah, as she speaks, points to the gathering storm, which appears to have burst in the face of the foe at the commencement of the battle: cf. $5^{4.5.20.21}$ (*notes*); Jos. *Ant.* V.v. 4" (C. F. Burney, *Book of Judges* [London, 1918], pp. 90 f.). Here both chap. iv and chap. v are treated almost as if they were straightforward eye-witness accounts to be conflated with one another to create a total picture.

[53]) So e.g. H. Gressmann, *Die Anfänge Israels* (Göttingen, [2]1922), pp. 15 f., where besides *Heldensagen*, the description *alten volkstümlichen Sagen* is applied to the Judges stories as a whole, inclusive of Jdg. iv. On pp. 190 ff., the commentary on chapters iv and v uses *die Sage* as a standing designation.

Deborah. Indeed, the song of chapter v more adequately fulfils both these functions than the present prose narrative. Moreover, it may be pointed out in passing that the difficulty of finding clear evidence that the present text was essentially an *oral*, as against an *ab initio written*, text places a significant question-mark against a basic assumption involved in its classification as "(hero-)saga".

On the other hand, I do not deny the likelihood that some sort of oral "hero-saga" underlies the present Deborah-Barak story—indeed, perhaps more than one—so far as such is the likely source of the traditions on which it draws. However, it is at least as important to recognize that such material has formed but the basic stuff out of which our narrator has woven an intricate pattern of plot and theme, a structure in which the inherent irony of the situation between the two men and the two women has become the dominant motif.

Thus, finally, we must all the more recognize and allow for the fact that the literary nature and purpose of this text entail that any historical assessment in detail must carefully consider how far purely narrative considerations have dictated the ordering and relating of events, characters, and locale. It seems indisputable to me, for example, that Barak's immediate appearance on the scene in *v.* 22 is motivated by tightness of plot-structure and dramatic effect, and cannot therefore by itself lead to any conclusion about the relative locations of Jael's tent and Harosheth haggoyim [54]). Indeed the claim of *v.* 16, that Barak pursued Sisera's troops all the way to Harosheth-haggoyim (wherever that may be), may itself be due to a desire to heighten the effect of Barak's victory in order to emphasize by contrast his ultimate defeat, and more immediately, to make clear his absence from the scene-of-action of Sisera's flight to Jael's tent, about to follow. And so one could go on. These examples are perhaps relatively trivial [55]), but they illustrate concisely the dangers inherent

[54]) As for example is drawn from it by Hertzberg, p. 176, on iv 17; J. Gray, p. 272, on *vv.* 17-22; among others. J. D. Martin's comment (*Judges* [Cambridge, 1975] p. 61), on iv 22, on the other hand, shows greater perception here of narrative exigencies: "In any case, the narrative may have telescoped the chronology of the events".

[55]) The same cannot be said of H. H. Rowley's use of similar features in the Joseph and exodus narratives as important evidence in the debate over the chronology of the descent into Egypt and the exodus in *From Joseph to Joshua* (London, 1950), p. 24: "It is of the essence of the Biblical tradition of the Exodus that the building operations on which the Israelites were engaged were close to the palace, so that at the time of the birth of Moses Pharaoh's daughter might find herself in the vicinity of the Israelites when she went out for a walk, and at the time when

in failure adequately to assess and take account of the nature of the text.

There is nothing startlingly new in these conclusions, yet it is remarkable how easily they may be left out of account. The trouble arises in part from the fact that too often scholars work from generalized categorizations inherited from an earlier phase of scholarship, which are then allowed undue influence in their approach to specific pericopes. It is because such inherited categories as "historical narrative", "report" and "hero-saga" suggest that Jdg. iv 4-22 sets out to be, in its present form, some sort of historical or quasi-historical account of Barak's battle against Sisera, that inappropraté assumptions have been brought to bear in its interpretation, and an adequate understanding and appreciation of its true nature has not had a proper chance to develop.

As seen in the mirror of earlier scholarship, this text reflected a distorted image, which failed to do justice to its true proportions. It would be naive, not to say arrogant, to suppose that we, on the contrary, have delineated it truly. Nevertheless, the image depicted by a (properly) literary analysis has gained in brilliance and clarity, and certainly in interest. This at least argues that we see it thereby more adequately. If so, and in other cases no less than this one, then Old Testament scholarship stands to gain a great deal by embracing and developing, as it shows every sign of doing [56]), a method which can contribute to a better understanding of the texts which are the sum and substance of its study.

Moses led them out they were still in the neighbourhood of the court"; cf. the whole discussion on pp. 23-8, and again on p. 132. But it is essential to the dramatic impact of the narrative that there should be a series of rapid and immediate confrontations between the principal actors. Thus the logically consequent proximity of the Israelite settlement and the royal residence *need* have no historical foundation, and ought not to be made the basis of a far-reaching historical argument without independent attestation.

[56]) Thanks especially to the work of James Muilenburg and Luis Alonso Schökel and their pupils. Gunkel's pioneering efforts in this field have hitherto been rather neglected.

Schematic Summary of the Structure of the Deborah-Barak Story. (Jdg. iv 4-22)

EPISODE 1:4-10		EPISODE 2:11-16
1. *Tableau* 4 f.: Deborah at home as prophetess and judge (Prologue to narrative)		1. *Tableau* 11: Heber encam near Kedesh (Proleptic parenthesis) (*3rd change-of-scene*: from Heber's encampment to Sisera's fortress: elliptical intra-episode)
2. *Initiating action* 6a: Deborah summons Barak		2. *Initiating action* 12a: reporting of Barak's preparations to Sisera.
3. *Speech* 6b f: Deborah mediates to Barak the divine command and undertaking		3. *Speech* (indirect) 12b: gone up to Mt Tabor
4. *Response* 8-10: (a) *Counter-speech* 8, 9a: Barak attaches condition to response: Deborah accedes to condition but attaches penalty (b) *Action* 9b, 10: initiated by Deborah's accompanying Barak in his battle preparations (effecting:— *1st change-of-scene*: Deborah's home to Kedesh [? and Mt Tabor]: smooth intra-episode)	(*2nd change-of-scene*: from the muster at Kedesh [? Mt. Tabor] to Heber's encampment: abrupt inter-episode)	4. *Response* 13: *Action*: Sisera prepares for battle and marches to the Kishon (effecting: *4th change-of-scene*: from Sisera's fortress to positi by Kishon: smooth intra episode) (*5th change-of scene*: from Sisera's position on Kish to Barak's position on M Tabor: slightly ellipti intra-episode)
		3′. *Speech* 14a: Deborah give summons to battle
		4′. *Response* 14b-16: *Action*: Barak joins battle, Siser forces routed, Sisera flee (effecting: *6th and 7th changes-of-scen* from Mt Tabor to battl site, thence to Sisera's fortress: smooth intra-episode)

Schematic Summary of the Structure of the Deborah-Barak Story. (Jdg. iv 4-22)

	EPISODE 3:17-21		EPISODE 4:22
	1. *Tableau* 17a[b]: Sisera in flight has reached Jael's tent		1. *Tableau* 22aα: Barak in pursuit of Sisera has reached Jael's tent
	2. *Initiating action* 18aα: Jael comes out to meet Sisera		2. *Initiating action* 22aβ: Jael comes out to meet Barak
	3. *Speech* 18aβ: Jael summons Sisera to enter		3. *Speech* 22aγ: Jael summons Barak to enter and see Sisera
	4. *Response* 18b: *Action*: Sisera enters and Jael covers him (effecting: *9th change-of-scene*: from outside Jael's tent to inside: smooth intra-episode)		4. *Response* 22bα: *Action*: Barak enters (effecting:— *11th change-of-scene*: from outside Jael's tent to inside: smooth intra-episode)
hange-of- from 's fortress tside Jael's abrupt episode)	3′. *Speech* 19a: Sisera requests a drink	(*10th change-of* *scene*: from Sisera and Jael inside Jael's tent to Barak approaching on outside: abrupt inter-episode)	1′. *Final tableau* 22bβ, γ: victor confronts vanquished
	4′. *Response* 19b: *Action*: Jael provides milk and covers Sisera (Ellipse of verbal response)		
	3″. *Speech* 20: Sisera re- quests Jael to keep watch		
	4″. *Response* 21: *Action*: Jael murders Sisera (Ellipse of verbal response)		

THE PHILISTINE INCURSIONS INTO THE VALLEY OF REPHAIM (2 Sam. v 17 ff.)

by

N. L. TIDWELL

Alsager

The topographical and chronological difficulties in the present narrative sequence of 2 Sam. v are the common stock of every commentary on the chapter and every text-book on the history of Israel. On the chronological side, the present order of the text places David's encounters with the Philistines in the valley of Rephaim *after* his capture of Jerusalem but the introduction to the account of the two battles presents at least the first of them as the immediate Philistine reaction to the anointing of David at Hebron *before* his successful assault on Jerusalem. From the topographical angle, the comment that in response to the Philistine invasion David "went down to the stronghold" (*v.* 17) makes better sense with reference to Adullam or some other hide-out of David's Hebron period than to the recently acquired "stronghold of Zion" (*vv.* 7, 9). In addition, the location of the Rephaim valley is itself uncertain [1]) and the setting of the second battle (*vv.* 22-25) in Rephaim is open to suspicion [2]).

No universally accepted solution to these difficulties exists. The evidence has been interpreted in three main ways, placing the capture of Jerusalem either before, after or between the two battles [3]). Behind every solution that has been proposed, however, there lies what appears to be a largely unexamined assumption that the historical *reference* of the stories in 2 Sam. v 17-25 in their *present setting* is essentially, or in some cases very specifically, correct and *original*. At the same time it is widely acknowledged today that the material in 2 Sam. v has undergone considerable adaptation and re-arrangement in the course of that process of tradition from which the present text

---

[1]) For the three main sites that have been advocated see C. E. Hauer, Jr., "Jerusalem, the Stronghold and Rephaim", *CBQ* 32 (1970), p. 573, note 10.

[2]) Cf. the remarks of E. G. Kraeling, *Rand McNally Bible Atlas* (New York, 1956), p. 198, and see further below.

[3]) A representative list of advocates of each of these views is given in Hauer, p. 571, notes 1, 2 and 3.

emerged [4]). At various stages in this history of tradition older material was adapted to serve new purposes and the earlier narrative or annalistic order of events was re-arranged to suit the needs of a larger narrative sequence. Thus, for example, before its incorporation into that chapter of the Deuteronomic History Work which forms our present book(s) of Samuel, the largest tradition (and possibly literary) complex to which 2 Sam. v belonged was the story of David's Rise [5]), of which it was apparently the concluding chapter appropriately culminating in the final defeat of the Philistines and the capture of Jerusalem. Within the larger context of the *Vorgeschichte Davids* 2 Sam. ii (46)—v has also been recognised as a separate unit representing a yet earlier stage in the gathering together of the material of this part of 2 Sam.[6]). In this smaller composition chapter v has again the character of an appropriate recapitulating conclusion (cf. Carlson, p. 49). This kind of tradition-history which is thought to lie behind the present form of 2 Sam. v is a clear enough warning that the present import of the materials in this chapter and the purpose they now serve may well not be their original import and purpose. At least an exact or necessary identity of their original and their present purpose cannot or ought not to be unquestionably assumed. But this is precisely the assumption which is made by all existing attempts to solve the problems presented by the two accounts of battles against the Philistines in the valley of Rephaim. Every existing solution, no matter how it relates these battles chronologically to the capture of Jerusalem, accepts that the stories describe, as in their *present setting* it is their obvious purpose to do, two *major clashes* between David and the Philistines which had *far-reaching politico-military consequences* for ancient Israel. The message of the present text is that by these two encounters Yahweh through David finally opened the way to the total fulfilment of the ancient promise of the Land.

That the accounts of the Philistine incursions into the valley of Rephaim have some such purpose in the present form of the text is

---

[4]) For the traditio-historical criticism of this chapter see especially, M. Noth, *Überlieferungsgeschichtliche Studien* I (Halle, 1943), pp. 63, 105, note 5; R. A. Carlson, *David the Chosen King. A Traditio-Historical Approach to the Second Book of Samuel* (Uppsala, 1964), pp. 52-57; J. H. Grønbaek, *Die Geschichte vom Aufstiegs Davids* (*1 Sam. 15-2 Sam 5*) (Copenhagen, 1971), pp. 242-52.

[5]) In addition to the literature cited in note 4 see also L. Rost, *Die Überlieferung von der Thronnachfolge Davids* 6 (Stuttgart, 1926).

[6]) Cf. H. Gressmann, *Die älteste Geschichtsschreibung und Prophetie Israels* [2] (Göttingen, 1921) pp. xiv ff.; also Carlson, pp. 41-49; Grønbaek, p. 254.

not to be denied. At the final stage in the tradition-history of 2 Sam. v that is how the Israelite "author" understood them and that may be how they were seen and interpreted at even earlier stages in their tradition. But was that their *original reference*? This is a form-critical rather than a tradition-history question and in view of the widely acknowledged, because immediately obvious fact of the close similarity in content and structure between the two Rephaim stories (*vv.* 17-21, 22-25) it is remarkable that so little attention has been given to the form-critical aspects of the text [7]). Almost universally the character of the materials in 2 Sam. v is held to be "fragmentary" [8]) and the chapter has been described as "a composite of several traditions narrating several different episodes" [9]). But if this is the case there is even less justification for assuming that the *present literary context* of any of these fragmentary traditions is a true reflection of or a reliable guide to its *original historical reference*. This is especially true in the case of the traditions about David's encounters with the Philistines in the valley of Rephaim.

It is widely held that *vv.* 17-25 have been removed at some stage in their tradition-history from an earlier position immediately following *v.* 3 [10]). This hardly affects the question of any serious change in their purpose in the narrative and, in itself, has led no one to suspect that the historical reference of the stories has been at all radically modified in the process. However it does indicate that the stories have suffered some degree of dislocation in the course of their tradition-history. In the view of some scholars [11]) 2 Sam. v 17-25 originally belonged with the general summary of David's victories in 2 Sam. viii and was drawn ultimately from court annals. In this case these Rephaim stories are in the *earliest stage of their existence* cut loose entirely from their present context and the historical validity of their location in 2 Sam. v must be decided either on the *a priori* grounds

[7]) H. W. Hertzberg, *I and II Samuel* (London, 1964), p. 272 (= *Die Samuelbücher* [2](Göttingen, 1960]) comments that the two episodes are juxtaposed "because of their content" and need not "therefore have been immediately consecutive in time", but does not follow this insight through to its logical conclusion.

[8]) Cf. Grønbaek, p. 246; Carlson, pp. 52-7; also P. Dhorme, *Les Livres de Samuel*, (Paris, 1910), p. 316, and J. Mauchline, *1 and 2 Samuel* (London, 1971), p. 215.

[9]) J. Flanagan, *A Study of the Traditions Pertaining to the Foundation of the Monarchy in Israel*, Diss., University of Notre Dame, 1971, p. 47 (University Microfilms).

[10]) This has been a commonplace of Literary Criticism since J. Wellhausen, *Die Composition des Hexateuchs* [2] (Berlin, 1889), p. 256.

[11]) Cf. especially A. Alt, "Zu II Sam. 8, 1", *ZAW* 54, (1936), pp. 149-52.

that the ancient tradents must have known what the stories originally referred to and have used them accordingly and with due respect for historical "fact", or on grounds of historical probability, or *in the light of the clues, if any, afforded by the stories themselves when examined in isolation from their present context.* So far as the first alternative is concerned we can at least say that, even if the biblical "authors" did not deliberately distort or falsify history for theological purposes, yet certainly they were rarely if ever motivated by a strict concern for historicity in what they wrote and their methods of composition often reveal the priority of literary or theological considerations over purely historical ones in determining the sequence of events and juxtaposition of stories [12]). In terms of the second alternative, two decisive encounters between David and the Philistines in preparation for or in reaction to his successful assault on Jerusalem (or in both circumstances) or a Philistine invasion in response to the anointing of David over a united Judah-Israel and another incursion to prevent or counteract his capture of Jerusalem all have considerable theoretical historical probability. But such theoretical reconstructions of Israelite and Philistine strategy have value only as an index of the imaginative creativity of their authors if they are not explicitly corroborated by the evidence of the biblical stories themselves. That is to say, the third alternative, the study of the stories *in isolation from their present setting*, is alone able to provide the grounds upon which a theoretical reconstruction in terms of historical probability may be reliably built. This however, necessitates a form-critical analysis of the relevant traditions which must begin with an attempt to identify their form(s) (*Gattungen*).

The form (*Gattung*) of the two stories of *vv.* 17-25 is that of "battle-reports" or, more precisely, "*short* battle-reports" although neither of them features in the discussions of this form by W. Richter [13]), J. Plöger [14]), J. Van Seters [15]), or D. M. Gunn [16]). Richter's analysis

---

[12]) For the various literary or theological features which may have influenced the placement of the two Rephaim battle stories see Hertzberg, p. 272 (similarity of content), Carlson, p. 58 f. (associative words), Campbell, (see n. 17) p. 69 (the common oracular element).

[13]) *Traditionsgeschichtliche Untersuchungen zum Richterbuch* (Bonn, 1963) pp. 292-6.

[14]) *Literarkritische, formgeschichtliche und stilkritische Untersuchungen zum Deuteronomium* (Bonn, 1967), pp. 16-19.

[15]) "The Conquest of Sihon's Kingdom: A Literary Examination", *JBL* 91 (1972), pp. 182-97.

[16]) "Narrative Patterns and Oral Tradition in Judges and Samuel", *VT* 24 (1974) pp. 286-317.

of this *Gattung* lays particular stress upon the verbs which recount four different stages of the action:

1. Verbs of movement (*Bewegung*): *yāṣā'*; *hālakh*; *bô'*.
2. Verbs of military activity (*Kriegstechnik*): *ḥānāh*; *nilḥam*; *'āsaph*.
3. Verbs describing the result: *lāqaḥ*, *lākhadh* (cities); *hikkāh*, *nāghaph* (persons); and *nûs*, *rādhaph* for flight, pursuit.
4. Conclusion briefly indicating the extent of the engagement: expressions with *min* + place name, *we'adh* + place name (or *he locale*) and summary statements of the *maggēphāh*/*makkāh gēdhôlāh* kind.

J. Plöger and A. F. Campbell [17]), who alone discusses the battle report form of 2 Sam. v. 17-25, concentrate on structure and content rather than terminology and recognise four main elements in this *Gattung*:

1. Description of confrontation of forces, including the assembling of troops and the location of the camp or battle (Plöger's *Situationsangabe*).
2. Consultation of the oracle (Plöger's *Preisgabe-(Übereignungs)-formel*).
3. Battle tactics [18]).
4. Results and consequences—e.g. flight, pursuit, slaughter, casuality figures, booty. (3 + 4 = Plöger's *Siegesmeldung und Aufzählung der militarische Ereignisse*).

Recognition of the existence of this convention in the recording of accounts of battles is important for historical criticism. In the light of this convention it may be seen that the close similarities in form between battle-reports throughout the Old Testament, and between 2 Sam. v 17-21 and v 22-25 especially, do not indicate that all the battles so described belong to *the same category of military engagement*. If 2 Sam. v 17-21 describes a large scale major clash with the Philistines as a whole it does not follow merely from its similarity in form that *vv*. 22-25 describe an encounter of the same magnitude, and vice versa. But in the context of the relatively fixed form of a conventional battle-report the individual historical character, the particularity of each battle, will be revealed most clearly by those features, whether

---

[17]) Campbell, *The Ark Narrative. A Form-Critical and Traditio-Historical Study* (*1 Sam. 4-6*; *2 Sam. 6*) (Missoula, 1975).

[18]) The actual contest is not normally described in these battle reports, according to Van Seters, p. 188.

major or minor, in which the one report differs from all others. Here, obviously, such details as the location of the camp or battle scene, the route of flight or pursuit and any integral or incidental features of local colour (e.g. *Ortskenntnis*) will differ from story to story and in each report may reflect something of the particularity of the original historical reference of a given battle. Equally obviously, the name of the enemy and any indication of the size of the forces or type of troops involved will be another possibly significant variable within the conventional form. So too the different battle tactics may be a revealing variable, and there may be a significant variation in the conventional terminology employed.

Now on the point of terminology an interesting feature of the battle-reports in 2 Sam. v 17-25 which receives little attention from commentators is the rare use of the verb *nṭš* (Niph.) in a military sense [19]) and the substitution of the not so common but (in a similar military sense) not very frequently used *pšṭ* in 1 Chron. xiv 9, 13 [20]). On the three cases of *nṭš* (Niph.) for which a general sense of "spread abroad, be let go" is given, BDB comments that in these three cases accompanied by *b loc* the sense is to spread out "for purpose of plunder". Here then is apparently a term describing that particular type of military activity, the razzia, whose aim is not to engage a foe in any decisive confrontation or pitched battle but to gather spoils, and whose distinctive tactics would be the use of a limited number of troops who could strike suddenly and swiftly and as suddenly and swiftly withdraw. The Qal Ptc. Pass. of *nṭš* may well have the same connotation as the Niph. in the context of a very full and illuminating account of such a raid "for purpose of plunder" in 1 Sam. xxx.[21]). Here the activities of a marauding "band" (*gᵉdhûdh*) are described in some detail. Their aim is not conquest nor slaughter but booty—in the form of slaves and goods: "they killed no one but carried them off" (*v.* 2; cf. *v.* 19)—and to this end they had "made a

[19]) It is employed only three times in the O.T. at Jgs. xv 9 and 2 Sam. v 18, 22. K. Budde, *Die Bücher Samuel* (Tübingen, 1902), p. 33, cites Löhr for the reading *wattināṭēš* for *wattiṭṭōš* at 1 Sam. iv 2 but G. R. Driver, "Studies in the Vocabulary of the Old Testament VI", *JTS* 34 (1933), p. 379, adequately explains MT as a form of $\sqrt{}$*ytš*, to clash together.

[20]) The military sense is apparent in 12 places in O.T.. Only Chronicles has *pšṭ* followed by the preposition *b*.

[21]) S. R. Driver, *Notes on the Hebrew Text and Topography of the Books of Samuel* [2] (Oxford, 1913), p. 263, compares 1 Sam. xxx. 16 with the Niph. usage. Consonantally, of course, the text requires no change to read(either the Qal Pass. Ptc. or the Niph. Ptc.

raid" (*pšṭ*) on the Negeb. To deal with them David first enquired of the oracle (*vv.* 7-8) and then set out with his six hundred men, of whom only four hundred were actually used in the final assault on the raiding party (*vv.* 9-10). David and his men came upon the marauders to find them (*v.* 16) "spread abroad over all the land (RSV. MT = *neṭûšîm*), eating and drinking and dancing (Heb. = *weḥōgheghîm*), because of the great spoil they had taken". It makes sense strategically to imagine that David took advantage of the fact that the band were widely scattered ("spread abroad") when he came upon them but it makes equally good sense in the context of the story to take the Ptc. *nṭš* here to be a general statement that they "were looting, plundering, all over the area", which is amplified by the three following participles and further qualified by the last clause of the verse. At any rate, in its context in 1 Sam. xxx *nṭš* is clearly a term appropriate for the specific activities of a raiding party. The "spreading abroad" in this case is not a deployment of troops in preparation for a pitched battle for which the more usual term would be *ʿārakh milḥāmāh* [22]). In 2 Sam. v 17 ff. a very general term of movement (*bôʾ*) introduces the first battle report (*v.* 18) but it is followed by the term for a specialized type of military activity (*Kriegstechnik*), *nṭš* (Niph.) and this significant "variable" should not be overlooked in any attempt to clarify the character of the battle here recounted. It is the term to describe such operations as that of a raiding party in search of plunder. It suggests not a large scale military action but a raid capable of being handled by and normally requiring a small detachment of troops no larger than a contemporary "battalion" [23]).

The impression given by the unusual terminology of 2 Sam. v 18 (22) is heightened rather than diminished by the Chronicler's preference for *pšṭ*. Wherever this term is employed in a military sense

---

[22]) Cf. Jgs. xx 22; 1 Sam. iv 2, xvii 8; 2 Sam. x 18, etc. The distinction still holds even in 1 Sam. xxiii 3 where the fear of David's men is grounded on the fact that their own "irregular" band of outcasts has to face the Philistine "troops of the line" (*maʿarekhôth pelištîm*). Cf. J. Wellhausen, *Der Text der Bücher Samuelis* (Göttingen, 1892), p. 126.

[23]) The normal size of a "battling unit" is set at 1,000 by A. van Selms, "The Armed Forces of Israel under Saul and David", in *Studies in the Books of Samuel*, OTWSA 3rd Meeting Papers (Stellenbosch, 1960), p. 64. B. Mazar, "The Military Elite of King David", *VT* 13 (1963), p. 314, regards 600 as the size of a "regiment" comprising two fighting units (of 200 men each) and one reserve. Y. Yadin, *The Art of Warfare in Biblical Lands* (London, 1963), p. 112, reckons a "company" as 250 men and refers to an assault unit of 300 men as a norm at Mari (p. 73).

it describes actions which, however much they may otherwise differ, have the common element of "making a dash", mounting a sudden and swift attack either from concealment [24]) or, as in the case of *nṭš* (Niph.), for purposes of plunder or robbery [25]). This latter sense is evident in Hos. vii 1 and Job i 17 and it is reasonably clear, especially from the context, in 1 Sam. xxvii 8, 10, xxx 1, 14; 2 Chron. xxv 13. This may also be the sense in 2 Chron. xxviii 18 if the "raids" on the Shephelah and Negeb of Judah stand in some contrast rather than in parallel to the "capture" (*lkd*) and "settlement" (*yšb*) of the towns there. It is, of course, worth noting that "raiding" (*pšṭ*) most frequently takes place in the border regions (Shephelah, Negeb); cf. 1 Sam. xxx 1, xxvii 10. In the case of Job i 17 the apparently irrelevant detail that the Chaldeans had "formed three companies" (*rā'šîm*) should not be taken necessarily to imply the involvement of a large military force. A division of a fighting force into three "companies" was standard military practice in ancient Israel and among her neighbours [26]). Even as small a force as 300 could be so divided (Jgs. vi 16, 20), and perhaps David's "six hundred" were reckoned as three "companies" of 200 men each (1 Sam. xxx 9-10). The same division into *rā'šîm* for the raid on Job's camels is also specified for the operations of the Philistine raiding parties from Michmash (1 Sam. xiii 17). Contextually it is clear that *nṭš* (Niph.) and *pšṭ* (Qal) used with reference to military manœuvres are virtually synonymous. By the time of the Chronicler and the Septuagint they must, indeed, have been fully interchangeable terms unless one (*nṭš*) was by then dropping out of use or had already become obsolete. The Chronicler therefore employs *pšṭ* for *nṭš*, substituting what was in his day the more common term in this technical military sense for the rarer and older usage [27]), and the Septuagint translated both by the same verb,

---

[24]) Cf. Abimelech's surprise "dash" on the gate of Shechem. (Jgs. ix 33, 44), and the ambush at Gibeah (Jgs. xx 37).

[25]) Cf. *BDB pšṭ* Qal 2, "especially of a marauding foray" and cf. 1 Sam. xiii, 17 and xxiii, 27.

[26]) Cf. Mazar, p. 314; Y. Yadin, p. 264. See especially Gen. xiv 15; Jgs. vii 16, ix 43; 1 Sam. xi 11, xiii 17; 2 Sam. xviii 2; Job i 17.

[27]) Wellhausen, *Text*, p. 165, remarks that *pšṭ* in Sam. generally is used in a sense inappropriate at *v.* 18, 22. There could have been confusion of *nûn* and *pe* in the old Hebrew Script together with the simple transposition of *shin* and *ṭeth* in the transmission of the text between the time of Samuel and Chronicles and LXX. This might explain the use of following *b* which is exclusive to *pšṭ* in Chronicles.

συμπίπτειν [28]). In the case of either verb the common *Kriegstechnik* implied is an operation by a small band for such a purpose as pillage or plunder. The use of *nṭš* at 2 Sam. v 18 (22) is a significant pointer to the original reference of the story to a raid by a detachment of Philistine troops and not to a large scale invasion by "all the Philistines" (*v.* 17).

It is widely held that 2 Sam. v 17-25 is somehow bound up with the traditions of David's heroes in xxi 15-22 and xxiii 8-17. Carlson believes that all three passages originally belonged together [29]) while M. H. Segal [30]), considering it possible that all three are derived from one literary source, reconstructs out of a compound of them all a sequence of three main Philistine campaigns in the time of David [31]). Eissfeldt has observed that 2 Sam. xxi 15 reveals an originally narrative context for these hero stories and is inclined to believe they were at one time the sequel to 2 Sam. v 17-25 [32]). The links between xxiii 13-17 and 2 Sam. v 17 ff. are fairly obvious to any reader [33]). It is important to bear these observations in mind when pondering the historical problems of 2 Sam. v. For example, 2 Sam. xxiii 11-12 describes an exploit of one Shammah who faced the Philistines alone at Lehi. There are a number of respects in which this brief notice about Shammah is important for the understanding of 2 Sam. v 17 ff[34].). In the first place the pointing of the Hebrew rendered "Lehi" by RSV is uncertain but both of the two possible pointings adopted by commentators and translators contribute something to this present study. MT points *laḥayyāh* to which commentators generally pay little heed. Now *ḥayyāh* appears to be a feminine of *ḥy* meaning a "clan" or some such family or social unit (1 Sam. xvii 18),

[28]) Acc. to Wellhausen, *Text*, p. 165, LXX 2 Sam. v 18 and 22 was influenced by the Chronicler's version in the first place.

[29]) pp. 56-7. Cf. also Budde, p. 224; Hertzberg, p. 405; L. H. Brockington, "I and II Samuel", *Peake's Commentary* (London, 1962), pp. 332, 336.

[30]) "The Composition of the Books of Samuel", *JQR*, N.S. 56 (1965/6) pp. 32-50.

[31]) The first, in Rephaim, comprises v. 17-18, xxiii 13-17 and v 19-21; the second, at Gob, includes v 22, xxi 15-19, xxiii 9-10, 11-12, v 23-25, and the third xxi 20-21, viii 1 at Gath.

[32]) *The Old Testament. An Introduction* (Oxford, 1965), p. 278 (= *Einleitung*^{3} [Tübingen, 1964], p. 371).

[33]) E.g. the common setting in Rephaim, the common "descent" to the stronghold, and, despite the vocabulary difference (*bqʿ/prṣ*), the common success in "breaking through" the enemy.

[34]) The Chronicler conflates the stories of Shammah and Eleazar and sets the scene of what is properly Shammah's deed in Pas-dammim.

i.e. a group of limited size, and thus here and two verses later (2 Sam. xxiii 13) it would denote a small military force, a raiding party [35]). MT 2 Sam. xxiii 11 would then mean "the Philistines gathered together in a raiding party" [36]), and the story of Shammah may then be added to the evidence that "raids" (*nṭš*, *pšṭ*) normally involved small detachments of troops. However, the words which follow *laḥayyāh* in the Hebrew (*watteʰhî šām*), argue strongly that *lḥyh* is a place name and is better pointed *leḥyāh* [37]). This possibility can also contribute significantly to our investigation. Lehi was somewhere *on the border* in the Shephelah [38]) and it is the very same place upon which the Philistines "made a raid" (*nṭš* Niph.) in Judges xv 9. They came up (*ʿālāh*) (general term of movement with a military overtone), encamped (*ḥānāh*) (general term of military activity) in Judah, and "made a raid" (term for a more specific military operation) on Lehi. Unless the exploits of Samson and Shammah at Lehi are derived from one and the same original we must conclude that Lehi was the target of such habitual "raiding" that it called frequently for heroic deeds from its young men and thus passed on to Israel and to our Old Testament two hero stories associated with it.

Be that as it may, another striking feature of the Shammah pericope is the disproportionate space devoted to the detail of a certain "plot of lentils" [39]). The brevity of the notices of the exploits of the Three reminds one of the list of Minor Judges (Jgs. x 1-5, xii 8-15) and the agricultural details of the Shammah story can hardly be less significant then the details of the offspring of Jair, Ibzan or Abdon [40]). Lehi, one suspects, was agriculturally a productive locality and it is not pressing the point too far to imagine that the "plot of lentils" is indicative of the goal of the Philistine raid which Shammah beat off.

---

[35]) Driver, *Notes*, p. 366, defines the term as a "*clan* making a raid together" and remarks that "No doubt the occasion also was the same" as in 2 Sam. v 18.

[36]) Cf. Mazar, who translates "the Philistines were arrayed in a fighting force". Mauchline, p. 316 offers "in a troop" as a possible reading of MT. Chronicles (see note 34) omits 2 Sam. xxiii 9b-11a and at *v*. 15 with *ḥōnāh* following substitutes *maḥᵃnēh* for *ḥayyath*; cf. Wellhausen, *Text*, p. 214.

[37]) So e.g. Driver, *Notes*, p. 365. LXX ἐπι σιαγόνα also presupposes *Leḥi*.

[38]) The precise location of Lehi is unknown but it was apparently somewhere in the region of Timnah and the rock of Etam in what Kraeling describes as the "garden district" of *wadi Arṭas* (*Rand McNally Atlas*, p. 164).

[39]) 1 Chron. xi 13 reads *śeʿārîm* (barley) for *ʿᵃdhāšîm*. This may be simply a result of the frequent confusion of *resh* and *daleth* (so Dhorme, p. 436).

[40]) The figure 30 also links David's heroes with the Minor Judges. 30 appears to represent the number of the companions of the head of a clan, Jgs. xiv 11; 1 Sam. ix 22. Cf. Mazar, p. 310.

The aim of the expedition, one may reasonably surmise, was the stealing of harvested crops to swell the Philistine food supply or the deliberate destruction of the ripened crops as a way of undermining the enemy and forcing (or maintaining) submission by starvation. It was the rescue of Lehi's harvest from plunderers and its defence against pillagers that earned for Shammah a place in the Israelite memory of "mighty men". This conclusion is confirmed by the similar circumstances of the Samson story that is set in Lehi, Jgs. xv 1 ff. It is an occasion when the Philistines "make a raid" (*nṭš* Niph.) on Lehi in order "to do to Samson as he did to them" (*v.* 10) and the mischief of Samson they wish to repay in kind was the burning of their crops at harvest time (*bîmê qeṣîr-ḥiṭṭîm*). Both its location on the border between the Philistines and Israelites and its reputation as a productive agricultural area may have made Lehi a site frequently raided and an area in which many a warrior became a hero. For this reason Lehi has provided for the Old Testament a rich store of hero stories and topographical aetiologies associated with a hero figure, Jgs. xv 14, 17, 19; 2 Sam. xxiii 1-12.

The time when crops are ripe for harvesting or have just been harvested and the threat of the razzia is imminent (cf. Jgs. vi 3) [41]) is also the setting for that story of the Three which stands closest of all to 2 Sam. v 17 ff. It was at harvest time (*qāṣîr*) that "a band of the Philistines was encamped in the valley of Rephaim" (2 Sam. xxiii 13) [42]). The situation implied by the story is that from a Philistine garrison [43]) at Bethlehem (*v.* 14), a small detachment (*ḥayyāh*) had gone out as a raiding party or patrol of some kind. This is, in fact, exactly the kind of picture of Philistine military activities in the days of Saul and the Hebron-period of David which the rest of the evidence paints. After Aphek major pitched battles involving large numbers are few and are generally the result of some serious provocation [44]) on

---

[41]) The present text implies a raid at seedtime (Jgs. vi 3) but the whole enterprise as well as the details of *v.* 11 require the season of wheat harvest. Possibly the original text had "seed", expressed or understood, as the subject of the first *ʿālāh*.

[42]) The expression *ʾel-qāṣîr* is unusual and some prefer to read with Chron. and LXX *ʿal-haṣṣûr*, taking this with the preceding *rōʾš* in the sense of "top of the cliff" (Mazar, p. 315). The indication of place, however, follows *ʾel-dāwîd* and a time indication such as *rōʾš qāṣîr* is possible and meaningful. Cf. Dhorme, p. 437; Budde, p. 321; Driver, *Notes*, p. 366. For a similar expression see Jgs. vii 19; Num. x 10.

[43]) MT *maṣṣābh* but 1 Chron. xi 16 *neṣîbh*.

[44]) See Hauer, p. 574, with notes 13 and 14. Y. Aharoni, *The Land of the Bible*, (London, 1967), p. 255, observes that in the narratives concerning David all the

the part of the Israelites. For the most part Israel is portrayed as a land garrisoned by the forces of an occupying power, e.g. the garrisons at Gibeath-elohim 1 Sam. x 5, at Geba (LXX Gibeah) 1 Sam. xiii 3, and at Michmash 1 Sam. xiii 23, xiv 1, 4, 6, 11, 15 [45]). The countryside around these garrisons doubtless needed patrolling from time to time and the garrisons must certainly have relied upon local produce for their food supply. Also, when they had guaranteed their own supplies, possibly the destruction of the ripened grain in the fields or on the threshing floors (1 Sam. xxiii 1) [46]) within striking distance of any garrison may have been one sure way to prevent supplies going to Israelite guerrilla groups and to keep the local population in submission (cf. the picture of the state of affairs of the local farmers in 1 Sam. xiii 19-22). For any one of these activities, however, only a small detachment of troops would normally be needed. Thus from the Michmash garrison three detachments (*rā'šîm*) of "raiders" were sent out. These "raiders" are a specific task force within the total Philistine host (*kol-hā'ām*) [47]) distinct from or at any rate distinguishable from the garrison (1 Sam. xiv 15). The RSV "raiders" is in the Hebrew *hammašḥîth*, defined by Driver as "a body of raiders, probably a technical term denoting that part of the army employed in ravaging and destruction" [48]). It is the term used to describe the effect of a bedouin razzia in Jgs. vi 4. Like *mašḥîth* and *ḥayyāh* (2 Sam. xxiii 13) another term used to indicate a small group engaged in raiding (*pšṭ*) and looting (?) (*nṭš*) (1 Sam. xxx 1, 8, 15, 16)

encounters with the Philistines "seem to be limited to border skirmishes and plundering raids".

[45]) In some instances it is not easy to decide whether a "garrison" or a "governor" (or even a "monument") is indicated by the terms used. 1 Sam. xiii 3 (*neṣîbh*) seems to be a "governor" or "victory stele"; cf. Kraeling, p. 180; J. Blenkinsopp, "Did Saul make Gibeah his Capital?", *VT* 24, (1974), p. 2, note 3.

[46]) Here the narrative speaks specifically of a foraging party robbing the threshing floors of Keilah somewhere in the Adullam region. According to Driver, *Notes*, p. 183, it was a noted corn-growing area and Budde aptly comments (p. 187) that the incident took place in midsummer, the favourite time for raiding, when the harvested crops lay exposed on the threshing floors often for several months.

[47]) The precise meaning of MT 1 Sam. xiv 15 is difficult to ascertain. LXX irons out some of the difficulties by substituting the conjunction for the preposition before *kol-(hā)'ām* (cf. *BHK*). But in both MT and LXX the distinction between the garrison, or main body of Philistine troops, and the "raiders" is quite clear.

[48]) The word, regarded as a collective is seen by M.T. Houtsma,, "Textkritisches", *ZAW* 27 (1907), p. 59, as applicable to that special section of an ancient army which had the task of "destruction" such as tree-felling, filling up wells and demolition of buildings.

or to refer to the action of "raiding" wich an eye to spoils (2 Sam. iii 22) is *g^e^dhûdh*. It is used of "marauding banditti" [49]) in such texts as Gen. xlix 19; 1 Sam. xxx 8, 15; 1 Kings xi 24; 2 Kings v 2, vi 23; Hos. vi 9; Job xxix 25. In 2 Chron. xxvi 11 it appears to denote a "division" or "detachment" of troops within an army. 1 Sam. xxx thus confirms that *pšṭ* and *nṭš* are both terms more appropriate to describe the activities of a small raiding party than to portray major troop movements preparatory to a large scale, decisive engagement.

It begins to appear that behind the stories which, by their present position in 2 Sam v, ostensibly refer to decisive encounters between David and the Philistines there lie accounts of what were originally nothing more than the successful routing of Philistine raiding parties engaged in foraging for supplies for local garrisons or intent on destroying the harvested crops of the Israelites as they lay exposed on the threshing floors or burning the ripened corn as it still stood in the fields. The very scene of these encounters may well point to the same conclusion for they both (at least in the present and final state of the text) are set, in common with 2 Sam. xxiii 13-17, in *ʿēmeq R^e^phāʾîm*. We have seen that Lehi may have fed several hero stories and aetiologies into Israel's tradition because it was a frequent target for raiding parties whose aim was to steal or destroy the ripened or harvested crops. The *ʿēmeq R^e^phāʾîm* may well be in the same category. Two of the three stories of military action against the Philistines in this valley characterise the Philistine presence there as "raiding" (*nṭš* Niph., or *pšṭ*) and the third (2 Sam. xxiii 13) speaks of a *ḥayyāh*, a small raiding party, active in the valley at harvest time. Now, like Keilah in the Shephelah, where a Philistine raid with the express purpose of robbing (*šsh*) threshing floors took place (1 Sam. xxiii 1), the valley of Rephaim was a noted corn growing area. It seems to have been to Judaeans of the eighth century BC a proverbially productive valley, Is. xvii 5, and it may well have been so even from the time before the Conquest.

The importance of the site as a source of food supplies is not the only common feature that the valley of Rephaim shares with Lehi. Both Samson and Shammah belonged to that class of *gibbôrîm* who were not simply mighty warriors but more precisely Israelite "cham-

---

[49]) So H. P. Smith, *A Critical and Exegetical Commentary on the Books of Samuel* (Edinburgh, 1899), p. 247. Driver, Notes, p. 222, speaks of its use to describe a "marauding or plundering band". The same term served for both the *Streifzug* and the *Streifschar* (Budde, p. 187).

pions" [50]) whose speciality was hand to hand fighting in single combat. The Samson story throughout tells of one who took on a whole army alone and to portray the action in which he finally met victory-in-death the Old Testament uses the technical term for "representative fighting" such as single combat, *śḥq* (Piel), Jgs. xvi 25 [51]). Shammah, of course was in any case one of the three *gibbôrîm* and, on the occasion of his mighty deed in the plot of lentils at Lehi, when the militia fled before the Philistines (*v.* 11) he alone "took his stand" (*yṣb* Hithpael; cf. Goliath in 1 Sam. xvii 16) and challenged the enemy. One of the battle-rituals performed by these "champions" was taunting (*ḥrp* Piel) (1 Sam. xvii 10, 25, 26. RSV = "defy") which Eleazar and David did to the Philistines according to MT 2 Sam. xxiii 9—Eleazar being in Chronicles the hero to whom Shammah's deed appears to be ascribed and resited at Pas-dammim (1 Chr. xi 12-14) [52]). Now the Philistine equivalent of Israel's "champions" were men like Goliath, Ishbi-benob [53]) and Saph who were technically known as *'îš habbēnayim* (1 Sam. xvii 4, 23) and were also classed somewhat more enigmatically as *yelîdhê hārāphāh* (2 Sam. xxi 16, 18) or *yulladh lehārāphāh* (*vv.* 20, 21). The Chronicler, together with most modern commentators, understood *hārāphāh* as equivalent to *rephā'îm* which elsewhere in the Old Testament is not only a term for the departed in Sheol (Job xxvi 5; Ps. lxxxviii 10; Is. xxvi 9, 14) but also describes the *'anāqîm* (Deut. ii 11, 20, iii 11), men of great stature, giants, who lived in pre-Israelite Transjordan. Both in 2 Sam. v 18, 22 and 2 Sam. xxiii 13 the Septuagint translates Rephaim by τιτάνες while the Chronicles translator preferred the synonym γιγάντες, 1 Chr. xiv 9, 13. There seem to be fair grounds for suspecting that the very name *'ēmeq rephā'îm* reflects the fact that this valley was frequently the arena for contests involving "champions" or warriors who be-

---

50) For *gibbôrîm*, *'ōzerê hammilḥāmāh*, etc., as "champions" see Mazar, pp. 317, 318, note 8; R. de Vaux, "Single Combat in the Old Testament" in *The Bible and the Ancient Near East* (London, 1972) pp. 122-35 (= *Biblica* 40 [1959], pp. 495-508).

51) For this technical term cf. de Vaux, p. 131; Y. Sukenik (Yadin), "Let the Young Men, I pray thee, Arise and Play Before Us", *JPOS* 21 (1948), pp. 110-16; O. Eissfeldt, "Eine gescheiterter Versuch der Wiedervereinigungs Israels", and "Noch einmal. . .", *KS* III (Tübingen, 1966), pp. 132-46; 147-50.

52) In the context of the ritual of representative fighting MT *beḥārephām* makes perfectly good sense.

53) Possibly MT (Q) *weyišbiw* (K: *wyšbw*) *benōbh* (2 Sam. xxi 16) should read *wayyēšebhû benōbh* (or *beghōbh*) and the Philistine's name is concealed in *wayyā'aph dāwīdh*. Cf. *BHK* and Wellhausen, *Text*, p. 209.

longed to some special military elite or guild known in ancient Israel as *y^e^lîdhê hārāphāh* or *r^e^phā'îm*.

In the last two decades the whole question of the connotation of the word *r^e^phā'îm* has been re-examined several times as a result of the publication of Ras Shamra Rephaim Texts (*CTA* 20-22). Without reference to Ugaritic F. Willesen [54]) has argued that in the phrases *yalîdh hārāphāh/yulladh l^e^hārāphāh* the second term is an appellative—thus the anomalous uncontracted *lamedh*—and the whole phrase denotes "one dedicated to a deity" (*yālîdh*) (p. 328) whose symbol was "the royal Syro-Palestinian scimitar" (*hārāphāh* related to *ḥrp* translated in 1 Sam xvii by ἅρπη, sickle) (p. 331). The Ugaritic Rephaim texts have not proved easy to interpret with any confidence [55]) but the Ras Shamra material as a whole shows the Rephaim (*rp'um*) to be in some cases semidivine beings forming a "military coterie of one or more of the high gods" [56]) and in other cases certain humans who form a guild of some kind, possibly a guild of warriors dedicated to the god *Rapha* and to the divine *Rephaim* [57]). One task of the members of the human guild of Rephaim warriors which is specifically mentioned in the Ugaritic sources (*CTA* 20 B, 3-7; 22A, 22-6) is the *visitation and inspection of plantations and threshing-floors at harvest time.* What the purpose of this task was is open to debate. Gray relates it to the New Year cultus and the enthronement of Baal and, on the basis of a meaning "confer fertility" for *rp'*, concludes that the Rephaim were a sacerdotal guild of "fertilisateurs" [58]). The disordered nature of the Rephaim Texts (cf. Caquot, pp. 75, 84, 91) hardly permits the construction Gray places on them but in the light of this present study the Ugaritic material might well point to the Philistine *y^e^lîdhê hārāphāh/hār^e^phā'îm* as a guild of warriors, experts in single combat, one of whose distinctive tasks was the securing of adequate supplies for their king and his army by either commandeering or forcibly seizing the stocks of grain available on the threshing floors of the land at harvest time. For this reason

---

[54]) "The Philistine Corps of the Scimitar from Gath", *JSS* 3 (1958) pp. 327-35.

[55]) For a useful survey of attempts cf. A. Caquot, "Les Rephaims Ougaritiques", *Syria* 37 (1960) pp. 75-93.

[56]) P. D. Miller Jr., *The Divine Warrior in Early Israel* (Cambridge, Mass., 1973), p. 43. At *CTA* 22B, 8-9 the term is paralleled with *mhr* "warrior, hero".

[57]) So B. Margulis, "A Ugaritic Psalm (RS 24, 252)", *JBL* 89 (1970), p. 302. Also identified by Margulis as "a divine guild of chariot-riding warriors akin to, if not identical with, the *mryn/maryannu*", p. 301.

[58]) J. Gray, "The Rephaim", *PEQ* 81 (1948/9), pp. 133, 136, 137.

they might well, as at Ras Shamra, visit and inspect the grain on the threshing floors and the fruit in the plantations of their own people and also add to their home produce by plundering the threshing floors and cornfields of their enemies, vassals and neighbours. Some such conception of the rôle of the "descendants of the giants" among the Philistines would certainly help to explain the common elements of single-combat, the exploits of "champions", harvest time, small-group actions (*ḥayyāh*, *mašḥîth*, *g^edhûdh*) and a *Kriegstechnik* expressed by the unusual *nṭš* Niph. or *pšṭ* which are present in so many of the stories of Israelite and Philistine clashes from the end of the Judges period to the time of David's capture of Jerusalem [59]. It would also help to explain how a well-known agriculturally productive area from which the Israelites several times repulsed Philistine raiding parties came to be called *ʿēmeq r^ephāʾîm* [60].

The general thrust of this study so far is towards the conclusion that both battle-reports in 2 Sam. v 17-25 originally referred to relatively minor encounters with Philistine raiding parties and were not records of large scale engagements that might have had that decisive or significant strategical importance which their present setting accords them, and such as every discussion of the historical problems of 2 Sam. v takes them to be. Both stories in their present form describe the Philistine action as foraging or plundering (*nṭš/pšṭ*). But other details in these stories run counter to this conclusion. They speak, for example, of the activity of the Philistines in general and not of a "band" or the like. At one point, indeed, the totality of Philistine involvement is expressed by the phrase "all the Philistines" (*v.* 17). On the other hand, in this first encounter "all the Philistines" are routed by an Israelite force comprising only "David and his men" (*v.* 21), 600 or the equivalent of only one standard fighting unit or battalion, but sufficient to deal with a band of marauders (1 Sam. xxx 9-10) or, indeed, to engage in such raids itself (1 Sam. xxvi 8-12).

---

[59]) The LXX verb συμπίπτειν is found in classical usage with special reference to champions engaged in hand to hand fighting, cf. H. G. Liddell and R. Scott, *Greek-English Lexicon* (revised and augmented by H. S. Jones and L. McKenzie, 9th edn, Oxford, 1968), p. 1683. J. Blenkinsopp, "Jonathan's Sacrilege", *CBQ* 26 (1964), pp. 423-49, notes how all but one of the single combat incidents of the Judges—David era involve the Philistines. The exception is the fighting with multiple representatives in 2 Sam. ii, (p. 427, note 16).

[60]) The combination *ʿēmeq* and *r^ephāʾîm* together offer several possibilities of double meanings, especially if any credence is given to the equation *ʿēmeq* = "strong (man), hero"; cf. A. A. Wieder, "Ugaritic-Hebrew Lexicographical Notes", *JBL* 84 (1965), pp. 162-3.

In this unbalance, one suspects, may be discerned the tension between the original reference of these battle-reports and the effort to fit them into their present setting at a later stage in their transmission. At the same time even within what one may suspect was original to these reports are to be found important differences belonging to the particularity of each event. The battle-tactics in *vv.* 17-21 are different from those in *vv.* 22-25 and, though both are set in the valley of Rephaim, yet the details of the locality (the spring (?) Baal-perazim and the *b*ᵉ*kā'îm* trees) are distinct. The very close similarity in form is the result of the use of the conventionalized battle-report in both cases but the differences in detail do not permit the conclusion that the second report is merely a duplication of the first. For the proper understanding of these stories it is necessary to give as much attention to all their *differences* as well as to their similarities and it is also necessary to try to distinguish as fully as possible those elemetns in the present text of the stories that are part of the original battle-reports from the connective comments and compositional devices which have been designed to fit the older stories into a new narrative sequence in the course of the formation of this part of the Deuteronomistic History Work.

The last part of 2 Sam. v divides logically into two reports comprising *vv.* 17-21 and 22-25 respectively. However, it is perfectly clear, especially in the light of the *Schlachtbericht* conventional form, that *v.* 17 is not properly part of the first battle-report but is an introductory comment setting *both* reports into a larger narrative sequence by connecting these incursions with the Philistine reaction to David's anointing (*v.* 3). The narrative sequence is maintained in *v.* 17 by the opening *wayyišm*ᵉ*'û* but *v.* 18, the old battle-report's original opening, breaks this sequence with its pluperfect construction *ûph*ᵉ*lištîm bā'û* [61]), Verse 18 contains precisely those verbs which are characteristic of the introduction to the battle-report: the verb of movement, *bô'*, and a verb of military activity, *nṭš* Niph. This original introduction also sets the scene unequivocally in the valley of Rephaim.

The present introduction to *vv.* 22-25 contains equivalent terminological elements and specifies a setting identical to that of 18-21: *'ālāh*, verb of movement, and *nṭš*, verb of military activity, in the

[61]) On *v.* 17 as "editorial" and *v.* 18 as the older introduction cf. Budde, p. 224; W. Caspari, *Die Samuelbücher*, (Leipzig, 1926), pp. 457, 458. For the syntax see Driver, *Notes*, p. 263, who compares 1 Sam. ix 15.

valley of Rephaim. Several commentators have suspected the artificiality of this introduction to the second battle. The infinitive *la‘^{a}lôth* is missing from 1 Chr. xiv 13 and this verb of movement, which may also imply a particular type of military activity [62]), deliberately connects the narrative to *v.* 17 [63]). At the same time 22b repeats 18b verbatim. The introduction to 22-25 appears to be a conflation of *vv.* 17 and 18. In its present form it is the work of the "author" of *v.* 17 or a later hand and it must be doubted whether any trace of the original introduction to the second battle-story remains in our present text. Even the setting in the valley of Rephaim is suspect. In the 1 Chr. parallel (xiv 13) this second battle is located simply "in the valley" (*bā‘ēmeq*). It may be that the context points so obviously to the valley *of Rephaim* (which one Hebrew MS, the Septuagint and Syriac supply) that little weight may be attached to this omission. Against this, however, as several commentators observe [64]) the *Ortskenntnis* of the second report suggests a setting in a valley *b^{e}khā'îm* and the consequent pursuit and rout from Geba/Gibeon [65]) to Gezer makes better sense if the site of the battle is north-west of Jerusalem and not south-west. Thus for this second encounter, either the (or another?) valley of Rephaim itself must be located north of the Jebusite city in the Geba/Gibeon area or we must conclude that Rephaim is not the original site of the battle at all. A valley of *bākhā'/b^{e}khā'îm* is mentioned in the notoriously difficult second half of Psalm lxxxiv (verse 7) [66]) and this may be the same as the original setting of 2 Sam. v 22-25. If this equation is sound then this second battle took place somewhere along one of the main routes to Jerusalem (from the north-west)? and possibly at some point on the final stage of the approach to the city on such a route [67]). This

---

[62]) Hauer, p. 575, note 19, remarks that "go up" in the battle accounts proper seems to mean "attack the enemy on his front, to confront the enemy directly".

[63]) Thus the form is *wayyōsîphû ‘ôdh .. la‘^{a}lôth* and not simply *wayya‘^{a}lû* or *ûph^{e}lištîm ‘ālû*. On the "redactional" character of *v.* 22 cf. Grønbaek, p. 252.

[64]) E.g. Mauchline, p. 220. Cf. also Kraeling, p. 198; G. A. Smith, *The Historical Geography of the Holy Land* (London, 1901), p. 150, and O. Procksch, "Der Schauplatz der Geschichte David's", *PJB* 5 (1909), p. 70.

[65]) MT reads *gebha‘* but LXX ἀπὸ Γαβαων and 1 Chr. xiv 16 *miggibh‘ôn*.

[66]) MT reads *‘ēmeq habbākhā* which LXX's τοῦ κλαυθμῶνος appears to identify with both 2 Sam. v and Jgs. ii 5 (*bôkhîm*).

[67]) The basis for this statement is the precise connotation of the term *m^{e}sillāh* in Ps. lxxxiv 6 as it has emerged in an investigation of that term in which the present writer has been engaged for some time now. Cf. also S. Mowinckel, *The Psalms in Israel's Worship* (Oxford, 1962) (= *Offersang og sangoffer* [Oslo, 1951]) Vol. I, pp. 170 f.

would certainly explain the present setting of the story in the context of David's capture of Jerusalem because it may well be the proper and original setting of verses 18-25.

That the beginning of the second battle-report has suffered some mutilation in the process of transmission is further indicated by a comparison of the oracle element in each report. Possibly because of the presence of Abiathar with David during his free-booting days (1 Sam. xxii 20-23) the consultation of the oracle seems to have played an important part in determining David's strategy, e.g. 1 Sam. xxiii 2-4, xxx 7-8; 2 Sam. ii 1. In each case as well as in 2 Sam. v 18-21 the whole process is described in typically Hebraic fashion. The question is asked—"shall I go up/pursue?"—and the answer given—"go up/pursue"—and sealed with the *Übereignungsformel*—"I will give x into your hand" [68]). In 2 Sam. v 22-25, the question part of the ritual of consultation is missing, the reply is, untypically, initially negative—"you shall not go up"—and the positive response —"go around (*hāsēbh*) to their rear..."—implies that the question answered (if not the question posed) was not simply to do battle or not to do battle but *how* to do battle. The question is one of tactics: should David make a frontal attack (*ʿālāh*)? No, rather adopt a flanking movement [69]). Furthermore the stereotyped formula assuring victory (*nāthan beyadh*) does not conclude this oracle in this case and what replaces it does not promise David the victory (cf. 1 Sam. xxx 7 "*you* shall overtake... and rescue") nor even acknowledge that he would be the human instrument "into whose hand" (1 Sam. xxiii 4; 2 Sam. v 19) Yahweh would deliver them. The whole action from the tactical planning to the final victory is Yahweh's who even in the actual assault "went out before" (*yāṣāʾ liphenê*) David. From the traditio-historical point of view the consultation of the oracle in both battle-reports, drawing attention as it does to David's reliance on Yahweh and setting him thus in contrast with Saul (so, for example, Campbell, p. 69, n. 1), may be the most important element in the stories in their present context but it is an over-simplification to think that both stories in this respect carry equal weight. Between the two there is a very considerable difference in degree that may amount to a difference in kind in the extent of

---

68) In 1 Sam. xxx 8 the equivalent element is the assurance that "you shall surely overtake and shall surely rescue".

69) Cf. Driver, *Notes*, p. 264. Budde, p. 225, regards *hāsēbh* as a military technical term.

the rôles played respectively by Yahweh and David. The oracle in the first report is typical of the story of David in his Hebron and earlier days, just, as we have already seen, as the whole character of this same battle-report (*vv.* 18-21) is typical of the activities of David and his men in the same period. In fact the first battle in the valley of Rephaim is said expressly to have involved, on the Israelite side, simply "David and his men" (*v.* 21), a group whose importance declined after the capture of Jerusalem (cf. Mazar, p. 320).

It is highly improbable that David's 600 would have taken on "all the Philistines" in a pitched battle and certain that, in such a circumstance, they would have considered a frontal attack tactically suicidal. Even if David's question to the oracle was not a tactical one (*ha'e'eleh* = should I make a frontal attack?) the aetiology of Baal-perazim implies something like a charge right into and through the ranks of the enemy [70]. In this respect, although the vocabulary is not identical nor the situation exactly the same, 2 Sam. v 18-21 calls to mind the other valley of Rephaim action, 2 Sam. xxiii 13 ff., when the three *gibbôrîm* "broke through" (*bq'*) the Philistine camp. In contrast with the situation implied or expressed in the details of the first battle-report the tactics of the second engagement are more suitable for a surprise attack by a military force which did not feel confident it could successfully face a possibly superior enemy force in a pitched battle [71]. In conventionalized battle-reports the actual contest is not described; thus the character of a military action, whether it was a large scale pitched battle or a much smaller action against a raiding party, must be gathered 1) from what the introduction of the report reveals about the troop movements involved, 2) from details about tactics and numbers provided by the report itself, 3) from the concluding summons of the consequences (and extent) of the engagement. So far all the evidence from 1) and 2) points to the first battle-report in 2 Sam. v 18-21 as the report of a relatively minor action by David and his men against a Philistine raiding party in David's Hebron period or earlier. But 2 Sam. v 22-25 seems to speak of something on a larger scale. The summary of consequences or concluding statement of the results of the two battle-reports confirms this conclusion.

70) The precise image which lies behind this aetiology is uncertain. It may be that of a hidden spring bursting out from the rock (Driver, *Notes*, p. 263) or of sudden torrential downpour in the hill country (Hertzberg, p. 274).

71) That the flank attack implies a superior Philistine force on this occasion is also the opinion of Mauchline, p. 220.

2 Sam. v 18-21 concludes with the curious comment, into which, one suspects commentators have often read far too much, that "the Philistines left their idols there, and David and his men carried them away". This has been seen as a reversal of the shameful defeat at Aphek, 1 Sam. iv 10-11, when the symbol of the presence of Yahweh, the Ark, was captured by the Philistines [72]), but if this is the case one can only remark that the "author" of 2 Sam. v has made surprisingly little of it. If *v.* 21 led directly into 2 Sam. vi the interpretation might sound more convincing, and had the Hebrew "author" himself hinted at all at the parallel with 1 Sam. iv it would seem less like a traditio-historical fantasy. Rather than discerning this pattern of typology in the event the Chronicler saw the threat of heterodoxy and for "they carried them away" substituted the deuteronomically orthodox "they burned them with fire" (1 Chr. xiv 12; cf. Deut. vii, 5, 25). In fact, so little is made of the abandonment of the Philistines "idols" in 2 Sam. v itself that it might be doubted whether, without the lead given by the Chronicler (reading *ʾelōhêhem*) and the Septuagint (τοὺς θεοὺς αὐτῶν), it would *in this context* be necessary to assume the meaning "idols" for *ʿṣbyhm*. From the basic general "root" meaning "something carved, fashioned or cut" the specific sense of "carved image (of a deity), idol" is only clearly apparent in poetical contexts where a parallel term (e.g. *massēkhāh*, Hos. xiii 2; *ʾelîlîm*, Is. x11; *gillûlîm*, Jer. 1 2) or qualification by the materials used (*keseph*, *zāhābh*, e.g. Ps. cxxxv 15) makes this sense obvious. In other cases in poetry the specific sense "idols" is not obvious from the context or it is suspect, e.g. Hos. iv 17 *BHK*. In the only four prose passages in which the pointing of *ʿṣby(h)m* indicates the translation "idols", one (2 Chr. xxiv 18) combines it with *ʾashērîm* as an object of the verb *ʿbd* and thus leaves no doubt as to its specific connotation; one is simply a reproduction by the Chronicler of the term as used in his Samuel source (1 Chr. x 9 = 1 Sam. xxxi 9) and the two remaining are both problematical, namely 1 Sam. xxxi 9 and 2 Sam. v 21. In the latter case the comment about the abandonment of the *ʿṣbm* answers to the record of booty taken which often forms part of the concluding section of the battle-report and is prominent in the conclusion to the accounts of the activities of David and his men; cf. 1 Sam. xxiii 5 (a passage identical in form with 2 Sam. v 18-21), 1 Sam. xxx 18-20 (note especially the additional remarks about David's spoil in *vv.* 26-

72) Cf. Campbell, p. 69; Hertzberg, p. 257; Carlson, pp. 41-9; Grønbaek p. 254.

31). A final note that David and his men carried off *the spoil abandoned by a Philistine raiding party* is, form-critically, what 1 Sam. xxiii 1-5 would lead one to expect at 2 Sam. v 21. It is not entirely inconceivable that *ʿṣbyhm*, perhaps, in these two cases may mean "vessels, containers" for carrying spoil [73]) just as their "cattle" (*miqnêhem*, 1 Sam. xxiii 5) seems to mean either specifically their "baggage animals" [74]) or simply their "property" [75]). 1 Sam. xxxi 9 would then make fair sense if translated "to spread the good news (*mᵉbhaśśēr*) of their vessels (of spoil) (*ʿṣbyhm*) and (to gladden) the people (with the good news)" [76]).

Whatever one makes of 2 Sam. v 21, as a concluding summary to the first battle-report it is in a different category from the final statement of the second report. In *v*. 25a the touch of the Deuteronomistic "author" is again discernible in the words "And David did as the Lord commanded him". 25b, however, may well be a part of the original battle-report since it is formulated in the conventional *min/ʿadh* of a battle-report conclusion and summarises the total result of the encounter by *wayyakh*, "and he smote". The extent of the rout is from Geba or Gibeon [77]) as far as Gezer, that is as far as the boundary of Israel's dominion, along a line which had been the main route of the Philistine penetration into the hill country [78]). It would be difficult to find fewer words to convey the idea of the final settlement of the Philistine problem than the half dozen words of 2 Sam. v 25b, which not only as a result of the whim of a "redactor" but also perhaps as a matter of actual history opened the way for the bringing back of the Ark [79]).

Behind 2 Sam. v 22-25 there appears to lie a battle-report of a

---

[73]) Cf. the probable meaning of *ʿeṣebh* in Jer. xxii 28.

[74]) The Philistines were robbing threshing floors yet David brought back only *miqnêhem*. G. B. Caird, " I and II Samuel", *IB* 2 (New York and Nashville, 1953), p. 1004, therefore concludes that "baggage animals" (complete with spoils) must be meant.

[75]) Mauchline, p. 159, prefers to translate "property" or "gear", i.e. the immediately available plunder.

[76]) MT reads *beth* (*ʿaṣabbêhem*) but *ʾeth* should certainly be read with LXX and Chronicles. Cf. Wellhausen, *Text*, p. 148; Budde, p. 191.

[77]) See note 66. A further pointer to the large-scale character of the engagement in the second battle report is its location in the Gibeon area, i.e. in a well known "campus" of ancient times. Cf. J. Blenkinsopp, *CBQ* 26 (1964), pp. 431-3.

[78]) Cf. Procksch, p. 70; Aharoni, p. 260; Blenkinsopp, *CBQ* 26, p. 433; D. Baly, *Geographical Companion to the Bible*, (London, 1963), p. 86, and Map IX.

[79]) The importance of 2 Sam. v as the link to 2 Sam. vi is stressed by Flanagan, p. 47; Carlson, p. 58.

major confrontation between Israel and the Philistines which either paved the way for or resulted from the capture of Jerusalem. This much may be deduced from what remains of the battle-report even though its original beginning is mutilated and its conclusion has been partially re-drafted. 2 Sam. v 18-21, however, is a battle-report still largely in its original form relating the successful routing of a Philistine raiding party by David and his men. Its historical setting is most likely David's Hebron period. It may refer to an occasion soon after David's anointing, and for that reason was brought into its present context or appeared at one time after *v.* 3, but it does not have to do with any large scale movement of Philistine forces acting in reaction to David's anointing. That was how things were in the beginning of the tradition. The course of the history of this tradition thereafter and down to the final form of the text is open to speculation. It may be that associative woıds played a part in bringing the two battle-reports together, that the oracular element drew them to one another or that similar content as a whole led to their juxtaposition [80]). It is very much to be doubted, however, whether a known chronology or any serious concern for accurate historiography [81]) influenced their placement beside one another.

---

[80]) See notes 7 and 12 for these possibilities.

[81]) These are the factors which Hauer, p. 574, and Caird, pp. 1069-70, consider to be of primary importance in explaining the sequence of stories in 2 Sam. v.

NOTIONS OF HISTORICAL RECURRENCE IN CLASSICAL HEBREW HISTORIOGRAPHY

by

G. W. TROMPF

Sydney

Since many fine scholars have emphasized a contrast between a linear view of time in the Bible and the cyclical conceptions of ancient Mesopotamians or Greeks [1]), it may appear audacious to defend the view that there are ideas of historical recurrence in OT historiography. Yet I will stand by an opening distinction between the notion of a cycle and that of recurrence in a wider sense. Along with the idea of cyclical change (which usually entails the belief that sets of historical phenomena pass through a fixed sequence of at least three stages, then returning to an original point of departure) one may find a variety of notions of recurrence. Those of the non-cyclical type which interest us in this article include the ideas of re-enactment and recurrently actualized retribution. It is a feature of some written histories that their authors have perceived re-enactments in the events being covered, and have thus brought into sharper focus pairs of occurrences that can be related to each other (and are significant). Historians have also been known to illustrate the divine distribution of rewards and punishments throughout a given period. In so doing they have put forward a reciprocal rather than a cyclical view of historical recurrence, or in other words a view that common types of events are followed by consequences in such a way as to exemplify a general pattern in history. In these and most other cases, I should make clear, it is not exact recurrence that is commonly presumed but the repetition of sorts of events, or event-types, complexes and patterns. We are concerned here with the historian's understanding of recurrence, not with the myth of eternal return or cosmological doctrines of conflagration and perfect reconstitution. In what follows I traverse well-trodden ground in a new way, analysing notions of re-enactment and recurrent retribution in the works

---

[1]) For relevant literature see G. W. Trompf, *The Idea of Historical Recurrence in Western Thought* 1 (Berkeley and Los Angeles, 1979), ch. 3, introd.

of the Deuteronomist(s) and the Chronicler(s) with the hope of shedding fresh light on Hebrew historiographical preconceptions.

The Re-enactment of Significant Events

As notions of re-enactment formed one important basis for the great Israelite festivals [2]), it is only natural that they should have been transferred to and re-developed in historiography. The Deuteronomic history affords some pertinent examples of how given actions (usually taken to be of real significance) have been repeated later in the deeds of others. In Joshua, for instance, the Jordan crossing was consciously likened to the Exodus and the traversing of the Red Sea (Josh. iv 23, and see verses 6, 7, 21, cf. Deut. vi 20; Exod. xii 26-27), and Joshua came to possess the attributes of a "second" Moses [3]). We are meant to recognize, too, that the first crossing of the Jordan was later re-enacted by Elijah and Elisha, who both struck the water with a mantle (2 Kgs ii 8, 14). The interesting Captivity-Exodus motif also makes an appearance. This motif was present in prophetic works at the time of the Exile, when a disaster comparable to the Egyptian bondage had occurred [4]). It was subtly appropriated by the Deuteronomist (cf. Deut. xxviii 68), and he alone among Biblical writers made the Egyptian experience a time of punishment for Israel (preceding deliverance), just like the exile to Babylon (cf. Jer. xxi 14-15, xxiii 7-8 on the Egyptian Exile/Babylonian Exile).

These are obvious suggestions of re-enactment, yet without elaborating on the well-known ground plan and basic theological standpoint of the Deuteronomist, there are more to note besides. He saw Moses, for example, not just as the dispenser of the Torah but as a prophet or "prophetic covenant mediator". Thus, despite his unique greatness (Deut. xxxiv 10), Moses was "the first in a series of prophets" (cf. xviii 15-22), and "what Moses did in Deuteronomy so also did

[2]) G. von Rad, *Die Botschaft der Propheten* (Munich and Hamburg, 1967), ch. 6; E. tr. *The Message of the Prophets* (London, 1968). This is based on *Theologie des Alten Testaments* 2 (Munich, 1960), ch. G 1; E. tr. *Old Testament Theology* 2 (Edinburgh and London, 1965).

[3]) Josh. iv 5-7, 14, v 15 (cf. Exod. iii 5), xxiv 25; D. Daube, *The Exodus Pattern in the Bible* (London, 1963), p. 11.

[4]) W. Zimmerli, "Le nouvel 'Exode' dans le Message des deux Grands Prophètes de l'Exil", *Maqqél Shâqédh, La branche d'amandier. Hommage à Wilhelm Fischer* (Montpellier, 1960), pp. 216 ff.; German tr. "Der 'neue Exodus' in der Verkündigung der beiden grossen Exilspropheten", *Gottes Offenbarung. Gesammelte Aufsätze zum Alten Testament* (Munich, 1963), pp. 192 ff. Cf. C. Chavasse, "The Suffering Servant and Moses", *CQR* 165 (1964), pp. 162 f.

the prophets during the course of Israel's history", for they all delivered the covenants and warnings of Yahweh [5]). Of all the prophets, Elijah is the one most strikingly presented as a new Moses, acting like the mediator of a covenant between Yahweh and his people from a mount, destroying his enemies with a curse, actually seeing God pass by, handing his work on to a successor, and being eventually taken up by God [6]). And there is another feature of interest partly connected with Moses, although it represents more a special parallel between two stages of development than a simple re-enactment. According to the Deuteronomic framework, the wilderness wanderings bore unfavourable comparison with the actual possession of the land, because, although Yahweh's commandments were delivered outside Canaan, the wilderness period was a time of grave disobedience [7]). When Joshua completed the work of Moses, however, Israel was obedient and worthy enough "to rest" (*nūaḥ*) before her enemies [8]). Now a parallel seems to have been purposely drawn between this early situation and a later one under David and Solomon. Of the two monarchs, David was the great and seminal figure comparable to Moses, and was the recipient of a new covenant (2 Sam. vii 8-17), yet in his time there was great turbulence, both internal and external. It was only under his successor that the people found complete rest before their enemies, and the temple was built [9]).

To show the re-enactment of significant events, then, to suggest how a given figure or set of conditions recalled prior developments, was hardly foreign to OT historiography, and such preoccupations do not stop short at the Deuteronomic historian.

The Chronicler's four volumes are also apposite. It is well known that his account of Israel's history from David to the Exile diverges somewhat from the Deuteronomic history, and the differences imply a good deal about special notions of recurrence in his work. Like the Deuteronomist, the Chronicler was not uninterested in paralleling the work of the great Israelite heroes. It has been recently argued,

---

[5]) E. W. Nicholson, *Deuteronomy and Tradition* (Oxford, 1967), pp. 117 f. (whence the quotations).

[6]) Cf. also J. N. M. Wijngaards, *The Dramatization of Salvific History in the Deuteronomic Schools* (Leiden, 1969), pp. 60-3.

[7]) Deut. i 26 f., 34 f., 43-5, ii 14 f., xxxii 51; Josh. v 4-12.

[8]) Josh. xxii 4, xxiii 1; cf. xi 23b, xiv 15b, xxi 44; Jud. ii 10.

[9]) 1 Kgs. v 4, viii 56; cf. iv 25 (but note 2 Sam. vii 1, 11a on David's time); G. Östborn, *Yahweh's Words and Deeds. A Preliminary Study into the Old Testament Presentation of History* (Uppsala and Wiesbaden, 1951), p. 32.

for example, that he "modelled the transition of rule from David to Solomon on that from Moses to Joshua"[10]). But it is his handling of geography and general cultural atmosphere, and his effort to expose similarities between certain event-complexes throughout his work that are of special relevance. Geographically, the Chronicler focused sharply on Jerusalem. Apart from the fact that the northern kingdom gained so little of his consideration, [11]) what happens in Jerusalem, where "Yahweh, the God of Israel, dwells forever" (cf. 1 Chr. xxiii 25) [12]), represents his central preoccupation. For a post-exilic writer, the fate of the Jerusalem temple and its cultus, and the restoration of community life in Jerusalem and Judaea were of crucial importance. There was a continuous story to be told from David's capture of "Jebus" (1 Chr. xi 4ff.) to the restoration period; and within that story the holy temple had been first built, eventually destroyed, and then rebuilt and restored—a point very much related to the idea of recurrence. According to the Chronicler, David was less a warrior and defender of his realm than a builder, architect and cult organizer [13]), and Solomon was treated far less as one wise beyond compare than as a king building and ordering the temple [14]). Now in the books of Ezra and Nehemiah, significantly, we find an intense interest in the architectural history both of the Second Temple and of the restored Jerusalem, and it is an interest which noticeably complements the characteristic treatment in the earlier(?) volumes. The Chronicler apparently selected and organized his material to draw parallels between religious life under the righteous Judaean monarchs and life under the restored community. To isolate the obvious ones, not only were David and Solomon both concerned with building projects and temple officialdom, but the more meritorious of their successors have a degree of involvement also, an involvement which looks ahead to the restoration situation [15]). It is also noteworthy that

[10]) H. G. M. Williamson, "The Accession of Solomon in the Books of Chronicles", *VT* 26 (1976), pp. 351 ff.

[11]) cf. 2 Chr. x 1-19, xiii 3-20, xvi 1-6, xviii, xx 35 f., xxv 17-24.

[12]) But see R. E. Clements, *God and Temple* (Oxford, 1965), p. 128, on 2 Chr. vi 18, 21, etc.

[13]) 1 Chr. xiii 1 ff., xiv 1 f. (= 1 Sam. v 11 f.), xv 1, xvi 4 ff., 37 ff., xvii, xxi 18-xxii 19, xxviii, xxix 1-5; cf. G. von Rad, *Theologie des Alten Testaments* 1 (Munich, 1957), p. 348 = E. tr. *Old Testament Theology* 1 (Edinburgh and London, 1962), p. 351, on David producing a "pattern" for Solomon like a "new Moses".

[14]) 2 Chr. ii 5-viii 16; cf. 1 Kgs. v-viii; but note 2 Chr. i 7-13, ix 1-12 and parallels.

[15]) 2 Chr. xxiv 1-14, xxiv 5, xxvi 9, xxvii 3 f., xxxii 5, xxxiii 14, xxxiv 8b-12a. Only in the case of Jehoiada and Josiah are there parallels in 2 Kings.

the northern kingdom becomes a real defence hazard in 2 Chronicles just as the "province beyond the river" (=Samaria) was to the restored Judaeans [16]. Material concerning the religious organization of the righteous kings of Judah, moreover, much of which is peculiar to Chronicles, forged yet another connection between the pre- and post-exilic situations, [17] and the priestly and levitical *leitourgiai* were taken to be ordered by monarchs—David, Solomon, and Hezekiah in particular—in a manner similar to those of the period after the restoration [18]. There are even signs that the Chronicler actually foisted a post-exilic Levitical organization on the kingly period (esp. 2 Chr. xxiii 2-11; cf. 2 Kgs. xi 4-10) [19]. As for the form and content of religion in the two "eras", his work suggests a variety of correspondences—in the form of temple dedications, for example (with their accompanying grand sacrifices), the keeping of the great feasts under righteous rulers, as well as purifications, exhortations, prayers and psalms [20].

The evidence overwhelmingly supports the view, then, that the material peculiar to Chronicles has been incorporated into those books because of their relatedness to the restoration scene. The events of the monarchical and (immediately) post-exilic periods have been consciously paralleled. Nowhere is this more obvious than in the writer's treatment of the two important kings Hezekiah and Manasseh. The former reigned after a time of "captivity" (cf. *baššᵉbī*) (one afflicted on Ahaz by the Assyrians; cf. 2 Chr. xxviii 20-22, xxix 9, om. 2 Kgs.); he also performed a work of restoration with regard to the temple (xxix 3, 35b, om. 2 Kgs.), and was later forced to build up the broken walls of Jerusalem in defence against Sennacherib (xxxii 5, om. 2 Kgs.). The latter actually experienced a "Babylonian exile", a

[16]) 2 Chr. xi 5-12, xvii 1, xxv 7 (all omitted in 2 Kings), xvi 1 ff., xxviii; cf. Ezra iv 9 ff., v 3 ff.; Neh. ii 9 f., iv 1 ff., etc.

[17]) 2 Chr. xv 12-15; Ezra x 5b; Neh. x 29 (oaths before Yahweh); 2 Chr. xvii 7-9, xix 9 f., xxxiv 30-2 (= 2 Kgs. xxiii 1-3); Neh. viii 1-4 (teaching and reading the Torah).

[18]) 1 Chr. xv, xvi 4; 2 Chr. v 5-13, vii 6, viii 14 f., xxxiv. Cf. A. C. Welch, *The Work of the Chronicler* (London, 1939), ch. 3; G. von Rad, *Theol.* 1, pp. 348 f., E. tr., pp. 351 f.

[19]) See, however, W. Rudolph, *Chronikbücher* (Tübingen, 1955), introd.; J. M. Myers, *I Chronicles* (Garden City, New York, 1965), pp. xlv ff.

[20]) E.g. 1 Chr. xv 12-14, xxii 7, xxiii 30 f.; 2 Chr. v 1-vi 42, viii 12 f., xx 21, xxix 15, xxx 13, 23, xxxv 1 f.; Ezra iii 3-8, 11, vi 16-22, viii 28 f., ix 6-15; Neh. viii, ix 1, xii 47. These connections count against H. G. M. Williamson's new thesis that the Chronicler was not the author of the books of Ezra and Nehemiah; see his *Israel in the Books of Chronicles* (Cambridge, 1977), pp. 35 ff., 67 ff.

punishment for his wickedness, but in his distress "he entreated the favour of Yahweh", and so humbled himself that God "brought him again to Jerusalem into his kingdom" (2 Chr. xxxiii 12-13, om. 2 Kgs.). On his return, Manasseh significantly built outer walls for Jerusalem (vs. 14a) and restored (*kūn*) Yahweh's altar in the temple (vs. 16) [21]). Thus the actions of both kings foreshadow and are re-enacted in the work of the restoration community. Such foreshadowing, perhaps, may be deemed a brand of typology, but we must guard against what has become the tyrannical propensity to uncover typological theology or literary motif without so much as a thought for specifically historiographic methods, techniques and interests. Thus when the Chronicler wished to suggest that older actions or activities were re-enacted in more recent times, and when he adjusted his description of older events to strengthen the desired impression, he was doing history as he understood it and his disclosure of significances in events was integral to his historiographic enterprise, and was not just passing theological reflection over and above his narrative.

Admittedly one should be cautious here. It is all very well to write of parallelisms, correspondences or even re-enactment in the Chronicler's history, but was he really concerned with historical recurrence? Were his chief concerns really rather different—to legitimate certain post-exilic cultic offices (von Rad), or to illustrate religious continuity between the monarchical and restoration periods (Ackroyd), or to write a series of *midrashim* on the Hexateuch (Goulder)? [22]) Certainly his sense of precedence and continuity cannot be denied, but why should we suppose that such a sense automatically excludes notions of historical repetition? We moderns, of course, tend to treat parallelism, foreshadowing and the like as a rather anaemic variation on the recurrence idea, suggesting the loosest, least precise of repetitions. We may even want to argue that once we include parallelism under the umbrella of recurrence then the idea of recurrence has be-

---

[21]) Parallel to Ezra vi 3, ix 7; Neh. i 3b ff., ix 27 ff. On *kūn*, see G. Lisowsky, *Konkordanz zum hebräischen AT* (Stuttgart, 1958), p. 672.

[22]) G. von Rad, *Theol.* 1, p. 349; cf. p. 329, n. 5; E. tr., p. 352; cf. p. 330, n. 6; P. R. Ackroyd, "The Age of the Chronicler; the great Reformers, 1" (lecture to the ANZTS, Melbourne, 17 August 1970); "History and Theology in the Writings of the Chronicler", *CTM* 38 (1967), pp. 508 ff.; "The Temple Vessels—a continuity theme", in *Studies in the Religion of Ancient Israel*, *Supp. to VT* 23 (1972), pp. 166 ff.; cf. *Continuity* (London, 1962); M. D. Goulder, unpublished manuscript on the Chronicler (by courtesy of the author).

come too broad to be meaningful. But can we impose our logical distinctions on archaic minds which share a different conceptual framework? The ancient historian usually worked out such correspondences, however allusively, with the utmost seriousness; they brought cohesion and deep significance to his narrative *qua* history. G. Östborn, although he has been over-eager to uncover patterns of cyclical thinking in the OT, has rightly noted that the Chronicler's general schema —a new and good order established under David and Solomon, in accordance with the law of Moses / disturbances of this order through the disobedience of kings / a new and good order established under Ezra and Nehemiah, in accordance with the law of Moses—also points in the direction which interests us (p. 41; cf. pp. 36ff.). And there remains the special emphasis on two great figures at both the beginning and end of the whole narrative. David and Solomon are brought into closer relationship than in the Deuteronomic history (1 Chr. xxii 6—xxiii 1, xxviii 1—xxix 25; cf. 1 Kgs. ii 1-9), and the originally quite separate careers of Ezra and Nehemiah are telescoped together (esp. Neh. viii 9; cf. Ezr. ix-x, Neh. ix-x). The most unqualified approval of these four, in contrast to evident reservations about the other rulers in between, even the more righteous ones, clearly calls for a re-evaluation of the Chronicler's historiographical presuppositions. While we have yet to examine his approach to retribution, it may be affirmed that his redaction indicates an interest in recurrent patterns, in both the re-enactment and foreshadowing of key religious practices, and in a special paralleling of spiritual conditions under the united monarchy and the restoration community.

The Recurrent Actualization of Retributive Principles.

The teaching that retributive principles were continually operative in human life is writ large in biblical historiography. This view is a variant of the reciprocal rather than the cyclical view of historical recurrence, since appropriate recompenses for good and bad actions are not necessarily meted out within a fixed sequence. It is significant, though, that the Israelite-Jewish writers came closest to stating a cyclical (or alternation) view of history through interpreting the laws of rewards and punishments. Judges ii, as part of the Deuteronomic history, is a central case in point. There one finds a pattern of events which may be described either as a four-staged sequence capable of repetition or as an undulatory process. The generation of those who possessed the land had passed, and the Deuteronomist introduced the new period of the Judges. The members of the new generation did not know Yahweh's past work for Israel, and they "did what was evil in the sight of Yahweh", "forsaking" him and "serving the Baʿals" and other gods. They provoked Yahweh's anger, so that

> *whenever* they marched out, Yahweh's hand was against them for evil, as he had warned and had sworn to them (cf. Deut. xxviii 15 ff.), and they were in sore straits (ii 10-15).

Then Yahweh raised up Judges to save them, although they did not listen nor obey God like their predecessors:

> *whenever* the Lord raised up Judges for them, the Lord was with the Judge, and saved them from their enemies all the days of the Judge,

because he was moved to pity by their groaning under oppression. But "*whenever* the Judge died they turned back and behaved worse than their fathers", and Yahweh, in his anger, said he would not drive out the nations left unconquered by Joshua, but let them test Israel (ii 16-22).

Christopher R. North has argued cogently that for the Deuteronomist (whose editorial work in these and subsequent passages is clear enough) [23]) the period of the Judges was "marked by a monotonously recurring cycle", a "process" which, once complete, was capable of being "set in motion all over again" [24]). The four stages of defection, oppression, prayer (the importance of which becomes obvious after ch. ii), and deliverance [25]), suggest a recurring sequence not unlike the biological paradigm of growth, acme and decay, or even Polybius' well known cycle of governments. The stages in Judges, moreover, could be described as a straightforward alternation between a low-point (oppression brought on by disobedience) and a high-point (liberation and security made possible by obedience under a Judge). Alternation (when one set of general conditions is regularly succeeded by another, which in turn gives way to the first) is technically distinguishable from cyclicism, although the two conceptions can very easily merge, as in talk about the rise and fall of empires. Thinking about the schema of Judges ii in terms of this second or alternation frame, interestingly, recalls other ancient Near Eastern

---

[23]) On the redaction criticism of Judges, see C. A. Simpson, *Composition of the Book of Judges* (Oxford, 1957), pp. 133 ff. The italics above are mine.

[24]) *The Old Testament Interpretation of History* (London, 1946), pp. 96 f.

[25]) For the sequence put in these terms, see J. M. Myers in *The Interpreter's Bible* 2 (New York and Nashville, 1953), p. 701.

theories in which "national" fortune and misfortune follow one another in undulatory fashion [26]).

The Deuteronomic schema remains uniquely Israelite, and it does not stand in its own right either, but only as one of a number of ways in which retributive laws were manifested in Israelite history. Admittedly, the Deuteronomist applies the pattern of Jud. ii with fair consistency in subsequent chapters [27]), even carrying it to the rule of Samuel, who was considered the last Judge [28]). And with the defection of the sons of Gideon, of Eli (also one who "judged" Israel) and of Samuel [29]), the Deuteronomist reinforced the cyclo-alternating process with a theme about the repeated disobedience of "second generation rulers". However, it is not strictly true that Jud. ii "states succinctly the Deuteronomic conception of history" (Myers, p. 107), for it merely approaches one aspect of it, and speaks only to a specific period of Israel's past. Certainly Judges makes those traditional distinctions between Israelite-Jewish and Graeco-Roman views of history look simplistic, even though the notion of the *kyklos* can hardly be read into a chapter deriving from an ancient Near Eastern milieu. But to lay too much stress on cyclical thinking in Jud. ii would in any case be to miss the point that, for this part of his account, the Deuteronomist specially appropriates a current model to strengthen his more general thesis about the recurring operation of retributive principles in the Israelite past. Besides, as we have already shown, notions of historical recurrence cannot be confined to cyclical notions. Either to exaggerate cyclical thinking in the OT or to exclude it altogether (especially on principle) is to ride rough-shod over a vital distinction [30]).

Within the Deuteronomic history, admittedly, the writer's belief in recurrent retribution is most vividly conveyed in Jud. ii. Although

[26]) M. G. Güterbock, "Die historische Tradition und ihre literarische Gestaltung bei Babyloniern und Hethitern bis 1200" (pt. 1), *Zeitschrift für Assyriologie* 42 (1934), pp. 13 ff.; E. A. Speiser, "Ancient Mesopotamia", in R. C. Dentan (ed.), *The Idea of History in the Ancient Near East* (New Haven, Conn., 1955), pp. 55 f.; H. Gese, "Geschichtliches Denken im Alten Orient und im AT", *ZTK* 60 (1958), p. 134. On the Babylonian-exilic provenance of the Deuteronomic History, see especially M. Noth, *Überlieferungsgeschichtliche Studien I* (Halle, 1943), pp. 96 ff., 197 ff.; P. R. Ackroyd, *Exile and Restoration* (London, 1968), pp. 65 ff.

[27]) Jud. iii 8 ff., iv 2 ff., vi 1 ff., x 7-9 (7b is secondary), xi 1 ff., xiii 2 ff.

[28]) 1 Sam. ii 22-31, iii 1, iv 1 ff., vii 2; cf. vii 3-17.

[29]) Jud. viii 33-ix 57; 1 Sam. ii 12-17, 34, iv 11 (cf. iv 18b), viii 1-3.

[30]) Against Östborn, pp. 60 ff.; von Rad, *Theol.* 1, p. 329, n. 5; E. tr., p. 330, n. 6.

the rest of his work lacks the symmetry of Judges, he was remarkably consistent in proving for his readers that transgression (that is, disobedience against the law delivered to Moses, which prefaces the history in the form of Deuteronomy, and rejection of Yahweh's *debārīm* uttered through the prophets) must needs be requited by God, and faithfulness, in turn, be rewarded. Not only is it true that the Deuteronomist explains the momentous disasters befalling Israel and Judah in terms of retributive logic, but there is abundant evidence of his interest in the distribution of recompenses throughout the whole period under his consideration. There are, of course, interesting variations on this important, if not central, theme. Recompenses for good may come in terms of peace (as with Solomon for example), yet it could also be found in something so grim as death (as in the case of Josiah, who was saved from worse troubles to come by being "gathered to his fathers") [31]). Punishments, for their part, could be meted out immediately or relatively quickly, or else deferred until a much later time [32]). Without reiterating what is common scholarly knowledge, however, I simply wish to emphasize the pains with which the Deuteronomic writer illustrated the recurrent experience of appropriate recompenses, the "the recurrent pattern of failure and grace", as Ackroyd puts it (p. 74). Most significantly, large stages of Israel's history from Moses to the Exile are interpreted in terms of retributive justice and in such a way as to provide the real unity of the D work. If the period of the Judges witnessed fluctuations, there were two great periods of righteousness, one under Joshua, when only Achan's sin marred the bright picture of success, and when the whole land (*kol-hāʾāreṣ*) was taken and the twelve tribes given settlement, and the other under David [33].) David, conspicuously, did not commit any outrage or sin of blood-guiltiness, and he was also forgiven by Yahweh for despising the divine word in taking Bathsheba and in numbering Israel, even though a price is paid in each case[34]). While acknowledging David's merits, however, the Deuteronomist

[31]) 1 Kgs. iii-x (cf. xi); 2 Kgs. xxii 20, xxiii 29 f.

[32]) Josh. xii 2-26; 1 Kgs. xiv 10, 21, 25 f., xv 29, xvi 10, xxii 34 f.; 2 Kgs. i 15-17, ix 30-7, x 27, 32, xiii 22 f. (not detained); 1 Sam. ii 34, viii 4-22; 1 Kgs. i 39, xiv 10-18; cf. Deut. xvii 14-17 (detained).

[33]) Josh. xi 23 (but cf. pre-Deuteronomic xiii 1b), xiii-xxii. See above on "rest theology".

[34]) 2 Sam. xii 9-18 (cf. xv-xviii), xxiv 11-16; and (on the avoidance of outrage), for example, 1 Sam. xxiv 6, xxvi 9 f., xxv 26, xxix 6, 8 f.; 2 Sam. iv 11 f., ix 3-8, xxi 7; 1 Kgs. ii 31-3, xix 22b, xx 3b.

paid much attention to the punishments borne by those who threatened such a righteous king—by Saul and later contenders for David's position [35]). And if such requitals came upon individuals during David's reign, the writer makes it plain that in times of general disobedience or as a result of evil kings, the whole people experienced them. The Deuteronomist did not paint an idyllic picture of the wilderness wandering, to take a key example, but held it to be a rebellious period. When disobedient, the Israelites were defeated by enemies (Deut. i 26, 43; cf. 19-46), and not until the warriors who transgressed had died off (ii, 14b-16) could progress be made (ii 21, 33-36, iii 6). Even Moses was punished for his disbelief (xxxii 48-52; cf. Num. xxvii 12-14) [P], and it was Joshua who was the hero of the almost transgressionless period of settlement which followed. As for post-Davidic times, Israel "rested" under Solomon only as long as his faithfulness lasted (cf. 1 Kgs. xi 14-25), and deterioration in his reign foreshadowed the general decline treated in 1 Kgs. xii—2 Kgs. xxv, when there was such great evil that only a great disaster could requite it.

Thus the Deuteronomist's work was a history of the recurring execution of appropriate recompenses, and Israel's past was viewed as if the same principles operated time and time again. Implicitly the nature of rewards and punishments was in accordance with the degree of merit or of incurred guilt, but these operations were ultimately dependent on Yahweh and not upon natural or "mechanical" laws. The main point is, however, that the writer bequeathed an account of about six centuries in which history, in a special sense, repeated itself. His picture of the repeated acts of transgression against God's commandments, and the repeated consequences of such disobedience, his characterization of recurrent "event-shapes"—typical transgressions, typical warnings, fitting deaths and recompenses—all reflect a preoccupation with historical recurrence. There is, of course, no exact repetition, and the cyclic alternations of Jud. ii are confined to only one part of the history. Yet so much of what is usually associated with Graeco-Roman historiography—recurring principles in history, lessons learnt for the future from the past—is present in a distinctively Hebraic form. The Deuteronomist almost certainly assumed that patterns of events similar to those he recorded would happen in the future, if the same kinds of transgressions and deeds were effected. By re-

---

[35]) 1 Sam. xiii 13 f., xv 19-23, 28, 35, xvi 14, xix 5-10, xxiv 20, xxvi 16, xxviii 3-17, xxxi 2 ff.; 2 Sam. iii 30, xviii 9-15; 1 Kgs. iii 31 f.

viewing their chequered past, then, the Israelites had much to learn for the future consolidation of their nation and their faith.

It remains true that the Israelites lacked the conceptual tools to convey the idea of historical recurrence more lucidly. But the genuine interest in repeated instances of retribution we have just analysed, as well as that special concern to document the re-enactment of events and re-appropriation of former conditions, persuades one that the otherwise eccentric Chevalier C. J. Bunsen was correct when he once asserted that the Hebrews, just as much as the Greeks, had a clear perception of "the moral law ruling human affairs", holding "that the divine principle of truth and justice ... will prevail" [36]). And this is confirmed by the development of retributive ideas in the Chronicler's work, which in 1-2 Chronicles overlaps with 2 Samuel-2 Kings.

Beside the Deuternonomic work, the Chronicler's treatment of retribution looks crude and almost mechanical. We have already noted how he extolled the two periods of the united monarchy and the restoration. He idealized both David and Solomon; they were virtually without sin, and in consequence, were more decisively supreme in war and prosperous at home. The time of restoration was one of righteousness, with both Ezra and Nehemiah working assiduously to avoid transgression and thus the punishments of the past.

The interim period, however, was tainted with evils which made the Exile inevitable. Whilst he was far less severe on certain of the monarchs of Judah [37]), the Chronicler's post-Solomonic pre-exilic history still remains one of repeated disobedience. Although Yahweh persistently sent messengers to the kings, they kept despising them, and the priests and people also acted unfaithfully, until no "remedy was left" (2 Chr. xxxvi 14-16). Recurring disobedience marked the pre-Davidic period also. The Chronicler provides an insight into his understanding of early stages of Israelite history in the famous prayer of Nehemiah (in Neh. ix). Although the Davidic-Solomonic era is not mentioned, Nehemiah reflects on the whole period from the patriarchs to the possession as a time of close relationship with Yahweh—the disobedience in the wilderness being glossed over quickly (ix 16-19, cf. Deut. i-ii, etc.)—and within the situation after the restoration, Nehemiah sought a return to that relationship (vss. 32-38).

[36]) *Outlines of the Philosophy of Universal History* 1 (London, 1854), pp. 5 f.

[37]) Cf. 2 Chr. xiii 1 ff., xiv 1 [MT], xvii 1-20, xxvi 4, xxvii 1 ff., xxix-xxxii, xxxiv-xxxv.

The times in between possession and restoration, however, (though we may exclude the highpoint under David and Solomon) were disobedient and rebellious days. In a manner reminiscent of Jud. ii, the prayer refers to the Israelites' rejection of both the law and the prophetic warnings, so that Yahweh gave them "into the hands of their enemies".

> But in the time of their suffering they cried to thee and thou didst hear them from heaven; and according to thy great mercies thou didst give them saviours who saved them from the hands of their enemies. But after they had rested they did evil again before thee, and thou didst abandon them to the hands of their enemies, . . . yet when they turned and cried to thee, thou didst hear them from heaven, and many times (*ʿittīm*) thou didst deliver them (Neh. ix 26-28).

Once more Israel's disobedience heads a sequence, and is followed by defeat, supplication and Yahweh's succour (vss. 29-31). Hence an undulatory model makes its appearance, with national misfortune (caused by disobedience) and deliverance (due to reliance on Yahweh) succeeding each other in turn. We may therefore assume that, even if we allow for the special period of "saviourhood" under David and Solomon, the Chronicler took not only the period of the Judges to be one of fluctuation (on the basis of Jud. ii), but also the monarchical period as well, from Saul to Zedekiah [38]). What we anticipate from Judaean kingly history, then, is an impression of alternation not strictly present in the Deuteronomic account. The Chronicler was admittedly bound to pay deference to the formal judgements of his major source as to the righteousness or wickedness of different monarchs, yet even in doing that, he actually managed to create a more symmetrical pattern of alternation than his predecessor. For the purpose of simplification, the Deuteronomist's picture may be construed as in Diagram I. The Chronicler modified these classifications, however, in order to ease certain transitions from high-points to low-points, thus creating the effect of a zig-zag line of development between two sets of general conditions. He both altered and added to his main source, and isolated different stages in the careers of certain kings along the way.

To create this new impression Saul is treated as a disobedient king only (1 Chr. x 13-14; cf. 1 Sam. ix-xvi); the latter, less promising period of Solomon's reign is shelved (yet cf. 1 Kgs. xi); Rehoboam

[38]) In this connection, note the Chronicler's special emphasis on crying to Yahweh in distress in 2 Chr. xx 9, xxix 8-10, xxxii 20 ff., xxxiii 12; cf. vi 24 ff., xii 7.

becomes blameworthy and reckoned as evil only after a period under the shadow of Solomonic prosperity (2 Chr. xii 1b-5, 8, 14; cf. xi 12-17, xii 1a, 12b, yet cf. 1 Kgs. xiv 21ff.); Abijah becomes a good ruler rather than a bad one (xiii 1-23 [MT]; cf. 1 Kgs. xv 3); Asa, although he begins faithfully (2 Chr. xiv 1-xv 19, so 1 Kgs. xv 11-15), eventually enters an alliance with Syria, commits cruelties against the seer who condemns him for it, pays for his crime by contracting a disease, and dies seeking physicians rather than Yahweh (2 Chr. xvi 2-3, 7-10, 12-13; cf. 1 Kgs. xv 16-24, there being little sense of retribution in vs. 23b). Jeshoshaphat's reign is then idealized (2 Chr. xvii-xx, cf. 1 Kgs. xxii 41-60 (that sharpens the contrast between his and the preceding rule), but a misdemeanour at the end of his reign (2 Chr. xx 35-37; cf. 1 Kgs. xxii 47-49) foreshadows a low-point which comes with the accession of Jehoram. Jehoram kills his brothers and leads Judah astray (2 Chr. xxi 4, 6b, 11; cf. 2 Kgs. viii 18-19). For this he faces internal revolts (2 Chr. xxi 8-10; 2 Kgs. viii 2-22), the vehemence of a letter from Elijah (2 Chr. xxi 12-15), the incursions of enemies (vss. 16-17) and an incurable disease (vs. 18) (all om. Kgs.). Ahaziah succeeds him, but as he reigns for only one year (xxii 2), and is killed according to God's will (xxii 7, 9), it does not disturb the Chronicler to consider him in close conjunction with Jehoram (=2 Kgs. vii 20-27 and 28 ff.), and to treat him as the end of a blameworthy stage (cf. 2 Chr. xxii 9βb). Joash's rule sees a return to faithfulness, whilst Jehoida is high priest (xxiv 2, 4 ff., cf. 2 Kgs. xii 2, 4 ff.), but the relevant difficulty then facing the Chronicler comes with the fact that the Deuteronomist had listed three kings immediately following Joash who did *ṭōb* in the eyes of Yahweh—Amaziah, Azariah (=Uzziah) and Jotham (2 Kgs. xiv 3-6, xv 3-5, 34). He solves this problem first by disclosing that there had been transgression during Joash's reign, which was largely the fault of the Judaean princes after the high priest's death (2 Chr. xxiv 17-19). The princes die violently for their sin (vs, 23b), and Joash, who listens to them, is eventually murdered (vs. 25); cf. 2 Kgs. xii 20, which lacks a sense of retribution. Secondly, the Chronicler paints an increasingly gloomy picture of Amaziah's rule. Amaziah does certain things that are right before Yahweh (xxv 2a, 4-13; cf. 2 Kgs. xiv 3a), but he is blameworthy (2 Chr. xxv 2b, cf. 2 Kgs. xiv 3b); he then turns from Yahweh (cf. 2 Chr. xxv 27) and worships the gods of Seir (vs. 14), for which heinous sins he receives an oracle of doom (vss. 15-16), is captured, at great cost to Jerusalem, by Jehoahaz of Israel (vss. 23; cf. 20, 23-24; cf.

2 Kgs. xiv 8-10), and is killed by conspirators at Lachish (vs. 27 = 2 Kgs. xiv 19). Finally, having portrayed Amaziah's reign as a low-point, the Chronicler conceives of Uzziah's and Jotham's rules as a progression upward. Uzziah does well (2 Chr. xxvi 4; 2 Kgs. xv 3-5), but, puffed up with pride, he desecrates the temple and so contracts leprosy (2 Chr. xxvi 16-21), whilst his son Jotham follows in his footsteps but does better by not falling into his errors (xxvii 2; cf. 2 Kgs. xv 34). Thus there is a return to a more righteous rule (yet note the foreboding: 2 Chr. xxvii 28b). The transitions from Jotham to Ahaz and on to Hezekiah as they stand in D suit the Chronicler's predispositions, but he re-writes the reigns of Manasseh and Amon, making Amon's rather than Mansseh's rule the next extreme point of departure from God's ways. Hezekiah is amongst the most prosperous of post-Solomonic rulers (2 Chr. xxxii 23, 27-30), and this because he is amongst the most righteous (xxix 1-xxxii 1), although the Chronicler has reservations about his pride (xxxii 25-26; cf. 2 Kgs. xx 1b), perhaps in expectation of new, more terrible developments under his successors. The first of these, Manasseh the idolater, commits dreadful crimes, and yet, in his temporary exile, he repents, returning to restore God's altar and city (xxxiii 10-16; cf. 2 Kgs. xxi 10-15). His reign, then, is contrasted quite favourably with Amon's, who does not humble himself like his father, but who "incurred guilt more and more", and is eventually murdered (2 Chr. xxxiii 22-24; cf. 2 Kgs. xxi 20-24). From then on. the Chronicler follows the Deuteronomic precedents, with the reforms of Josiah, and the cluster of wicked kings who remove all "remedy" from the situation.

The overall result of the Chronicler's interpretation has been characterized in Diagram II, and this diagram reveals how he actually concerned himself with a process of historical recurrence. Indeed it is this concern which explains why the Chronicler's ascription of good and evil to the Judaean monarchs differs from the judgements of the Deuteronomist; it is this concern, I maintain, which accounts for most of the divergences between the two writers.

This patterning was reinforced by the Chronicler's somewhat shallow analysis of retributive principles. Every illness, for instance, had to be accounted for in terms of requital, the violent deaths of kings seen as punishments (even that of Josiah), and every defeat as a sign of disobedience [39]). By contrast, material prosperity accom-

[39]) E.g. 2 Chr. xii 5-12, xiii 15, xiv 12, xvi 12-14, xxi 16-20, xxii 7 ff., xxv 20-2, xxvi 21, 27, xxviii 5 ff., xxxii 21, 24 f., xxxiii 11, xxxvi 5 f.

DIAGRAM I

The Deuteronomic picture of monarchical rule from Saul to Zedekiah (Judaea)

Good Kings:	Saul (1)+	David Solomon (1)	Asa Jehoshaphat	Joash	Jotham	Hezekiah	Josiah	
			Azariah (= Uzziah)					
Evil Kings:	Saul (2)	Solomon (2) Rehoboam Abijah	Jehoram Ahaziah	Amaziah	Ahaz	Manasseh Amon	Jehoahaz Jehoiakim Jehoiakin Zedekiah	Exile

DIAGRAM II

The Chronicler's picture of monarchical rule from Saul to Zedekiah (Judaea)

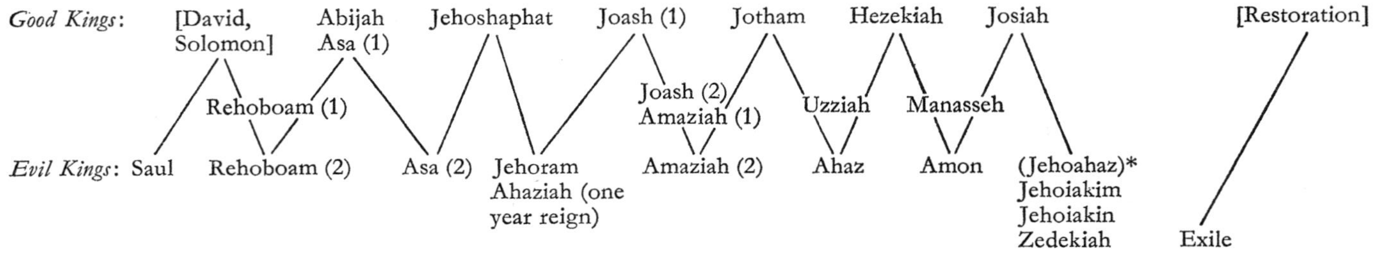

+ Bracketed numbers denote identifiable stages in certain kings' reigns
* The Chronicler does not inform us whether this king did or evil or right before Yahweh

panied almost blameless rule (*supra*, cf. esp. 2 Chr. xvii 5, xx 20 [om. 1 Kgs.]. xxxii 27 ff., cf. 2 Kgs. xx 12 ff.), and except for the murder of the prophets, the violent deaths of those who did not deserve them were overlooked (cf. esp. 2 Kgs. xxv 18-21, om. 2 Chr.). In Chronicles, moreover, oracular activity manifests itself with greater regularity than in the Deuteronomic work [40]), and in all, then, we find in this later history an eclectic intertwining of relevant themes—of re-enactment, continuity, retribution, and of alternation between two sets of general conditions.

Various theoretical conclusions may be drawn from the above interpretations. I have presented these in detail elsewhere, together with a critique of important contributions by Bertil Albrektson and Hartmut Gese [41]). It suffices to close here with the assertion that "the linear-cyclical dichotomy", or the forced contrast between "straight-line" and "cyclical" views of history, should be seriously qualified. Even apocalypticists expecting the imminent end of the known order could describe the course of the past in terms of cycles [42]), and it can hardly be considered un-Hebraic that the Deuteronomist and the Chronicler, neither of whom indulged in eschatology yet who both traced long paths of Israelite history towards more limited *teloi*, disclosed different kinds of recurrences to teach lessons about Yahweh's dealings with his people. The two historians probably made use of current Near Eastern paradigms in their efforts, for their readers stood face to face with Mesopotamian *Weltanschauungen*. This being the likely case one ought not belabour the contrast between Hebrew and non-Israelite views of history; yet the distinctively Hebraic characteristics of these two writings—especially their highly sophisticated organization, scope, epic quality and Yahwist theology—remain.

---

[40]) cf. G. von Rad, "Die levitische Predigt in den Büchern der Chronik", *Festschrift Otto Procksch* (Leipzig, 1934), pp. 113 ff. = *Gesammelte Studien zum AT* (Munich, 1958), pp. 248 ff.; E. tr. "The Levitical Sermon in *I* and *II Chronicles*", in *The Problem of the Hexateuch and Other Essays* (Edinburgh and London, 1966), pp. 267 ff.

[41]) In a submission to *History and Theory*; cf. my *Historical Recurrence* (see n. 1 above), ch. 3, introd.

[42]) Jewish Sibyll. Bks. III 158-60, 289, 563, 649, 728; 2 Bar. liii 5 ff., lvi-lxxiv; cf. A. C. B. Kolenkow, *An Introduction to II Bar.* 53, 56-74; *Structure and Substance* (Harvard doctoral dissertation, Cambridge, Mass., 1971), ch. 2. On the New Testament, see especially J. Jeremias, *Jesus als Weltvollender* (Gütersloh, 1930), pp. 8 ff.

SALOMO — DER ERSTGEBORENE BATHSEBAS

von

T. VEIJOLA
Hyvinkää, Finnland

Dem Gedächtnis des Hethiters Uria gewidmet

In der Genealogie Jesu am Anfang des Matthäusevangeliums (Mt. i 6) steht die Aussage „David zeugte den Salomo von dem Weib des Uria". Eigenartig in dieser Aussage ist, daß sie anstelle von „Bathseba" von „dem Weib des Uria" spricht und dadurch die skandalöse Geschichte wachruft, die hinter der Geburt Salomos lag. Ja, wer wollte, könnte sie sogar dahingehend verstehen, daß Salomo das im Ehebruch gezeugte erste Kind Davids und Bathsebas war — was allerdings kaum der alte Sinn der genealogischen Notiz sein dürfte. Aber ganz abgesehen davon reizt diese Möglichkeit zur näheren Prüfung der Geburtsverhältnisse Salomos.

I

Neuerdings hat E. Würthwein in seiner Studie *Die Erzählung von der Thronfolge Davids — theologische oder politische Geschichtsschreibung?* (Zürich, 1974) [1]) exkursartig die Frage angeschnitten, ob die Erzählung vom Tod des ersten und von der Geburt des zweiten Kindes von David und Bathseba (2 Sam. xii 15b-24a) überhaupt zu der alten Thronfolgeerzählung gehört habe; d.h. ob nicht in Wirklichkeit Salomo der Erstgeborene Bathsebas gewesen sei. Er zitiert zuerst einige ältere Autoren, die an dieser Stelle bereits ihre Bedenken geäussert haben [2]), und nennt sodann zwei Beobachtungen, die gegen die Ursprünglichkeit der Erzählung vom Tod des ersten Kindes geltend gemacht werden können: „1. Die Geschich-

---

[1]) Neuere Literatur zum Thema bietet W. Dietrich, „David in Überlieferung und Geschichte", *VF* 22 (1977), S. 44-64.

[2]) J. Marquart, *Fundamente israelitischer und jüdischer Geschichte* (Göttingen, 1896), S. 26; S. A. Cook, „Notes on the Composition of 2 Samuel", *AJSL* 16 (1899-1900), S. 156 f.; E. Auerbach, *Wüste und Gelobtes Land* I (Berlin, [2]1938), S. 228, Anm. 1.

te von der Geburt des im Ehebruch gezeugten Kindes ist nicht zu Ende geführt; es fehlt ihr die zu erwartende Namengebung, die man in xii 24b finden könnte. 2. Die Erzählung von der Geburt Salomos als des zweiten Sohnes greift zeitlich dem Folgenden weit voraus"(S. 32).

Dennoch ist Würthwein von der Kraft dieser Argumente nicht vollkommen überzeugt, sondern meint, daß man die Sache letztlich nicht sicher beweisen kann (S. 32). Nun liegt es wohl in der Natur der Sache, daß man sie nie absolut sicher beweisen kann, doch scheint mir, daß sich mit den von Würthwein gemachten Beobachtungen, zusammen mit einigen neuen, noch einiges mehr zeigen läßt.

II

Es ist in der Tat sehr auffallend, daß in der Erzählung von der Geburt des im Ehebruch gezeugten Kindes die Namengebung fehlt. Ein unbefangener Leser, der etwas Sinn für die hebräische Erzählungskunst hat, wird nach dem jetzt abschließenden Satz „und sie gebar ihm einen Sohn" (xi 27a) rein gefühlsmäßig fragen: „Und wie nannte sie ihn?" Denn normalerweise wird in Geschichten, die über die Geburt eines Kindes berichten, auch die Namengebung mitgeteilt [3]). Sie scheint — der Bedeutung des Namens entsprechend [4]) — für die hebräischen Erzähler ein besonders wichtiges Moment darzustellen. Wo die Namengebung fehlt — was äußerst selten der Fall ist —, da müssen besondere Gründe vorliegen:

In der Erzählung von dem Salomonischen Urteil (1 Reg. iii 16-28) berichtet eine Dirne, wie sie und eine andere Dirne kurz nacheinander Kinder zur Welt gebracht haben (V. 17-18), ohne jedoch ihre Namen zu nennen. Aber wer würde es in diesem Zusammenhang überhaupt erwarten? Es handelt sich ja um eine *paradigmatische* Erzählung über die richterliche Weisheit des Königs, der — den neutestamentlichen Paradigmen ähnlich [5]) — jedes *biographische* Interesse fremd ist; sogar der König, dessen Name (Salomo) aus

---

[3]) Abgesehen von dien vielen genealogischen Geschichten in Genesis vgl. Stellen, die wie 2 Sam. xi 27a „und sie gebar (ihm) einen Sohn/eine Tochter" lauten, daran aber die Namengebung anschließen: Ri. viii 31, xiii 24; 1 Sam. i 20, iv 19-21; Jes.viii 3; Hos. i 3-4, 6, 8-9; Rt. iv 13, 17.

[4]) J. Pedersen, *Israel* I-II (København, ²1934), S. 190: „Der Name ist ein Teil der Seele."

[5]) Vgl. M. Dibelius, *Die Formgeschichte des Evangeliums* (Tübingen, ⁵1966), S. 46 f.

dem weiteren Kontext erschlossen werden kann, bleibt in der Erzählung selbst anonym [6]).

Ähnlich verhält es sich mit dem Wunderbericht über Elisa und die sunemitische Frau (2 Reg. iv 8-37). Durch Elisas Wunderkraft (V. 16) wird die Frau schwanger und gebiehrt einen Sohn [7]), dessen Name aber aus durchsichtigen Gründen nicht erwähnt wird: An der Stelle, wo man die Namengebung erwarten könnte (V. 17), steht die in diesem Zusammenhang viel wichtigere Mitteilung, nach der der Sohn gerade um die Zeit geboren wurde, die Elisa der Frau angekündigt hatte (V.16). Hier liegt die Pointe der Erzählung. Außerdem bleiben uns in der langen Geschichte auch die Namen der Mutter und des Vaters des Kindes unbekannt. Nur die auch sonst bekannten Hauptakteure der Prophetenlegende, Elisa und sein Diener Gehasi, sind namentlich genannt; darüber hinaus interessieren biographische Fragen diese Erzählung überhaupt nicht [8]).

Ganz anders liegen die Dinge in der Thronfolgeerzählung, die auch Familiengeschichte Davids genannt wird [9]). Für sie ist biographisches Interesse im allgemeinen charakteristisch, besonders ausgeprägt in bezug auf das davidische Königshaus. Um so mehr wundert es, daß der Erstgeborene Davids und Bathsebas in *dieser* Überlieferung nicht mit einem Namen belegt ist.

Man könnte zwar versuchen, die fehlende Namengebung *historisch* so zu rechtfertigen, daß man die neutestamentliche Überlieferung (Lk. i 59, ii 21) zu Hilfe nimmt, nach der die Namengebung gleichzeitig mit der Beschneidung des Jungen am 8. Tag erfolgte, und sie mit der Angabe von 2 Sam. xii 18 kombiniert, wonach das Kind am 7. Tag starb. Danach hätte das Kind noch keinen Namen bekommen können. Dagegen spricht jedoch allein schon die Namengebung des „zweiten" Kindes (xii 24), die nichts von einer Frist von 8 Tagen ahnen läßt, und vor allem die mangelnde Evidenz für die Gültigkeit des neutestamentlich bezeugten

[6]) Es handelt sich um eine volkstümliche Wandererzählung, deren Stoff nicht genuin israelitisch ist, s. M. Noth, *Könige* (Neukirchen, 1968), S. 47; E. Würthwein *Die Bücher der Könige* (Göttingen, 1977) S. 36 f.

[7]) 2 Reg. iv 17: *wtld bn* wie in 2 Sam. xi 27 und xii 24.

[8]) Genausowenig Biographisches bietet die entsprechende Erzählung der Eliaüberlieferung (1 Reg. xvii 17-24).

[9]) Siehe z.B. Cook, S. 155; A. F. Puukko, *Vanhan Testamentin johdanto-oppi* (Helsinki, 1945), S. 100; E. Sellin — G. Fohrer, *Einleitung in das Alte Testament* (Heidelberg, [10]1965), S. 241; F. Langlamet, „Pour ou contre Salomon?", *RB* 83 (1976), S. 345.

Brauchs bereits in älteren Zeiten [10]). Vielmehr gewinnt man aus den alttestamentlichen Berichten über Namengebungen [11]) den Eindruck, daß dem Kind der Name unmittelbar nach seiner Geburt gegeben wurde [12]). Hätte die im NT vorausgesetzte Gewohnheit trotzdem für soviel ältere Zeiten Gültigkeit — was allerdings eine sehr hypothetische Möglichkeit ist —, könnte man sich kaum dem Verdacht entziehen, daß das Kind eben deswegen am 7. Tag sterben *mußte*, damit es noch ohne Namen auskommen konnte. In beiden Fällen verrät der Bericht somit seine historische Unwahrscheinlichkeit.

Sowohl historische wie auch formgeschichtliche Erwägungen sprechen also dafür, daß auch das erstgeborene Kind einen Namen bekam. Dazu kommt noch das literarische Argument, das bereits von S. A. Cook (S. 156f.) und E. Würthwein (*Thronfolge*, S. 31f.) geltend gemacht worden ist: Der Satz *wyqrʾ ʾt šmw šlmh* (xii 24bβ) würde zu dem abrupten Ende der Erzählung von der Geburt des ersten Kindes in xi 27a eine tadellose Fortsetzung bilden [13]). Der unmittelbar vorangehende Satz *wtld bn* (xii 24bα) wäre dann eine dem Kontext geschickt angepaßte Wiederaufnahme des gleichen Satzes in xi 27a, die zeigte, daß alles, was zwischen diesem Ring liegt (xi 27b-xii 24a), einen sekundären Einschub bildet.

Auf den ersten Teil des Einschubs, die Nathan-David-Szene (2 Sam. xi 27b-xii 15a) brauche ich nicht mehr näher einzugehen, denn ihr sekundärer Charakter an dieser Stelle ist schon längst und mehrfach erwiesen [14]). Immerhin, auch diese Szene gibt ein

---

[10]) Die priesterschriftliche Überlieferung kennt zwar die Beschneidung am 8. Tag (Gen. xvii 12, xxi 4; Lev.xii 3), aber ohne Namengebung. Aus Gen. xxi 3-4 geht eher hervor, daß der Junge den Namen schon vor der Beschneidung erhielt.

[11]) Vgl. z.B. die Benennung der Kinder Jakobs in Gen. xxix 32 - xxx 24, weiter Gen. xix 37, 38, xxxv 16-18; Ri. xiii 24; 1 Sam. iv 19-21 u.ö. Wenn Mose seinen Namen ausnahmsweise lange Zeit nach der Geburt (Ex. ii 2) erhält (V. 10), hängt das eng mit der Eigenart der Überlieferung zusammen: Mose hatte einen ägyptischen Namen, den er nicht von seinen hebräischen Eltern bekommen konnte.

[12]) So auch M. Noth, *Die israelitischen Personennamen im Rahmen der gemeinsemitischen Namengebung* (Stuttgart, 1928), S. 56, und R. de Vaux, *Les Institutions de l'Ancien Testament* I (Paris, 1958), S. 74.

[13]) Ein vielsagendes Zeichen dafür, daß xi 27a nicht als ein befriedigender Erzählungsabschluß empfunden wird, ist Buddes Versuch, xii 25aβb hinter xi 27a zu setzen (K. Budde, *Die Bücher Samuel* [Tübingen/Leipzig, 1902], S. 257), was aber nur eine literarisch und sachlich unbegründete Rettungsaktion ist.

[14]) Siehe F. Schwally, *ZAW* 12 (1892), S. 153-5; Cook, S. 156; Budde, S. 254; W. Nowack, *Richter, Ruth u. Bücher Samuelis* (Göttingen, 1902), S. 194;

in diesem Zusammenhang beachtenswertes Argument an die Hand. Die von Nathan dem David verkündete Strafe (V. *10-12) [15]) deutet merkwürdigerweise mit keinem Wort den Tod des im Ehebruch gezeugten Kindes an; erst die später hinzugefügte deuteronomistische Überleitung (V. 13-14) trägt das Schicksal des Kindes in die Gerichtsbotschaft ein, sie auf diese Weise mit der nachfolgenden Erzählung ausgleichend [16]). Es fragt sich also, ob nicht die alte Nathan-David-Szene in einer Zeit bzw. Umgebung entstanden ist, wo die Geschichte vom Tod des Erstgeborenen unbekannt war [17]).

Wenn wir uns jetzt noch näher der Wiederaufnahme in 2 Sam. xii 24bβ zuwenden, müssen wir in dem Satz *wyqrʾ ʾt šmw šlmh* die Nennung von David als Subjekt als ein wenig störend empfinden, weil es nämlich bis zum 9. Jahrhundert Sitte war, daß die Mutter dem Kind den Namen gab [18]), was man auch nach 2 Sam. xi 26-27a für normal halten würde. Es gibt jedoch eine Lösung auch für dieses Problem. In 2 Sam. xii 24 ist neben der Keṯīb-Lesart *wyqrʾ* als Qerē auch die feminine Lesung *wtqrʾ* überliefert, die außerdem durch mehrere Handschriften und einige Übersetzungen bezeugt ist (*BHS*). Sie vertritt ohne Zweifel die ältere Textform [19]), die aus einer Zeit stammt, als es noch üblich war, daß die Mutter ihrem Kind den Namen gab, während die maskuline Form *wyqrʾ* die später veränderten, patriarchalischen Verhältnisse in der Namengebung widerspiegelt.

H. Gressmann, *Die älteste Geschichtsschreibung und Prophetie Israels* (Göttingen, [2]1921), S. 156 f.; H. P. Smith, *A Critical and Exegetical Commentary on the Books of Samuel* (Edinburgh, [4]1951), S. 322; vgl. auch W. Dietrich, *Prophetie und Geschichte* (Göttingen, 1972), S. 132,und Würthwein, *Thronfolge*, S. 24.

[15]) Auch diese Verse sind deuteronomistisch überarbeitet (s. Dietrich, *Prophetie und Geschichte* S. 127-31), was jedoch hier keine Rolle spielt.

[16]) T. Veijola, *Die ewige Dynastie* (Helsinki, 1975), S. 113.

[17]) L. Rost, *Die Überlieferung von der Thronnachfolge Davids* (Stuttgart, 1926), S. 97, versucht die Existenz von 2 Sam. xii 15b ff. mit der Nathan-David-Szene zu begründen: „Erst durch die Hereinnahme Nathans wird die sonst nur lose angefügte Erzählung vom Sterben des Kindes zu einem wichtigen Glied des Ganzen." Was geschieht aber mit der „nur lose angefügten Erzählung", wenn die Begründung falsch ist?

[18]) Das Material zusammengestellt bei S.Herner, „Athalja", *Vom Alten Testament, Festschrift für K. Marti, BZAW* 41 (1925), S. 137-41; vgl. auch Noth, *Namengebung*, S. 56; de Vaux, *Les Institutions* I, S. 74; J. J. Stamm, „Hebräische Ersatznamen", *Festschrift für B. Landsberger* (1965), S. 414.

[19]) So auch J. J. Stamm, „Der Name des Königs Salomo", *ThZ* 16 (1960), S. 287, 295.

Nun scheint es aber weiter, daß die jüngere, maskuline Lesung mit der Erzählung vom Sterben des ersten Kindes eng zusammenhängt. In dieser Erzählung konzentriert sich nämlich alle Aufmerksamkeit auf David, dem der Erzählung nach offenbar viel daran liegt, daß er ein zweites Kind anstelle des verstorbenen bekommt. Bathseba spielt hier überhaupt keine Rolle, sie tut nur das, wozu David nicht fähig ist: sie gebiert (V. 24), aber für alles Sonstige, die Namengebung eingeschlossen, trägt David selber die Verantwortung. Demnach setzt die ältere, feminine Lesart *wtqr'* offensichtlich *nicht* die Geburt des zweiten, sondern die des ersten Kindes voraus, bei der Bathseba zwar auch eine bescheidene, aber doch eine etwas aktivere Rolle als bei der zweiten spielt (vgl. xi 26-27a mit xii 24abα). Für David dagegen konnte die Geburt des ersten Kindes kein besonders fröhliches Ereignis werden, denn dazu war die Vorgeschichte des Kindes doch etwas zu düster. Folglich kann man von ihm auch keine besondere Lust zur Namengebung erwarten, die nach dem damaligen Brauch ohnehin die Sache der Mutter war.

Wie nannte Bathseba nun aber ihren Sohn? Es war im alten Israel üblich, daß das Kind einen symbolischen Namen erhielt [20]), der eine Anspielung auf die Umstände aus dem Leben der Mutter enthalten konnte [21]). Der Name *Šᵉlomō* gehört nach J. J. Stamm zu der Gruppe der sog. Ersatznamen [22]) und bezeichnet das Ergebnis der im Verb *šlm* Pi. ausgedrückten Tätigkeit „ersetzen, unversehrt machen", bedeutet also: „seine Unversehrtheit" [23]), oder mit G. Gerleman [24]) in Weiterführung von Stamm vielleicht besser: „sein Ersatz". Stamm und Gerleman sehen in dem Namen eine Erinnerung an das zuvor gestorbene Kind [25]). Aber war das erste Kind mit seinem dubiösen Hintergrund nach der Geburt des „zweiten" wirklich noch so wichtig, daß Bathseba — oder noch weniger David nach dem jetzigen Wortlaut — seine Erinnerung wach halten wollte? Ganz anders sehen die Dinge aus, wenn man von dem Tod des

---

[20]) Vgl. J. Barr, „The Symbolism of Names in the Old Testament", *BJRL* 52 (1969), S. 11-29.

[21]) So z.B. Gen. iv 1, xxix 31 — xxx 24. Seltener ist es, daß Umstände aus dem Leben des Vaters die Namengebung bestimmen (Ex. ii 22); vgl. de Vaux, *Les Institutions* I, S. 75.

[22]) Zu ihnen s. Stamm, *Festschrift für Landsberger*, S. 413-24.

[23]) Stamm, *ThZ* 16, S. 297.

[24]) „Die Wurzel *šlm*", *ZAW* 85 (1973), S. 13; vgl. Ders., „*šlm*", *THAT* II (1976), Sp. 932.

[25]) Stamm, *ThZ* 16, S. 296; Gerleman, *ZAW* 85, S. 13.

ersten Kindes vollkommen absieht und in „Salomo" eben dessen Namen erblickt, den Bathseba ihm zur Erinnerung ihres vor kurzem verstorbenen Ehemannes Uria gab. Denn in diesem Fall hatte Bathseba vollen Anlaß, ihren erstgeborenen Sohn „seinen Ersatz" zu nennen, nämlich den Ersatz Urias, den sie neulich durch den Krieg auf eine, wie *sie* glauben mußte, ganz natürliche Weise verloren hatte. Den Grundsatz „Das Schwert frißt bald so, bald so" (xi 25) konnte Joab in Urias Fall kaum ganz ernst nehmen (vgl.xi 15), für Bathseba dagegen war er die einzige mögliche Erklärung für das Schicksal ihres Ehemannes. Der Ernst der Lage für Bathseba bestand jetzt darin, daß sie als Witwe ohne Kinder [26]) in eine sozial äußerst ungesicherte Situation zu geraten drohte [27]). In diesem Augenblick war es für sie ein besonderes Glück, daß sie ein Kind erwarten konnte, und zudem noch ein Kind für den König. Darin öffnete sich für sie eine ganz ungewöhnliche Chance, sich aus der Notlage einer Witwe zu retten. Als Gattin des Königs und Mutter eines Sohnes war sie vollkommen berechtigt, ihrem Sohn im Blick auf Uria den Danknamen [28]) „sein Ersatz" zu geben, denn das war Salomo wahrhaftig für sie. Andererseits wollte sie durch diesen Namen auch die Ehre ihres königlichen Gatten retten, indem sie die Umgebung, der die näheren Umstände nicht bekannt sein konnten, verstehen ließ, daß das Kind von ihrem ehemaligen Mann Uria gezeugt war; d.h. sie wollte durch die kluge Wahl des Namens eben das erreichen, was David nicht gelungen war, als er Uria nach Jerusalem befahl [29]). Wer etwa moralische Bedenken gegen diese Art der Namengebung hat, der muß sich zunächst von späteren (Vor-)Urteilen freimachen und sich dann auch vergegenwärtigen, daß moralische Skrupel den Charakter Bathsebas offenbar wenig belasteten (vgl. 1 Reg. i).

Es versteht sich von selbst, daß man später Anstoß an einen Namen als Namen des großen Königs Salomo nahm, der eine Anspielung auf den gemordeten Ehemann Bathsebas enthielt. Ein vielsagendes Zeichen für das hier empfundene Unbehagen und

---

[26]) Von früheren Kindern Bathsebas wird jedenfalls nichts gesagt.

[27]) Zur Lage der Witwe z.B. de Vaux, *Les Institutions* I, S. 69. In Bathsebas Fall wäre wahrscheinlich die Leviratsehe nicht ohne weiteres in Frage gekommen, weil ihr verstorbener Mann ein Ausländer war.

[28]) Das war der Name Salomo nämlich auch, s. Stamm, *Festschrift für Landsberger* S. 421.

[29]) Dagegen lag nichts Ungewöhnliches darin, daß David eine kurz zuvor verwitwete Frau ohne akuten Anlaß heiratet (vgl. Abigail 1 Sam. xxv 39).

zugleich für das Bewußtsein von der ursprünglichen Bedeutung des Namens „Salomo" unter den späteren Lesern der Thronfolgeerzählung ist die stark glossenhafte Fortsetzung zu Salomos Namengebung (xii 24bγ-25) [30]), wo die göttliche Liebe zu diesem Kind hervorgehoben und es mit einem neuen, ganz orthodoxen Namen *Jedidja*, „Jahwes Liebling", umbenannt wird.

Hier entstehen im Blick auf den heutigen Wortlaut allerlei Fragen. L. Delekat z.B. fragt, warum Jahwe eigentlich den zweiten Sohn Bathsebas öffentlich zu seinem Liebling erklärt; und Delekat fügt hinzu: „Der Erzähler tut nichts, das zu erklären. Der Eindruck, der entsteht, ist: Jahwe hat seinen Unmut zu erkennen gegeben, lenkt dann aber seinem Auserwählten zuliebe rasch wieder ein" [31]). Es ist aber unfair und auch unnötig, dem alten Verfasser eine solche Gemeinheit zur Last zu legen, denn die Umbenennung Salomos durch Nathan ist ein allzu durchsichtiger, nachträglicher [32]) Versuch, dem König einen makellosen neuen Namen zu verleihen, der sich dann freilich nicht mehr durchsetzen konnte. Demselben Ziel diente — mit viel größerem Erfolg — auch die vorgeschobene Erzählung von der Erkrankung und dem Tod des ersten Kindes, denn daran anschließend konnte Salomo tatsächlich als „*sein* Ersatz" betrachtet werden [33]).

III

Die bisherigen Beobachtungen und Überlegungen haben schon vielerlei Bedenken gegen die Echtheit der Erzählung vom Tod des ersten und von der Geburt des zweiten Kindes (xii 15b-24a) hervorgerufen. Die von Würthwein (*Thronfolge*, S. 32) erwähnte

---

[30]) Zur Stelle vgl. Würthwein, *Thronfolge*, S. 29 f.; auch nach Langlamet, *RB* 83, S. 136, 506, ist sie sekundär.

[31]) L. Delekat, „Tendenz und Theologie der David-Salomo-Erzählung", *Das ferne und nahe Wort, Festschrift für L. Rost*, *BZAW* 105 (1967), S. 32.

[32]) Der sekundäre Charakter der Stelle verrät sich auch dadurch, daß der Namengeber der späteren patriarchalischen Sitte gemäß Nathan ist (vgl. Herner, S. 139). Der masoretische Wortlaut von V. 25a, der vor den vielen Korrekturvorschlägen doch den Vorzug verdient, kann wohl nur bedeuten: „und er (Jahwe) sandte (Botschaft) durch den Propheten Nathan und dieser nannte seinen Namen Jedidja" (vgl. z.B. Stamm, *ThZ* 16, S. 287; *Jerusalemer Bibel* [auf deutsch] und *Traduction Œcuménique de la Bible*).

[33]) T. N. D. Mettinger, *King and Messiah* (Lund, 1976), S. 30, schreibt in treuer Nachfolge des Ergänzers: „The death of the child implies that the Davidic dynasty does not bear the blame in the matter of Bathsheba. The author of the SN (Succession Narrative) is also anxious to make it clear that Solomon is not to be mistaken for the illegitimate child."

zeitliche Schwierigkeit mit zwei Geburten während der Belagerung von Rabbath Ammon ist jedoch noch nicht zur Sprache gekommen.

Nach 2 Sam. xi 1 fand die Mobilisierung des Heeres „bei der Rückkehr des Jahres, um die Zeit, da die Könige ins Feld zu ziehen pflegten" statt. Danach — und nach Parallelbelegen (1 Reg. xx 22, 26; 1 Chr. xx 1; 2 Chr. xxxvi 10) — würde man denken, daß es sich um einen der normalen Feldzüge handelte, die die altorientalischen Herrscher mehr oder weniger regelmäßig zu einer festen Zeit im Jahre [34]) unternahmen. Es kann natürlich geschehen, daß ein Feldzug aus unerwarteten Gründen länger dauert als geplant. Aber können die Israeliten Rabbath Ammon nahezu zwei Jahre belagert haben, die man etwa braucht, um zwei Geburten unterbringen zu können?

Hätten wir allein den Bericht über de Belagerung (2 Sam. xi 1a, xii 26-31) ohne die Bathseba-Geschichte, würde niemand an einen so langen Zeitraum denken. Auch die entsprechende Darstellung des Chronisten (1 Chr. xx 1-3), in der die Bathseba-Affäre aus moralischen Gründen weggelassen ist, erweckt keineswegs den Eindruck einer so langen Belagerung. Außerdem muß in Betracht gezogen werden, daß der Ammoniterkrieg nicht allein mit Davids Söldnern durchgeführt wurde (x 7, xi 1, 11, 24), sondern der ganze Heerbann Israels war mit der heiligen Lade ausgezogen (xi 1, 7, 11, xii 28, 31) und unterlag der Pflicht der sexuellen Enthaltsamkeit (xi 11, 13, vgl. Jos. iii 5; 1 Sam. xxi 6) [35]). So fragt es sich, ob ein solcher Jahwekrieg, der eine gemeinsame Angelegenheit aller wehrpflichtigen Männer in Israel war, sei es aus praktischen oder aus theoretischen Gründen [36]), fast zwei Jahre dauern konnte.

Bereits K. Budde hat die hier vorliegende zeitliche Schwierigkeit klar gesehen, wenn er sagt: „Es versteht sich ganz von selbst, daß

---

[34]) Die Zeitbestimmung „Rückkehr des Jahres" (*tšwbt hšnh*) bezieht sich wahrscheinlich auf den Übergang des Winters zum Sommer, also auf das Frühjahr, das auch nach den Angaben der assyrischen Annalen die normale Zeit für den Auszug des Heeres war, s. J. Begrich, *Die Chronologie der Könige von Israel und Juda und die Quellen des Rahmens der Königsbücher* (Tübingen, 1929), S. 88 f.; de Vaux, *Les Institutions* I, S. 289 f.

[35]) Vgl. G. von Rad, *Der Heilige Krieg im alten Israel* (Göttingen, [5]1969), S. 7, 35 f.

[36]) Eine lange andauernde Belagerung wäre eine *petitio principii* einer Kriegstheorie, zu der Jahwes entscheidendes Eingreifen als konstitutives Element gehört (vgl. von Rad, *Der Heilige Krieg*, S. 12 f.; F. Stolz, *Jahwes und Israels Kriege* [Zürich, 1972], S. 187-91). Als Einschränkung muß allerdings die Frage gestellt werden, ob es damals überhaupt schon eine Theorie des „heiligen Krieges" gegeben hat (vgl. G. H. Jones, „'Holy War' or 'Yahweh War'?", *VT* 25 [1975], S. 642-58).

nicht alles, was bis hieher erzählt ist, Empfängnis und Geburt zweier Kinder und gar die Übergabe des zweiten an einen Erzieher [37]), sich vor der Beendigung des Ammoniterkriegs abgespielt hat" (S. 258). Die Lösung des Problems meinte Budde darin zu finden, daß der Verfasser den angesponnenen Faden zunächst bis zu seinem Ende verfolge und dann wieder zu früher geschehenen Ereignissen zurückkehre (xii 26-31) (S. 258). Es fällt aber nicht leicht, dem erzählerisch sehr hochstehenden Verfasser der Thronfolgeerzählung eine derartig gezwungene Lösung zuzumuten. Wenn er eine Nachholung im Sinne von Budde beabsichtigt hätte, hätte er das wahrscheinlich doch auch dem Leser irgendwie kenntlich gemacht. Nun denkt der unbefangene Leser ja ganz selbstverständlich, daß die Bathseba-Geschichte sich bis zu ihrem Ende, zur Geburt des zweiten Kindes, während der Belagerung von Rabbath Ammon abspielt.

In einem etwas anderen Licht erscheint das zeitliche Problem wiederum, wenn man der von Budde (S. 250) angegriffenen Interpretation folgt, nach der der Ammoniterkriegsbericht (2 Sam. *x, xi 1, xii 26-31) eine eigenständige Quelle vertritt, die erst sekundär mit der Bathseba-Geschichte kombiniert wurde. Eindeutig ist der Befund freilich auch dann nicht, denn zwei Vertreter dieser Auffassung, S. A. Cook (S. 156 f.) und L. Rost (S. 74-80, 97 f.), sind verschiedener Meinung über Salomos Herkunft: Nach Cook war er der erste, nach Rost dagegen der zweite Sohn Bathsebas. Aber man könnte im Sinne von Rost — der selber auf unser spezielles Problem allerdings nicht eingeht — argumentieren und sagen, daß der Verfasser hier zwei ganz verschiedene Stoffe miteinander in Verbindung gebracht hat, wodurch leicht chronologische Unausgeglichenheiten entstehen können. Nun gibt jedoch Rost (S. 92) selber zu, daß die Bathseba-Geschichte den Ammoniterkriegsbericht als *Rahmen* voraussetzt; also ganz mechanisch sind die zwei Überlieferungen doch auch nach ihm nicht nebeneinandergeraten.

Wenn man einmal versuchsweise die *prinzipielle* Richtigkeit der Rostschen Theorie von der Eigenständigkeit des Ammoniterkriegsberichts akzeptiert [38]), muß man jedoch unbedingt eine Korrektur

---

[37]) Budde, S. 257 f., macht in xii 25 die seit J. Wellhausen, *Der Text der Bücher Samuelis* (Göttingen, 1871), S. 185, übliche Textkorrektur *wyšlm* statt *wyšlḥ*.

[38]) Rost, S. 80, gibt als Umfang der „Quelle" 2 Sam. x 6 - xi 1, xii 26-31 an und begründet ihre Selbständigkeit mit stilistischen Argumenten (S. 75 f.), die beim heutigen Stand der Literaturwissenschaft kaum jemanden noch überzeugen können.

an ihr vornehmen. 2 Sam. xi 1 kann unmöglich Teil allein des Feldzugsberichts sein, da dieser Vers nicht Einleitung nur zum Kriegsgeschehen, sondern gleichzeitig auch zu den unheimlichen Ereignissen in Jerusalem ist: Um die Zeit, da die Könige ins Feld zu ziehen pflegten, sendet David Joab mit den Söldnern und dem israelitischen Heerbann aus, bleibt aber selber in der Stadt. Damit sind die Weichen für die nachfolgende Geschichte gestellt, die Spannung des Lesers geweckt, der jetzt neugierig darauf wartet, was in der von wehrfähigen Männern leeren Hauptstadt wohl noch geschehen wird. Zugleich ist aber eben dieser Vers in literarischer Hinsicht die Stelle, an der der Ammoniterkrieg und die Bathseba-Geschichte sich zeitlich überschneiden, was zeigt, daß wenigstens dem Verfasser dieses Verses, d.h. dem Verfasser der Thronfolgeerzählung, sehr viel an der Gleichzeitigkeit der Ereignisse an der Front und in der Stadt lag.

Man könnte natürlich noch einen Schritt weitergehen und einwenden, daß es sich trotz der Gleichschaltung in der Thronfolgeerzählung *historisch* gesehen um zwei verschiedene Kriege handelt, wie Rost [39]) offenbar annimmt. Das ist jedoch eine sehr kühne Hypothese, die noch besonders bewiesen werden müßte; denn die heutige Fassung der Erzählung bietet kaum Anhaltspunkte für ihre Richtigkeit. Sowohl nach dem Ammoniterkriegsbericht (xii 26, 27, 29) wie auch während der Bathseba-Geschichte (xi 16-25) handelt es sich um die Belagerung einer Stadt, die nach der Einleitung (xi 1) und dem Kriegsbericht (xii 27, 29) Rabba heißt [40]). Nach beiden Berichten ist der König David an dem Kriegsgeschehen nicht persönlich beteiligt, die Führung des Krieges liegt in den Händen des Joab (xi 6, 7, 14, 17, 18, 22, 25, xii 26, 27), wie auch der Verfasser in der Einleitung (xi 1) feststellt. Hier wie dort geht es um ein gemeinsames Unternehmen der Söldner und des Heerbannes (xi 7, 11, 24, xii 28, 29, 31), wie ebenfalls die Einleitung voraussetzt (xi 1). Unter diesen Umständen bleibt derjenige den Beweis schuldig, der hier trotzdem zwei verschiedene Kriege finden möchte. Solange das nicht

---

[39]) S. 77: „Wir wissen gar nicht, ob der Krieg, in dessen Verlauf die Uriageschichte spielt, wirklich jener Ammoniterkrieg von xii 26 ff. war." Die Begründung lautet: „In xi 2 ff. erfahren wir — von xii 9 abgesehen — nie den Namen der Gegner Davids, geschweige den Namen der belagerten Stadt" (Rost, S. 77). Ähnlich denkt offenbar auch Cook, S. 157.

[40]) Die Dreiteilung des Stoffes in „Kriegsbericht", „Bathseba-Geschichte" und„ Einleitung" ist lediglich ein Versuch, das Material von dem Gesichtspunkt Rost's aus zu betrachten.

gelungen ist, besteht zwischen dem Ammoniterkrieg und der Bathseba-Geschichte mit zwei Geburten eine zeitliche Diskrepanz, die nicht wegzuerklären ist.

IV

Nach allen Anzeichen, die wir bis jetzt zusammengestellt haben, scheint „die Erzählung von dem ersten gestorbenen Kind der Bathseba" tatsächlich „eine Legende" zu sein, „die von Salomo den Makel nehmen will, daß er als Frucht eines ehebrecherischen Verhältnisses geboren sei." [41]) Das erfordert allerdings, daß wir eine Erklärung auch für den sonderbaren Charakter der Legende (2 Sam. xii 15 b-24 a) geben können.

Nach dieser Legende benimmt sich David ja *vor* dem Tod des Kindes wie man sich gewöhnlich *nach* dem Tod zu benehmen pflegt (V. 16-17, 21) und gibt zu seinem Verhalten eine Erklärung, die merkwürdig rational(istisch) klingt (V. 20-23). Die Sache ist natürlich schon immer aufgefallen und hat vielerlei, teilweise sogar recht komische Deutungen unter den Auslegern gefunden. Nach K. Budde (S. 257) ist Davids Verhalten „Beweis gesunden Menschenverstands und männlicher Haltung", nach A. Schulz [42]) dagegen der „Willensstärke in der Überwindung unnötigen Schmerzes", während nach W. Caspari [43]) der König „mit Rücksicht auf den augenblicklichen Kriegszustand" auf die Trauergebräuche verzichtete. Für L. Rost (S. 98) wird in Davids Antwort an seine Diener „die Anerkennung der unbeugsamen Gerechtigkeit Gottes" sichtbar, für H. W. Hertzberg [44]) dagegen die „übergeordnete Erkenntnis", daß „die Sache zwischen Gott und ihm (David) nunmehr wirklich in Ordnung" sei. Den größten Einfluß hat jedoch die Erklärung der Stelle durch J. Pedersen [45]) gehabt. Nach ihm verrät sich in Davids Benehmen eine ganz neuartige, liberale Einstellung zum Tod und zu den altisraelitischen Trauerbräuchen. David zeige durch sein Verhalten, daß er die Konsequenzen nicht kennt, die die vom Tod verursachte Unreinheit nach der traditionellen Denkweise für das Menschenleben mit sich brachte. „Er beurteilt die Handlungen nur nach ihren Resultaten." Auch E. Würthwein (*Thronfolge*, S. 26) hat sich die Deutung

[41]) Auerbach, S. 228 Anm. 1.
[42]) *Die Bücher Samuel* II (Münster 1920), S. 135.
[43]) *Die Samuelbücher* (Leipzig, 1926), S. 534.
[44]) *Die Samuelbücher* (Göttingen, ⁴1968), S. 259.
[45]) *Israel* III-IV (København, 1936), S. 345.

von Pedersen zu eigen gemacht; im Unterschied zu Pedersen betont er aber mehr die Rolle des Verfassers, der uns dieses Charakterbild von David in *kritischer* Absicht vermittelt hat. Die Episode enthalte somit implizite Kritik an David von der Seite des Verfassers der Thronfolgeerzählung. Es ist aber nicht leicht, eine solche kritische Tendenz in der Darstellung zu erkennen, wie schon die oben angeführten, ganz andersartigen Stellungnahmen zu ihr zeigen [46]), und auch Würthwein selber ist von der Richtigkeit seiner eigenen Interpretation nicht vollkommen überzeugt (*Thronfolge*, S. 32).

Die Lösung des Problems ist m.E. viel einfacher, wenn man einmal den sekundären Charakter der Episode anerkannt hat. Von besonderer Bedeutung ist dann die Aussage von xii 18, nach der das Kind am 7. Tag starb. Diese Mitteilung ist kaum rein zufällig entstanden, denn die Zeitspanne von 7 Tagen als Lebenszeit [47]) des Kindes paßt in diesen Zusammenhang besser als jede andere. Einerseits dauerte die normale Trauerzeit eben 7 Tage (Gen. 1 10; 1 Sam. xxxi 13; Jdt. xvi 24; Sir. xxii 12), andererseits war nach den Reinheitsvorschriften jede Frau während ihrer Menstruation 7 Tage lang im Zustand der Unreinheit (*ṭm'h*) in dem sie nicht angetastet werden durfte (Lev. xv 19-24, xviii 19, xx 18); dasselbe galt auch von einer Mutter, die einen Sohn geboren hatte (Lev. xii 2), während die Mutter einer Tochter doppelt so lange unrein war (Lev. xii 5).

Bevor wir jetzt einige Schlußfolgerungen ziehen können, müssen wir noch eins in Betracht ziehen: daß nämlich nach einer Notiz in 2 Sam. xi 4 Bathseba sich gerade „von ihrer Unreinheit (*mṭm'th*) gereinigt hatte" [48]), als David sie zum ersten Mal zu sich holen ließ. Ihr Bad bedeutete also die notwendige Reinigung von der eben abgelaufenen Regel, und damals wurde sie sofort schwanger.

[46]) Eine von ihnen noch abweichende Erklärung bietet G. Gerleman, „Schuld und Sühne", *Beiträge zur Alttestamentlichen Theologie, Festschrift für W. Zimmerli* (Göttingen, 1977), S. 132-9. Nach ihm (S. 138) beruht der Dissens zwischen David und seinen Höflingen auf der unterschiedlichen Ausgangsposition der beiden: „David wußte, daß der Tod des Neugeborenen eine Sühne war, durch welche Jahwe ein in Gang gekommenes Böses aufhob", was der König aber seinen Dienern verschleiern wollte. Diese Auslegung ist leider auf der unhaltbaren Voraussetzung gebaut, daß 2 Sam. xii 15b ff. die Nathan-David-Szene (xii 1-15a) kennt; die deuteronomistischen Verse 13-14 sind sogar der Schlüssel der Interpretation (S. 133-6), s. jedoch oben Anm. 14 und 16.

[47]) Im Duktus der Darstellung hindert nichts, den 7. Tag als 7. *Lebenstag* des Kindes zu betrachten.

[48]) Die verspätete Stellung der Bemerkung (ihr Platz wäre eigentlich in V. 2) sowie ihr pedantischer Charakter lassen vermuten, daß sie als Vorbereitung für die Legende xii 15b-24a von deren Verfasser konzipiert wurde.

Nun wollte der spätere Verfasser, der den Tod des Kindes am 7. Tag eintreten ließ, damit zweierlei verständlich machen. Einerseits wollte er dem Leser den Gedanken suggerieren, daß Bathseba nach 7 Tagen, als David zu ihr kam (V. 24), sich wieder in demselben Zustand befand wie beim ersten Mal und auch jetzt sofort schwanger werden konnte. Andererseits gab die siebentägige Lebenszeit des Kindes dem Erzähler die Gelegenheit zu demonstrieren, daß David ein frommer Mann war, der nichts unterließ, um dem Kind durch intensives Beten und Fasten das Leben zu retten. Gleichzeitig konnte David die üblichen Trauerriten im voraus durchführen, was also nicht in erster Linie aus „aufgeklärten", sondern aus zeitlichen Gründen geschah. Hätte David nämlich die Trauerriten erst *nach* dem Tod des Kindes begonnen, wäre die für die Empfängnis günstige Zeit bei Bathseba nach der Meinung des Verfassers vorbeigegangen, was er nicht mehr in Kauf nehmen konnte.

Freilich bleiben hier auch einige offene Fragen. Rein biologisch gesehen dürfte es höchst unwahrscheinlich sein, daß eine Frau 7 Tage nach der Entbindung schon wieder schwanger wird [49]). Zudem sagt unser Erzähler nichts davon, wie denn Bathseba mit ihrer Trauerzeit nach dem Tode ihres Kindes fertig wurde. Nach dem Tode ihres Mannes hatte sie auf jeden Fall die Trauerzeit gehalten (xi 27). Diese Probleme sind natürlich keine Einwände gegen die Richtigkeit unserer These. Vielmehr sprechen auch sie für den legendarischen Charakter der Erzählung und müssen als der Tribut betrachtet werden, den der Ergänzer zollen mußte, als er zwei Geburten während des Ammoniterkrieges unterbringen wollte. Er konnte nicht bis zu dem nächsten Monat warten, weil er wußte, daß der Ammoniterfeldzug sich durch seine Einmischung sowieso in eine bedenkliche Länge ausdehnte. Die biologische Unwahrscheinlichkeit der Sache dagegen hat der (männliche) Erzähler kaum bemerkt [50]), und Bathsebas Gefühle beunruhigten ihn wohl wenig.

---

[49]) Auch die priesterschriftliche Gesetzgebung, die nach ihrem Stoff jedoch älter ist (s. M. Noth, *Das dritte Buch Mose* [Göttingen, ^{3}1973], S.82), nimmt Rücksicht auf eine länger andauernde Blutung der Wöchnerin, während der sie nicht kultfähig ist (Lev. xii 4-5); sexuellen Umgang mit ihr verbietet diese Vorschrift jedoch nicht.

[50]) Ebensowenig kann man von ihm die Kenntnis davon erwarten, daß die größte Empfängnisbereitschaft der Frau nicht 7, sondern 14 Tage nach Einsetzen der Regel liegt. Für ihn war die Hauptsache zu zeigen, daß Bathsebas Schwangerschaft beide Mal zum gleichen Zeitpunkt einsetze, was auch biologisch durchaus glaubwürdig klingt.

Es genügt, daß David sie „tröstet" (xii 24); dann kann David schon zu ihr gehen und ihr beiwohnen.

Viel wichtiger war es in den Augen des Erzählers, dem Leser *psychologisch* verständlich zu machen, wie David unmittelbar nach dem Tod des Kindes zu Bathseba gehen konnte. Hier zeigt er auch ein besonders feines Gefühl. Nachdem er dargestellt hat, wie David die Trauerriten im voraus durchführt und das Kind stirbt (xii 16-19), schildert er im Detail — viel ausführlicher als eigentlich notwendig wäre —, wie David von der Erde aufsteht, sich wäscht und salbt, andere Kleider anzieht, in das Haus Jahwes geht und betet, nach Hause kommt und ißt (V. 20). All das, worüber die Hofleute staunen (V. 21), ist ein Zeichen dafür, daß der König sich getröstet hat und wieder zum normalen Ungang mit anderen Menschen fähig ist — auch zum Umgang mit seiner Frau Bathseba. Denn die eben beschriebenen Maßnahmen erscheinen, mehr oder weniger vollständig aufgezählt, häufig auch als Vorbereitung eines sexuellen Aktes [51]). Einige von ihnen tauchen sogar unter den Zwangsmaßnahmen auf, mit denen David bestrebt ist, den von der Front heimgeholten Uria zum sexuellen Kontakt mit Bathseba zu bringen. Er sagt zu ihm: „Gehe in dein Haus hinab und wasche deine Füße" (xi 8) [52]). Auf die Frage, warum er doch nicht nach Hause gegangen war, antwortet Uria u.a.: „Sollte ich in mein Haus gehen, um zu essen und zu trinken und bei meinem Weibe zu schlafen" (xi 11). Beim zweiten Mal versucht David sein Ziel zu erreichen, indem er Uria einlädt, bei ihm zu essen und zu trinken, um ihn dabei trunken zu machen (xi 13). Wir sehen also, daß der Verfasser, der David sich nach dem Tod des Kindes mit allen gebührenden Mitteln „fit" machen läßt (xii 20), ein sensibler Mann war, der wußte, wie „fließend die Grenzen zwischen der Physiologie und der Psychologie sind" [53]) und wie die schwierige Aufgabe, die er sich gesetzt hatte, mit Takt und Raffinesse durchzuführen war.

V

Um etwas über den geistigen und geistlichen Hintergrund dieses Mannes zu erfahren, empfiehlt es sich, kurz auf die Art einzugehen,

---

[51]) Koh. ix 7-9; Rt. iii 3; Ez. xvi 9 ff.; vgl. auch Gen. xxix 22; Ri. xiv 10; Cant. i 3, iv 10; Est. ii 12, 18.

[52]) Das Wort *rglym* enthält hier vielleicht eine sexuelle Anspielung (vgl. Ex. iv 25; Jes. vi 2, vii 20; Rt. iii 4, 7), so Hertzberg, S. 254.

[53]) R. Smend, „Essen und Trinken — ein Stück Weltlichkeit des Alten Testaments", *Beiträge zur Alttestamentlichen Theologie, Festschrift für W. Zimmerli*, S. 448.

wie er seine Erzählung eingeführt hat. Er begründet den Tod des Kindes mit einem irrationalen Eingreifen Jahwes: „Jahwe aber schlug (*wygp*) das Kind ..., sodaß es krank wurde" (xii 15 b). Die hier gebrauchte Ausdrucksweise, nach der ein Mensch plötzlich durch einen Schlag (Verb *ngp* Qal) von Jahwe umkommt, hat in den Davidüberlieferungen zwei Parallelen, die aber beide in Zusammenhängen stehen, die eines Zusatzes verdächtig sind.

In der Nabalgeschichte (1 Sam. xxv) erscheint die Aussage „Etwa zehn Tage danach *schlug* Jahwe den Nabal, sodaß er starb" (V. 38) als eine sachlich überflüssige, theologische Korrektur zu der Feststellung des vorangehenden Verses „Es erstarb ihm sein Herz in seinem Inneren, und er wurde zu Stein." Nabal war m.E. auch nach der hebräischen Anthropologie damit schon tot genug und brauchte keinen zusätzlichen Schlag mehr [54]).

Die andere Stelle, die von einem Jahwe-Schlag zu berichten weiß, steht in 1 Sam. xxvi 10, in einer Rede, wo David es dem Abisai wehrt, den schlafenden Saul umzubringen, weil David nämlich meint, daß „Jahwe ihn *schlagen* wird, oder seine Stunde kommt, da er sterben muß, oder er in den Krieg zieht und weggerafft wird." Aber auch hier handelt es sich um keinen originären Zusammenhang, wie die unnötige Doppelung der Redeeinleitung (V. 9/10), die Wiederholung eines ganzen Satzes in Davids Mund (V. 9b/11a) und die inhaltliche Spannung mit dem nächsten Kontext (V. 11b/12a) uberdeutlich zeigen [55]).

Auch diese Beobachtungen zur Terminologie [56]) bestätigen also von einer neuen Seite das Ergebnis, daß wir es in der Erzählung vom Tod des ersten Kindes Bathsebas mit bearbeitender Tätigkeit zu tun haben. In der Thronfolgeerzählung selbst gibt es freilich keine Aussage, die mit der Einleitung dieser Erzählung wörtlich übereinstimmt. Aber es gibt doch einige Stellen, die in ihrem theologischen Gehalt ihr sehr nahekommen. Vor allem sind hier die drei geschichtstheologischen Notizen zu nennen, von denen ausgehend G. von

---

[54]) H. W. Wolff, *Anthropologie des Alten Testaments* (München, 1973), S. 69, gelingt es jedoch, hier einen Schlaganfall mit Gehirnblutung zu diagnostizieren.

[55]) Etwas zu gewaltsam ist die Lösung von H.-U. Nübel, *Davids Aufstieg in der Frühe israelitischer Geschichtsschreibung*, Diss.theol. Bonn (1959), S. 54, der auch V.9 dem Bearbeiter zuschreibt.

[56]) Auch das Substantiv *mgph* im Sinne einer von Jahwe verursachten Plage hat in den Davidüberlieferungen ausschließlich sekundäre Bezeugung: 2 Sam. xxiv 21, 25 (s. Veijola, S. 109).

Rad [57]) meinte, die eigentliche Intention der Thronfolgeerzählung erfassen zu können, die sich jedoch später — teilweise schon früher — als sekundäre Einschübe entpuppt haben.

Die erste dieser Notizen, die deuteronomistische Kommentierung am Ende der alten Bathseba-Geschichte (xi 27 b) [58]) ist mit ihrem moral-theologischen Charakter vielleicht noch etwas weit entfernt von der Aussage in xii 15 b, die die irrationale Seite des schicksalhaft wirkenden Jahwe betont. Ihr entspricht aber gut die zweite von G. von Rad hervorgehobene theologische Deutestelle, die am Ende unserer Episode steht, 2 Sam. xii 24bγ („und Jahwe liebte ihn") [59]), und die nach von Rad (*Ges. Stud.*, S. 183) „von der ganz irrationalen Liebe Gottes zu diesem Menschen" zeugt. Sie paßt ausgezeichnet mit dem Auftakt derselben Erzählung („Jahwe aber schlug das Kind ...") zusammen. Die dritte, für von Rad (S. 183 f.) die wichtigste geschichtstheologische Notiz, 2 Sam. xvii 14b, will im Zusammenhang des Absalom-Aufstandes zeigen, wie ein menschlich kluger Rat durch Jahwes Eingreifen zunichte gemacht wird: „Jahwe hatte nämlich befohlen, den guten Rat des Ahitophel zu vereiteln, um das Unheil über Absalom zu bringen." Niemand wird bestreiten, daß diese Aussage inhaltlich auf einer Linie mit 2 Sam. xii 15b („Jahwe aber schlug das Kind ...") steht.

Nun hat Würhwein (*Thronfolge*, S. 33-42) nachgewiesen und darin schon bei F. Langlamet (*RB* 83, S. 350-56) Bestätigung gefunden, daß die zuletzt erwähnte, dritte theologische Deutestelle nicht eine isolierte Eintragung, sondern Bestandteil einer umfangreichen Bearbeitungsschicht ist, die Ahitophel als Ratgeber in ein ungünstiges Licht setzen will [60]). Zusammenfassend sagt Würthwein (S. 42) über diese planvolle Bearbeitung, daß in ihr „die Hand eines sehr konsequent verfahrenden, aber auch sehr fähigen Mannes am Werk ist". Das läßt sich wohl ohne Übertreibung auch von demjenigen sagen, der die Erzählung vom Sterben des Erstgeborenen Bathsebas

[57]) „Der Anfang der Geschichtsschreibung im alten Israel" (1944), *Gesammelte Studien zum Alten Testament* (München, 1958), S. 181-6.

[58]) Dazu Dietrich, *Prophetie und Geschichte*, S. 132; vgl. ihm zustimmend Würthwein, *Thronfolge*, S. 24; auch Langlamet, *RB* 83, S. 136; dagegen wehren sich H. Seebass, „Nathan und David in II Sam. 12", *ZAW* 86 (1974), S. 210, Anm. 18, und Mettinger, S. 30.

[59]) Zum sekundären Charakter der Stelle s. Cook, S. 157 Anm. 31; Budde, S. 257; Würthwein, *Thronfolge*, S. 29 f.; vgl. auch Wallis, *ThWAT* I (1973), Sp. 122.

[60]) Würthwein, *Thronfolge*, S. 34-42, rechnet zu dieser Schicht: 2 Sam. xv 16b, 31, xvi 21-23, xvii 5-14, 15b, 23, xx 3. Vorschnell ist Mettingers Schlußfolgerung, 2 Sam. xvii 5-14 sei deuteronomistischer Herkunft (Mettinger, S. 29).

konzipierte. Weiter stellt Würthwein (S. 42) über die von ihm gefundene Bearbeitung fest, daß sie „ganz im Dienste der Dynastie steht", also „am Hofe zu vermuten ist". Anders kann es sich auch kaum mit einem Mann verhalten, der dem mächtigsten Exponenten der davidischen Dynastie eine anstoßfreie Herkunft fabrizierte. Zudem hebt Würthwein (S. 42) den „weisheitlichen Einfluß" hervor, der in der Bearbeitung der Ahitophel-Szenen „deutlich fühlbar ist" [61]). Eben aus diesem Einfluß würden sich auch die „aufgeklärten" Züge in Davids Verhalten nach dem Tod des ersten Kindes (xii 20-23) [62]) erklären.

Wie aus all diesen Verbindungslinien eindeutig hervorgeht, weist die Legende vom Tod des ersten Kindes eine erhebliche geistige Verwandtschaft mit einer anderen, breiteren Bearbeitungsschicht innerhalb der Thronfolgeerzählung auf. Der Gedanke, diese zwei Schichten von ein und derselben Hand abzuleiten, liegt verlockend nahe [63]). Bevor das jedoch definitiv behauptet werden kann, müßte die Thronfolgeerzählung in redaktionsgeschichtlicher Hinsicht noch gründlicher als bisher durchgearbeitet worden sein [64]).

[61]) Auch Langlamet, *RB* 83, S. 117, 128, 135 f. u.ö., postuliert eine „theologisch-weisheitliche" Bearbeitung, die zugleich auch prodavidisch und prosalomonisch ist. Früher hat vor allem R. N. Whybray, *The Succession Narrative* (London, 1968), S. 56-95, die Verbindungen der Thronfolgeerzählung mit der Weisheit hervorgehoben. Infolge der Undifferenziertheit in literarischen Fragen scheint Whybray jedoch, ohne es zu wissen, mehr die Bearbeitung als die Urfassung der Thronfolgeerzählung ins Auge gefaßt zu haben.

[62]) Vgl. noch besonders V. 23 mit dem typisch weisheitlichen Vergleich 2 Sam. xiv 14a (dazu Whybray, S. 81) in der Episode von der weisen Frau aus Thekoa (2 Sam. xiv 2-22), die Würthwein, *Thronfolge*, S. 46, insgesamt für einen „weisheitlichen Einschub" hält (vgl. auch Langlamet, *RB* 83, S. 136).

[63]) In diesem Zusammenhang kann die Tatsache nicht unerwähnt bleiben, daß Bathseba Ahitophels Enkelin war (vgl. 2 Sam. xi 3 und xxiii 34). Es könnte durchaus sein, daß Bathsebas Heirat in die königliche Familie ein Zerwürfnis mit ihrer alten Sippe mit sich brachte, nachdem der Hintergrund des Todes von Uria den Verwandten bekannt geworden war. Folglich versuchte Ahitophel durch seine antidavidische Tätigkeit während des Absalom-Aufstandes den Meuchelmord des Uria, der wie sein eigener Sohn zu „den Dreißig" gehörte (2 Sam. xxiii 39), zu rächen. Als Gegenschlag wollte literarische Hofpropaganda — wahrscheinlich erst später — von Salomo die unangenehme Erinnerung an Bathsebas Vergangenheit entfernen und zugleich den gefährlichsten Vertreter ihrer Sippe, den Ratgeber Ahitophel, psychisch und physisch töten. Für diese Kreise scheint der Tod die angemessene Lösung zum Problem unbequemer Persönlichkeiten darzustellen (2 Sam. xii 18, xvii 23).

[64]) Ein verheißungsvoller Anfang bei Langlamet, *RB* 83, S. 349-79, 481-528. Langlamet betont selber nachdrücklich den vorläufigen Charakter der von ihm erzielten Ergebnisse, er beendet seine glänzende Studie mit dem Satz: „Mais ce n'est encore là qu'une hypothèse de recherche que seule une étude détaillée de la rédaction ‘prodavidique' en *Samuel* pourrait infirmer ou confirmer" (S. 528).

VI

Wir kommen jetzt zu *Schlußfolgerungen. 1.* Für die Frage, von der wir ausgegangen sind, bedeuten die oben gemachten Beobachtungen und Überlegungen, daß Salomos Stellung als Bathsebas Erstgeborener nicht mehr in den Bereich bloßer Vermutungen gehört. Vielmehr scheint sie mir das historisch Wahrscheinliche zu sein.

Man könnte freilich die Kritik noch ein Stück weiterführen und sagen, daß die alte Geschichte von Salomos Geburt in einer so boshaften Absicht niedergeschrieben worden sei, daß wir ihr kein historisches Vertrauen schenken können. In Wirklichkeit wüßten wir also überhaupt nichts Näheres von Salomos Geburt. Es gibt jedoch eine historisch fest verankerte Angabe, die gegen diese radikale Skepsis spricht: der Name des Königs Salomo. Wenn die Bedeutung des Namens „sein Ersatz" ist und wenn dem Vorgänger Salomos der historische Boden entzogen ist, dann kann der Name sinnvoll nur als Anspielung auf den gefallenen Ehemann Bathsebas, den Hethiter Uria, aufgefaßt werden.

Allenfalls läßt sich fragen, ob Salomo nur scheinbar oder auch wirklich „sein Ersatz" war. Die positive Antwort auf diese Frage würde voraussetzen, daß die Geschichte von Davids Ehebruch eine nur im Volksmund entstandene, historisch wertlose Anekdote sei [65]), und sie würde bedeuten, daß Bathseba in Wirklichkeit Urias Sohn auf den Thron der Doppelmonarchie gebracht hätte. Diese Möglichkeit ist nicht ganz von der Hand zu weisen, aber ebensowenig auch zu beweisen.

2. Im Blick auf die Darstellungsweise und Intention der alten Thronfolgeerzählung bringt die Entfernung des legendarischen Einschubs mehr erzählerische Geschlossenheit und inhaltliche Schärfe mit sich [66]). Die Bathseba-Affäre mit all ihren Unheimlich-

---

[65]) Aus formgeschichtlichen Gründen nannte Gressmann, S. 156, die Bathseba-Geschichte eine „Sage", meinte jedoch, daß „man schwerlich David etwas so Ehrenrühriges nachgesagt hätte, wenn man keinen Grund dazu gehabt hätte." Ist die Begründung aber nach den heutigen Erkenntnissen noch stichhaltig? Vgl. Würthwein, *Thronfolge*, S. 32.

[66]) Unnötig zu sagen, daß das gewonnene Ergebnis nicht im geringsten die von Rost, S. 128, für die Thronfolgeerzählung angenommene Zielsetzung unterstützt, nach der sie *in majorem gloriam Salomonis* geschrieben worden sei (so noch Mettinger, S. 31). Aber z.B. auch der „pattern" von J. Blenkinsopp, „Theme and Motif in the Succession History (2 Sam. xi 2 ff) and the Yahwist Corpus", *VTSuppl* 15 (1966), S. 47 f., leidet einen erheblichen Schaden, indem

keiten wird mit der bekannten Subtilität geschildert. Am Ende konstatiert der Thronfolgeerzähler ganz nüchtern: „Nachdem aber die Trauerzeit vorüber war, schickte David hin und nahm sie zu sich in sein Haus. So wurde sie seine Frau und gebar ihm einen Sohn und gab ihm den Namen Salomo" (xi 27a, xii 24bβ). Er kommentiert das unerhörte Geschehen nicht einmal mit einem halben Wort — sei es theologischer oder moralischer Art —, sondern geht unter völligem Stillschweigen, das allerdings mehr spricht als tausend Worte, zum letzten Akt des Ammoniterkrieges über (2 Sam. xii 26-31).

Über Salomo schweigt der Thronfolgeerzähler dann eine geraume Zeit. Der tritt auf die Bühne erst in 1 Reg. i [67]), zusammen mit seiner ehrgeizigen Mutter und dem intriganten Propheten Nathan, die eine Konterrevolution gegen Salomos älteren Bruder Adonia und dessen Anhänger organisieren [68]). Mit einem meisterhaften Trick gelingt es Nathan und Bathseba, dem alterschwachen David — „Pape trompé par la Curie" [69]) — einen angeblich einmal geleisteten Schwur abzulisten, mit dem sie den Thron für Bathsebas Sohn sichern (1 Reg. i *11-49). Auch diese Ereignisse kommentiert der Erzähler mit keinem Wort, sondern schreitet ohne Aufregung zur nächsten Phase fort, zur Darstellung der Säuberungswelle, die den politischen Gegnern Salomos den Garaus macht (1 Reg. i *50-53, ii *13 ff.). Einer nach dem anderen werden sie geköpft, sogar unter Verletzung des Asylschutzes des Heiligtums (ii 28-31a,

---

der Ehebruch und seine Strafe (der Tod des Kindes) auf verschiedene literarische Stufen geraten.

[67]) Für die nähere Interpretation von 1 Reg. i-ii s. Veijola, S. 16-29; dazu in der Hauptsache übereinstimmend Langlamet, *RB* 83, S. 323-79, 481-528 (mit Literatur), und Würthwein, *Das Erste Buch der Könige*, S. 2-28.

[68]) Auch Langlamet, *RB* 83, S. 522, 525, hebt den inneren Zusammenhang in der Darstellung von 2 Sam. *x-xii und 1 Reg. *i-ii hervor. Er meint jedoch, daß der Thronfolgeerzähler zu David eine andere Einstellung als zu Salomo habe: „En dépit de son amertume, il ne met pas en cause l'autorité de David. Il ne s'oppose ni à David ni à la monarchie davidique. Il n'ignore certes pas les fautes et les faiblesses du roi défunt: il les a, semble-t-il, évoquées lui-même en rédigeant les premiers chapitres de son 'histoire de la succession', où il précise, à sa manière, les circonstances de la naissance de Salomon" (S. 525). In derselben Richtung schreibt auch Dietrich, *VF* 22, S. 53: „Der Erzähler macht David mE. nicht schlechter, als er es in diesem Fall wirklich war." Lassen sich diese Urteile noch aufrecht erhalten? Salomos Geburt aus dem Ehebruch war sicherlich nicht *seine* Schuld, und wer war überhaupt in der Lage zu wissen, *wie* David in diesem Fall *wirklich* war? Vgl. Würthwein, *Thronfolge*, S. 22.

[69]) Langlamet, *RB* 83, S. 525.

34) [70]), aber wieder enthält sich der Thronfolgeerzähler jeder expliziten Stellungnahme, stellt lediglich nach der letzten Enthauptung lakonisch fest: „So war das Königtum fest in der Hand Salomos" (1 Reg. ii 46b). Er hat es uns überlassen, das Urteil über den theologischen und moralischen Wert der geschilderten Vorgänge zu bilden.

---

[70]) Auch in Adonias Fall verstößt Salomo gegen das Asylrecht (i 50, 51abα, 53 — V. 51bα [*l'mr*], 51bβγ und 52 sind sekundär, s. Langlamet, *RB* 83, S. 500-502)—obwohl Adonia erst später hingerichtet wird (ii 25)

THE ORIGINS OF THE TWENTY-FOUR PRIESTLY COURSES

A Study of 1 Chronicles xxiii-xxvii

by

H. G. M. WILLIAMSON
Cambridge

There is only one explicit reference in the Old Testament to the division of the Jewish priesthood into twenty-four courses, namely 1 Chron. xxiv 7-18. It is, nevertheless, clear from a growing wealth of evidence that the arrangement outlined there remained largely unchanged throughout the following centuries until the fall of the second temple. Since this fact is now widely recognized, there is no need to deal with it again here [1]).

At present, however, there is much less evidence on which to come to a decision about the time of origin of this system, even though such a decision is a prerequisite for establishing why it developed in the first place. The later sources do not provide much help here. E. Schürer [2]) was able to show that they are not incompatible with a post-exilic date, but hesitated to be more specific. Similarly, studies

---

[1]) In addition to the works discussed more fully below, reference may be made in support of this statement to the following publications of texts and discussions based upon them: Y. Avi Yonah, "A List of Priestly Courses from Caesarea", *IEJ* 12 (1962), pp. 137-9; idem, "The Caesarea Inscription of the Twenty-Four Priestly Courses", in E. J. Vardaman and J. L. Garrett (ed.), *The Teacher's Yoke: Studies in Memory of Henry Trantham* (Waco, 1964), pp. 46-57; J. T. Milik, *SVT* 4 (1957), pp. 24-5; G. M. Steindler, "Le *mišmarōt* in una iscrizione di Beit Ḥaḍir (Yemen)", *AION* 34 (1974), pp. 277-82; S. Talmon in C. Rabin and Y. Yadin (ed.), *Scripta Hierosolymitana* 4 (1958), pp. 168-76; P. Winter, "Twenty-six Priestly Courses", *VT* 6 (1956), pp. 215-17; Y. Yadin, *The Scroll of the War of the Sons of Light against the Sons of Darkness* (Oxford, 1962), pp. 204-6. References that have long been known were recognized to have supported this conclusion, though they could not establish it with quite the precision of the more recent discoveries; cf. 1 Macc. ii 1; Lk. i 5-9; Josephus, *Ant.* vii, §§ 365 f., and *Life*, § 2; on *Against Apion* ii, § 108, cf. J. Jeremias, *Jerusalem zur Zeit Jesu* (Göttingen, ³1962), p. 231 (ET, London, 1969, pp. 204-5); and a number of later Jewish sources, such as M. Sukkah v 6-8 and M. Taʿanit iv 2.

[2]) *Geschichte des jüdischen Volkes im Zeitalter Jesu Christi* II (Leipzig, ⁴1907), pp. 286-9 (ET II/1, pp. 216-20).

of the history of Old Testament priesthood [3]) tend either to avoid or to stop short of the issue, while those who approach the matter from the angle of the first century A. D. [4]) can legitimately afford to leave the matter unresolved for their particular purposes.

Of the few who hazard a more specific discussion, the majority seem to favour the reforms of Nehemiah as the most likely setting for this development. Thus, for instance, although J. Liver [5]) is right to reject the view of Y. Kaufmann [6]) that there is an explicit reference to the institution in Neh. xiii 30, yet he feels compelled to agree that there is no good reason why such a date should not be regarded as the most probable.

The present article, by contrast, will argue for a somewhat different conclusion, based on a more exact analysis of the setting of 1 Chron. xxiv 7-18 within its wider context of 1 Chron. xxiii-xxvii. Two main problems will need to be dealt with. First, various literary levels have often been detected within these chapters even though no particular analysis of them can be said to enjoy a consensus. An attempt will here be made to improve on this situation. It will be suggested that there are in fact only two such levels, that 1 Chron. xxiv 7-18 belongs to the secondary level, and that the various passages which make up this secondary level are all ideologically inter-related. This is an important point because it gives the analysis a greater measure of self-authentication and at the same time provides a reasonable explanation, associated with the origins of the twenty-four courses, for the later process of expansion itself. Secondly, a number of commentators have observed that there is a close link between 1 Chron. xxiii 2 and xxviii 1, so that from a narrative point of view xxiii 3-xxvii 34 seems to be intrusive. It will be necessary to examine this view also in order to be able to arrive at a closer dating of the material in relation to the date of the Chronicler's composition as a whole.

To start with the "internal" analysis of these chapters, it should be observed at the outset that in their present position the context of

---

[3]) Reference need be made only to A. H. J. Gunneweg, *Leviten und Priester* (Göttingen, 1965), and A. Cody, *A History of Old Testament Priesthood* (Rome, 1969). R. de Vaux, *Les institutions de l'Ancien Testament* II (Paris, 1960), pp. 233, 242 and 246 (ET, London, [2]1965, pp. 372, 379 and 382) refers these chapters to the post-exilic period, but gives little further detail.

[4]) For instance J. Jeremias, *Jerusalem zur Zeit Jesu*, pp. 224-34; F. F. Bruce, *New Testament History* (London, 1969), p. 139.

[5]) *Chapters in the History of the Priests and Levites: Studies in the Lists of Chronicles and Ezra and Nehemiah* (Hebrew. Jerusalem, 1968), pp. 31-49.

[6]) *The History of Israelite Religion* IV (Hebrew. Tel Aviv, 1972), pp. 358-9 (ET, New York, 1977, pp. 411-12).

these various lists is provided by xxiii 3-6*a* [7]). This makes clear (a) that David was personally responsible for the organization of the Levites into divisions [8]); (b) that only Levites were involved at this stage; and (c) that the Levites were sub-divided into four classes, namely those who had charge of the work in the house of the Lord, officers and judges, gatekeepers, and musicians [9]). In what follows, however, there is included a number of passages which are either not governed by this context or which may be held to contradict it. There is thus a *prima facie* case for assuming that some of the subsequent material has been added later, an assumption which other considerations also support.

The list of gatekeepers in xxvi 1-19 provides a convenient starting point for our analysis [10]). It is widely agreed first that verses 4-8 are intrusive, both because they interrupt the treatment of the family of Meshelemiah in verses 1-3 and 9, and because the house of Obed-edom, with which they deal, is not linked genealogically with the Levites, whereas the other two main families in the list are (Meshelemiah is linked with Korah in verse 1 and Hosah with Merari in verse 10). Furthermore, the numbers attributed to Obed-edom (sixty-two, verse 8) are out of all proportion with those attributed to Meshelemiah (eighteen, verse 9) and Hosah (thirteen, verse 11) [11]).

---

[7]) Despite most English translations, verse 6*a* (to *maḥleqôt*) should be taken with what precedes, while the remainder of the verse is the heading for the following list; cf. A. C. Welch, *The Work of the Chronicler. Its Purpose and its Date* (The Schweich Lectures, 1938; London, 1939), p. 84.

[8]) It is universally agreed that the lists in their present form do not in fact go back to David's time, but reflect the arrangement of the post-exilic cult. Most telling in this regard is comparison with the related lists in Ezra-Nehemiah.

[9]) The four groups of Levites are listed here in descending numerical order, whereas in the following more detailed lists which comprise the primary layer they are dealt with rather on the basis of their relationship to the centre of worship in the temple.

[10]) Cf. J. W. Rothstein and J. Hänel, *Kommentar zum ersten Buch der Chronik* (Leipzig, 1927), *ad loc.*, followed by G. von Rad, *Das Geschichtsbild des chronistischen Werkes* (Stuttgart, 1930), p. 116. Welch, pp. 91-3, also accepts the outline of Rothstein's literary analysis, though he reverses the historical development by which Rothstein explained his findings. W. Rudolph, *Chronikbücher* (Tübingen, 1955), pp. 171-3, by contrast, argues that the passage is a unity. His view depends, however, on a rather different approach to these chapters as a whole which does not, in my opinion, do justice to the various lines of argument developed in this article which all point in the same direction. His discussion of the present paragraph is unsatisfactory because it does not get to grips with the substance of the arguments in favour of a literary division.

[11]) It may be noted in passing that a progression can be outlined in the development of the lists of the gatekeepers in the post-exilic literature in terms of names,

If this is correct, then verses 12-18 must also have been included by the reviser, since the reference to Obed-edom (verse 15) is quite secure in its present context, and cannot be detached in the way that it could in verses 4-8. Two other considerations independently support the conclusion that verses 12-18 are secondary:

(a) Meshelemiah is here called Shelemiah. In itself, this causes no difficulty (the same man is referred to as Shallum in 1 Chron. ix 19), but we should certainly have expected that the same spelling would have been used within the same passage were it all to derive from the same author.

(b) The whole process of lot-casting for duties described in these verses seems to contradict the context as established by xxiii 3-6*a*. There, the organization of the Levites is ascribed to David, but here he is not mentioned and the implication of verse 13 is that the gatekeepers were themselves responsible for the arrangement of their duties.

Verse 19, finally, with its reference to the Korahites and the sons of Merari, seems best to be understood as the original conclusion to verses 1-3, 9-11 (cf. verses 1, 10). We may thus conclude that 1 Chron. xxvi 1-19 is composite. Verses 1-3, 9-11 and 19 have been later supplemented by the addition of 4-8 and 12-18. The first block of material is a simple list of gatekeepers, arranged on a genealogical principle. The revision, however, has two effects. First, it introduces into a Levitical context the family of Obed-edom. Uncertainty about his status is reflected also in 1 Chron. xv-xvi, where it can be shown that the Chronicler himself included him amongst the singers, while a later reviser insisted that he was a gatekeeper [12]). His inclusion amongst the gatekeepers only at the stage of revision in chapter xxvi thus agrees with a development attested elsewhere. Secondly, the revision supplies considerable detail about the nature of the gatekeepers' duties, arranged by the casting of lots. The numbers in verses 17-18 amount to a total of twenty-four. This cannot be directly equated with the twenty-four priestly courses, since, unlike the latter, they all functioned together, not by rotation. Nevertheless, the possibility cannot be ruled out that the number is not coincidental, and that it points to the same type of approach to cultic organization.

---

numbers and levitical status, namely Ezr. ii 42 (Neh. vii 45); Neh. xi 19, xii 25; 1 Chron. ix 17 ff. and xxvi 1-19. It is thus of interest to note that Obed-edom is also missing from 1 Chron. ix 17 ff., which otherwise has very close links with xxvi 1-3 and 9.

[12]) For details, see my forthcoming commentary on 1 and 2 Chronicles in the New Century Bible series.

Moving back now to the lists of musicians in chapter xxv, we find that the passage falls into two distinct parts. Verses 1-6 give a list of the musicians and their duties divided into three under the leadership of Asaph, Jeduthun and Heman. Verse 7 introduces the remainder of the chapter, since its figure of 288 is exactly the 24 × 12 of verses 9-31. This part gives an orderly presentation of the division of the singers into twenty-four courses.

Examination of these two parts of the chapter reveals that, although there are many points in common between them, there is also a number of unevennesses, indicating that here again the chapter was not originally a unity [13]). Not all the points noted here are of equal weight by any means, but it is suggested that when taken together they present a strong case for such a division of the chapter.

(a) In verses 1-6 there is a considerable emphasis on David's personal ordering of the musicians (verses 1, 2, 5, and 6), whereas in 7 ff. not only is David not mentioned but also the musicians decide their duties by lot-casting (verse 8).
(b) Verses 2, 3 and 6 state that the musicians performed under the direction of their father. It is difficult to see how this could have worked out in the system of verses 9 ff., where they are divided up into twenty-four separate courses.
(c) A similar point may perhaps be made about the use of instruments. In verses 1-6, these are to some extent distributed amongst the three groups (see especially verse 3), implying that they all needed to play together. In the system of twenty-four courses in 7-31, however, it must be assumed that each separate course would have contained those who could play on each type of instrument (though cf. point (f) below).
(d) Despite the practice of casting lots, verses 7-31 show a considerable degree of orderliness, and in many ways this corresponds to the order in verses 1-6 [14]). Nevertheless, this correspondence is not com-

---

13) For some of the following observations see, in addition to the commentaries, D. L. Petersen, *Late Israelite Prophecy: Studies in Deutero-Prophetic Literature and in Chronicles* (Missoula, 1977), pp. 64-8, although in other respects both the analysis and the conclusions presented here differ considerably from those of Petersen.

14) See the diagrammatic presentation in Rothstein-Hänel, p. 453, repeated by Petersen, p. 67. Particularly striking is the fact that the order in verses 9-31 keeps together at the end the curious names of verse 4*b* which have been recognized as comprising either a hymnic fragment or a catalogue of five "incipits"; for the former view, see originally H. Ewald, *Ausführliches Lehrbuch der hebräischen Sprache des alten Bundes* (Göttingen, [8]1870), p. 680, and its development in various ways

plete: Joseph occurs first in verse 9, against the order of verse 2, and a few of the names occur in the two passages in slightly different forms [15]). This slight divergence within substantial overall agreement points away from the literary dependence of one passage upon the other, and indicates rather that the lists are based on the actuality of the situation at the time of composition, but that this had changed slightly between the two halves.

(e) The word *mispār* is used in different ways in verses 1 and 7. Despite the objections of most commentators [16]), its use in verse 1 with the meaning "list" is quite acceptable as is shown by the fact that at 1 Chron. xi 11 it is introduced by the Chronicler with exactly this meaning against his *Vorlage* (2 Sam. xxiii 8). In verse 7, however, it is used with its more normal meaning of "number", "total". An important subsidiary conclusion resulting from this observation is that it is no longer necessary to regard verses 2 ff. as intrusive in their present context, as the commentators referred to in note 16 above were obliged to do. Our much simpler analysis of the chapter into two straightforward parts is thus strengthened.

(f) Finally, I consider it possible that different types of music are intended by the two lists. In verse 7, the music is described as *šîr*, which, when used absolutely as here, means "singing". In verses 1-6, however, attention is focussed exclusively on the playing of instruments, and it is significant that when *šîr* is used (once only, in verse 6), it is immediately qualified by the words "with cymbals, harps, and lyres". Thus RSV correctly renders *šîr* in this verse by "music".

If, for these reasons, it is legitimate to detect two hands at work in this chapter, the question must be asked, which is secondary? Two main factors point quite clearly to verses 7-31 as the later addition.

---

by (in addition to the commentators) E. Kautzsch, *ZAW* 6 (1886), p. 260; P. Haupt, *ZAW* 34 (1914), pp. 142-5; H. Torczyner, *JBL* 68 (1949), pp. 247-9. For the latter view, cf. J. M. Myers, *I Chronicles* (Garden City, 1965), p. 173. Whatever be the origins of this curious phenomenon, it is sufficient for our present purposes to observe with Rudolph (pp. 166-7) against Welch (pp. 88-90) that the words are certainly used as proper names in the present context of both halves of the chapter.

[15]) Apart from cases where the differences are merely orthographical, note *yiṣrî* (verse 11) for *ṣ^e^rî* (verse 3), *ʿ^a^zar'ēl* (verse 18) for *ʿuzzî'ēl* (verse 4) and *šûbā'ēl* (verse 20) for *š^e^bû'ēl* (verse 4).

[16]) E.g. I. Benzinger, *Die Bücher der Chronik* (Tübingen and Leipzig, 1901), p. 75, and R. Kittel, *Die Bücher der Chronik* (Göttingen, 1902), p. 94, followed by Rothstein-Hänel, Welch, p. 88, et al. Their views were opposed by E. L. Curtis and A. A. Madsen, *A Critical and Exegetical Commentary on the Books of Chronicles* (Edinburgh, 1910), p. 276, but for unsatisfactory reasons.

First, verses 1-6 relate closely to the context established by xxiii 3-6*a*. David is responsible for organizing the musicians, while the emphasis on the use of instruments corresponds exactly to what we would expect on the basis of xxiii 5. This is not true, however, of verses 7-31. Secondly, verses 7-31 have instead two links with xxvi 12 ff., which we have already argued are secondary. Most impressive here is the close similarity between xxv 8:

> And they cast lots for their duties, small and great, teacher and pupil alike

and xxvi 13:

> And they cast lots by fathers' houses, small and great alike, for their gates.

Linked with this is the orderliness of the duties in the two secondary passages, which is based upon the system of courses, and yet which is lacking in the earlier lists.

We may thus conclude our analysis of chapter xxv by noting the similarities to the results already achieved in chapter xxvi. The earlier strand (verses 1-6) contains genealogically based lists which correspond exactly with xxiii 3-6*a* and which, it will be argued later, are fully compatible with other parts of the Chronicler's work. The secondary material, on the other hand, seems to reflect the same outlook as that already detected in chapter xxvi.

We are now in a position to move back to the lists of Levites and priests in xxiii 6*b*-xxiv 31. First of all, there is a fair measure of agreement that xxiii 25-32 cannot come from the same hand as the earlier part of the chapter [17]). This is principally because on the one hand verses 6*b*-24 (with the exception of the intrusive verses 13*b*-14 [18])) give a genealogically related list of Levites who were to do the work for the service of the house of the Lord (verse 24), thus corresponding exactly with the context governed by xxiii 4, whereas, on the other hand, verses 25-32 link together both this type of Levite and the Levitical singers (verses 30-31), thereby ignoring the distinctions made in verses 4-5, distinctions which, moreover, the lists of 6*b*-24

[17]) Cf. Rudolph, p. 156, etc.

[18]) The explanatory expansion included in these verses is out of place in a list of heads of fathers' houses. Its outlook, however, fits in closely with the concerns of the priestly reviser who, it will be argued, was responsible for the rest of the secondary material in these chapters, together with a few short interpolations elsewhere in Chronicles.

and xxv 1-6 evidently maintain [19]). In addition, it is clear from verses 28, 29 and 32 that the main purpose of these verses is to spell out the distinction between priests and Levites, in which the duty of the Levites was merely "to assist" or "to attend". Here again, there is nothing in the context which would have led us to expect concentration on such a topic. In contrast with all this, however, the genealogical list which remains fits admirably after the heading in 3-6*a*, and provides, we may now observe, just the same sort of amplification of the first category of Levite mentioned in verse 4 as xxv 1-6 and xxvi 1-3, 9-11 and 19 do for those in verse 5 [20]).

Moving on now to "the divisions of the sons of Aaron" in xxiv 1-19, we see at once that several factors already familiar from the preceding discussion mark the section in its entirety as secondary:

(a) It is intrusive in a context that is dealing exclusively with Levitical lists. It is true that priests are mentioned in xxiii 2, but the heading to the lists in question comes only in verses 3 ff., and there the priests are not referred to. (In xxiii 2, the reference to priests is introduced only as a part of the stereotyped threefold division of the population current in his time; cf., for instance, 1 Chron. xiii 2; 2 Chron. xxx 25,

---

[19]) It may be mentioned here that some scholars argue towards the same conclusion on the basis of the discrepancies in verses 3, 24 and 27 over the age at which the Levites entered on their service. Welch, p. 81, for instance, makes it the start of his whole analysis of these chapters. In fact, however, 24*b* and 27 are much later additions altogether, so that they cannot be drawn into our main discussion at all. 24*b* interrupts the connection between 24*a* and 25 (so Rothstein-Hänel, p. 419). Since verse 25 stands at the head of the passage from the reviser, 24*b* must be later still. For Levitical service to start at twenty years old is not envisaged in the Pentateuch, though cf. 2 Chron. xxxi 17; Ezr. iii 8. Probably the age was changed from time to time under the pressure of circumstances. We may then surmise either that the glossator wished to invoke Davidic authority for the practice current in his own time, or that he simply aimed at explaining away the difference between 1 Chron. xxiii 3 and 2 Chron. xxxi 17. Verse 27 also interrupts the evident continuity between verses 26 and 28. It is a misplaced gloss on 24*b*, seeking to explain the discrepancy with verse 3. It is not very apt, however, because the whole extended section, introduced at xxiii 1, is properly to be regarded as "the last words of David".

[20]) Many scholars have argued that there were originally twenty-four heads of fathers' houses in this passage, even though the present text gives only twenty-two (or twenty-three, according to Curtis-Madsen, pp. 263-6); in addition to the commentaries, particularly the older ones, cf. M. Berlin, "Notes on Genealogies of the Tribe of Levi in 1 Chron. xxiii-xxvi", *JQR* 12 (1900), pp. 291-8. There is no primary textual evidence for such speculations, however; they are based merely on the prior assumption, contested in this article, that the twenty-four courses should be reflected here. In the absence of other evidence, it is better method to accept the text as it stands.

xxxv 8; Ezr. ii 70, etc. 1 Chron. xxiii 1-2 serves as an introduction to the whole of xxiii-xxix, and does not, therefore, oblige us to find specific references to each of the categories which it mentions in xxiii-xxvii alone, *contra* Curtis-Madsen, pp. 260 f.)

(b) That this is so is confirmed by the fact that xxiv 1 links closely with the end of xxiii, already seen as secondary.

(c) Contrary to what the context would lead us to expect, David does not act alone, but "with the help of Zadok ... and Ahimelech" (verse 3, and cf. verse 6). This provides the first link with material already noted as secondary in xxv and xxvi.

(d) A further such link is that the courses of priests are organized by lot, rather than by royal appointment. In particular, we should note verse 5: "They organized them by lot, all alike (*ʾēlleh ʿim ʾēlleh*)", which is similar to the distinctive expressions in xxv 8 and xxvi 13 noted earlier.

(e) A final link with the other secondary material is provided by the fact that the courses number exactly twenty-four, a situation nowhere reflected in the primary material.

The passage as a whole is favourable to the priesthood. This is clear not only from its connection with the end of xxiii, but also from the way in which a past failing of the priestly house is covered over (verse 2; cf. Lev. x 1-2; Num. iii 4). The pro-priestly inclinations of the reviser, apparent now from this chapter, as well as from xxiii 13*b*-14 and 28 ff., will enable us later to link the whole of his work in xxiii-xxvii with some other comparable revisions elsewhere in 1 Chronicles.

At the end of chapter xxiv there is appended a fragmentary list of "the rest of the sons of Levi" (verses 20-31). On the whole, it continues the genealogy of xxiii 6*b* ff. one generation further by recapitulating parts of it in the same order and then extending it. All reference to the family of Gershon, however, is omitted. This provides us with the first piece of evidence that the passage cannot have been included by the original author of xxiii, for, as Welch (p. 84) observes, when David was organizing the Levites into divisions (xxiii 6), "he could not have both included and excluded the Gershonites: nor could he have set over his courses at the same time a body of men and their sons". In support of this conclusion we may observe first that the paragraph is integrally tied to xxiv 1-19, itself secondary (compare verse 31 with verse 3, and note too the comparison with "the sons of Aaron"; the expression *leʿummat ʾaḥêhem* also occurs at xxvi 12), and, second, that the Levites cast lots for their duties rather than being organized by David.

Why did the reviser add this curious section? Clearly, he was bringing the situation up to date, which seems to have involved the addition of one generation [21]). In addition to this, however, verse 31 suggests that he intended to reach a total of twenty four courses for the Levites as in the previous case of the priests, thus marking an advance over the list in xxiii. Quite how he did so is not clear to us, especially as the sons of Gershon (xxiii 7-11) are not taken into account here, but appreciation of his intention is sufficient for our present purposes.

At the end of chapters xxiii-xxvii, there are two passages which have not yet been dealt with. Both raise many questions which cannot be discussed here. We shall confine our remarks exclusively to the prior issue of their literary status.

First, in xxvi 20-32 details are supplied of the duties of various Levites. Although many commentators divide it into several unconnected sections, it does in fact constitute a single unit because of the overarching genealogical framework supplied by the four Kohathites listed in verse 23 (cf. xxiii 12) [22]). It seems probable that the paragraph has been extracted from some other more extensive source because (a) despite their introduction in verse 23, and unlike the other three families mentioned there, the Uzzielites are not referred to in the sequel, and (b) some of the people mentioned here have already been listed in xxiii 6*b* ff.; as it is unlikely that they served simultaneously in two of the four categories of xxiii 4 f., this discrepancy points to the separate origin of the material.

Such a slight inconsistency is insufficient in itself, however, to relegate the paragraph to the secondary level, for even if he was aware of it the compiler of the primary layer had strong motive to include this extract, namely that its reference to some Levites who acted as "officers and judges" (verse 29) corresponds to the fourth category listed in the heading at xxiii 4 f. Moreover, such other considerations as there are support the view that this passage is primary: all those listed are Levites, and they are grouped genealogically, as elsewhere in the primary material. Similarly, David's authority over them is

---

[21]) The text certainly seems to have suffered corruption in some places, but the emendations suggested by the majority of commentators do not alter the position set out above.

[22]) So correctly in this respect Rudolph, pp. 176-7.

exercised directly (vese 32). At the same time, however, none of the features of the secondary material is to be found here.

Finally, the whole of chapter xxvii is to be regarded as secondary, since it is neither related to the Levites, nor deals with David's final arrangements, but describes rather his reign in general. It is thus quite unrelated to the context governed by xxiii 3-6*a*. The numbers in verses 1-15 (twelve divisions of 24,000 each), though not found elsewhere, reflect the orderly outlook of material already established as secondary; cf. especially xxv 9-31 [23]). Thus, while I believe it can be shown that for each of the four paragraphs which make up this chapter the reviser was drawing on earlier material and that he has reshaped this to make it serve his own particular purposes, yet nevertheless what matters for us in the present context is that none of this is to be attributed to the primary layer of 1 Chron. xxiii-xxvii.

We may now summarize the discussion so far by observing that there are two main strands of material in 1 Chron. xxiii-xxvii. The primary strand is made up of xxiii 6*b*-13*a*, 15-24, xxv 1-6, xxvi 1-3, 9-11, 19, and xxvi 20-32. It may be stressed that each of these four short sections is governed by one of the categories of Levite listed in xxiii 3-6*a*. In each case David is himself responsible for their organization, and they each present little more than a genealogically based list (though there is rather more elaboration in the final paragraph).

Most of the secondary material likewise has a number of factors in common, a fact which lends support to the literary analysis for which I have argued. These have been noted during the discussion. Historically, the most significant of these is that only in this secondary layer, and then consistently, do we find reference to the twenty-four

[23]) The artificial nature of xxvii 1-15 is clear from the fact that (a) the names of the commanders are drawn from the list of David's heroes in xi 11 ff., even though historically they could not also have been commanders of large divisions; Asahel (verse 7), for instance, was killed before David became king over the whole of Israel (2 Sam. ii 18-23), and though the inclusion of "his son Zebadiah after him" shows awareness of this difficulty, it does not in fact remove the anachronism. It may be noted, however, that there are enough small differences between the two forms of the list to suggest that the dependence was not direct; and (b) a national, conscripted army, unlike a professional standing army, was called to arms only in time of war; cf. de Vaux, II, p. 29 (ET, p. 227). There is no evidence whatever for the very improbable suggestion of this paragraph that civilians were conscripted for a month's service each year, despite the characteristically spirited discussion by Y. Yadin, *The Art of Warfare in Biblical Lands* (London, 1963), pp. 279-84. In view of all this, the probability that the reviser was here working under the influence of the recently introduced system of twenty-four courses, which he has extended in a utopian manner to other areas of David's secular administration, is enhanced.

courses. Since this revision must at the earliest be later than the date of the Chronicler himself, it enables us to establish a *terminus post quem* for this development on more reliable grounds than those of general probability, and rather later than what was noted at the start of this article as the general view.

Is it possible, however, to be yet more specific? I believe it is, provided (a) the relationship of the primary layer to the work of the Chronicler himself can be established, and (b) there is some indication of the length of time between this layer and the work of the reviser.

Several factors favour the inclusion of the primary layer into his work by the Chronicler himself, despite the contrary view of many commentators, to be examined shortly. First, some such material is to be expected on the basis of the general context. From 1 Chron. xvii onwards, the Chronicler's overriding concern is David's preparations for the building of the temple. Just as in chapters xv-xvi he is concerned to explain the new role of the Levites after the ark has been brought to Jerusalem, so it is not at all surprising to find that he goes on at this point to make some reference to the preparation by David for their ordering in the future temple. This point is further supported by such passages as 2 Chron. viii 14, xxiii 18 and xxxv 4, where explicit reference is made to David's ordering of the Levites. If we regard the whole of xxiii-xxvii as secondary, these passages are left without adequate antecedent. The same point may be urged even more specifically on the basis of 1 Chron. xxix 8, which clearly presupposes xxvi 21, but which (despite Rudolph, pp. 185 and 191) there is no reason to regard as a later addition [24]).

Secondly, the reconstructed lists of the primary layer fit in well with the stage of development in the Levitical orders during the post-exilic period reflected in other parts of Chronicles, while the revision isolated here is similarly of a piece with that found elsewhere. A full discussion of this would take us far beyond our subject [25]), but one or two of the most obvious examples may be briefly referred to.

[24]) Since Rudolph regards the whole of 1 Chron. xxiii-xxvii as additional, he is obliged also to regard various other allusions in 1 Chron. xxviii-xxix as introduced later under its influence. Some of these become unnecessary in the context of the present analysis. The only convincing example is xxviii 1, where the titles seem to be based on those of xxvii. I should agree that here the reviser has continued his work for a few lines beyond the end of xxvii by including these titles after xxviii 1*a* in order to integrate his additions with the continuing narrative of the Chronicler.

[25]) The most detailed single collection of material for such comparative purposes is J. Liver, *Chapters in the History of the Priests and Levites*, though my conclusions differ quite markedly from his.

The post-exilic development in the guilds of singers has been analysed in some detail by H. Gese [26]). He isolates the following four stages:

I. At the return from the exile, the singers are simply called "sons of Asaph", and are not yet reckoned as Levites (Ezr. ii 41; Neh. vii 44);

II. Neh. xi 3-19 and 1 Chron. ix 1-18, from Nehemiah's time. The singers are now reckoned as Levites, and are in two groups, the sons of Asaph and the sons of Jeduthun;

III. A. 1 Chron. xvi 4 ff.; 2 Chron. v 12, xxix 13 f., xxxv 15. The levitical singers are now in three groups, Asaph, Heman and Jeduthun;

III. B. 1 Chron. vi 31 ff. and xv 16 ff. Jeduthun is replaced by Ethan, and Heman is now more prominent than Asaph.

In the passage under discussion, the singers in xxv 1 are listed in the order Asaph, Heman and Jeduthun, which is the same as Gese's III A. However, the numbers attributed to each family indicate the increasing prominence of Heman (verse 5), thus bringing it a little closer towards III B. Against Gese, I take stage III B to reflect the period of the Chronicler himself [27]). He could thus well have included xxv 1-6 in his account, whereas any attempt to make these verses later than him is virtually ruled out by the fact that Jeduthun has still not been replaced by Ethan.

Similarly, in the case of the gatekeepers it was shown above that Obed-edom was only included amongst them by the reviser, not by the primary layer. Although this is admittedly only negative evidence, this latter reflects the same outlook as the Chronicler himself, whereas it is the reviser of 1 Chron. xv-xvi who insists on his status as a gatekeeper (cf. xv 21 and xvi 5, but contrast xv 18, 24 and xvi 38). Conversely, if xxvi 1-3, 9-11 and 19 be set within the development of the lists of gatekeepers in Ezra, Nehemiah and Chronicles, it will be found that it fits the period of the Chronicler admirably [28]).

The clearest, though by no means the only, evidence that the work of the Chronicler has been revised by some one with priestly sym-

---

[26]) H. Gese, "Zur Geschichte der Kultsänger am zweiten Tempel", in O. Betz, M. Hengel and P. Schmidt (ed.), *Abraham unser Vater: Juden und Christen im Gespräch über die Bibel. Festschrift für Otto Michel zum 60. Geburtstag* (Leiden, 1963), pp. 222-34, = *Vom Sinai zum Zion. Alttestamentliche Beiträge zur biblischen Theologie* (Munich, 1974), pp. 147-58.

[27]) Here I can only refer to my forthcoming commentary, especially on 1 Chron. xv-xvi, for details. In fact, my main point holds even on Gese's view.

[28]) Cf. note 11 above for the material.

pathies comes from 1 Chron. xv-xvi [29]). Thus, for instance, though "the sons of Aaron" occur in xv 4, they are not mentioned in the more detailed list which follows (verses 5-10). Again, though "the priests Zadok and Abiathar" are referred to in verse 11, David goes on to address only "the heads of the fathers' house of the Levites" in verse 12. Further, although "the priests and the Levites sanctified themselves to bring up the ark" in verse 14, verses 15 and 25 ff. refer only to the activity of the Levites. It is likely, therefore, that these references were added by someone who took his cue from the mention of sacrifices later on, just as the inclusion of "trumpets" in xv 28 (contrast their absence from the list of 19-21) probably led to the addition of 24b*a* on the basis of the fact that in the Pentateuch and elsewhere it was the priests alone who blew them (Num. x 8, xxxi 6; cf. Neh. xii 35, 41).

It may thus be concluded both that the primary layer of 1 Chron. xxiii-xxvii can be attributed to the Chronicler [30]), and that it has been subjected to the same type of revision, even if more extensive, as his work in other passages.

Why, then, have so many commentators adopted a contrary view? The answer is simply that the passage as a whole appears to interrupt the connection between xxiii 2 and xxviii 1 [31]). Such an argument is not sufficient to overthrow our earlier conclusion. First, once it is realized how relatively small is the amount of material to be attributed to the primary layer, full weight may be given to R. J. Coggins's comment that "this would not have been regarded as an

---

[29]) I should nevertheless dissociate myself quite emphatically from the radical divisions of the Chronicler's text proposed in different forms by Rothstein-Hänel, Welch, and K. Galling, *Die Bücher der Chronik, Esra, Nehemia* (Göttingen, 1954). Nor do I find nearly so much scattered secondary material as Rudolph; for one example, cf. my *Israel in the Books of Chronicles* (Cambridge, 1977), pp. 71-82. The pro-priestly reviser's work generally consists of little more than the addition of a verse or two here and there to make clear the distinction between priests and Levites. Thus his treatment of 1 Chron. xxiii-xxvii is quite unparalleled in its extent.

[30]) Where there are some slight inconsistencies (actually barely noticeable in the primary layer), on which Rudolph particularly lays heavy emphasis, they may be explained as due to the Chronicler incorporating originally independent material without feeling the need to make them conform in every particular. This too is attested elsewhere in his work; for an example, cf. my "Sources and Redaction in the Chronicler's Genealogy of Judah", *JBL* forthcoming.

[31]) So, for instance, M. Noth, *Überlieferungsgeschichtliche Studien 1* (Halle, 1943; Tübingen, [2]1967), pp. 112-15; Rudolph, p. 152; T. Willi, *Die Chronik als Auslegung: Untersuchungen zur literarischen Gestaltung der historischen Überlieferung Israels* (Göttingen, 1972), pp. 196 f.

interruption by the original readers in the way that we should so consider it" [32]). We have always to beware of imposing modern standards of literary appreciation on an ancient author.

Secondly, closer examination of xxiii 2 and xxviii 1 leads us to question whether they really support the process of interruption which has been claimed. If the material was inserted quite so clumsily as is suggested, we should not have expected any overlap between xxiii 2 and xxviii 1, whereas if a later scribe were trying to point out the interruption we should have expected him to repeat the sentence exactly. In fact from the point of view of vocabulary they have very little in common (for instance, the word for "assembled" is different in each case, xxiii 2 using *'sp*, xxviii 1 using *qhl*).

Thirdly, what we do have here is a literary device that seems to have been quite popular at this time and which is found elsewhere in the Chronicler's work, namely "repetitive resumption" [33]). Other examples of this device show both that it need not involve verbally exact repetition, so long as the resumption is clear, and that it is used precisely to allow the inclusion of material germane to the author's main purpose which does not, however, exactly fit his narrative sequence. This, it may be suggested, was just the Chronicler's position. He wanted to include details of David's final ordering of the Levites because of their great importance to his overall interests, but could not find a point at which to fit them smoothly into his narrative. His use of this device, therefore, far from supporting the view of those who regard the whole of xxiii-xxvii as secondary, encourages us rather to trace the inclusion of the Levitical lists in their original short form back to the Chronicler himself.

The date of Chronicles remains a controversial issue, but one in the later part of the Persian period, around 350 BC, still seems to satisfy the evidence best [34]). Most recently the attempt has been made by

---

[32]) *The First and Second Books of the Chronicles* (Cambridge, 1976), p. 118.

[33]) The term seems to have been coined by S. Talmon, *The Interpreter's Dictionary of the Bible, Supplementary Volume* (Nashville, 1976), p. 322, who gives examples from Ezra-Nehemiah. See also the remarks of P. Welten, *Geschichte und Geschichtsdarstellung in den Chronikbüchern* (Neukirchen-Vluyn, 1973), pp. 190 f., and T. C. Butler, *VT* 28 (1978), p. 146. The device is found, *inter alia*, at 1 Chron. iv 1 (see the article referred to in note 30 above), v 3 (resumption of v 1*a*), xv 11 (resumption of the substance of verses 4-10), xvi 37 (resumption of xvi 4-7), and so on.

[34]) See *Israel in the Books of Chronicles*, pp. 83-6, for a survey of the main points at issue.

several scholars to revive the theory of a sixth century date [35]), but I have set out elsewhere my reasons for disagreeing with this position [36]). The important question that remains, however, is the length of time between the work of the Chronicler and that of the reviser. Our preceding discussion has revealed one or two factors that suggest it was not more than a single generation.

First, in the case of the supplement to xxiii 6*b*-24 in xxiv 20-31, it was necessary to add only one generation to the earlier material, presumably amongst other things to bring it up to date. Secondly, it was found that the differences in order and names of the singers between the two halves of chapter xxv could best be explained on the basis of a development of the actual situation at the time of composition. Since these differences are only slight, and since overall there is substantial agreement, the time gap is likely to have been quite short. I thus conclude that the priestly reviser worked only a single generation after the Chronicler himself, and that he already presupposed the completed development of the system of twenty-four courses. A date for this development at the close of the Persian period thus seems most probable [37]).

The only evidence which might tell against this conclusion is the reference to Jehoiarib in xxiv 7. It has been argued by a number of scholars that since in other lists he occurs further down, if at all, the present order can date only from the Maccabean period, since the family of the Maccabees belonged to this family (1 Macc. ii 1) [38]). This point is not sufficient, however, to overthrow our previous conclusion. First, the most that this evidence could prove would be that the position of Jehoiarib within the list had been altered through

---

[35]) F. M. Cross, "A Reconstruction of the Judean Restoration", *JBL* 94 (1975), pp. 4-18; J. D. Newsome, "Toward a New Understanding of the Chronicler and his Purposes", *JBL* 94 (1975), pp. 201-17; D. L. Petersen, *Late Israelite Prophecy*, pp. 57-60. These writers acknowledge the stimulus of an earlier, brief article by D. N. Freedman, "The Chronicler's Purpose", *CBQ* 23 (1961), pp. 436-42.

[36]) In the course of an article entitled "Eschatology in Chronicles", *Tyndale Bulletin* 28 (1977, but published in 1979), pp. 115-54.

[37]) This date, of course, depends on accepting my date for the composition of Chronicles as a whole. Nevertheless, the literary analysis of 1 Chron. xxiii-xxvii and the consequent *relative* dating of the two strands presented above is not affected by this, and may be judged separately on its own merits.

[38]) This argument goes back at least as far as Schürer. In addition to a number of the commentaries and other works already referred to, see the cautious remarks of P. R. Ackroyd, "Criteria for the Maccabean Dating of Old Testament Literature", *VT* 3 (1953), pp. 113-32 (126-7).

later influence [39]). Liver, for instance, has argued (pp. 36-7) that, since the sectarians at Qumran presupposed the existence of the twenty-four courses in their alteration of it to twenty-six, the system itself must pre-date the Hasmonaean period. Secondly, however, it is not necessarily so certain that the family of Jehoiarib was not prominent before the rise of the Maccabees. Rothstein-Hänel, pp. 433 ff., argued that he was on the basis of his ascendancy through some of the lists in Ezra, Nehemiah and Chronicles, though it must be admitted that not all would accept the integrity of the text in the passages they cite. Others have argued towards a similar conclusion on the basis of the phraseology of 1 Macc. ii 1 itself [40]). Finally, Myers (pp. lxxxvii and 165), on the basis of the attestation of Chronicles from Qumran, finds it hard to accept that any part of it could derive from so late a date, though this argument is questionable. We may nevertheless conclude that various explanations for the position of Jehoiarib in 1 Chron. xxiv 7 are possible, and that therefore the date for the origins of the twenty-four courses argued for above on the basis of wider and more reliable considerations is not affected by it.

The sources available do not suggest any particular reason for the development of the system of twenty-four courses, nor are we sufficiently well informed about the situation in Jerusalem at the end of the Persian period to do more than indulge in speculation on this issue. It is possible that it represents no more than another, though in this case ultimately definitive, step in that development which has often been traced through the historical books of the post-exilic period. On the other hand, it seems more probable that some specific cause underlies what must have been a quite widespread reform of the temple personnel. Two possibilities may be suggested. First, a strong case has been made out for the view that at about this time a substantial number of priests left Jerusalem for Shechem, where they became an important element in the development of the Samaritan community as known from later times [41]). This secession would

[39]) This is the view, for instance, of Curtis-Madsen, p. 269, and de Vaux, p. 266 (ET, p. 397), and it is allowed, at least, by Rudolph, pp. 161-2.

[40]) P. R. Ackroyd, p. 127, n. 2, develops this suggestion with appeal to the comments of F.-M. Abel, *Les livres des Maccabées* (Paris, [2]1949), p. 30. It is also assumed in the recent major commentary of J. A. Goldstein, *I Maccabees* (Garden City, 1976), p. 17, and see the discussion of the issue by M. Stern, in S. Safrai and M. Stern (ed.), *The Jewish People in the First Century* II (Assen, 1976), p. 589.

[41]) Cf. H. G. Kippenberg, *Garizim und Synagoge. Traditionsgeschichtliche Untersuchungen zur samaritanischen Religion der aramäischen Periode* (Berlin, 1971), pp. 50-9, and my development of his arguments in *Israel in the Books of Chronicles*, pp. 137-8.

certainly have necessitated a measure of reorganization in Jerusalem, and it is noteworthy in this respect that the list of priests in xxiv 7-18 has far less contact with earlier lists of priests than do the lists of other cultic officials in the revision of 1 Chron. xxiii-xxvii with their antecedents.

A second possibility relates to the rather obscure incident related by Josephus (*Ant.* xi §§ 297-301), which tells how the high priest Joannes murdered his brother in the temple, as a result of which the Persian Bagoses (Bagoas)

> defiled the sanctuary and imposed tribute on the Jews, so that before offering the daily sacrifices they had to pay from the public treasury fifty drachmae for every lamb,

a measure which we are told lasted for seven years. Since this incident is to be dated to our period [42]), and indeed may not be unconnected with the first possibility outlined above, the disruption it undoubtedly caused to the regular temple services may have contributed to the development of the courses.

The main conclusions of this discussion may now be briefly summarized. There are two main literary layers in 1 Chron. xxiii-xxvii. The earlier, very much shorter, layer was part of the Chronicler's original composition. The second was added about a generation later by a pro-priestly reviser under the impact of the institution of the system of twenty-four courses. This establishes a date for the introduction of this institution in the closing years of the Persian period, a time when at least two events for which we have independent evidence connected with the Jerusalem priesthood might well have demanded such a reorganization.

---

[42]) See my discussion in "The Historical Value of Josephus' *Jewish Antiquities* xi. 297-301", *JTS*, ns 28 (1977), pp. 49-66. M. Stern, pp. 589-90, also draws attention to the relevance of this incident to our present concern, but he dates it considerably earlier than I do.

INDEXES

AUTHORS CITED

REFERENCES

Biblical

Apocrypha and Pseudepigrapha